...men, Ward Beadles and Grooms

VICTORIA'S YEAR

VICTORIA'S YEAR
English Literature and Culture, 1837–1838

Richard L. Stein

New York   Oxford
OXFORD UNIVERSITY PRESS
1987

Oxford University Press

Oxford   New York   Toronto
Delhi   Bombay   Calcutta   Madras   Karachi
Petaling Jaya   Singapore   Hong Kong   Tokyo
Nairobi   Dar es Salaam   Cape Town
Melbourne   Auckland

and associated companies in
Beirut   Berlin   Ibadan   Nicosia

Copyright © 1987 by Oxford University Press, Inc.

Published by Oxford University Press, Inc.,
200 Madison Avenue, New York, New York 10016

Oxford is a registered trademark of Oxford University Press

Library of Congress Cataloging-in-Publication Data

Stein, Richard L.
  Victoria's year.

  Bibliography: p.
  Includes index.
  1. English literature—19th century—History and criticism. 2. Great Britain—Civi-
lization—19th century. 3. Great Britain—History—Victoria, 1837-1901. 4. Victoria,
Queen of Great Britain, 1819-1901—Coronation. I. Title.
PR461.S78   1987   820'.9'008   87-17347
ISBN O-19-504922-5

Parts of this book have appeared previously. Much of chapter 6 appeared in the
author's essay, "Remember the Téméraire," in *Representations*, no. 11 (Summer 1985),
pp. 165–200, © 1985 by The Regents of the University of California. Reprinted by
permission of The Regents. A small portion of the last section of chapter 3 is drawn
from an essay published in the Fall 1980 issue of *The Victorian Newsletter* (no. 58), pp.
5–9. Finally, the second section of chapter 5 is based on an essay, "Milk, Mud, and
Mountain Cottages: Ruskin's *Poetry of Architecture*," that appeared in *PMLA*, vol. 100,
no. 3 (May 1985), pp. 328–341, reprinted by permission of the Modern Language
Association of America. © Copyright 1985 by The Modern Language Association of
America.

1 3 5 7 9 8 6 4 2

Printed in the United States of America
on acid-free paper

*For Carole,
Rebecca, and Sarah*

"Il faut," as M. de Tocqueville has said, "une science politique nouvelle à un monde tout nouveau." The whole face of society is reversed. . . .

John Stuart Mill, "Civilization" (1836)

All things are in revolution; in change from moment to moment, which becomes sensible from epoch to epoch: in this Time-World of ours there is properly nothing else but revolution and mutation, and even nothing else conceivable.

Thomas Carlyle, *The French Revolution* (1837)

Young, fair, trusted, beloved, new to business and to life, the Sovereign of England commences a reign, that in the course of nature will last beyond the generation who hailed in the Reform Bill—the charter of new liberties—the transition to a new stage of British civilization.

Edward Bulwer in the *Westminster Review* (1840)

ACKNOWLEDGMENTS

I am grateful to the various libraries, archives, and collections of prints, paintings, and drawings, whose generous assistance made *Victoria's Year* possible: the University of Oregon Library, with special thanks to Richard Heinzkill of the Reference Department, and to the Department, of Inter-Library Loans (and its director, Joanne Halgren) for bringing books to Eugene that were difficult to find anywhere in America; the library of the University of California at Los Angeles; the Huntington Library, San Marino, California; the William Andrews Clark Memorial Library (where I began some of the earliest research towards this book working with their collection of George Cruikshank, and where an imaginative, courteous staff always made searching for obscure materials a pleasure); the British Library, London, and the British Museum Department of Prints and Drawings; the library of the Victoria and Albert Museum, London; the Guildhall Library, London, including the Department of Prints and Maps; the Tate Gallery, London; the Royal Archives, Windsor Castle (and the Registrar, Miss Jane Langton, who offered encouragement and sage advice), and the Royal Archives Collection of Prints and Drawings. Thanks are due also to numerous other museums and collections around Britain, who offer information and warm assistance to even the casual visitor; they, more than anyone, have taught me how to observe.

Several grants assisted this project at different stages. I am grateful to the National Endowment for the Humanities, the William Andrews Clark Memorial Library, and the University of Oregon Graduate School and Office of Research, for their support.

For permission to reprint portions of this book that have appeared elsewhere, I wish to thank *PMLA, The Victorian Newsletter,* and *Representations.* A preliminary portion of the section on *The Poetry of*

Architecture was delivered at the annual meeting of the Modern Language Association of America in December, 1983. Sections of "Signs, Scenes, and Sketches" were presented at the annual meeting of the Philological Association of the Pacific Coast in November, 1983, and at the first annual conference of the Interdisciplinary Nineteenth-Century Studies Association (INCS) in April, 1986. Some of my comments on Cruikshank were developed from a paper given at the Northwest Conference on British History, April, 1982.

Through many stages of writing and revision, an overworked but always efficient staff in the University of Oregon English Department cheerfully transformed my jumbled notes into a legible text. Heartfelt thanks are due to Germaine Beveridge, Donna Holleran, Lori Peterson, Marilyn Reid, and Mike Stamm for efforts well beyond the call of duty.

I wish to give special thanks to the colleagues who read and commented on *Victoria's Year* in manuscript, in part or as a whole: Carl Dawson, Richard Dunn, U. C. Knoepflmacher, John McCoubrey, Carlisle Moore, I. B. Nadell, Kathleen Nicholson, Stanley Pierson, and an anonymous reader for Oxford University Press. All of them helped me see the relation between the forest and the trees, and to understand both more clearly. Randall McGowen read the manuscript in its entirety, commented extensively, and helped me find the way to some of the most difficult and important revisions. The advice of these readers resulted in new insights gained and the correction of a number of mistakes; the errors that remain are, of course, my own.

The last but hardly least important category of thanks is for familial encouragement and support: to my parents, Jay and Lorayne Stein, unstinting in their confidence and generosity, always ready to put me up (and put up with me) during research in the Los Angeles area; to my mother-in-law, Sally Abbey, my sisters-in-law and brother-in-law Joan Abbey, Lorrie Levin, and Al Levin, for hospitality, good humor, patience, and more dinners than I dare to compute. My largest debt of all is to my wife and daughters, for gifts too extensive to be described, which the dedication of this book can only begin to acknowledge.

Eugene, Oregon
June 21, 1986

R. L. S.

CONTENTS

ILLUSTRATIONS

VICTORIA'S YEAR

Introduction:
The New Map of London

The year 1837, except for the death of the old King and the accession of the young Queen, was a tolerably insignificant year.

Walter Besant, *Fifty Years Ago* (1888)

... the conclusion I reached was that the real, central theme of History is not what happened, but what people felt about it when it was happening. ...

G. M. Young, *Portrait of an Age*

How utterly the wretched shred of Time
Which in our blindness we call Human Life,
Is lost with all its train of circumstance,
And appanage of after and before,
In this eternal present; that we Are!
No When,—No Where,—No How,—but that we Are,—
And nought besides. ...

Richard Monckton Milnes, "The Marvel of Life" (1838)

... the present itself is unknown to us. ...

Thomas Carlyle, *Chartism* (1839)[1]

Princess Alexandrina Victoria, just past her eighteenth birthday, was informed of the death of her uncle, King William IV, in the early morning of June 20, 1837. It was the first day of a reign that was to last for more than six decades, and was to imprint the Queen's name on a variety of styles and manners, on the experience and culture of nearly a century inside and outside Britain. This book concerns the literature and culture of the first year of that reign in England, 1837–1838—Victoria's Year, as I will call it. That phrase does not, of course, refer to a precise chronological year, and any reader who has glanced at the Table of Contents will have observed that the book's three parts span a period from 1836 to 1839. But (as Virginia Woolf might ask) what is a year? My concern is not with a period of exactly 365 days but with a vaguer moment, registered within the consciousness of those who lived in it: the beginning of Victoria's reign as a mode of experience rather than a span of time. What was the feel of things—of the physical world, of mental and moral life? What did contemporaries understand about their own time, and what did they fail to understand? To what extent did the first year or so of the new reign have a definite character of its own, or to what extent was it seen as having one? If it is possible to characterize this brief historical period from within, what is the relation of the image so constructed to the "portrait of an age" drawn by later generations? Were there early signs of what came to be known as Victorianism? Does the experience of 1837–1838 necessitate any reexamination of that term, any redefinition of it from our own perspective one hundred and fifty years later?

Often such questions are answered (in literature or history) by reading backwards. One first assumes that 1837 was a starting point and then searches for corroborative evidence. It is a dubious methodology, and, as I hope to show, the epistemological issues it raises were themselves highly topical in the late 1830s. But that does not make it any easier to solve the problem of what Hazlitt termed "the spirit of the age." Those first years themselves, considered by themselves, provide ambiguous evidence, which also seemed ambiguous at the time. The new Queen's subjects were less than confident that something important was beginning and less than certain about the prospects for the future. The evidence for this is partly negative. Victoria herself had not yet become a public symbol, nor was it clear she would become one. Her accession produced predictable efforts to mythologize her life; but in the week or so before and after the death of William IV, the recitation of significant biographical incidents referred as much to him as to her. The *Times,* politically sympathetic with the old regime, managed to extol the very dullness of the "Sailor King" as a notable virtue in paying tribute to "the memory of his inoffensive nature." He "committed no wrong, provoked no enemy.... " Perhaps he never had opportunity to:

> He met with no adventures on a wide scale. He displayed no gross, nor great, nor memorable attributes.... He was not a man of genius nor of superior talent, nor of much refinement, but he was diligent.... William IV manifested on the throne the best qualities of a private English gentleman.[2]

In a final demonstration of these passive virtues, the patriotic monarch had begged his doctors to "tinker me up" so he could live through one last anniversary of the victory at Waterloo (June 18).[3] Nor was this image tarnished when, after his death two days later, a generous provision in his will led to public disclosure of a second liaison and a number of illegitimate children; this was regarded as merely providing further evidence of the late King's "social and domestic virtues."[4] The straining to adulate domesticity, especially where its existence is so dubious, is a kind of parody of Victorianism, before the fact.

What of the Queen herself? The first legends about Victoria tell of youthful acts of charity, early lessons in thrift—but these can be seen as much as attempts to familiarize as to mythologize her. She "was almost entirely unknown to her subjects," Lytton Strachey observed.[5] She had not been well known as a princess (the King had not allowed her to be). Her very name caused confusion, and the decision to reign as Queen Victoria required the alteration of a number of official forms that had included Alexandrina too. Perhaps that name was struck off to dispel associations with her German family, to make her seem a more genuinely native monarch. The most enthusiastic early accounts emphasized her British character. One periodical writer even reported that she was named Victoria in honor of the victory at Waterloo.[6] It is plain that her English identity was a sensitive issue, a sign that the Queen had what modern heads of state might call an image problem. Even at the time of her coronation, a year later, the *Times* could claim that there was far less public enthusiasm for her than for the Duke of Wellington. The adjective "Victorian" was not to be coined for a number of years, and in 1837 only the requirements of normal legislative usage produced reference to the "first Victoria Parliament." Did she really belong to the age, or it to her? Could anyone in 1837 have thought of it as Victoria's Year? The closest approach to an impressively symbolic use of her name to stand for the period resulted from a "ludicrous" mistake: a writer trying to keep up with shifting legal forms accompanying the change of monarchs dated a writ "In the Year of our Lady, 1837."[7] The *Times* reported the story to make sure its readers could laugh at this twofold ignorance—of verbal convention and the character of the times.

My own concern in surveying this period is with its cultural and intellectual rather than its political or social character—less, that is, with the Queen than with her subjects, and less with their lives than their thoughts. This means first of all that I will pay close attention to writing. *Victoria's Year* is primarily a literary study, although it is by no means restricted to that. In many chapters the focus shifts from literature as usually defined to historical writing and philosophy, to popular journalism, to the other arts, to science and technology, and even to public events. The breadth of this survey distinguishes it, I think, from the other single-year study of Victorian literature, Carl Dawson's fine book *Victorian Noon,* which surveys English literature (or, as Dawson says, "literary culture") in 1850.[8] I have called my book a study of literature and culture, but it might be more accurate to say literature in culture, for the goal is not so much to present a comprehensive survey as it is to define the interconnections—and discontinuities—with a larger world that give the writing of this time its special flavor. I hope to identify that flavor as precisely as possible, in terms of contemporary taste. And in terms of contemporary concerns: who are we? where are we going? Over and over such questions surface, or else remain conspicuously beneath the surface, as if nothing were more urgent than identifying the nature of the present time. I plan to show how that issue was addressed and also how it was evaded in spite of the pressure to address it—to show how men and women did and did not come to terms with the nature of their own time, in various forms of writing and speaking and graphic art. The aim, then, is not simply to describe what happened or what was produced, but to suggest the ways in which all the varied "arts" of the late 1830s engaged in a common project of self-portraiture, a collective effort to understand the present as part of history. When my focus changes—especially as it moves away from what is usually defined as the subject of literary studies—it is in an effort to preserve the contemporary sense (or senses) of self, the feel of the present to those who actually lived in it. G. M. Young regarded this as the fundamental subject of his classic study of early Victorian England, *Portrait of an Age:* "the real, central theme of History is not what happened, but what people felt about it when it was happening: in Philip Sidney's phrase, 'the affects, the whisperings, the motions of the people'; in Maitland's, 'men's common thoughts of common things'; in mine, 'the conversation of the people who counted.'"[9]

Even claims of this kind raise annoying questions: which whisperings? who counts? who's counting? Our own contemporary critical theory makes it difficult to make sweeping claims of complete inclusiveness or objectivity, or even to provide final readings of particular texts. One feels even more hesitant about this when the texts being considered are, in many cases, neglected or forgotten—and often justly, since many of these are second-rate works, not the kind sometimes described on dust jackets as minor classics. Some conspicuous examples of the latter simply are left out of this book: Thackeray's *Yellowplush Papers,* Tupper's *Proverbial Philosophy.* There is no discussion of *Pickwick,* and very little of such promising young poets as Elizabeth Barrett and Robert Browning. Some of the non-literary omissions may seem more serious: party politics, popular movements (Chartism, for instance, or the Tractarians). I will grant from the start that my choices of materials as well as my responses to them may be eccentric, that they have been shaped by a variety of personal and cultural assumptions that make this version of Victoria's Year very different from one that might be constructed by another person at another time. Perhaps another writer wouldn't feel the need to construct one at all: the beginning of Victoria's reign might seem too transparent, or too trivial, or simply too confused. But I have chosen to immerse myself in all those qualities—the transparencies, trivialities, and above all the confusions of the late 1830s. If this has not revealed the "main currents" of early Victorian thought, that may be due to my own predilection for undercurrents. In some cases these will seem to be transitory or shallow; in some they are powerful and deep. In either case, my aim is to illuminate patterns of feeling and thought—of consciousness, and unconsciousness—excluded from more familiar categories of literary and cultural history. Yet at the same time I will try to remain alert to the cultural spaces in which pattern breaks down, in which connections and relationships are mainly noticeable by their absence. This project began by questioning whether a clear literary and cultural image of the first year or so of Queen Victoria's reign could be constructed at all. To a significant extent, the answer is no—particularly if the end in view is any single unity, any coherent early Victorian frame of mind. The voices of these years are rarely in agreement, with one another or themselves—not even on the subject of discourse itself. The links between them often are tenuous, abrupt; it is difficult to rediscover smooth lines of connection. Thus, if there is a pathway through the culture of the late 1830s, it tends to be twisting and confused, often very little like a path at all. *Victoria's Year,* nevertheless, attempts to follow it, even when it leads nowhere, or turns back upon itself, or moves among disparate disciplines or intellectual modes—if not to create a crisp portrait image then at least to draw a rudimentary map.

Later in this chapter I will deal with actual maps and other modes employed to render a complex reality orderly and legible; for now, I wish to offer my own map of the book as a whole. *Victoria's Year* begins with that issue of legibility, connected with the question of seeing and representing familiar and unfamiliar aspects of the world, explored in a series of graphic and literary "sketches" from 1836. I will argue that there is something distinctly contemporary about them, both about the "sketch" technique and the conditions it is designed to capture. The second chapter moves to various forms of even more self-consciously "modern" writing of 1837 and 1838, to the problem of whether that period was then or now can be considered a distinct "golden year." This question in turn leads to an investigation of one of the most topical areas of early Victorian writing, the responses to new forms of social and scientific thought—their literary adoption, and avoidance. I have devoted the fourth chapter to a more curious contemporary theme, the pervasive fable of a kidnapped child, which recurs in a number of minor works and is best remembered for its adaptation by Dickens in *Oliver Twist*. That novel, with its emphasis on seeing, comprehending, and finding one's way through a confusing new world, leads to a consideration of books on epistemology, and especially the epistemology appropriate to travellers, including one of the classic scientific/ travel books of the century, Darwin's *Beagle* journal. The next chapter turns to another celebrated nineteenth-century ship, Turner's *Fighting Temeraire,* as an image of what it meant in 1839 to memorialize the relatively recent past, and what it meant to create new forms of memory appropriate to the experience of a new age. The Conclusion, shifting from Turner's glowing sunset to the "Sun Pictures" produced in 1839 by the earliest experiments in photography, uses those images as a way of identifying a more general transformation in contemporary self-consciousness—from varied and tentative responses to an unknown world to a new, more fixed mythology, including a new mythology of the Queen herself.

Victoria's Year thus moves from 1836 to 1839, from perceiving to remembering, and returns again and again to the problems of representation posed by new forms of experience—or those regarded as new. It is debatable, of course, whether that contemporary sense of a new world is ever justified, fully or even in part. But there are some facts of the late 1830s that seemed urgent and unprecedented to those confronting them for the first time. Five years after the Reform Bill of 1832, the threat of revolution lingered, if only in the form of a persistent nightmare. Although historians continue to debate whether this fear was justified, there is general agreement that it was felt, and in some cases acted upon. Explosive potential of another sort was associated with the unprecedented power of steam—demonstrated in the rapidly increasing numbers of railroads and steamships, and in their more than occasional wrecks. Special uncertainties also arose from the fact of a new reign, and particularly from having a young Queen on the throne; what if the new character of the age proved to be feminine? (Thomas Hood connected these last two modern phenomena through a visual-verbal pun in a drawing titled "Trains Are Coming In" published in the *Comic Annual*.[10]) And what often was regarded as the most extraordinary contemporary phenomenon of all—the most clearly unprecedented fact of the age—can be summed up in a single word: London.

By all accounts, London was a scene of incomprehensible, thrilling, and sometimes terrifying vitality. Over and over the writers of the 1830s reminded their readers, and themselves, that nothing like it had ever been experienced before or could be found elsewhere in the modern world. It seemed to surpass all powers of description. As a writer in *Chambers' Edinburgh Journal* observed three days before Victoria's accession to the throne, "There is no word in our language capable of defining what London is. . . . It is an enigma—a mystery even to those who have been born and bred in it."[11] The *Penny Magazine* explained that the lack of any satisfactory account of the city resulted from its "almost limitless variety. . . . London is a world in itself. . . . Adequately to chronicle and to describe such a city as London, a man should have sounded every depth and shallow of the accumulated facts of the past, and what is more, have plunged into the deepest recesses of the present."[12] The city seemed important enough to merit analysis in books (such as James Grant's *The Great Metropolis* in 1836 and John Hogg's *London As It Is* in 1837), a long series of articles entitled "The Looking-Glass of London" that ran throughout 1837 in the *Penny Magazine,* and numerous short pieces in a variety of other periodicals. The subjects of discussion differed, as did the opinions of urban life. The final installment of "The Looking-Glass of London"— on "London Extremes: Hyde Park and Rag Fair"—suggested not only that there were several radically different cities within the city, but that different observers might experience them in radically different ways. London as a whole could be summed up best by what is offered as a modernized version of "our Great Dramatic Poet":

> How rich, how poor, how abject, how august,
> How complicate, how wonderful, is London.[13]

The only issue on which everyone agreed was the phenomenal nature of the city itself. "We are sixteen hundred thousand, men, women, and children," announced *Blackwood's,* comparing London and Rome to the advantage of the former. "We inhabit the greatest, the richest, and the noblest city that the world has ever seen."[14]

Much of this could have been said of eighteenth-century London. It might be objected that all of these commentators avoid the central fact of urbanization in the 1830s, when the most unprecedented forms of growth and change were to be found in the new industrial cities of the North.[15] But this only confirms the point in another way: the explanations of the contemporary city don't quite work; all of them simultaneously face and evade their subjects. Those catalogues make us aware of how much lies outside the scope of any catalogue, especially when its subject is the modern city. And catalogues in the 1830s multiplied, in varied and sometimes astonishing forms. London itself—even if its novelty was, in fact, already old—seemed to require a series of special guides: maps and guidebooks, dictionaries of local slang, lists of proper carriage charges, names of "low haunts" to be avoided (why else would they have been located so precisely?), handbooks, tables of mileage between the center and surrounding villages, street directories with principal public buildings and clubs pictured alongside their addresses, keys to shop signs, new versions of old publications reprinted to take account of new buildings, new neighborhoods, and particularly the new extensions of the railway into the city. The very quantity of this literature makes the point in another way. London now requires guidebooks, and multiple ones at that: no untrained perspective, no single perspective of any kind, however well-informed, is adequate to the complexity of the city. Perhaps the best word for the contemporary sense of this is not complexity but confusion, although some publications attempted to treat London's size and intricacy as an amusing rather than a confusing fact. This is apparent in the existence of a puzzle based on this jumble, called *Labyrinthus Londinensis, or the Equestrian Perplexed.*[16] Another more straightforward topographical work—Tallis' *London Street Views* (1839)—promised to provide something implicit in all these varied guides: a "Description of Every Object Worthy of Notice. . . . Intended to Assist Strangers visiting the Metropolis through all its Mazes."[17] That final, vaguely ironic term again suggests that such accounts can never be complete, or completely satisfactory.

To some extent, this outpouring of topographical materials can be attributed to advances in surveying and map-making techniques. Yet these are developments of the 1820s, when the first trigonometric surveys were made. The maps issued in the late 1830s are almost without exception reprints of earlier ones, with a few place names added or altered (in some cases mistakenly) to justify the claims of the covering page that each represents a "new" map taking account of the latest changes—"Comprehending the Various Improvements to 1839," as the map issued by E. Ruff and Company declared (Figure I.2). That map, in fact, is a later edition of a map of 1827, which as recently as 1835 had the names of the original mapmakers, C. and J. Greenwood, on it, as well as acknowledgment that the "Actual Survey" on which it was based had been conducted from 1824 to 1826.[18] The "improvements" noted to bring this map up to date are drawn so roughly that the revised portions are clearly distinct. Thus the Royal Palace has been relabeled the "Queens Palace"; the word "Queens" *(sic)* is printed in a slightly finer typeface (looking more like a hand-scrawled imitation of type) to make it fit the space that formerly had served to refer to the King. It is as if the publishers are too uncertain about the permanence of the new reign to make it the occasion for creating an expensive new design. Victoria's ascendency will be acknowledged, or rather squeezed in, yet it is not significant enough (even though this map is "Humbly Dedicated" to her) to call for an altered image of the city, a major publishing venture. There was, in fact, no genuinely new map of London made in 1837, or even by 1839.[19] Had one been created, of course, it would have been much easier to argue for the reality of Victoria's Year—its reality, that is, to the people who lived in it. As it is, this piece of evidence simply is missing: it is an event, a moment in publishing history, that never took place.

Should cultural or literary history take account of such a nonevent—and if so, how? What are the consequences when it does, or when it does not? One answer (or example by way of answer) can be found in one of the first Jubilee surveys of Victoria's reign, Walter Besant's *Fifty Years Ago*. "The year 1837," it declares, "except for the death of the old King and the accession of the young Queen, was a tolerably insignificant year."[20] Looking back from the perspective of 1887–1888, Besant can only marvel that so much has been achieved from such modest beginnings. He insists that 1837 was still part of the eighteenth century. From the secure historical position of a proud, prosperous Jubilee, he regards the first year of Victoria's reign at times with amused curiosity, at times with open condescension. The subject at best is charming, often simply trivial. When it does seem to engage Besant's interest, it is the progressivism of 1837 that he finds appealing—the promise, whatever lesser matters were in the air, that great developments were leading England to the glorious condition it enjoys in his own day, and perhaps to new futures more glorious still. Thus he finds it difficult to focus on the single year he has chosen:

> The nineteenth century actually began with steam communication by sea; with steam machinery; with railways; with telegraphs; with the development of the colonies; with the admission of the people to the government of the country; with the opening of the Universities; with the spread of science; with the revival of the democratic spirit. It did not really begin, in fact, until about fifty years ago. When and how will it end? By what order, by what ideas, will it be followed?[21]

It is not simply that Besant, like so many other chroniclers of the past, has high hopes for the future. He has high (or at least rigid) standards of history, too, at least about what constitutes history and what does not. In his list of major developments, 1837 itself remains fundamentally unimportant—although not so much that he cannot turn it into an entertaining commemorative volume—and radically distant from the present, "a time so utterly passed away and vanished that a young man can hardly understand it." As Jerome H. Buckley observes, Besant lingers "over quaint customs long outmoded, as if contemplating the strangeness of a remote antiquity."[22] There are, of course, subjects of interest—clubs, schools, sports, scientific advances, writing, hard work of many kinds (to mention some of the main topics he considers in nineteen chapters). Yet the conclusion is clear: "We have all grown richer, much richer."[23] The remark applies to culture and society generally as well as to the financial wealth of the nation. For all his efforts to evoke the spirit of that distant age, Besant cannot disguise his sense that the beginning of the Victorian period appears impoverished, defined above all else by what it lacks.

Yet this Besantine approach cannot simply be ridiculed, although its tone is dated. As I have tried to suggest, the absences he laments may exist; and they can tell us a great deal, perhaps even more than the sort of tangible presences he would take as the tokens of an "important" age. Perhaps this conclusion simply reflects post-structural biases; perhaps it reflects post-Freudian ones. Certainly it underscores the differences between Besant's approach to the past and ours. For much modern and post-modern theory, no task seems more urgent than to recover a sense of the events and ideas once relegated to marginal realms of insignificance, the dimensions of experience that people found easiest, or most convenient, to forget. The same theoretical perspectives lead us to place at least as much emphasis on discontinuities as connections, on diversity as unity, on the dissonances among competing languages (in M. M. Bakhtin's sense of the word) as their harmonies. To some extent, we scrutinize these differences to discover new ways of identifying underlying unities. But our interest in such patterns exists alongside an equally intense (or perhaps even greater) interest in the ways and places a pattern breaks down or begins to come undone. Similarly, the confusions of an age can tell us a great deal about it, particularly when, as is more than occasionally the case, they are portrayed as understandings—mistakes disguised as choices made, questions hidden behind apparent certainties, blindness represented as insight (Paul de Man might have added that this is always the case). A revolution that does not succeed; a literary argument that falls apart midway; a picture that reveals how little its subject really has been seen or known. Each of these may help us reconstruct the explicit or implicit models by which things were attempted, understood, judged, and represented: the canons and paradigms that were designed to shape practice. They may, then, help us perceive the unsettling of those paradigms, the moments when someone stumbled over a gap in the ordinarily seamless contemporary conception of truth. Perhaps that final phrase makes the most important point of all: we must always speak of someone's truth, embraced with reference to particular interests and particular ends. For any conception of truth—our own, as well as those advanced in the past—is politicized and value-laden. Thus, in dismissing 1837 as unimportant, Besant (and he is not alone in this) associates genuine historical achievement, and the conception of a genuine historical period, with power; his list of major institutions progresses effortlessly to universities and science and democracy from steam, and in a sense all of those institutions are versions of that harnessed, technologized natural force. What conceptions of history and society do our distinctions of major and minor, true and false, serve? To what extent are we bound by them in reasserting the "significance" of familiar cultural monuments?

It is impossible to escape such limiting assumptions completely, although we can become increasingly aware of their constraints. For literary studies, this means in part viewing our canons critically, reconsidering the ways the idea of literature itself enforces distinctions and exclusions of certain kinds of "lesser" writing. What is being lost, or ignored, when we emphasize "major" rather than "minor" writers, "successful" rather than "immature" works? I will devote a good deal of attention to early works by writers who went on to far more impressive achievements; but it is also necessary to consider works by those who did not. If, for instance, one cannot study the 1830s without discussing Dickens and Carlyle, it becomes all the more important to examine their work in relation to what are usually considered less distinguished productions of less distinguished names, or in relation to writing that cannot be attached to any name at all. I have in mind especially the popular press, an essential frame of reference if only to remind ourselves of the proximity of "literature" to other modes of verbal expression. Can one describe the literary transformation of commonplace reality without examining the representation of similar subjects in more commonplace sources? Was there a set of standard subjects and situations outside of literature itself, an iconography of the normal that structured even the most casual writing? What were the most familiar stories and sentiments, the readiest verbal reflexes? When an ordinary writer wanted to reach an ordinary audience, what language did he or she speak? Was there an "ordinary language" in which one might choose, or be compelled, to treat ordinary reality? Throughout *Victoria's Year* I make use of material of this kind, from newspapers particularly, as much for the texture as the text (to paraphrase Nabokov), for getting the feel of a period we cannot be sure we know for sure with our conventional cultural instruments. Carlyle's 1838 essay on Sir Walter Scott praised the Waverley novels for helping people discover "that the bygone ages of the world were actually filled by living men."[24] To make this discovery again, as fully as possible, we must read Scott and Carlyle but also read other sources as well: read unimportant stories, from ordinary sources, and read them carefully enough so we do not smooth out their discontinuities and contradictions into something simpler, clearer, or more polished—into "literature."

Here I want to consider one such story—an ordinary account of an ordinary (well, relatively ordinary) person—from the *Times*. I will discuss it at some length—partly because it seems representative and partly because it does not (and I say "seems" to admit again that the issue of representativeness itself is clouded, one of the shoals on which the most ambitious historical ventures often wreck), and partly because it stands out as a narrative of real life with much of the power and complexity we ordinarily associate with fine fiction. An unimportant story, by Besant's measure and many others, which only found its way into the newspaper at all because contemporary law assigned suicide to the category of crime. Under the Police Notes for July 21, 1837, just a month after the new Queen's accession, the *Times* printed the story of an apparent suicide attempt. "BOW STREET: Yesterday a miserable-looking cripple, who said that his name was Michael Minch, was . . . charged with having attempted to drown himself in the river, at Strand-stairs." The attempt (if that is indeed what it was) was thwarted when the man was pulled from the water by a police constable (identified only as F34), to whom he gave a confused account of himself. First Minch explained that he wanted to put an end to his miseries. Then his story changed. In the new version he said that he had "plunged into the water to save the life of a man with whom he had been conversing a few minutes before, and who had expressed his determination to commit suicide to avoid starvation." Minch was a glass-cutter from Cork. The second man, "with whom he was acquainted, and who was wholly destitute like himself," was called "Cotter" (although this spelling of the name may be an English transcription of Irish speech). In the course of their conversation, Cotter complained that he could not live without "grub," and suggested that both jump into the river; when Minch agreed that he had equally little reason to live, Cotter leapt in, crying, "then follow me." "At that moment a cloud came over the moon and he lost sight of Cotter." Minch immediately threw himself into the water to attempt a "rescue," but his clothes weighed him down. He was pulled out after struggling, apparently alone. The magistrate ordered that the river be searched for this mysterious second party, and that the prisoner be sent back to Sheerness, his legal place of settlement.

Our own most immediate response to such an account could be described as post-Freudian, although it is partly post-Dickensian as well. We assume the story has been fabricated, consciously or not, and that the mysterious Mr. Cotter is an alter-ego for the glass-cutter from Ireland: Cotter and Minch, Jekyll and Hyde—an extra syllable distinguishes between the self and a double. It is interesting, though, that the magistrate conducting the examination both did and did not acknowledge this fantastic element. Minch was punished for his suicide attempt, but the river also had to be dragged. The tale is improbable, but not necessarily more than real life. (And who should "judge" such matters better than a magistrate?) But the intricacies of the newspaper account only begin here. For the story concerns a moment of simultaneous recognition and distancing: Cotter is familiar and unfamiliar to Minch ("known and unknown," Tennyson would say); it is a classic instance of the Freudian uncanny. Even assuming that the story is true, its narration stresses this contradictory conception of the Other: he is both fellow-sufferer and Satanic tempter; the darkened moon only further allegorizes this dual identity. And if we assume (as apparently did the *Times* reporter) that the story is false, the confusions deepen, for the being so distanced belongs to Minch himself. Now "Minch's Narrative" (how often does a phrase of that sort introduce an interpolated tale within a Victorian novel?) becomes a complex piece of self-defining fiction: not just the story of self-division, it constitutes a divided self in the process of narration.

When was this elaborate account created, and how consciously: was there a pause between the first and second explanation to the constable while Minch recalled a story already planned ("this is what I planned to say"), while he created one for the first time ("this will save my skin"), or while he groped in simple confusion ("what if it really happened another way?")? Clearly enough, Minch was in desperate straits; to some extent his circumstances produced this story, perhaps because starvation can induce hallucinations. We cannot be sure that Minch is a simple liar, or even a complex one (in Wilde's sense of the word). As the magistrate's sentence reminds us, such an act normally is considered criminal. Minch had little choice but to compose sentences of his own to try and evade punishment—in a sense the law compelled him to conjure up those self-divisions. Did he in an instant of panic come upon an aspect of himself to which he could respond only in terror? Or was it simply the familiar fear of the police that motivated his tale? It is a story of what we would term schizoid behavior, yet this divided self may have been created in response to an intolerable situation, in the manner described by R. D. Laing. Perhaps a "wretch" like Minch has no choice but to invent a second self.

Where, then, in these murky, swirling waters of confusion, does the "true story" lie? Who (to ask a question out of John Fowles) is Minch? Out of what shadows does he come? I do not know. Neither, perhaps, did Minch himself and neither did that magistrate, although that did not delay sentencing any more than it kept the *Times* reporter from the "sentencing" that transforms these uncertainties into a narrative. The newspaper account remains interesting in large part because it discloses that process of transformation, the construction (or reconstruction) of Minch into a specific role. For the genteel reader of the *Times,* this becomes a story of one of those Others who is defined and distanced in "the eyes of the law" (a phrase that will gain added significance when we read *Oliver Twist*), a being who need never be known in any full human way at all as long as the proper judicial—and narrative—forms are followed. Legal procedures and narration here become versions of one another; they replace knowing or the need for knowing, provide a way of defining clearly what otherwise might have remained disturbingly obscure. It is that very obscurity I have attempted to recapture in reexamining this account, as I will with other narratives in *Victoria's Year.* The reason has something to do with my own interpretive procedures, and something to do with the character of the time. For what we are confronted with here is not so much a single narrative as the collision of many, or many possible narratives: not simply the distinct perspectives represented in Minch's own story, the legal response to it, and the journalistic account of both, but the multiple interpretive possibilities that can be glimpsed within each of these. And it is a multiplicity we will see again. What is important, then, is not to determine the best or most plausible version of an uncertain truth but, quite the reverse, to avoid discriminations that would limit that indeterminacy (or overdetermination). The task is to employ a method that does not understand too well, too clearly—that does not rationalize the densest texts or events out of existence.

Throughout *Victoria's Year* I have tried to respect the ambiguities of the materials being considered, their inconsistencies and contradictions, and to acknowledge the inevitable tension between explanatory abstractions and the elusive experience they are supposed to represent. This can become a kind of juggling act: how many possibilities can be kept in the air at once? But the necessity for intellectual legerdemain is confirmed by the shifting categories of explanation that emerge so conspicuously in the late 1830s. Nothing seems more certain about the time than its uncertainties, beginning with the uncertain character of the "year," the "period," as such. Nothing seems so continuous as the pattern of discontinuity (apparent within single voices as well as among many). There are fewer resolutions than failures to resolve, or failures that try to conceal themselves beneath unconvincing gestures at success. There is a continuing search for connections, although more often than not this only leads to a continuing reemergence of gaps. Something is lost when an account of these differences reduces them to an excessively neat sameness, when the clarity of a map disguises the roughness of the landscape, or when our own explanatory "sentences" begin to impose, judicially, an alienating otherness on our "subjects."

It is essential, then, to remain alert for such juridical structures in the past as well as the present. The *Times* report on Minch's apparent suicide attempt signals its own detachment (and ours) in the ironic disdain with which it first refers to him as a "miserable cripple." I will cite several other examples, if only to suggest how easily narration, while apparently in the service of representational accuracy or vividness, slips into a less neutral mode. One appears in another police report, from the *Times* of September 5, 1837.

> *Lord Mayor:* "What are you?"
> *Prisoner:* "What am I? Why I gets my living in the streets."
> *Lord Mayor:* "I see you do."

I have printed this exchange in standard dramatic layout because that is how the *Times* printed it: the very typographical format of the interchange becomes a way of distancing it, reducing a human situation to a humorous one. In this case, the prisoner was charged with stealing a leg of pork, for which he was sentenced to the treadmill. "What!" he responds when sentence is passed. "For carrying away my own wittles? You wouldn't do such a thing, would you? I an't a thief, *upon* my honour. (A laugh)." This laughter, in the courtroom and in the newspaper account of the proceedings, renders people as characters, caricatures, curiosities rather than something more complex, or more demanding of our interest or sympathy. When Besant mentions the most grisly and sensational crime of 1837, he too reduces it to drama, starring the murderer, Greenwood, himself:

> never was there a hanging more numerously or more fashionably attended. The principal performer, however, is said to have disappointed his audience by a pusillanimous shrinking from the gallows when he was brought out.[25]

It is a bad joke, but Greenwood was a bad man. These descriptions (including the treatment of Minch in the *Times* story) are constructed to render their subjects "tolerably unimportant," imposing, or preserving an otherness we, too, sometimes may feel relieved we can "hardly understand."

The question of otherness is one I have found especially prominent in surveying the writing of the late 1830s. It can, as in the case of Minch, become a question of self-knowledge, a vision of the self as Other, or a vision of the otherness concealed within a familiar self. Even more commonly, it involves an uneasy glance across barriers that normally divide individuals, classes, and nations from one another: a glance at gypsies, at "the poor," at "foreigners" of all sorts, particularly the "savages" who reside in the miserable conditions of distant jungles and deserts (although some live within the modern city, too). The main section of *Victoria's Year* concludes with an examination of Darwin's *Beagle* narrative, to consider (in part) the relation between his maturing scientific interests and his somewhat less mature, less scientific responses to the natives of the countries visited during his "Surveying Voyages." Darwin was only able to travel to South America and gather the specimens and insights that would form the basis for his great work of 1859 and after because the Crown commissioned a series of voyages to draw up maps; and as we will see, his interest in the divisions and connections between different natural phenomena—the developmental structure of the physical world—was not unrelated to the official interest in clarifying political and topographical divisions, in reducing a confusing, distant world to a known regularity, and classifying its unfamiliar inhabitants within that structure.

Darwin was not alone in struggling to develop a new epistemology adequate to the description of a new world. Harriet Martineau considered this her first task in writing a series of books about America. John Stuart Mill suggested that it ought to be the task of anyone trying to make sense of modern Europe, a world that was changing so rapidly that no traditional ways of knowing could serve: "'Il faut,' as M. de Tocqueville has said, 'une science politique nouvelle à un monde tout nouveau.' The whole face of society is reversed."[26] The same conviction is visible throughout Thomas Carlyle's *French Revolution,* arguably the most influential and significant book of 1837. A new kind of writing for a new kind of historical experience—the same characterization could be used for the other major literary production of the year, *Oliver Twist.* Both Carlyle and Dickens create new narrative forms partly in response to the radically new experience associated with the modern city, not incidentally including the explosive violence that seems so close to the surface in the frightening, faceless urban mob. Once again, then, the problem of knowing is related to the presence of Others, whose obscurities pose a powerful threat. No wonder Dickens' novel is filled with descriptions of people gazing with fierce determination, surveying (quite as literally as in Darwin) one another and the City itself, as if their very lives depended on the possibility of transforming the chaos of urban experience into maplike order. And on this possibility, apparently, the life of their society as a whole also depends. As in *The French Revolution,* the greatest threat to the stability of institutions comes from those whose external and internal conditions remain unknown and unacknowledged, creatures so debased that everyone forgets how firmly the structure of society is based on them. (This is the subject of a fine modern historical novel about the 1830s in Wales, Gwyn Thomas' *Leaves in the Wind.*) They are the inhabitants of a *terra incognita* within the known world of apparent order. Unless that undiscovered country is visited, surveyed and mapped, tallied and enumerated, it may threaten to absorb the known, orderly world within itself.

Knowing and mapping, then, are at least in part political activities, at least in part exercises of power. No wonder they encounter resistance. The Act for Registration of Marriages, Births, and Deaths was made law in 1837, and its imposition of centralized records met with opposition from those who feared systematization as such, as well as those simply nostalgic for the sanctity of the parish register. Some even regarded maps as posing a similar threat. The most powerful recent account of this appears in Brian Friel's play *Translations,* about a British military surveying expedition to Ireland in 1833. The drama explores the conflict precipitated by the coercive dimensions of map making itself, which in this case included the substitution of English "translations" for traditional Gaelic place names. Hugh, a Latin scholar who is master of the local hedge-school, understands best the implications of placing new names on a new map.

> *Hugh:* But remember that words are signals, counters. They are not immortal. And it can happen—to use an image you'll understand—it can happen that a civilization can be imprisoned in a linguistic contour which no longer matches the landscape of . . . fact.
> *Owen:* We're making a six-inch map of the country. Is there something sinister in that?
> *Yolland:* Not in. . . .
> *Owen:* And we're taking place-names that are riddled with confusion and . . .
> *Yolland:* Who's confused? Are the people confused?
> *Owen:* . . . and we're standardizing those names as accurately and sensitively as we can.
> *Yolland:* Something is being eroded.[27]

That final remark might stand as another epigraph to *Victoria's Year,* not just for the way it speaks about that time but for the way it speaks about it to us. The late 1830s are scarred by erosions, some actually made by humans in an effort to provide clearer markings on a landscape already deformed and defamiliarized by natural changes (such as the geologic shifts described by Lyell and Darwin). But the regularity of a map may in the end only heighten our sense of the irregularities of the physical world, its assymetries, its deviations from the legibility of a plan. And that discrepancy in turn makes us aware of the power exerted in the attempt to make the world correspond to our maps of it, to mold reality to fit an imagined scheme. Perhaps there is wisdom in evading such tasks, in only drawing provisional surveys, in only adapting old maps rather than constructing new ones. Perhaps it is those who do not attempt to impose new maps on the world who are most aware of its intricate topography, its radical resistance to geometric order. The truest seer may be the one who admits how little he can see, who declares with Carlyle in *Chartism* that "the present itself is unknown to us."[28] Perhaps. But such reticence is rare, especially among map makers, especially in Carlyle. For every glimpse of the elusiveness of reality in Victoria's Year, we find a parallel and corresponding reflex of assertion, a claim for certainty made all the more absolutely on account of the uncertainty it attempts to cover. This has predictable political consequences, and familiar psychological roots. It is one of the most disturbing reminders, as we look back on the beginning of Victoria's reign from the sesquicentenary of her accession, that this distant, unfamiliar age is in fact very much like our own.

I

PROLOGUE—1836

1

Signs, Scenes, and Sketches

Nay, our commonest emblems or symbols are losing their force and significance.... Is not old Time himself becoming very old ...?

Penny Magazine (1838)

Perhaps, after all, the whole of human philosophy is nothing more than construing signs, translating one language into another, reading individual facts in general principles, and general principles in individual facts.

Quarterly Review (1840)

Lord Mayor: What are you?
Prisoner: What am I? Why I gets my living in the streets.
Lord Mayor: I see you do.... *Times* (1837)[1]

I

In December 1836 the seventeen-year-old Princess Victoria was visiting Claremont House, in Surrey, the home of her uncle Leopold, King of the Belgians. On a road nearby, she observed a family of gypsies camped. They evoked her immediate interest and sympathy. When one of the women gave birth to a son during the next year, the Princess sent food and blankets; she even considered asking the woman to name the boy Leopold! The extent of this fascination is revealed by almost two months of entries in her journals and well over a dozen drawings in her sketchbooks. Marina Warner includes three pictures from this group in her edition of *Queen Victoria's Sketchbook,* and they offer a representative sample of the Princess's response. We see the gypsies in groups and individually, but the figure that emerges over and over is a woman Warner terms "the tribe's mother," Sarah Cooper, whose "formidable appearance" particularly attracted the Princess: "There is so much mind and soul in it ... I *do so* wish I could take her likeness from nature! What a study she would be!"[2] In fact, the "likenesses" in the sketchbooks are drawn, as their labels remind us, "from recollection" rather than nature. Perhaps it was not seemly for the future monarch to draw some of the poorest of her future subjects in their normal setting; perhaps it simply was too cold. At any rate, although the images we have do manage to capture some out-of-doors flavor, they are informed mainly by the idealizing imagination of the royal parlor. In one (Figure 1.1), the six children with Sarah (her nephew and nieces, as Victoria's caption on the drawing explains) are poorly dressed but clean-looking, their dark eyes round, alert, and friendly; several seem to be smiling; all are wearing shoes. Sarah's hair is pulled across her forehead and coiled at the back, a coiffure that, combined with the cloak draped over her shoulders, gives her an almost regal appearance. Another image (Figure 1.2), a portrait sketch, depicts Sarah alone and in profile; and although the drawing emphasizes the gypsy curve of her nose, its tone is set by the treatment of her eyes and mouth and the upturned angle of her head—an ardent, meditative pose. She could be an aristocrat, or the heroine of a historical painting. The woman on the left of another image (Figure 1.3) also takes a thoughtful glance upwards, while the head of the woman beside her (carrying a bundle on her back) is set off in front of her circular hat, as if by a halo.

Victoria would not have been the only genteel young lady of her day to encounter gypsies, nor the only one to have made records of her meeting in words and pictures. What I find interesting in these images is not their uniqueness but their typicality—a typicality based in the use of pictures to mediate what might have proved an unsettling experience. There are no signs that Victoria felt threatened or even uneasy in those encounters, or that she regarded conditions in the gypsy camp as evidence of more general conditions, such as the problem of poverty. Her journals reveal little questioning of social structures or social disproportions. There are outbursts of indignation, but less in response to the conditions in which gypsies live than to the way they are regarded by others in Victoria's own class. They are, in the words of her journal, a "greatly wronged people." "It is atrocious," she adds in 1837, "how often these poor creatures have been falsely accused, cruelly wronged, and greatly ill-treated."[3] She is sympathetic, to be sure, and eager to see those sympathies shared by others in a position to offer material and moral assistance. But that sympathy has clear limits. For one thing, the Princess exhibits the familiar nineteenth-century aversion to formal institutional solutions for social problems; and the plight of these gypsies is not considered, as I have indicated already, a general social problem at all. One might be tempted to praise Victoria for this, for her insistence on the particularity of a situation she has seen and of human beings she has met—except that these sketches and journal entries suggest that she was not fully prepared to acknowledge that humanity; she generalizes, but in other ways. In spite of her sympathy, the gypsies remain "creatures," a class of Others removed from and fundamentally different from the genteel observer, who reconstitutes her own privileged position in even her most humane gestures towards this group of social inferiors. Her charity towards the newborn child exhibits this relationship, for it defines Victoria as the Generous Outsider, part of the legion of leisured ladies who visited the poor with their baskets. But the Princess does not simply visit, smile, and bestow: she records (or "takes") the "likenesses" of those Others in words and pictures. And those descriptive sketches, as much as her gifts, reassert her superiority to the ones being observed. As artist, she identifies herself with that well-established role of aristocratic spectator, who studies the poor as curiosities and maintains her own distance by treating them as aesthetic objects. This is, as I have suggested already, a reflex rather than a deliberately chosen strategy, and it is all the more effective for the ease with which Victoria yields to it. "We met two Gipsies, an old and a young woman," she writes in the first journal reference to the group (December 3 1836): "the young one was beautiful and so picturesc! [*sic*] Drew."[4]

Once again I should stress how typical this remark is for an aristocratic girl in the 1830s or for anyone in a class above the gypsies themselves. William Howitt, a writer with considerable social sophistication and conscience, treats gypsies within the category of "Picturesque and Moral Features of the Country" in *The Rural Life of England:* any picture of that life "which should omit those singular and most picturesque squatters on heaths and in lanes," he explains, would be "wholly defective."[5] And he intersperses his own account with references to the long tradition of verbal and pictorial evocations of their poetic character. Similarly Victoria's drawings—and the other treatments of the gypsies elsewhere in her journals—remind us how fully her responses were mediated by a variety of conventions and prior experiences. She acknowledges one of those herself on December 17, when she "Read in or rather looked over (for I have read it through before)" a book called *The Gipsies' Advocate.* This book, published in 1831 by James Crabb ("Author of 'The Penitent Magdalen'"), stresses the gypsies' "many genuine features of humanity" in order to incite "an energetic benevolence toward this despised people," especially among judges and clergymen, to whom the volume is dedicated.[6] Victoria continued to reread this book, and to underline passages heavily, well into

January 1837, and echoes it in her recollections of the gypsies' familial attachment, gratitude, and cleanliness. Crabbe provides her with a language that is at once sympathetic and detached; the stress on typical virtues allows Victoria to avoid inquiring too closely into particular conditions, or particular lives. This literary and moral model at times even allows her to forget that these are poor gypsies at all. Of the "*extreme* cleanliness" of the newborn boy she notes, adding the emphasis herself, that "it was quite as clean and neat as you would wish any child or infant to be."[7] "There is," she remarks on December 21, "something lofty and very peculiar in their carriage and demeanour, very unlike peasants."

To some extent the Princess is only following her most refined aesthetic instincts, recording information charming or picturesque enough to deserve notice. Yet such aesthetic categories also conceal social standards while bolstering them through the recording of "significant"detail. In *The Dark Side of the Landscape* John Barrell shows that the representation of the rural poor in eighteenth- and nineteenth-century landscape painting involved a similar concealment, disguised as realistic portrayal.[8] In effect, the pastoral scene became a form of visual reassurance, an image of the proper appearance of poverty through the eyes of a monied class. Victoria's debt to this pictorial tradition is apparent in her sketches of the gypsies, where they look "very unlike peasants" indeed. They are more conventionalized, more colorful and dramatic; if there is a model for these images it may be found in Victoria's own drawings of the theater, her favorite subject in the year or so before she ascended the throne. The dignified profile portraits of Sarah Cooper in particular bear a striking resemblance to the Princess' numerous drawings of Madame Grisi, her favorite actress, in a variety of heroic operatic roles. What we are seeing, then, is several times removed from reality—a conventionalized treatment of someone striking a conventionalized pose. How derivative the treatment was is indicated by Marina Warner, who notes that all of Victoria's sketches are handled in the formal, academic manner she learned from her drawing-master, Richard Westall. As it happens, Victoria had just learned of Westall's death on December 6, and this may suggest another reason for the stylization of her gypsy pictures. Westall himself was poor; he had no other pupils, but refused to take money for instructing her. Victoria had "hoped, at a future time to make him comfortable"; now, mourning his loss, she regrets that she will be "denied this satisfaction."[9] Perhaps these pictures of theatrical gypsies render payment in a less direct way, if only to Westall's memory—an artistic tribute, demonstrating how fully his precepts had been followed. She has learned her lessons well, and uses her sketches to impose stylized aesthetic form on a reality far different from the world she knows. At the same time, a word like "impose" makes her too much a conscious actor in this process. It is less likely that she deliberately set out to beautify these subjects than that the aesthetics evident in her sketches informed her first glimpses of them. There may never have been a moment in which she saw them in any other form. Her sketching is a way of confirming what she felt she had discovered, a way of turning mere experience into "Art."

I am assuming that these drawings are romanticized; perhaps they were more accurate than that. It is possible, for instance, that the gypsies Victoria encountered "by chance" camped deliberately in her path in order to become objects of her charity. It is equally possible that they would have presented themselves to genteel observers according to the models most likely to prove inoffensive: to dress cleanly, as they appear in the sketches; to hide their men (never seen in Victoria's pictures), whose roughness might be more difficult to disguise. But this elaborate scenario, if true, would only confirm further the extent to which the "reality" of this experience was structured by an elaborate theater of class, a set of socioeconomic and moral guidelines expressed in aesthetic form. Whatever Victoria actually saw, and whatever conditions or motives preceded the sight, the form in which she understood and represented it was to a great extent determined for her by the assumptions and requirements of an art that was anything but value-free.

To some extent, this is what all art does, or has the potential to do. But I have begun with these relatively casual drawings by the future Queen because the art of the sketch—or some particular forms of it—took on special importance in 1836, and because it helps us understand an important dimension of the experience of that time. That importance is suggested in a notable literary fact: 1836 was the year the first collected edition of *Sketches by Boz* appeared, an event that can be said to mark the arrival of Dickens on the literary scene and the beginning of a new form of writing that would be closely associated with his name. Some of its qualities are suggested in the word "sketch" itself. The term implies an analogy between the brief verbal description and a hastily drawn picture, an analogy stressed in the publicity for the series as an interrelated display of words and images: "Sketches by Boz and Cuts by Cruikshank." But the word also connotes effortlessness, and thus the work of a genteel amateur; as in Victoria's drawings of the gypsies, the observer can remain interested but detached because of a portraiture that does not pass beyond certain limits of scope and specificity. Of course Dickens is not really the same sort of artist as Victoria, and his sense of the sketch differs from hers in at least one crucial respect. For his is not a borrowed style, or his only available one. It is used in connection with certain kinds of subjects. In some situations, no more sustained attempt at representation will be appropriate: nothing other than a sketch will do—nothing less, and nothing more. It is almost as if, like Poe (who reviewed a pirated edition of the *Sketches* in 1836, praising the "unity of effect"[10]), Dickens imagines an audience incapable of sustained concentration, for whom a brief, compact expression of truth is the only "poetic principle" possible. But there is another reason his own verbal portraiture must be vivid and direct. Modern reality is varied, changing, evanescent—especially the reality of the city. Boz is an urban artist who introduces us to the sketch as the inescapable urban mode. F. S. Schwarzbach, who links the *Sketches* with several roughly contemporary attempts to record different aspects of urban life (including Leigh Hunt's "The Streets of the Metropolis" of 1834–1835 and William Trotter's *Select Illustrated Topography . . . of London,* 1837–1839), points out that there was something unique in the Dickensian approach: the "now-ness" of his vision, based on the same quality of the city it depicts. "His excellence," explained a *Westminster* reviewer, "appears . . . to lie in describing just what everybody sees every day."[11] Boz sketches a new art of the urban ordinary, "Illustrative of Every-Day Life and Every-Day People," as the subtitle puts it. That is what makes it both like and unlike those sketches by the Princess: after all, she did not see "Every-Day People" every day.

Sketches are hasty and unfinished drawings, preparations, studies in outline; they are also virtuoso performances, imitations, displays. Dickens creates sketches in all these senses. Boz is the historian of an external world that must be captured quickly, because it is changing, and in a distinct, virtuoso style, because what seems most significant about it, and most subject to change, is an atmosphere closely related to that style, and which only a style of that sort can preserve. We are constantly becoming aware of the artist in motion: strolling—and Boz is an ancestor of Baudelaire's *flâneur*—while he addresses us in a style as mobile as the city itself. Even the tokens of an apparent fixity and lifelessness are animated by this vision, as in the famous description of the human histories suggested by the fluttering costumes on display in the secondhand shops of Monmouth Street. "We love to walk among these extensive groves of the illustrious dead," Boz remarks, and his own motion becomes associated with a vital energy within the disembodied clothes.[12] Elsewhere his wanderings transform successive accounts of separate streets and buildings into a continuous, almost cinematic montage; particular places seem to come alive and enact their histories before our eyes. The succession of images creates the illusion of an animated cartoon or time-lapse photography, or (to mention one source of both of these) the small books of slightly differing images set in motion when we flip the pages with our thumbs. The form is experimental, as if no wholly traditional form would do. The city is somehow too large, too varied, too active to be represented by established narrative techniques. It is also too vast. The specificity of the sketch frames and limits a reality that never could be represented or even known in its entirety, and perhaps would prove unpleasant if it were. "The first thing which strikes a person on his visiting London, for the first time," writes James Grant in *The Great Metropolis* (1836), "is its amazing extent. . . . To walk over such an extent of ground amidst the everlasting jostling and interruptions which one has to encounter in the crowded thoroughfares of London, is no easy task. Those who have once achieved such a pedestrian feat, will feel no disposition to repeat it."[13]

Even when Boz becomes a fixed observer, withdrawn from the bustle of the moving crowd, the result is to accentuate further the energy of his surroundings. As in "The Streets—Morning" and "The Streets—Night," he occupies a still point around which the rest of the world turns, so that the shifting focus of the prose comes to express the shifting character of the urban scene.

> The pavement is already strewed with decayed cabbage-leaves, broken hay-bands, and all the indescribable litter of a vegetable market; men are shouting, carts backing, horses neighing, boys fighting, basket-women talking, pie-men expiating on the excellence of their pastry, and donkeys braying.[14]

Above all, the emphasis is upon change, the succession of new impressions that must be recorded to convey accurately the density of urban life. Boz makes us aware of the uniqueness of any of those impressions—events, people, things—when contrasted with a more stable sense of reality, when contrasted, that is, with anything that is not London. It is as if Dickens, too, recognizes the extraordinary nature of the everyday. He sketches to freeze what is in motion, to give permanence to what is continually taking new forms. For part of the uniqueness of urban experience is the fact that it is perpetually vanishing, perpetually on the verge of being lost. "Perhaps," Grant remarks, "there is no place in the world which so frequently changes its inhabitants as London. They are constantly shifting. . . . It is like a great vortex, drawing persons from all parts of the world into it, and, after whirling them about a short time, again throwing them out."[15]

In *Sketches by Boz,* the city is a scene of perpetual displacements: the old by the new, the new by the newer. Yet as much as Dickens seems to exult in the vigor of this urban flux, he laments the passing of certain urban events and types that cannot sustain their identities in a setting where the character of everything is transient. Again and again we are confronted with his nostalgia. The clothes-biographies of "Meditations in Monmouth Street" are motivated by it. Elsewhere Boz mourns the disappearance of favorite vehicles, buildings, hardware (such as door-knockers), and landmarks. The crowd in the Scotland Yard ale-house cannot believe that the world will survive its modern changes, a fear that is realized in the demolition first of London Bridge and then of the ale-house itself. Hackney coaches are beginning to be painted, their wheels made uniform, and Boz can only "say it with regret." "These are innovations," he adds, summing up a list of such changes, and, "like other mis-called improvements, awful signs of the restlessness of the public mind, and the little respect paid to our time-honoured institutions. Why should hackney-coaches be clean?"[16] Even nature is threatened. "The First of May" acknowledges the disappearance of a purer, pastoral existence, and with it some of the vitality of the season. The sketch begins recounting some of "the old scenes of . . . early youth. . . . Magic scenes indeed; for the fairy thoughts of infancy dressed them in colours brighter than the rainbow, and almost as fleeting." But Boz is nostalgic for more than memories. "In former times," he declares,

> spring brought with it not only such associations as these, connected with the past, but sports and games for the present—merry dances round rustic pillars, adorned with emblems of the season, and reared in honour of its coming. Where are they now! Pillars we have, but they are no longer rustic ones; and as to dancers, they are used to rooms, and lights, and would not show well in the open air. Think of the immorality, too! What would your sabbath enthusiasts say, to an aristocratic ring circling the Duke of York's column in Carleton-terrace—a grand *poussette* of the middle classes, round Alderman Waithman's monument in Fleet-street,—or a general hands-four-round of ten-pound householders, at the foot of the Obelisk, in St. George's-fields? Alas! romance can make no head against the Riot Act; and pastoral simplicity is not understood by the police.[17]

It would violate the spirit of the *Sketches* to treat this simply as a lament for the world destroyed by modern urban life. Boz is a Londoner, as the humor of the passage attests. The wit that takes over midway through ("Think of the immorality, too!") is the most marked feature of his style, and serves a function not wholly different from the stylization in Princess Victoria's drawings of the gypsies. For humor holds excess sympathy in check and keeps nostalgia at a distance. Our longings for the past, for the picturesque remnants of other worlds we remember, do not seem any less real in the medium of this style, but they seem far less serious. The point is emphasized by the narrative tone: changes in the world are inevitable, as inescapable as growing up. Humor owes its existence to this process. Boz reminds us of the fact as he explains what it means to revisit Astley's, home of the Londoner's earliest theatrical delights: "there is no place which recalls so strongly our recollections of childhood." Now, of course, everything is changed. Yet if our childhood mood cannot be recovered, it is not the place which is to blame. "Astley's has altered for the better—we have changed for the worse. Our histrionic taste is gone, and with shame we confess, that we are far more delighted and amused with the audience, than with the pageantry we once so highly appreciated."[18] Childish amazement has given way to the witty detachment of maturity. Humor allows the spectator to occupy a Wordsworthian middle ground between past and present, balancing their pleasures and gains against one another. The limited scope of the sketch achieves the same purpose. It provides the earliest structural principle for what Robert Garis terms The Dickens Theater, the art of creating any particular mood or insight in its fullest possible form without being committed to it as an unvarying position in a full fictional text. Literary sketching opens the possibility of a limited, flexible style— or, more accurately, one unlimited because of its flexibility, a flexibility that allows Dickens to explore a particular situation or character or event and then move on to explore others in other ways. Humor, too, is mobile, suited to the physical and intellectual mobility of the sketcher who strolls freely through the city without becoming fixed in any particular place or stance. It is a link between the protean variety of London and the sympathetic yet detached mind of the observer, who manages to look at it as both an insider and an outsider. Humor enables Dickens to see in several ways at once.

Above all, then, humor is unsystematic. Boz makes it clear that the witty, intimate approach to city life is an alternative to other ways of seeing and understanding, equally (or perhaps even more) modern but far less flexibly humane. Most notably, the casual realism of the sketch is deliberately contrasted with the formality of numbers. Thus, in "A Visit to Newgate," Boz announces what sort of writing he will not engage in:

We do not intend to fatigue the reader with any statistical accounts of the prison: they will be found at length in the numerous reports of numerous committees, and a variety of authorities of equal weight. We took no notes, made no memoranda, measured none of the yards, ascertained the exact number of inches in no particular room; are unable even to report of how many apartments the gaol is composed.

"We saw the prison," he concludes, "and saw the prisoners; and what we did see, and what we thought, we will tell at once in our own way."[19] The target of this disclaimer is statistics or any other formal method of representing London and its institutions quantitatively. The Statistical Society of Manchester had been founded in 1833, and that of London in the following year, just before this account was written; Boz already takes pains to distinguish his own approach from theirs. Asa Briggs has observed that throughout the period Victorians "approached the growth of their cities first and foremost in terms of *numbers*."[20] Dickens recognizes the tendency in its earliest stages, and resists.

A more general resistance is taking place here as well, although it is easy enough to mistake this for neglect, or even youthful innocence. The casual detachment of Boz's tone sets "A Visit to Newgate" apart from everything else Dickens ever wrote on prisons and from the other prison literature of its time as well. Philip Collins, in *Dickens and Crime,* remarks on the "vagueness" and "non-committal" quality of some of the descriptive passages, and adds that this "account of the prison is ... the least critical of any that I have seen from this period."[21] By "critical" here he means something like socially and morally self-conscious, the sort of stance we associate with Dickens' more "mature" writing, the vision that is established at least by the time of the publication of *Oliver Twist* several years later, and that had begun to emerge in the *Pickwick Papers* as well, certainly in the episodes concerning the Fleet Prison (issued in mid-1837). That new perspective is also evident in the 1839 edition of the *Sketches,* where Dickens adds a footnote to "A Visit to Newgate" approving recent changes in prison regulations. It is precisely this sort of direct social commentary that the sketch in its original form avoids. This is not to say that the potential for other approaches is wholly lacking: we are informed, for instance, of the clean, orderly conditions for women prisoners; and the very eagerness with which Dickens undertook the "Visit" in 1835[22] (for this was one of the few sections added to the previously published *Sketches* and written for the collected edition) suggests that he already had been touched by the contemporary interest in prison reform. Yet the sketch technique itself permits, or even requires, Boz to preserve a distance from his subjects, one that precludes a fully developed moral or political stance, just as it precludes a fully developed sympathy. The focus is less psychological than architectural; although Boz takes us inside the building, we remain outside its inhabitants. Newgate to a great extent remains a place, distinct from those inhabitants, another monument to be scrutinized for traces of life associated with the past. Thus cells are described in far more detail than are the people in them, and the longest account of a convict's state of mind concerns an imaginary being, conjured up within the gloom of a vacant condemned cell. There are, of course, real prisoners in Newgate, but Boz almost never focuses at any length upon them or even attempts to enter their minds. To do so would be to sacrifice the detached perspective of the casual observer, his humor, his calm.

Boz's equanimity as a social observer contrasts with another celebrated literary experiment of the same time—also conceived in relation to an unfamiliar form of experience, also treating a place of confinement, although in this case it is not actually a prison. The January 1836 number of the *Monthly Repository* contained two poems, signed only by the initial "Z," in which we hear only the single voice of a single speaker, apparently closed off from the rest of the world. When reissued in 1842 they would appear under the heading "Madhouse Cells," and a reference to that claustrophobic setting is implied even without the added title. "Z" turned out to be "B"—for these are Robert Browning's first published dramatic monologues—and it is almost as if the pseudononymous initial has been chosen to emphasize the proximity of "B" to B-O-Z, to close the gap of their identities by one letter. Yet in spite of that alphabetical gesture, their styles—their approaches to the characters they depict—are not in most ways similar: in place of Dickensian humor we have the first forms of Browning's grotesquerie; in place of the theatrical spectacle of various cityscapes we have the forced confinement of the cell. Of course, the madhouse is not wholly different from the prison, and Dickens would explore the Browningesque subject of psychic imprisonment imposed by madness and crime a year later in the famous account of "Fagin in the Condemned Cell" in *Oliver Twist*. But what seems most unlike Boz is the intense scrutiny of Browning's dramatic monologue technique. The creation of that dramatic "I" prevents us from distancing these bizarre figures—"Porphyria's Lover" and "Johannes Agricola in Meditation"—as mere clinical curiosities. The dramatic monologue gives us access to a world otherwise closed, not just to the rooms in which these men are confined but to the innermost "cells" of their beings, to what Pater would call "the narrow chamber of the individual mind."[23] This is observation that penetrates to the very soul of its object; we are engaged far more closely than what we experience with Boz. Michael Mason has argued that the reference to "Madhouse Cells" grows out of a contemporary debate over more humane treatment of lunatics; there was a new insistence on recognizing the rationality of madness, on the importance of precise observation as a therapeutic tool.[24] Yet the fixity and depth of this gaze also suggests observation closer to the model proposed by Michael Foucault; if we feel as if we are within the cell, we also seem to be peering into it with the intensity of a keeper. As we will see, there were others in the 1830s who shared this perspective; Dickens would become one of them before long. Yet in the *Sketches by Boz* observation is less intrusive, less intense. To some extent this does involve vagueness, including moral vagueness; Dickens's determination to add a sketch on Newgate reminds us that a clearer moral position would not be long in developing. But for now, at least, in 1835 and 1836, the sketch serves as an alternative to more passionate engagement in such matters. Its ease of manner is bound up in the persona of Boz, and in this sketch at least his detachment also contributes to our sense of the identity of the beings he depicts. By keeping those inmates so much at the margins of his sketch, Dickens preserves something of their independence, their integrity. There is a recognition of their humanness here, and it is respected. That respect persists even when Boz follows a character into a prison from the streets.

"The Last Cab-Driver" examines another disappearing London type, a figure "who awakened in our bosom a feeling of admiration and respect, which we entertain a fatal presentiment will never be called forth again by any human being."[25] Once again, we can imagine the same material introduced in a very different key. Nearly extinct types and dying institutions might call forth a more apocalyptic vision, the more violent clashing of old and new we associate with Dickens in those later and more Carlylean novels *Hard Times* and *A Tale of Two Cities*. Conflict here is of a very different sort. It is not that *Sketches by Boz* lacks consciousness of social change, but that the consciousness is untroubled: the Dickensian brow remains unfurrowed; that Carlylean struggle of epochs here is largely comic, a mock battle. Thus "The Last Cab-Driver" moves quickly from picturesque details—the "gorgeous" colors of the vehicle, its driving habits and trick of reappearing in the most unlikely times and places—to a humorous contest between the driver and the law, his "influence . . . over the risible muscles of justice itself." On the "last time we saw our friend," the cabman is threatened with arrest by an upset customer. Calculating that there is no escape, he "knocked the little gentleman down, and then called the police to take himself into custody, with all the civility in the world." Here is one London character who will face the threat of extinction in style. And it is interesting that, as in the remarks on May Days, the disappearance of the type is a by-product of the extending influence of law itself; perhaps all eccentricity will die out in a wholly civilized society, certainly all eccentricity will if it displays itself like this in public. Yet we are not allowed to dwell on the darker implications of this episode, for the sketch is not concluded here. As Boz hastens to add, "A story is nothing without a sequel." The narrative only ends when the cab-driver is encountered once more—although at a distance, for now Boz does not actually see him. Visiting the Middlesex prison "in search of our long-lost friend," Boz hears a voice "pouring forth its soul in the plaintive air of 'All round my hat,' which was then just beginning to form a recognized portion of our national music." The Governor explains that the singer is a prisoner who refused to work on the wheel, was ordered to solitary confinement, and there "lies on his back on the floor, and sings comic songs all day." We immediately recognize the character; his triumphant independence reads like a parable of the comic spirit itself. More importantly, it epitomizes the movement of narration throughout the *Sketches*. There is no question about the direction the world is taking. London is coming increasingly under the sway of officialdom; many of the city's most colorful people and institutions are disappearing as society becomes increasingly ordered, rational. But it remains possible to imagine a compromise—a comic compromise—between a new society and the colorful figures of the past.

It is important to recognize, though, that this compromise is largely imagined. The cab driver is not visited in his cell; Boz merely hears his voice. As he later explains, "Our heart had not deceived us." There is a wish fulfillment about this conclusion that Dickens makes no effort to disguise: the cab driver may be the last of a dying type, but he remains cheery, undaunted. The closing description of him is wholly theatrical, in Garis' sense of the word; it is, to use the subtitle of the section in the *Sketches* from which this account is taken, a "scene." To some extent, then, Boz's equanimity is made possible by a reduction of this figure in another way. Not unlike the police reports considered earlier, this construction of experience into comic drama "sentences" the cab driver to a life that is not his own. Yet there remains something more complex and more tentative about the Dickensian scene. As that word suggests, this is only a small portion of a larger drama, and that drama might take on a very different tone. If it is still possible to laugh, other responses are not ruled out. It is still possible, that is, for the cab driver to laugh, and still possible for Boz himself, but we can imagine both viewing the scene in a very different way. Victoria's sketches display no evidence of a sense that there are alternatives to seeing those gypsies in the way she does, no sense that other conditions might await them than the one she depicts. Dickens presents us with an art of alternatives, which proposes its conclusions lightly, tentatively, even putatively (is that really the voice of the cab driver?), with a sense of their precariousness strongly underscored. Why, after all, is this the last cab driver? Why is this to be the last time Boz will ever see him? More severe "sentences" could be imposed, and perhaps they will be. Comedy here, as comedy always, alludes to the tragedies that might have been—but alludes only, then refuses to invoke them. It is comedy in spite of everything, comedy after all. In later Dickens fiction, this precariousness will grow more and more difficult to sustain; by the time of the darker novels, it will be a comedy increasingly difficult to believe in, but only because of a shift in a balance we can see struck with this very first published book. As early as *Oliver Twist* that balance shifts, but that change of tone only serves to make the achievement of 1836 seem all the more impressive. It is still possible to contemplate a rapidly changing world with equanimity. But there are signs that this won't be true for long.

II

The London and Greenwich Railway was opened in 1836, the first constructed in the "neighbourhood" of the metropolis, as the *Penny Magazine* pointed out.[26] The magazine devoted the lead article in its issue of 9 January 1836 to the new line, or more precisely, as the headline indicates, to "The London and Greenwich Viaduct and Railway"—not just to the railway system but also to its most impressive piece of engineering, the great arches on which the tracks are carried as they cross Bermondsey and Deptford. The front page of that issue is dominated by a woodcut of the scene (Figure 1.4). Indeed, we almost feel that the woodcut is dominated by the scene it tries to depict: instead of the usual vertical format, this picture is placed so the magazine must be turned in order to study it. It is one of the earliest railway pictures, perhaps the earliest showing a line connecting to London, and it is important in precisely the way the sketches by Victoria and Dickens are—as an indication of how in 1836 people conceived and represented reality, especially the new forms of reality that were being encountered for the first time. Yet in another way this is a fundamentally different sort of art from what we have seen in those other examples. Victoria's sketchbook is a private record, informed by the standards of her class and the graphic style she learned from her drawing master, Richard Westall; it is not intended to address any specific audience. Dickens clearly is writing for a wide body of readers, yet in doing so he creates a simultaneously public and personal voice, as embodied in the persona of that witty and omnipresent observer, Boz. The *Penny Magazine* speaks in a far less individualized manner and claims to offer something far less narrowly personalized than mere impressionistic sketches. It is, after all, a publication of the Society for the Diffusion of Useful Knowledge, as we are reminded on every cover. Here, then, are facts, information; we are expected to regard these essays and illustrations, as useful records of the truth. Yet clearly enough this is a rendition of facts, truth represented in a particular aesthetic form. What sort of truth does it represent, and how? What are the concerns and values that inform this "scene"?

For it is a scene—both as presented in the *Penny Magazine* and, according to the essay that begins beneath the illustration, when visited in reality. The anonymous author is enthusiastic enough about this "metropolitan improvement" (an earlier London book of this title had been illustrated by Cruikshank) to describe it as a "scene" or a "picture," so pleasing to gaze upon that we might imagine it had been arranged for our visual gratification. It is a "fine spectacle," the writer explains, "really worthy of the term frequently applied to it, 'magnificent.'" The railway is presented more as a work of art, or part of a beautiful landscape, than a mere machine or industrial tool. It is idealized, no less than Victoria's pictures of the gypsies—perhaps even more so when we realize that this picture was made before the construction was complete (like the contemporary railway maps that recorded projected lines as part of the cityscape); the scene it depicts does not yet fully exist in reality. To some extent the article faces this issue, for it speculates on how the completed line will live up to such lofty expectations. The arches have been designed to house businesses, and paths have been laid out to maintain a thoroughfare beneath the tracks: will the presence of the railway disturb the scenic beauty the writer anticipates? He insists that it will not. Some "individuals" are quoted to explain: the noise, for instance, will be no more unsettling (or, implicitly, no less natural) than that of suddenly passing thunder, or else (another man says) like that of a "heavily-laden wagon, the noise of which did not at all disturb his comfort." It is not important to decide whether such reports are exaggerated or whether the tolerance for noise in 1836 was higher than it is today. What is interesting here is that the same sorts of questions are raised that we might pose—questions of environmental impact, we would term them—but they are answered decidedly in an affirmative voice. The only concern expressed by the writer is for the smooth operation of the trains themselves: if the arches are used as planned to house private dwellings, the smoke from them could make the tracks impassable; therefore gas stoves have been installed "to prevent the annoyance of the smoke." The annoyance, that is, to the railway! Railroads will not intrude on normal life, or vice versa, the *Penny Magazine* reassures us. The new technology belongs.

All of this is implicit in the questions raised, and the answers given, in the *Penny Magazine* essay; and the same strategy of justification can be seen in the illustration that goes with it. There, if anything, the impulse to aestheticize the railway is even more evident, as is the technique by which this is accomplished. The "scene" is laid out according to well-established formats of iconography and allusion. The image is framed by two willowy trees at either side, with an unbroken gray sky overhead and well-cultivated gardens in the foreground below. The woodcut may have been designed by, or based on the work of, G. F. Bragg, whose *Six Views of the London and Greenwich Railway* (1836) (Figure 1.5) places the long, arched viaduct in the background of pastoral scenes, with sheep grazing or canal horses at rest—and even those animals look up in undisturbed interest at the distant, passing carriages.[27] The most fundamental effect of such an arrangement is to naturalize the railway. We might be in a prosperous country town rather than a few miles from London Bridge. The buildings of a more populous area are seen at a distance, but the people visible here are strolling at leisure and admiring the views (one man is pointing out some distant sight to a boy). Perhaps the area did retain a village atmosphere in the 1830s, but the very creation of a short railway line suggested the possibility of a present or future increase in density in the area; the *Penny Magazine* estimates traffic will be 4,000 people per week. The image avoids reference to this growth by insisting on another set of social conditions: suburban peace and pastoralism, in spite of or perhaps even under the protection of the new technology. Those arches, after all, look less like a modern railway construction than a Roman aqueduct. This allusion comes from the design of the arches themselves, examples of what George L. Hersey calls the architecture of associationism.[28] The illustration exaggerates the associational effect, making the arches seem slightly higher and more slender (i.e. nobler) than in fact they are, calling attention to the pattern of the brickwork, and obscuring the railway carriages themselves so that the viaduct remains at the center of interest. As George Rennie commented a year later, on plans for the London Grand Junction Railway that made use of arches like those on the Greenwich line, "The eye dwells with pleasure on the undulating line of the arches—and when the series is of some length the effect is still better. The admiration excited by the Aqueducts at Rome and Lisbon is a proof of this."[29] The inescapable allusion to Rome suggests imperial power, wealth, and dignity; above all, it connotes a world of romantic landscapes. Industrial England begins to look Mediterranean.

   Sir John Summerson points out that when the first London Bridge Station was built in 1844 (as a terminus for the London and Greenwich Railway and several other southeastern lines), the design was an Italian villa resembling a mansion Charles Barry recently had completed for Lord Tankerville at Walton-on-Thames. "Raised on ground that was made up to the level of the viaduct which carried the line to Greenwich, the station with its tower and belvedere must have made a pretty picture."[30] Such pictures helped legitimate the impact of the railways on the world they entered. In this sense, Summerson misses the point when he remarks on the incongruity of Philip Hardwick's elaborate classical portico at the entrance to Euston Station (1835–1840): it was "the kind of thing which noblemen were accustomed to build at the entrances to their parks. . . . The problem of a railway station as an architectural subject was not brought into focus."[31] But in another way, precisely that problem is focused on, and not so much solved as deliberately overshadowed by traditional aesthetic forms. A frank, truly "modern," railway architecture would have been too stark, and thus posed a serious problem indeed. The function of those Greenwich line arches, or the image of them in the *Penny Magazine,* is to persuade us that we have not yet arrived at a crisis that forces us to choose between the new and the old. The new technology can be sustained beautifully on traditional supports.

I have left one crucial detail of this illustration unremarked until now because in a sense it sums up all the others: the church spire, rising high above the arches, over the smoking engine of the railway train itself, in the background of the picture. It almost rises out of those vertical arches, although its line also partly mirrors the only other slender verticals in the illustration, the trees at the edges of the print. The church has a meaning in both contexts: it is a symbol of the faith which arose from the "paganism" of Rome and which provides much of the unifying force in the English pastoral myth. These associations are strengthened further by the fact that it is a Greek Revival church of the 1820s (St. James's, Thurland Road, by James Savage, 1827–1829, although it is not so labelled in the woodcut).[32] Once again, we are shown the classical tradition rising to its culmination in Christianity, as indeed, the picture suggests, does the power of the railway itself. The engine of the railway train is almost invisible against the shadowed side of the church; in effect the church merges with it, and the smoke almost seems to be coming from the church as well. The church is the integrating visual image in the picture, the presiding force that organizes all of its elements into a unified scene in the first place, the pious "genius of the place." The vertical spire, then, connects all the varied human activity in the picture with some higher purpose. If it were not for its presence, both the railway carriages and the buildings on the distant hillside would be more prominent. Our eyes would be forced to move randomly between the different elements of the picture—foreground, background, right, and left—and the horizontality of the image would emerge far more strongly than it does. As an image of a civilized place, a town, and one closely associated with the city of London, it would become more

diffuse, less centralized, losing itself in its endless growth rather than sta-
bilized by the institutions at its center. We would have a sprawling, suburban, horizontal city, instead of the orderly, vertical world imaged in the
print. The woodcut solves these aesthetic problems in a conventional way.
It is not the only representation of the contemporary world to call our
attention to such contrasts.

III

The notion of contrasts receives one of its most important formulations
in 1836, in one of the best-known of all nineteenth-century accounts of the
state of the environment. It is given by an architect named Augustus
Welby Pugin, whose views are proclaimed in the very title of his most
famous book: *Contrasts; or A Parallel between the Noble Edifices of the
Fourteenth and Fifteenth Centuries, and Similar Buildings of the Present
Day; Shewing the Present Decay of Taste.* It is one of the classic writings
of the Gothic Revival, and Kenneth Clark credits it with originating "a
new conception of the Middle Ages."[33] This conception also involves a
new way of regarding the present: not just a new attitude towards the modern world but a new method of evaluating it, a new epistemology in which
architecture becomes the basis for the analysis of the whole of society.
Pugin creates a Gothic grid against which nineteenth-century reality can
be placed, measured, and judged. His image for this evaluative process is
the scale: the final illustration of *Contrasts* shows a medieval church being
weighed against, and overbalancing, several modern ones. But most of the
illustrations depend less on such a metaphoric balancing process than a
specific, point-by-point comparison of medieval and modern buildings,
down to some of their most minute details. We are meant to treat the former as a visual norm against which any of the latter's deviations can be
seen and denounced. I have used the term "grid" to describe this analytic
structure because the dense specificity of the plates emphasizes contrasting
patterns, patterns of architecture in the fourteenth and nineteenth centuries. Gothic, then, is literally a frame of reference. Pugin's subject is the
total design of a world, the structure composed out of all the disparate
elements of a material culture. And his text is copiously illustrated, so we
can see what he means. Clark points out that some of the plates make their
points through Pugin's own pictorial style as much as through distinctions
in historical architecture. "The dignified panelling of the modern Contrasted Altar might seem to us preferable to its fussy Gothic counterpart

were it not made repulsive by an ingenious trick of shading and the dis-
proportionate hugeness of its church furniture."[34] But such tricks are
needed because Pugin is as interested in general atmosphere as in the treatment of specific details. The real subject is the impact of architecture on
those who use it, the experience of the world that it creates. It is a much
larger subject than architecture alone. Were it not for the limits of space,
Pugin remarks, he could have shown that the Revived Pagan Principle
"has invaded the ordinary forms of speech, and is discernible in modern
manners and government."[35] The book concerns pervasive moral contrasts, expressed by the most minute details as well as the broadest lines
of architecture.

The lines Pugin admires most enthusiastically are vertical. They dominate his own architectural work, as can be seen in the imaginary grouping
of the two dozen favorite churches he had designed, in the frontispiece to
An Apology for the Revival of Christian Architecture in England (1843).
The picture looks like a competition of spires; as Phoebe Stanton notes, it
gives many of the churches on paper "spires they were never to acquire"
in reality.[36] But as in the designs for individual churches (such as St.
Mary's, Derby, which was begun in December 1837 and which Pugin
etched at the time of its completion in October 1839 with an imaginary
spire that does not even appear in the frontispiece of the *Apology*),[37] the
point is to create an effect, and to emphasize a quality he felt was implicit
in all of his work. For Pugin conceived of himself not only as a modern
Gothic architect, but as the architect of a new *civitas dei,* in which architecture serves as the ever-present symbol of the connection between the
secular and the sacred. *Contrasts* campaigns for Gothic, or what was called
the Pointed Style, because, quite literally (in one of the verbal-visual metaphors Pugin loves to employ), it points the way to the True Faith. "Great
height and vertical lines," he explains, "have been considered by the Chris-
tians, from the earliest period, as the emblem of the resurrection" (3). In
the first of the contrasting plates in the revised edition of 1841, showing a
"Catholic town in 1440," (Figure 1.6) the vertical movement is overwhelming, for most of the public buildings have tall spires and even the
houses have steep roofs. The illustration of "The Same Town in 1840"
contains few of those medieval holdovers; the continuous horizontal band
of modern rooftops dominates the scene, broken only by the regular thin
forms of smokestacks, with a few wavy lines of smoke to remind us how
they pollute the clear air England used to breathe. A more fearsome part
of the new, secular city is the square-enclosed octagonal building squatting
low in the foreground. Pugin calls it "The New Jail," but it is clearly based
on Bentham's panopticon. The radical simplicity of such geometric build-

ing is precisely what Pugin wishes us to find repulsive in modern design, and modern social theory. This is the architectural embodiment of a utilitarian nightmare, a world wholly rationalized into oppressive, deadening regularity. The drawing presents the aesthetic form of this social and philosophical decline. It is building without aspiration, building that binds itself to the earth, building that traps the eye and the mind in a repetition of a few limited forms. The same monotony forms the visual pattern of the whole New Town: identical windows laid in bands across undecorated factory walls suggest the observer's sense of exclusion, the inhabitant's sense of imprisonment. This is the Horizontal City, bound to the material world, binding and dehumanizing its citizens. And barely seen on the furthest horizon, mirroring the repetitive utilitarian mechanization of architecture and life in such a place, barely visible through the smokey atmosphere, is the long, arched viaduct of a railway line, almost identical to the one on the cover of the *Penny Magazine.*

There are almost no other references to railways in *Contrasts,* but the book voices a sustained denunciation of the entire series of modern innovations that literally have broken up the harmonious medieval world. We can see this vandalism for ourselves, Pugin explains, by visiting any "renovated" example of our ancient parochial churches, and he lists the outrages:

> The aisles cut to pieces by galleries of all sizes, and heights; the nave blocked up with pews; screens cut away; stalls removed from their old position in the chancel, and set about in odd places. . . . Large portions of the church, for which there is no use, walled off, to render the preaching place more snug and comfortable; porches enclosed and turned into engine houses, and a host of other wretched mutilations. . . . (32)

Modern construction in reality is destruction. Pugin once again seems to be speaking literally in one of the Appendices to the edition of 1841 when he refers to "the leveling and destructive feelings produced by real Protestantism" (70).

Some of this can be seen as the anti-Protestant ranting of a rabid Catholic, yet what makes Pugin's theology interesting is that it takes a consistently architectural form. He reads the decline of England after Henry VIII as an unending campaign of architectural violence: "from this period, we have only to trace a melancholy series of destructions and mutilations" (23). The failures of Protestantism are especially visible when it tries to ape the forms of Catholic building.

A follower of John Knox himself, as in the Scotch conventicle in London, may build a meeting-house with pointed windows, arches, and tolerably good detail, but these will always look like the scattered leaves of a precious volume that have been bound up by an unskilful hand, without connexion [*sic*] or relation to their meaning. (57–58)

By extension, this is the problem of the modern city as well: it is a disunity, a formerly and potentially still-cohesive social unit that has been shattered and dispersed (like those ecclesiastical possessions) by a Reformed society. Part of what makes the town of 1840 so disturbing is its lack of a center. Even if the abbey grounds that were at the center of the Catholic town four hundred years earlier still exist, we cannot see them behind the forbidding walls of those riverside factories. The only possible center of things, and the closest thing to a circular building in the picture, is the Benthamite jail: the octagon within a square. The octagon reappears later in "Contrasted Residences for the Poor"—a sterile modern poor house, commanding an almost uninhabited landscape. Here, then, is the organizing unit of nineteenth-century life, requiring only the addition of a last enclosing wall to be converted—should the growth of another new town make this necessary—from a house of charity to a house of correction. In either case the contrast with the Middle Ages is dramatic: the poor are confined, not cared for. Pugin suggests (not unlike Foucault) that the cornerstone of modern social architecture is the power of surveillance and coercion.

Yet in spite of this vision of dehumanization, *Contrasts* is not fundamentally a gloomy book, at least not in the first edition of 1836. Phoebe Stanton points out that revisions made the second edition considerably harsher. "Little of Pugin's wilful but amusing enthusiasm of 1836 remained in 1841;"[38] some of the passages he had "discarded had qualified and lightened the satire of the earlier book."[39] The tone had become "disagreeable," for Pugin's battle against the Revived Pagan Principle "was at least in part inspired by his dismay and despair over the state of society."[40] Somehow in 1836 this mood could be held in check. There is, to be sure, the bleak vision of a Horizontal City, a medieval Catholic world wholly levelled; yet it remains possible to conceive of the trend being reversed, of a new Pointed Style emerging from the ashes of the old one and bringing society to a Gothic rebirth. Perhaps the most telling indication of this surviving, vertical possibility appears in the two-line motto to the penultimate chapter, "On the Present Degraded State of Ecclesiastical Buildings." It is printed, as we might expect in heavy Gothic type.

> The spot that angels deigned to grace,
> Is blessed though robbers haunt the place.   (35)

The passage might serve as an epigraph to *Oliver Twist,* which began to appear a year after *Contrasts.* Yet there it would be ironic, so difficult to accept so that even the "blessed" characters of the novel must move away from London by the end of the book. Pugin in 1836 alerts us to the same irony but is still able to rise above it on the vertical lines of his architectural utopianism. Perhaps 1836 was the last year in which he would be able to sustain such a vision. Perhaps it was one of the last years for some time when anyone could. It was becoming increasingly difficult to mediate past and present, to remain confident of the moral direction of the pervasive spectacle of change.

IV

I have not yet discussed signs, unless the term is used in its semiotic sense as referring to all signifying features, as in the pictures by Victoria, Pugin, and the *Penny Magazine,* or the language of *Sketches by Boz.* This is not a wholly modern connotation. The word was used in similar if slightly different ways in the 1830s; and it is that contemporary sense of and interest in signs that I wish to explore briefly here. The starting point for this investigation must be Carlyle's classic essay of 1829, "Signs of the Times," which alludes to Christ's words in Matt. 16:3 as a way of insisting upon the urgency of the present need for attentiveness and interpretation. Within a few years the title phrase had become commonplace, although usually without Carlyle's apocalyptic undertones attached. It could at times take on an even more modern connotation, though, especially when reexamined with reference to the chapter on "Symbols" in *Sartor Resartus.* Thus William Sewell, reviewing Carlyle's writings for the *Quarterly* in 1840, conjectures, "Perhaps, after all, the whole of human philosophy is nothing more than construing signs, translating one language into another, reading individual facts in general principles, and general principles in individual facts."[41]

There is an even more common, and more literal, sense of this word current in the 1830s. It is related to the problem of "construing signs" that Sewell mentions, and to the nostalgia for familiar, traditional forms of life that we have seen in *Sketches by Boz.* For one of the tokens of the disappearing, premodern urban culture Dickens writes about is the old-fash-

ioned shop-sign—an outmoded form of art connected with an outmoded
form of trade, a memorial to a simpler mode of life associated with a simpler economy. There is an essay on such "Signs" in *Chambers' Edinburgh
Journal* for December 23, 1837, and another on shop-signs in the *Penny
Magazine* of 12 March 1836. Both examine the historical roots of modern
signs. All people, says *Chambers'*, echoing Carlyle on "Symbols," are sign
users, and the essay traces various forms of this from ancient cultures
down to the present; it is as if signs are at once primitive relics and tokens
of our progress. This contrast is even more evident in the *Penny Magazine,*
where it is pointed out that some traditional symbols are still in use, and
that others have become obscure and require explication. All signs, simple
or complex, tell us something about the ability of individuals to express
themselves and something about the state of the societies in which they
live. It is not surprising, then, to find another contemporary picture (Figure 1.7), another "scene" of modern urban life, almost totally filled with
signs, that peculiarly modern form we know as advertising posters. It is,
in effect, a picture of words, a symbol of symbols. It is dated 1835, although
internal evidence suggests that it was reworked until 1837—thus its central
imagery concerns the nature of those symbols in the year or so just before
Victoria ascended the throne: the signs of the times, especially insofar as
those signs take on a particular form in London.

The picture, a watercolor by a little-known painter named John Orlando
Parry, is entitled "A London Street Scene," although we see less of an
actual street, or street life, than of the backdrop against which street activity usually takes place. That backdrop is not completely usual, though,
since it is under construction. This is an image of London changing, London being rebuilt. A dozen figures are depicted in front of a low construction fence and an old building wall. On it are pasted dozens of paper posters. The wooden fence is pasted with them, too, and there is even one
behind the fence on the scaffolding that holds up the old building. In the
distance, rising over the single street lamp, is the dome of St. Paul's. All in
all, it is a site we can imagine actually seeing; nothing in the image is
extraordinary, as the title promises. "Street scenes" are common forms of
urban genre painting, records of actual life. But the phrase usually refers
to the people on the streets. Here the emphasis on surfaces and the physical
presence of buildings connects the title to the layout of London as much
as anything else; as in Pugin, or in the illustration of the London and
Greenwich Railway in the *Penny Magazine,* the subject is the state of the
urban environment. The scene is the material, nonhuman street, and Parry
shows us enough of it, in enough detail, to lead us to question its nature.

What does London look like as a material entity? What will it look like in the future, when this construction is complete? How is that future related to what existed before? The dome of St. Paul's, inset at the left-hand corner like an iconographic rubric beginning (if we read from left to right) the rest of the visual exercise, forces us to consider the relation of the modern city to its form in the past century, or the even more distant past. And St. Paul's is even further bracketed in the picture by those scaffolding boards and the construction fence: what are we making out of our heritage?

Such generalized, abstract questions occupy our interest more forcefully than any of the human figures in the lower foreground of the picture. There are three groups of them (four and two and five people, respectively, with an additional dog in the left-hand group balancing the numbers and bringing the total to a dozen beings in all). At the left, a guardsman talks with a top-hatted policeman, whose pocket is being picked by a young thief. At the right, two women, two men, and a butcher's boy stand around a chestnut brazier, two of them watching the bill-sticker at work in the center of the picture. Near the center, with his back towards us, is "a stunted chimney sweep."[42] Yet even his central position does not call attention to his poverty, or his deformity. The most important characteristic of this boy is his craned neck: his head leans far backwards to watch the new bill being unrolled above him; he returns our attention from the human world back up to the signifying words. The pickpocket, similarly, seems to have been introduced as a comic touch rather than for his rags—a Hogarthian detail, although unlike Hogarth Parry does not allow us to linger over such figures. The pickpocket marks the lower corner of a visual triangle that again draws our eyes away from the human action and back to those pasted walls; similarly, the very darkness of the chimneysweep's clothing makes his presence less prominent. None of the figures stands out at first sight, not just because of the brightness of the printed letters behind them but because they are all frozen in place, figures from a tableau. The mass of printed imagery immediately behind them is like a stage curtain dropped behind actors fixed at the narrow edge of a theater platform; only here the curtain becomes the main presence on the stage, the leading character in the action. The drama of the picture lies in this very fact, for in normal terms it isn't dramatic at all. What we are shown, then, is the backdrop becoming foregrounded, humans fading into insignificance before, alongside, and within the city to which they supposedly give life. This "Street Scene" is quite literally a scene of the street—a scene about this place as a visible, palpable presence. We are observing animated life slowly dying out, or already dead, in spite of the white smoke from the brazier or the allusions of those posters themselves to "living theater" acted in other times and places. People in the urban world are less convincingly alive than in the world of the stage, or in the references to the stage made by popular advertising.

Dickens explores the same relation between our sense of the theater and our response to printed words in the section on "Astley's" from *Sketches by Boz.*

> We never see any very large, staring, black Roman capitals, in a book, or shop-window, or placarded on a wall, without their immediately recalling to our mind an indistinct and confused recollection of the time when we were first initiated into the mysteries of the alphabet. We almost fancy we see the pin's point following the letter, to impress its form more strongly on our bewildered imagination; and wince involuntarily, as we remember the hard knuckles with which the reverend old lady who instilled into our mind the first principles of education for ninepence per week, or ten and sixpence per quarter, was wont to poke our juvenile head occasionally, by way of adjusting the confusion of ideas in which we were generally involved. The same kind of feeling pursues us in many other instances, but there is no place which recalls so strongly our recollections of childhood as Astley's.[43]

As I observed earlier, Dickens goes on to "confess" that his infantile taste for the Astley's performances has diminished. He does not indicate whether there has been a corresponding alteration in his sense of printed letters. But his remarks provide another way of regarding Perry's "scene," and understanding its connection with a world related to yet removed from the one we knew as children. Parry invites us to reexperience that childhood sense of wonder at the presence of the letter. It is as if we are scanning print once again for the first time, with a sense of its drama and mystery and life.

This fascination with words and letters is connected with our experience of people, and our experience of the city. For it is precisely the blankness of London's walls, created in part by the new construction that erects fences and scaffoldings and treats old buildings as surfaces to be remade, that opens new possibilities for posting bills, and diminishes the importance of the human drama by comparison to the vitality of the changing material world. In effect the city itself is recreated as a temporary surface, open to infinite and perpetual redecoration, relabelling. A writer in the Dublin *Evening Post* in 1840 would refer to London, in contrast to Paris, as "neither new nor old," but rather "a sort of *Provisional City,* a multitudinous congregation of houses, that are constantly . . . in a state of transition of being run up or run down."[44] *The Great Metropolis* had made the same observation about the city's population: "There is no place in the world which so frequently changes its inhabitants as London. They are constantly shifting."[45]

If a continually changing London has become merely "provisional," it becomes necessary to view its people in a new provisional character as well—in terms of their most prominent eccentricities at any particular moment, in terms of the poses they assume or the roles they fill within particular settings or circumstances. Grant, commenting on the isolation and anonymity of London life, suggests that it would be possible to "walk on all fours in the public streets, without any one staying to bestow a look on you."[46] The implication, of course, is that this may actually be the case. Impersonality breeds peculiarity, perhaps even animalistic behavior (which Grant documents in his later descriptions of the lower classes), and whatever other extremes of behavior are adopted to establish individuality within the urban mass. This is one of the important assumptions of Dickensian characterization, already at work in *Sketches by Boz.* It is the method of Parry's "Street Scene" as well. We view these figures in a moment of suspended animation, as caricatures. They are less permanent, and perhaps less convincingly real, than the letters of the posters behind them. Yet their alphabetic immobility makes it possible to shift our attention back upwards to the real letters on the wall, and then lower our gaze again to those figures "from life." Figures and posters blend together to create the "characters" of an enormous theatrical spectacle, an elaborate urban tableau, so heavily stylized that we have no alternative but to attempt to "read" its messages.

There is a fundamental connection, then, between those posters on the wall and the people on the streets below, although it is a connection that at first glance seems ironic or paradoxical. There are just a dozen living beings in this "scene," yet we cannot even count the posted bills. The figures on the street are frozen in an eternal present, while the bills (printed and attached in the past) refer to events that were still in the future when they were new—and (as I will show at more length) events that are in many cases based on famous episodes from the historical past. The disorder of the posters resembles a dense archeological site, in which one vertical slice reveals many separate historic periods copresent in a single physical area. This collapsing of time is most clearly imaged in the newest addition to the wall, the poster that is being stuck during the present moment of the picture's existence. This poster, and the act of sticking it, implies a coexistence of past, present, and future, as well as a simultaneity of legibility and that which cannot be seen. The blank, pasted side of the poster is the center of the entire painting, the apex of triangles formed by the side groups, the spot towards which the three figures looking upwards (a sweep, a sailor, and the bill-sticker himself) gaze; it is the central point of both color and significance. No wonder it is being watched so intently. It is above all an image of the frozen, precarious quality of the present. We are watching to see what modern London will become.

What is there to see in that central patch of white? Nothing less than the future unrolling from the past. The bill being pasted now was printed earlier—to refer in turn to a later performance of a classic play from the past *(Othello)*. Another place is referred to—the stage on which the play will be performed—yet we cannot see what or where it is, or rather will be. The top third of the poster remains obscure, a future that cannot be wholly known. And if we try to imagine the conditions under which it will be known, we discover that more knowledge only brings further confusion. For in the few seconds it will take for the bill-sticker to complete his task, the rest of the clarity of this "scene" will dissolve into the ordinary jumble of the streets: the butcher's boy will move on, the pickpocket will flee (perhaps pursued by the guardsman, the policeman, or the barking dog), the chestnut-woman will turn her head to see if her bellows have taken effect. Perhaps the bill-sticker will begin to affix another poster. In another instant, that is, life will resume.

Parry's watercolor exploits our curiosity about the seen to confront us with the proximity of the unseen, the invisible futures suggested by the visible forms of the present. It draws us towards the imagining of such futures through the centrality of that nearly pasted, nearly posted bill. We are compelled to "read" the future as well as the present, a process that because of the outdated material on the other posters, and because of the traditional costumes of the figures on the street, also involves reading the past. In this sense, the "scene" of those letters on the wall becomes representative of the "scene" of London life generally. We are presented with an intricate confusion that requires interpretation, a partly living rebus composed of the layered interpenetrations of past, present, and future. It is an instant frozen from a living world, an archeological fragment of a complex civilization—how complex, how much alive, is suggested by the incompletion of what we do manage to perceive. What is in the other half of the poster? What is behind the wall? What will happen next? Such questions are inescapable, and the answers unavailable. The image cries out for decoding: some of the posters barely can be made out, and strain our eyes to read; we want to move closer, change perspective, discern the key to the puzzle. Yet it resists clarification. The attempt to read reveals what we can and what we cannot know. The precision with which Parry has represented those alphabetical characters gives way to a growing sense of uncertainty

in the character of the scene as a whole, an uncertainty found above all in
the rigid forms of the other supposedly living characters. We cannot penetrate their immobility to the life behind. The theatricality of poses that
makes them so explicable also involves a reduction, a suspension, of their
real, ordinary lives. Like the posters on the wall, they must be seen in a
partial fixity, or not seen at all—at least, not seen with the completeness
required for our own interpretive activity, not seen within a fully rationalized "scene." Perhaps this theatricality, like that of Victoria's picturesque gypsies, results from the artist's necessary distance from life. Perhaps
it is intentional: as in the case of Dickens' last cab driver, we are not
allowed to intrude on the privacy of inner being. In either case, we cannot
crack the code.

Thus far, I have referred only generally to the words on those posters,
the specific signs that attract our attention as strongly as any of the living
figures in the picture. They are almost all theatrical posters, and thus again
remind us of the staged character of the "scene" below. The references are
to popular plays and playhouses: *Othello, The Last Days of Pompeii, Tom
and Jerry;* the Adelphi, Astley's, St. James', the English Opera House.
More than this actually can be read—or in another sense less, since even
some of these words are shown only in part and must be reconstructed
from the hints of a few letters (or fragments of letters). But this is related
to the interpretive activity that the picture necessarily stimulates: we recreate fragmented statements, and create new ones out of the juxtapositions
of different fragments alongside one another. The effect is like that of those
popular childhood skits ("sketches") based on rapid changes of the radio
dial: cooking lessons merge with news reports and advertisements with
soap operas; it is the effect Orson Welles exploited in creating his brilliant
radio version of *War of the Worlds*. Sensory confusion becomes collage,
which can produce horror or laughter, and part of its fascination is that we
never feel completely sure how to respond, how to classify such art. It col-
lapses the borders between artifice and reality and forces us to reexamine
our normal insistence on making clear generic distinctions. Welles, for
instance, proved dramatically that the taste for science fiction involved
some fundamental anxieties about the nature of the everyday world. Parry
is doing something not wholly different. We are not simply being reminded
of the most popular stage presentations of the past few months, or the most
colorful posters found on London's walls. This is an arranged randomness,
suggesting something about contemporary preoccupations and tastes. It is
a collection of thoughts, memories, recreations, fantasies: a collage of the
popular mind—which may explain why it is conceived suspended over the
heads of these figures, who seem to be walking in their sleep while their

daytime dream-work stands out more vividly than they do themselves. What, then, does this unconscious language tell us? What is on everyone's mind?

Above all, I think, the possibility that civilization is approaching a catastrophe. The most common motif in all those semilegible signs is the contrast of past and present, only here it is presented even more dramatically (even more theatrically) than we saw in Dickens or Pugin—even more than in the 1841 edition of *Contrasts*. The words and phrases that emerge from that swirl of competing posters include Pompeii, Jerusalem, Vauxhall, Paris, Comet, Last Days. The single most prominent poster in the whole collage is the one advertising Pompeii at the upper right, the corner to which our eyes are drawn from the lines of figures on the left, continuing past the folded poster at the center. As we examine other posters in the scene, the Pompeii reference is repeated and echoed. We are looking back from the present to some of the most dramatic and disastrous settings of the past: "King Arthur Every Evening This Week"; Jerusalem; the partially concealed letters of several other posters may spell out, or simply suggest, Venice (we see only the last half of the word) or Greece. A second Pompeii poster can be seen almost in full over the head of the guardsman at the left: "The Destruction of Pompeii Every Night." It is not, of course, a general reference to Pompeii or Vesuvius alone. What we can see of that large poster on the right is advertising a stage adaptation of Bulwer's popular novel.

ADELPHI THEATER
EXTRAORDINARY HIT
THE LAST DAYS OF
POMPEII!

But the novel itself reflected a larger and older taste for disasters, volcanoes and Vesuvius in particular. Firework displays of its most famous eruption were performed at Vauxhall and the Surrey Zoological Gardens; it was one of the most popular subjects of panoramas from 1824 until the late 1840s.[47] The "Destruction of Pompeii" poster at the left of Parry's picture refers to one of those performances. A contemporary viewer would have recognized the theatrical event and perhaps even the poster itself.

What makes the representation of so many signs fascinating is how Parry's juxtaposition of all of these graphic *objets trouvées* creates a context of reference beyond the specific performances and events they were printed to advertise. Even the contemporary viewer might have seen familiar items of the collage in new ways. The name of a new express coach in this context suggests (in a sort of pre-Eliot free verse) the possibility of mass catastrophe:

COMET!
In 24 Hours
LIVERPOOL

King Arthur, Othello; Pompeii, Jerusalem, Paris, even (perhaps) Venice or Greece. As a collection of words, the posters begin to speak in unison about ancient forms of heroic life and the destruction of great centers of civilization. This may help explain the archeological motif of the "scene" as a whole. Is this the next great archeological site? The general interest in apocalyptic scenes and historical catastrophes is related to a sense of uncertainty about the future of England following the French Revolution and the Reform Bill; if France was turned to rubble overnight, will England suffer the same fate? The comparison of London to Jerusalem, Pompeii, Venice, and Tyre appears frequently in the 1830s and 1840s, culminating in Ruskin's *Stones of Venice* in 1851. Parry alludes to the kind of question Ruskin would ask in heavily Biblical rhetoric: is London, too, destined to sink into ruins?

Perhaps it has begun to already. Reviewing Ranke's *History of the Popes* in 1840, T. B. Macaulay would describe a future visitor from New Zealand standing on the ruins of London Bridge to sketch the rubble of St. Paul's; the idea was to be echoed in Blanchard Jerrold's *London: A Pilgrimage* (1872), which cites Macaulay and includes a Doré woodcut of the lone New Zealander surveying the scene.[48] It was an idea of tremendous power, and tremendous endurance. As those customers in Boz's Scotland Yard tavern observed, London Bridge had been destroyed once already; is "modernization" of the City really only the prelude to its ultimate wreck? In *The Great Metropolis,* James Grant imagines the reflections "a Christian" might engage in "were he to station himself on the top of St. Paul's . . . and look down on the houses and streets within a circle of five miles."

> The painful and humiliating thought would intrude itself on his mind, that in those houses and streets there were no fewer than two millions of his fellow-beings, and yet that of this vast number, though now as busy and bustling as if this world were to be their eternal home, there will not, in all probability, ere the lapse of a century, be one solitary individual whose body is not mouldering in the dust.[49]

Does the half-realized outline of St. Paul's in the background of Parry's watercolor allude to the same possibilities? The figures in the foreground seem barely alive. And the street itself, disfigured and obscured as it is by that mass of theatrical posters, enjoys a precarious existence, as if its surfaces are held together only, and only for the moment, by paper and paste. Parry shows us very little of a London we can be sure we know: St. Paul's in the distance, walls covered with placards, and some traces of new construction. But construction here clearly involves demolition, too. The buttress behind the wooden fence may be supporting an old wall while a new building goes up alongside it, and it may be used because that old wall itself is being removed. The posters can be on those walls only because the surfaces are temporary, provisional; thus they tell us not only about a succession of cultural events but about a continuous process of urban renewal. We may even begin to wonder about that dome, suspended unconvincingly (like an image from a theatrical backdrop) behind the fence at the left. How much more of St. Paul's remains in its usual condition, and for how long?

The buttress next to the dome supporting the placarded wall introduces the fundamental motif of the image: temporary stability. It is hardly accidental that this buttress is marked, almost inexplicably (for how would any bill-sticker reach that spot?) with a single poster bearing the name of "Mr. Parry." This is in effect the artist's signature—referring to his farewell musical performance of June 24, 1837—and, in a crucial way, his point.[50] For those walls not only fill the picture with posters, they are supported by them, they *are* them—the posters become the walls, become London. The scene, and the City, is sustained by the power of art. The painter creates a frozen moment that interrupts the confusion and dissolution of London, buttresses it by reference to its arts and to its preoccupation with the past. There are no sources of stability in the present, in the "real" world of the image. The guardsman is posed like a store mannequin (with a stuffed dog at his feet) and the policeman stands stiffly nearby, his body paralleling the rigid line of the wooden support over his head. They are ineffectual, as the pickpocket demonstrates. The church seems implicated in this uselessness as well; not just because it rises directly over their heads, but because it is awkwardly two-dimensional, walled off from the "life" of the street, such as it is. Authority has already receded into the past.

Yet I must resist my own temptation to overliteralize these images or oversolemnize Parry's charming genre scene. Even if we treat the imagery seriously, it is not in the end a picture of hopelessness. We might recall Pugin's epigram in connection with that group of officers apparently at the mercy of a young criminal, with St. Paul's dome floating overhead:

> The spot that angels deigned to grace,
> Is blessed though robbers haunt the place.

The imagery is double-edged. Certain possibilities are absent, yet that absence itself recalls them as potential in the future: King Arthur, Jerusalem. Some of the posted bills seem to warn us not to treat any of these allusions too seriously: "Have you seen the industrious fleas?"; "Bull & Mouth." Another detailed poster refers (again) to John Parry in connection with what appears to be a production of "The Sham Prince"—but the covering edge of another poster makes us only guess at this reading, so that it also suggests the artist's reference to his own "Sham Print" in the image before us. Such confusion, in the end, is entertaining, fun. The conflict of imagery leaves meaning, a resolution of these varying messages, to what E. H. Gombrich in *Art and Illusion* calls "the beholder's share." And that very openness tells us something about urban experience. If the world has become a delightful spectacle, as in *Sketches by Boz,* it is not enough to move through it passively. The figures in the picture are lifeless, unconscious; we are being urged to a more intensive mental life. The challenge of the painting is to observe, to make sense of the urban world by observing. This is the "message" that is repeated more than any other in the various posters: "Have you seen . . . "? The first sign we encounter (assuming again that we begin reading from the left) is translatable into similar terms (if we reconstruct what is hidden under another advertisement for "Musical Fun"): "If You Watch This . . ." The last poster we will see, if our eyes move from left to right and bottom to top, invites us to have our hats renovated on the Strand in the following intimidating language: "Are You Aware . . . "? How can we study this image and not be aware—aware, that is, of the need for awareness itself?

Parry earned his living as a musician; perhaps it makes sense to compare his picture to a medley, to which we respond by trying to identify the various motifs that comprise the whole. But the analogy of music also suggests that we can regard the English words printed on these posters as another kind of notation, another language, one it requires training to decipher. A few years later, Darwin would sum up his experience as naturalist aboard the *Beagle* by invoking the metaphor of musical notation for the complex beauty of the landscape in South America: "I am strongly induced to believe that, as in music, the person who understands every note will, if he also possesses a proper taste, more thoroughly enjoy the whole, so he who examines each part of a fine view, may also thoroughly comprehend the full and combined effect. Hence, a traveller should be a botanist."[51] Parry requires a correspondingly sophisticated science of modern life. We cannot simply look at London street-life; we must know how to read its notations, its codes. As in Darwin we confront a strange, foreign world. The city is ultimately a kind of perceptual jungle, a *terra incognita.*[52]

Where precisely does Parry's scene take place? It is London, yet the signs allude to other places: Pompeii, Jerusalem, Paris; Liverpool, Surrey, Chester. We are everywhere, and nowhere, in this scene. What at first seems to be the simple two-dimensionality of a highly conventional image opens into something far more complex—a four-dimensional world (since much of the dislocation is caused by reference to different periods of historical time), a world that requires new modes of perception and new modes of art. Parry did not, as far as I know, create other pictures of this sort, and these complexities may suggest one reason why. Surveying this strangely dislocated scene, we are glimpsing also the dislocation of art, art at the end of its normal possibilities. The art represented in this painting is wholly commercialized (advertising art), and it is wholly based upon other arts (such as the theater) rather than upon any unmediated external reality or truth. It is art that must become increasingly flamboyant, dramatic, in order to compete with other art works and with the increasing confusion of the city. What, then, will the future mean, for London or its arts? All we can be certain about is that traditional forms will not suffice. To some extent, neither does Parry's untraditional response. In spite of the layers of possibility embedded in the scene (or perhaps because of them) the image never becomes wholly convincing. Nor do I intend my own exploration of it to suggest some clear, stable, final structure of meaning. The picture is interesting because of its tensions, particularly the ones that are not and cannot be resolved. And this is also what makes it so central an artifact of the 1830s. Parry—like Princess Victoria, Dickens, and Pugin— is grappling with new forms of reality, yet his solution seems far more uneasy than any of theirs, far more precarious, far more provisional. And what he shows, and does, in this painting, is prophetic of a crisis that would become increasingly apparent in the late 1830s, as various people attempted to understand, or simply represent, the rapidly changing contemporary world. As we approach Victoria's Year it becomes increasingly evident that traditional modes will not do. It is becoming more and more difficult to read the signs of the times, because the signs, as well as the times, are changing.

II

VICTORIA'S YEAR
1837–1838

2

The Golden Year

Is it not as if this swelling, simmering, never-resting Europe of ours stood, once more, on the verge of an expansion without parallel; struggling, struggling like a mighty tree again about to burst in the embrace of summer, and shoot forth broad frondent boughs which would fill the whole earth?

Thomas Carlyle, *Chartism* (1839)

What, is there no space for golden mean
And gradual progress?

William Wordsworth, "At Bologna, In Remembrance
of the Late Insurrections, 1837, Continued"

Ah! when shall all men's good
Be each man's rule, and universal Peace
Lie like a shaft of light across the land,
And like a lane of beams athwart the sea,
Through all the circle of the golden year?

Alfred Tennyson, "The Golden Year"

Well! but the pictures. What struck me in this Suffolk St exhibition was the want of conception and ideality—which is a serious want to people like me, who can understand and enjoy in a picture, nothing beside. But it is the defect of the age—is it not?

Elizabeth Barrett to Mary Russell Mitford, 1837

In life as it is, lies the true empire of modern fiction.... Unquestionably, there is more food for the philosophy of fiction in the stir and ferment, the luxuriant ideas and conflicting hopes, the working reason, the excited imagination that belongs to this era of rapid and visible transition, than in the times of "belted knights and barons bold."

Edward Bulwer in the *Edinburgh Review,* "Lady Blessington's Novels" (1838)[1]

I

"The death of a king is always an awful lesson to mankind." So Sydney Smith declares in a "Sermon on the Duties of the Queen," published within a few weeks of Victoria's accession to the throne.[2] Taking his text from Dan. 4:31 ("Oh King, thy kingdom is departed from thee"), Smith alternates between prophetic hopefulness and sober realism as he portrays the possibilities and dangers awaiting the new monarch. This young woman needs to be reminded of the consequences of her power and its risks, including the ultimate ones. Beginning his survey of royal duties with popular education, he blandly observes that "the arm of the assassin may be often stayed by the lessons of his early life."[3] The warning would have seemed increasingly prophetic. Victoria received two threats against her life in 1837, the first of half-a-dozen or so, including several assassination attempts, in the first six years of her reign. But the sermon centers on more immediately practical matters. Smith urges Victoria to attend to the education of the people, to maintain "a state of profound peace," to avoid ambition and suspect flattery, to remain above fanaticism and a sectarian spirit, to become, in short, what he calls a "patriot queen." His idealizing culminates in a "painting" of this perfect monarch, the image that would come to life if his words were heeded.

> Here is a picture which warms every English heart, and would bring all this congregation upon their bended knees before Almighty God to pray it may be realized. What limits to the glory and happiness of our native land, if the Creator should in his mercy have placed in the heart of this royal woman the rudiments of wisdom and mercy; and if, giving them time to expand, and to bless our children's children with her goodness, He should grant to her a long sojourning upon earth, and leave her to reign over us till she is well stricken in years? What glory! what happiness! what joy! what bounty of God![4]

The rhetoric is conventional; what is more surprising is the caution with which Smith hedges his bets. An eighteen-year old monarch may seem capable of reigning for many years; but the likelihood of wisdom is another matter. After all we are considering a "young queen, at the period of life which is commonly given up to frivolous amusement." Can we be assured that the actual woman will correspond to the picture-book model, who "sees at once into the great duties of her station"?[5] Smith's greatest fear is not that some assassin's bullet will find its mark, but simply that a lively young woman will take too long to grow up.

One might expect the first responses to a new, youthful queen to be hyperbolic. But the early images of Victoria—in words and pictures—temper idealism with evasion; few of her subjects seem prepared to fantasize unambiguously when the subject of their hopes is so little known. A sonnet in *Blackwood's Edinburgh Magazine,* straining for confidence, almost entirely obscures its central figure in a metaphorical haze:

> When some fair bark first glides into the sea
> Glad shouts of thousands echo to the sky
> And as she leaves the land fond hearts beat high
> With hope and fear. . . .
> Even so thy subject's hopes and prayers, fair Queen!
> Go with thee:—Clouds above thy bark may brood,
> And rocks and shoals beset thine unknown way;
> But thou in virtue bold may'st steer serene
> Through tempests. . . . [6]

The impulse to substitute platitude for portraiture takes pictorial form in J. H. Nixon's painting of *Queen Victoria's Progress to the Guildhall on November 9, 1837.* For all its vivid color and energy, the picture (Figure 2.1) depicts the stately procession and cheering crowd with far more specificity than the figure who is supposed to be at their center: we can make out the members of the Lord Mayor's party distinctly (after all, the painting was commissioned by the Guildhall, where it now hangs), but Victoria is vague, a few dabs of paint within her more carefully delineated coach. And this is only a better-finished example of a tendency, visible in other images of the new Queen, to conventionalize her almost beyond recognition (see Figures 2.2, 2.3, and 2.4). No wonder *Blackwood's* refers to her in December 1837 as "the best beloved and worst painted Queen." In the picture by Nixon only her crown is clearly suggested. It is as if the office rather than the woman promotes so much excitement. That is the way it was put by the *Times,* which muted its enthusiasm for political reasons, commenting on the coronation at the end of June 1838. The great outbursts of feeling on this occasion were not, we are told, really directed at Victoria herself. The people "thought of her not as an individual to be loved with headlong zeal or played upon by corrupt adulation." They "regarded her as in herself *an institution.* They saw the monarchy in Queen Victoria." Besides, the leader adds, the cheering was much louder for the "illustrious" Tory Duke of Wellington; Victoria "was in some measure on her trial," receiving only "on trust" the praise she still must learn to merit.[7]

Some observers commented that the Queen never could be much more than this, that it was a cruel mistake to expect (or worse, to urge) her to

aspire to something more. The *Quarterly,* ostensibly reviewing Sydney
Smith's sermon, can only lament the "youth and inexperience" of this
"innocent, and lovely creature committed by a combination of accidents
to Melbourne's temporary guardianship"; naturally she "cannot ... be
fully acquainted with the extent of her interests or her duties in the present
chaos of public affairs."[8] The *Westminster Review* belittles the "glaring
absurdity" of expecting "a young Queen" to pursue any decisive plan of
action. "Common sense points out but one course for her Majesty to
adopt: in conformity with the example of her predecessors, which her own
extreme youth renders it particularly advisable that she should imitate;
that is, the course of leaving things as she finds them, taking the advice of
the ministers who happen to be in office, and allowing her youthful will
and judgment to make their influence on public affairs as little perceptible
as possible."[9] The essay, signed "E" (Charles Buller, according to the
Wellesley Index of Victorian Periodicals), may have been influenced by the
views of John Stuart Mill, who as the journal's functioning editor,
expressed strong opinions concerning the line the *Westminster* ought to
follow. "It seems to me that if we occupy ourselves with the Queen at all,
we ought to make her believe that people feel interested about her just at
present from mere curiosity, and not because they really believe she can
do much; and that unless she has the qualities of Elizabeth she will be
nothing."[10]

There is something condescending in Mill's remarks, all the more surprising (as his modern editors observe) in view of his well-known feminist
sympathies. He claims a more disinterested perspective: the issue, he
insists, is the conception of monarchy as such in an increasingly democratic society. Can a progressive journal find the right tone to address this?
Not, apparently, if the writer is Harriet Martineau, whose essay (which
Mill rejected) is "altogether contrary to the character which we are trying
to give to the Review." "H. M." misrepresents the character of the Queen
as well:

> She always treats the Queen like a young person. Now the Queen cannot be
> young, except in ignorance of the world, and kings and queens are that even
> at sixty. She always treats the Queen as *artless.* She cannot be artless, as a
> person full of anxieties, or who will be so, about doing her duties to her sub-
> jects. I am convinced she is just a lively, spirited young lady, thinking only
> of enjoying herself, and who never is nor ever will be conscious of any diffi-
> culties and responsibilities,—no more than Marie Antoinette, who was a
> much cleverer woman and had much more *will* and *character* than she is
> ever likely to have. She is conscious, I dare say, of good intentions, as every

other young lady is; she is not conscious of wishing harm to any one, unless they have offended her, nor of intending to break any one article of the Decalogue. That is the nature of the well-meanings of a person like her, and if we wish to give her any higher feelings or notions about her duties, we cannot go a worse way to work than H. M. does.[11]

Mill's point is that we cannot expect any ordinary individual, especially from this class, to exercise a decisive influence in the 1830s. Yet the tone is more than a little nasty towards Victoria, Martineau, and women generally. The rejected essay is "what a woman's veiw of practical affairs is supposed to be, and what the view of a person ignorant of life always is." This may be "all very well from a woman to a woman, but not such as should be addressed by a body of men who aim at having authority *to* a woman and the public *of* that woman." Mill is determined that Victoria's image be constituted for her by others, by men.

It was, of course, still an age in which men insisted on speaking for women. The year 1837 marked the publication (perhaps to capitalize on the interest in Victoria) of *Memoirs of Celebrated Women,* edited by G. P. R. James. Two years after its appearance, an "almost mystical" tract on woman's influence was issued under the name "Sarah Lewis"; it turned out to be the translation of a volume titled *L'Éducation des Mères* by a French cleric, Aimé-Martin.[12] But the problem in writing about Victoria is a special case of this general reluctance to let women tell their own stories. Mill's language reveals this: "I am convinced . . . ," "I dare say, . . . ," "a person like her." The Queen is simply an unknown, a blank for commentators to fill as best they can. When the adjective "Victorian" was coined, it came to be associated with a widespread sense of confidence, direction, and identity. The uncertainty about the new Queen in 1837 is a token of a general uncertainty about the present. This is one reason why the death of a king is such an "awful lesson," for it represents the passing of a central symbol of the kingdom as a whole. What new symbol is going to take its place? What will Victoria herself stand for? Such questions lead in a circle: we cannot understand a symbol without a better sense of what it symbolizes; to some extent the prior issue is constructing an adequate context of understanding in which Victoria, or any other representative figure, can find a place.

That was the project of modern literature. Perhaps it always is. But the writing of the 1830s concentrated upon the contemporary world with particular intensity, informed by the urgency of basic unanswered questions. What sort of era was it, if it could be called an era at all? To what extent did it resemble or differ from the past? Was it in any sense of the word "classical"? The *Edinburgh Review* of July 1838 brushed aside the suggestion that a new Golden Age of painting was likely to begin in England.[13] Was there any other way in which contemporaries could feel justified in regarding 1837–1838 as a "golden year"?

II

If any poet deserves to be identified with this insistent historical self-consciousness, it is Tennyson. In a sense, the whole of his career is a continuing search for an appropriately modern verse, the period leading up to publication of *In Memoriam* in 1850 above all. It was in this spirit that he wrote a poem for the Queen's accession in June 1837. It is hardly one of his triumphs—"little more than newspaper verse," by his own description; he sent it off to a friend (James Spedding) to be offered to the *Times* and other papers. Yet it is not quite as journalistic as that remark suggests. What makes it interesting are the lapses of confidence in what we might expect to be heartier verse. Optimism does not come easily to the young poet. As a toast in eleven stanzas, "The Queen of the Isles" deliberately aims at the conventional and celebratory. Yet Tennyson cannot propose this without acknowledging the uncertainties he wants the new reign to resolve:

> And since Time never pauses but Change must ensue,
> Let us wish that old things may fit well with the new,
> For the blessing of promise is on her like dew—
>   So a health to the Queen of the Isles.[14]

Do we join in this toast because of our hopes or our fears? The aim is to produce a spirited celebratory verse, and it doesn't succeed. Tennyson only whets our appetite for more knowledge, and better poetry.

  That hunger is partly satisfied in "The Golden Year," a more substantial poem about the character of the times written two years later. Here there are conversations, and characters, at least one of whom comes alive. Still, the verse is marked by ambivalence, although in this case it is clear that Tennyson is exploring his own uncertainties rather than trying to pass over them. The exploration centers on the phrase in the title: what does it mean, or what can it? Are we living in a genuinely classical "golden" time? If so, what are the proofs, and in what form can they be represented in poetry? This is a self-conscious poem about the problem of writing modern poetry.

One of the central characters is a poet; it is his hopeful song from which the title comes. But our understanding of that song, around which the whole poem is arranged, alters as the surrounding frame develops; much as in those portraits of Victoria, an image must be viewed in relation to its setting. The song expresses lyrical optimism, but the rest of the poem qualifies and complicates that mood.

The opening lines begin the process of qualification even before their subject has been introduced:

> Well, you shall have that song which Leonard wrote:
> It was last summer on a tour in Wales.

This is a holiday poem, we are being warned—only the mood of a summer's day, and at that one that has passed. The poet, Leonard, distances his own song even further as "my work of yestermorn" (21). Within this framework, the emphasis of the song shifts from envisioning the golden year to measuring its distance from the present:

> 'We sleep and wake and sleep, but all things move;
> The Sun flies forward to his brother Sun;
> The dark Earth follows wheeled in her ellipse;
> And human things returning on themselves
> Move onward, leading up the golden year.
>   'Ah, though the times, when some new thought can bud,
> Are but as poets' seasons when they flower,
> Yet oceans daily gaining on the land,
> Have ebb and flow conditioning their march,
> And slow and sure comes up the golden year.'   (22–31)

How slow? How sure? Leonard's last stanza is somewhat less confident:

> 'But we grow old. Ah! when shall all men's good
> Be each man's rule, and universal Peace
> Lie like a shaft of light across the land,
> And like a lane of beams athwart the sea,
> Through all the circles of the golden year?'   (47–51)

The main process of qualification takes place outside the song, where this questioning is questioned further. As soon as Leonard stops singing, he is answered by another voice: James, "you know him,—old but full / Of force and choler, and firm upon his feet" (60–61). The poem becomes their dialogue, an early Victorian dialogue of self and soul, realism and hope.

Even before it is resolved we are aware that no single vision is sufficient, that no single perspective can capture the potential of modern reality.

At first James dismisses Leonard's song in a single outburst: "Ah, folly!" (53). But that makes him sound more cynical than in fact he is. What he objects to in the song is not optimism but the romantic mood in which it is cast, the distancing of such ideals in the past or future.

> 'What stuff is this!
> Old writers pushed the happy season back,—
> The more fools they,—we forward: dreamers both'. . . . (64–66)

He counterposes an optimism couched in simpler and more modern terms, echoing Thomas Carlyle's *Sartor Resartus* as well as Goethe's image of a historical seed-time, which Carlyle also cites.[15] Our first responsibility is to live. Questioning, hesitating, miss the spirit of life:

> . . . as if the seedsman, rapt
> Upon the teeming harvest, should not plunge
> His hand into the bag: but well I know
> That unto him who works, and feels he works,
> This same grand year is ever at the doors.   (69–73)

It isn't more certain than Leonard's vision, but it is more concrete. Time is what we make of it. We have returned to the hopes of the original song, in a new and more convincing form.

But can anyone speak for an "age"? In "The Golden Year" neither of the main characters alone settles the central question, although clearly James comes close. Thus when the dialogue ends, the poem doesn't. The concluding lines offer an odd confirmation for James' earthy confidence.

> He spoke; and, high above, I heard them blast
> The steep slate-quarry, and the great echo flap
> And buffet round the hills, from bluff to bluff. (74–76)

The emphasis has shifted from gold to slate: it requires a commonplace mixture of Carlylean labor and modern technology to open the veins of genuine hope in the age. This is also the way to open the veins of genuinely contemporary poetry. The dialogue has presented the conflict of two kinds of poetic language. The mining blast resolves that contest dramatically in a burst of pure sound. Tennyson commented that the final lines reproduce "the echo of the blasting as I heard it from the mountain on the counter side, opposite to Snowdon."[16] But the echoing is more complex than this, more than an exercise in onomatopoeia, as the movement from romantic mountain scenery to slate mining should suggest. It is a double or even a triple echo: verse imitates a sound that is in itself echoed by the landscape from human origins. We hear the violence of industry converted into poetry through the mediation of nature. This half-jarring "music" implicitly answers the questions raised in Leonard's idealizing song. There is no need to wait for a new classical age, or a new classical art. It may, however, require special tools to create it.

The problem of imagining 1837 as a golden year, then, is partly bound up in the difficulty of regarding the new forces of the age, including science and technology, as poetic material. Early in "The Golden Year" we learn that Leonard has failed to achieve this: "They said he lived shut up within himself, / A tongue-tied Poet in the feverous days" (9–10). He grants the justice of this complaint, bemoaning that he was "born to late" to find appropriate poetical subjects. He cannot create verse from

> . . . the fair new forms
> That float about the threshold of an age,
> Like truths of Science waiting to be caught. . . .
> (15–17)

A cancelled passage from the manuscript makes clearer what sort of material Leonard has rejected. He attempted to acquaint himself with new scientific thought, only to turn back to our "grand old sires" in the past, who

> . . . laughed and let the earth go round, nor knew
> The noiseless ether curdling into worlds
> And complicated clockworks of the suns.
> Motion: why motion? were it not as well
> To fix a point, to rest?. . . .

Christopher Ricks observes that this imagery is drawn from Charles Babbage's *Ninth Bridgewater Treatise* of 1837, a book Tennyson owned, which mentions the curdling of nebular light.[17] But the point is that Leonard dismisses such metaphors, and the general aims behind them as well.

Babbage's volume summed up the eight treatises prepared (according to the terms of the will of the Earl of Bridgewater, establishing the series in 1829) to demonstrate "the power, wisdom, and goodness of God as manifested in the creation."[18] What might have made Leonard particularly uneasy is Babbage's claim for the broad cultural value of the project. In the spirit of the Bridgewater Treatises generally, he promises that the advancement of scientific knowledge will produce a finer poetry, a new mythos. Babbage hints that it may have produced this already.

At the present period, when knowledge is so universally spread . . . , facts and arguments are the basis of creeds, and convictions so arrived at are the more deeply seated, and the more enduring, because they are not the wild fancies of passion or of impulse, but the deliberate results of reason and reflection.[19]

By contrast with this confidence in the unity of modern thought, Leonard seems a narrow, specialized thinker, not only less modern but less humane. After he dismisses the idea of nebular motion, he suddenly appears more futile too, a Blakean geometer whose universe is centered on himself.

> And here, methought he seemed to grasp
> A pair of shadowy compasses, with these
> To plant a centre and about it round
> A wide and wider circle. . . . [20]

At this point in the manuscript, James speaks again, "Right in his rhythm and cadence," as another cancelled line puts it.[21] His earthier voice provides a corrective needed to bring poetry closer to the contemporary world, closer to the "facts" of which Babbage speaks. But he still refers only vaguely to "that same grand year." And his language finally must give way to that other sort of poetry in the closing description of the mining blast. Tennyson has not found a human spokesman for the age, or even for his own measured assessment of it. The poem is inconclusive; the ending comes too quickly, seems too mechanical (in several ways); it is too "bluff." The poem's questions are terminated, not solved.

Literary endings, as Frank Kermode explains, reveal a great deal about the way writers understand the order of things outside their works. Beginnings do too. Both end points of a text mark the links between it and the world, and when it is difficult to conceive the present precisely we would expect to see some consequences in opening or concluding words of poems. Thus in "Godiva" (1840), Tennyson must introduce the historical-legendary materials of his story with a self-conscious reflection on how such stories can be told, or understood, from a modern perspective. It is so self-conscious that the reflection takes place twice, in an awkward pair of beginnings that openly search for ways to make the leap into the past.

> *I waited for the train at Coventry;*
> *I hung with grooms and porters on the bridge,*
> *To watch the three tall spires; and there I*
> *   shaped*
> *The city's ancient legend into this:—*
>
> Not only we, the latest seed of Time,
> New men, that in the flying of a wheel

Cry down the past, not only we, that prate
Of rights and wrongs, have loved the people
    well
And loathed to see them overtaxed; but she. . . .
                        (1–9)

Tennyson again is writing about writing, about writing a poem about Godiva. In what ways is this figure accessible to a modern sensibility? What does it mean in 1840 to say, as the poem does in the final line, that "she built herself an everlasting name"? The problem of writing is linked to the problem of remembering; in searching for an apt poetic form Tennyson seeks appropriate form for what we might call (using Paul Fussell's phrase) modern memory, recollection shaped out of and for the conditions of contemporary life.

I think this issue becomes particularly urgent by 1839, and I will explore it in the context of that year in chapter 6. But the problem of modern memory preoccupied Tennyson earlier, especially in the years following Hallam's death in 1833. These are the years in which he began work on *In Memoriam,* and he explores what would be the central issues of that poem in most of his work at this time: given the acuteness of the modern sense of loss, is it still possible to create genuine poetry—poetry that will seem genuine, that is, to the modern sensibility? One set of answers comes in the series of poems called the *English Idyls,* a group of unpretentious contemporary stories that follow Theocritus both in their title and in being set within an external narrative frame.[22] Thus we find (as in "Godiva," which is part of the series) a story within a story, the presentness of modern materials held at arm's length to be studied. John Dixon Hunt terms this the poetry of distance: "passion and thought are presented already achieved and formulated in verbal icons; myth and history are constantly offered as completed speech and narration, as artefact rather than chronicle."[23] But this way of framing the problem of modernity in poetry is not always a satisfactory way of solving it. We often feel an unresolved tension between memory and contemporary experience, and this often increases as Tennyson tries to bring his frame narratives to a satisfactory conclusion.

"The Epic," another of the *English Idyls,* overtly addresses the issue of modern memory, especially in its highly self-conscious conclusion. It was written to provide a frame for the earlier "Morte d'Arthur," the first published portion of what would become the *Idylls of the King.* The frame allows Tennyson to speculate on how such medieval materials might be used in a contemporary setting. In "The Epic," we are "At Francis Allen's on the Christmas-eve." The conversation is fast-paced and wide-ranging. Eventually it will get around to the poetry of one of the guests, Everard Hall, who will read the sole surviving section (i.e., "Morte d'Arthur") from what was once a twelve-book epic. But first other topics are considered, so many that the narrator only barely keeps up:

> And half-awake I heard
> The parson taking wide and wider sweeps,
> Now harping on the church-commissioners,
> Now hawking at Geology and schism;
> Until I woke, and found him settled down
> Upon the general decay of faith
> Right through the world, 'at home was little left,
> And none abroad: there was no anchor, none,
> To hold by.' Francis, laughing, clapt his hand
> On Everard's shoulder, with 'I hold by him.'
>
> (13–23)

That gesture and remark define the central problem of the poem in another way: can traditional poetry provide a substitute for traditional human ties? Can it provide real solace for modern anxieties, real alternatives to discredited beliefs? The poet himself is dubious.

> 'Nay, nay,' said Hall,
> 'Why take the style of those heroic times?
> For nature brings back not the Mastodon,
> Nor we those times; and why should any man
> Remodel models?'   (34–38)

As that brief scientific reference ought to remind us, the age demands new forms of thought. Yet Hall remains ambivalent. He has burned his epic in disgust—all but one book: "keep a thing, its use will come." The nature of that "use," the very possibility of it, is explored in the last section of the frame.

After the central poem is finally read, all the auditors return to their rooms to sleep on what they have heard. Did it touch them with any meaningful truth? Will they respond in any meaningful way? The situation is directly parallel to the one described within the "Morte d'Arthur" itself, where a sceptical Sir Bedivere finds it difficult to understand and obey the king's final, apparently bizarre requests. Faith and fealty break down together. The medieval poem is not simply about a king's death, it is about the waning power of his words and the waning respect for his mythic status. The modern frame-poem considers whether such a precarious myth can exert any power in the nineteenth century. The answer, such as it is, comes to the poem's speaker in two dreams, the second merging almost imperceptibly with the first at the approach of dawn, "when dreams/Begin to feel the truth and stir of day." In fact, both dreams finally merge into that day, into reality.

> To me, methought, who waited with a crowd,
> There came a bark that, blowing forward, bore
> King Arthur, like a modern gentleman
> Of statliest port; and all the people cried,
> 'Arthur is come again: he cannot die.'
> Then those that stood upon the hills behind
> Repeated—'Come again, and thrice as fair;'
> And, further inland, voices echoed—'Come
> With all good things, and war shall be no more.'
> At this a hundred bells began to peal,
> That with the sound I woke, and heard indeed
> The clear church-bells ring in the Christmas-morn.   (289–303)

There is something unconvincing here; and, for all the fervor of the rhetoric, it is a highly contingent moment. This is only dreaming, after all, and it is difficult to say whether those pealing bells satisfy or merely sharpen the dreamer's desires. Has something been achieved or merely wished for?

The subject of "The Epic" is the longing for heroes, one Carlyle would explore in his lectures of 1840. But that longing is satisfied far less in Tennyson's poetry than Carlyle's prose. There is no suggestion in the poem how hero worship can be translated into action, how it can shape or become part of "the truth and stir of day," even on Christmas. If a new kind of day is dawning, it has not been described. We have only a vague sense of the kind of era the poet would like to invoke, or the kind of "modern gentleman" he would place at its center. Tennyson, of course, has Hallam in mind, but nothing in "The Epic" has prepared for such a reference. Nor is there any clear topical reference that contemporaries might have recognized—there are no obvious candidates for the role of modern-medieval hero, and that would be the point of Carlyle's lectures. Later on, the figure in the poem would be associated with Albert, but that allusion would be premature in 1838; Victoria's marriage was still several years away. Surely it cannot be associated with King William—an inadequate hero, and no longer available. The uncertainties of the poem grow directly out of the uncertainties of the new reign. The death of a king is always an awful lesson for mankind.

III

If the loss of kings cannot be remedied with new, extraordinary, heroic figures, perhaps the most appropriate response is to concentrate on ordinary beings, and ordinary life. By the late 1830s the ordinary and familiar had become the most pervasive motif of contemporary literature. It forms the basis for the great outpouring of popular comic writing, a genre that includes Dickens and Thackeray as well as such less-remembered writers as Theodore Hook and Thomas Hood. There is an equally notable emergence of simple rural life as the subject of "a somewhat new class of writing, . . . the unaffected prose pastoral," as R. H. Horne observed in 1843 in *A New Spirit of the Age*.[24] Horne cited especially Mary Russell Mitford, author of *Our Village*, (which appeared in various forms from 1819 to 1832), *Belford Regis: Sketches of a Country Town* (1835), and, most recently, *Country Stories* (1837). There were also William and Mary Howitt, whose respective books of 1838, *The Rural Life of England* and *Birds and Flowers and Other Country Things*, extended the genre from prose (his book) to poetry (hers). The growing statistical movement represents a less literary version of this fascination with ordinary facts; J. R. McCulloch's *Statistical Account of the British Empire* (1837) begins with a chapter on "The Face of the Country." To some extent the same impulse finds its way into drama; at least, in Horne's view, it ought to. "The Drama should be the concentrated spirit of the age," he insists, yet it is in the fiction of Dickens, Hood, Mrs. Gore, and Mrs. Trollope, rather than the plays of Sheridan Knowles and William Macready, that a "living and real" expression of modern life appears. He does allow, however, that Knowles "personifies our age . . . in his truly domestic feeling. The age is domestic, and so is he. Comfort—not passionate imaginings,—is the aim of every body, and he seeks to aid and gratify this love of comfort."[25]

Domesticity is at the center of the Victorian period as a whole, and its significance grows through the 1830s. Some of the landmarks of this process are pictorial. In Daniel Maclise's *Interview Between Charles I and Oliver Cromwell* (exhibited at the Royal Academy in 1836), history is collapsed into family life (Figure 2.5). Charles turns away from the fateful encounter to gaze fondly at his children and his dog. The painting in effect dramatizes the development of a middle-class domestic prototype from an older heroic model, and is structured around the contrast of familial roles and a more traditionally heroic masculine image.[26] A similar conception of the Cavalier monarch helps advance the plot of a novel of 1837, Benjamin Disraeli's *Henrietta Temple*. The hero, Ferdinand Armine, comes upon the title character copying a miniature of Charles: "A melancholy countenance!" he remarks. "It is a favorite of mine," she replies.[27] An alert reader would know at once that their marriage is inevitable. Of course, Disraeli's is a modern love story, but that is part of the point. Charles I is associated with a new set of values, with emotions we all share.

For many, then, the new age required new modes of both art and life.

Harriet Martineau suggested this in an obituary essay on Sir Walter Scott, which she tried to make into an obituary for the historical novel and all the flamboyant forms of behavior idealized by it. Romantic love, like the romantic exploits associated with the "helm and cuirass," must be replaced in fiction by something more modern, more familiar. "The same passions still sway human hearts, but they must be shown to be intensified or repressed by the new impulses which a new state of things affords."[28] The point became commonplace. A writer in the *Edinburgh Review* (identified in the *Wellsley Index of Victorian Periodicals* as Edward Bulwer) made it in July 1838, reviewing "Lady Blessington's Novels." "Unquestionably, there is more food for the philosophy of fiction in the stir and ferment, the luxuriant ideas and conflicting hopes, the working reason, the excited imagination that belongs to this era of rapid and visible transition, than in the times of 'belted knights and barons bold.'"[29] The culmination of this shift from the heroic to the domestic appears in Sir Edwin Landseer's great pictorial study of the royal family, *Windsor Castle in Modern Times* (painted in the early 1840s). As the title suggests, the emphasis of the portrait (Figure 2.6) is on the "new spirit" of monarchal life: the Queen and Prince Albert are depicted as ideal wife and husband, surrounded by dogs, children, and the game he has just brought in from hunting. This is domesticity elevated into the form of a myth, one that would become increasingly widespread in the 1840s. And it is built out of that older mythology of the hunt: the violence of the chase has been softened to accord with the elegant but still domestic interior, especially through the image of the Princess Royal playing with a dead kingfisher in the lower left-hand corner. The orderly drawing room replaces a rugged landscape; family harmony subdues conflict or daring. Domesticity, then, in part means domestication, including the domestication of masculine power.

Women might be expected to find this transformation particularly congenial; that is only partly the case. Elizabeth Barrett, writing to Mary Russell Mitford in May 1837, finds the familiar qualities of contemporary painting disappointing.

What struck me in this Suffolk St exhibition was the want of conception and ideality—which is a serious want to people like me, who can understand and enjoy in a picture, nothing beside. But it is the defect of the age—is it not? It is terrible to be dragged captive, not by a King in purple and fine linen, not by a warrior in the glittering of his arms, but by a poor paltry counting-house Utilitarianism—along a rail road instead of a Via Sacra.[30]

Barrett's own poetry of this period, however, often follows the same domesticating route. In two poems that appeared in the *Athenaeum* just after Victoria's accession, she tries to humanize the monarch with vignettes based on newspaper accounts of Victoria's first Council session and her first public appearance as Queen. Given these sources, it is not surprising that "The Young Queen," much like the conventional tributes to Victoria I discussed before, is unconvincing as the portrait of an actual person. She sounds a bit like an average, pious cottager, and in a sense that is the point. Above all, Barrett insists, Victoria is like us. Although she is a queen, she is also a young woman.

> And eke our youthful Queen
> Remembers what has been,
> Her childhood's peace beside the hearth, and sport upon the sod!
> Alas! can others wear
> A mother's heart for her?—
> But calm she lifts her trusting face, and calleth upon God.[31]

"Victoria's Tears," published a week later (June 8 1837), takes this pastoral innocence as a token of God's affection for England:

> She saw no purples shine,
> For tears had dimmed her eyes:
> She only knew her childhood's flowers
> Were happier pageantries!
> And while the heralds played their part
> For million shouts to drown—
> "God save the Queen" from hill to mart—
> She heard through all, her beating heart,
> And turned and wept!
> She wept, to wear a crown.[32]

These poetical sketches of Victoria reappeared in Barrett's collection of 1838, *The Seraphim, and Other Poems,* the central poem of which contains an even more ambitious expression of the domestic impulse. "The Seraphim" brings angels down to earth. Literally: the poem centers around a dialogue between two seraphs during their descent from the heavens to view the Crucifixion. Barrett's preface explains that she decided on the subject while translating that classic of the heroic tradition, Aeschylus' *Prometheus Bound* (her translation appeared in 1833). That project led her to speculate on what the Greek poet might have written had he been alive at a later period.

I thought, that, had Aeschylus lived after the incarnation and crucifixion of our Lord Jesus Christ, he might have turned, if not in moral and intellectual yet in poetic faith, from the solitude of Caucasus to the deeper desertness of that crowded Jerusalem where none had any pity; from the "faded white flower" of the Titanic brow, to the "withered grass" of a Heart trampled on by its own beloved; from the glorying of him who gloried that he could not die, to the sublimer meekness of the Taster of death for every man; from the taunt stung into being by the torment, to HIS more awful silence, when the agony stood dumb before the love!

By this more human standard, the Promethean story, "leaving man's heart untouched," is "dwarfed." "Has not LOVE a deeper mystery than wisdom, and a more ineffable lustre than power? I believe it has." Even the Greek poet would have turned from the "demigod ... to the Victim, whose sustaining thought beneath an unexampled agony was not the Titanic 'I can revenge,' but the celestial 'I can forgive!'"[33]

It is not simply that Barrett wishes to recreate classical poetry in a new key. She proposes a translation of contemporary religious values as well, or at least a shift of emphasis. The image of a merciful God of Love is defined in clear opposition to that of a vengeful God of Power—an evangelical, Old Testament figure. Yet it remains heroic, although in a new (and New Testament), more human sense of the word. For Christ's sacrifice is both greater and more humble than it usually is conceived to be. "Are we not too apt to measure the depth of the Saviour's humiliation from the common estate of man, instead of from His own peculiar and primaeval one?" Even the seraphim must descend to a lower, more human conception of Christ's suffering and majesty. Barrett contrasts the emotions of two seraphs—a "weaker" one overwhelmed by fear, a "stronger one by a more complex passion"—with the "voluntary debasement of Him who became lower than the angels, and touched in His own sinless being, sin and sorrow and death."[34] The seraphs are humanized in this encounter, discovering the paradoxical strength-in-weakness of Christ's submission to pain.

> O crownèd hierarchies that wear your crown
>   When His is put away!
> Are ye unshamèd that ye cannot dim
> Your alien brightness to be liker him,
> Assume a human passion, and down-lay
> Your sweet secureness for congenial fears,
> And teach your cloudless over-burning eyes
>   The mystery of his tears?   (292–299)

The last phrase is important in two ways. Angels, as sinless creatures, cannot produce actual human tears.[35] They also must learn to sympathize with a condition they cannot share, a "mystery of . . . tears" that encompasses the mystery of humanity as well as Christ's sacrifice.

The first stage in the humbling of the angels involves a recognition of their own limits, the limits of power alone. Zerah the Bright One confesses to his companion, Ador the Strong, how fully he feels his own weakness as he gazes into the eyes of Christ on the Cross.

> Zerah.   I cannot bear—
> Ador.   Their agony?
> Zerah. Their love. God's depth is in them. From his brows
>   White, terrible in meekness, didst thou see
>   The lifted eyes unclose?
>   He is God, seraph! Look no more on me,
>   O God—I am not God.   (589–594)

Seraphs can be too exalted. At the heart of the poem, Zerah realizes that the nobility of meekness enables humans to exceed the angels in their love of God. "Do we love not?" Ador asks. "Yea," Zerah responds,

> But not as man shall! not with life for death,
> New-throbbing through the startled being; not
> With strange astonished smiles, that ever may
> Gush passionate like tears and fill their place. . . .
> Oh, not with this blood upon us—and this face,—
> Still, haply, pale with sorrow that it bore
> In our behalf, and tender evermore
> With nature all our own, upon us gazing. . . .
> Alas, Creator! shall we love thee less
> Than mortals shall?

Ador replies simply, "Amen! so let it be." "Blessèd they, / Who love thee more than we do: blessèd we, / Viewing that love which shall exceed even this." Imperfect humans can love God more than "sinless seraphs," for they can sympathize with Christ's suffering (665–697). Men and women, then, are ennobled most of all by their capacity for genuine grief. "Tears! what are tears?" Barrett asks in a sonnet of 1844: "Thank God for grace, / Ye who weep only."[36] This is a lesson of "The Seraphim" too:

> Zerah. Little drops in the lapse!
>   And yet, Ador, perhaps
>   It is all that they can.
>   Tears! the lovingest man
>   Has no better bestowed
>   Upon man.
> Ador.   Nor on God.   (501–504)

I have been emphasizing the domesticity of this poetic vision, but it is equally important to point out its femininity, for its values are deliberately played off against those associated with a masculine tradition of heroic action. At times Barrett minimizes those feminine values, as if this is "mere" women's writing. Her sonnet "To Mary Russell Mitford, In Her Garden" apologizes for her own "Low-rooted verse, . . . as nature-true / Though not as precious" as her friend's; only Mitford is "unperplext" enough to "preach a sermon on so known a text!" But "The Seraphim," dramatizing the limits of what is usually thought of as masculine power (Barrett's angels are clearly sexless), makes larger, more feminist claims for a woman's perspective, and a woman's writing. It is as if only a woman can retell the story of the Crucifixion for modern readers. The preface to Barrett's volume of 1844 makes the same assertion for the story of the Fall, in defense of her new poem, "A Drama of Exile." Eve's grief in particular, "considering that self-sacrifice belonged to her womanhood, and the consciousness of originating the Fall to her offense,—appeared to me imperfectly apprehended hitherto, and more expressible by a woman than a man." This is what finally distinguishes her version of the Biblical story from Milton's. His, in effect, is a view from inside—the view from within official patriarchal tradition, a view from inside the Garden itself: "within, I thought, with his Adam and Eve unfallen or falling,—and I without, with my EXILES,—*I* also an exile! [37] Barrett goes on to qualify her claims of poetic rivalry, but not those of her own unique perspective. She writes in a modern post-heroic, post-Miltonic world, for which and to which a more humble exile's voice—the voice of a woman—is particularly suited to speak.

Women in the late 1830s found their voices most clearly in fiction, in narrating the realities of ordinary modern life. I will consider some of these stories elsewhere in *Victoria's Year,* but it is important to focus on one notable example now, a novel that at least as deliberately as Tennyson's poetry explores the problems associated with turning life into literature. It is a provincial novel to end all provincial novels, a domestic story exposing the dark undercurrents in the myth of domesticity, an "unaffected prose pastoral" concerned in great part with the destructive effect the whole pastoral tradition has had on the lives of those who have had to contend with actual rural existence. And it can speak of such damaging illusions with special force because the author is a woman, writing to show how often women are the particular victims of this deceptive mythology. In *Deerbrook* (1839), Harriet Martineau attempts to write a story in keeping with the warnings and possibilities she had outlined in her essay on Scott. She attempts, that is, to adhere to a fundamental realism: in a straightforward depiction of ordinary lives, in a skepticism about the possibilities available for heroic action or dramatic reversals of fortune. Like George Eliot after her, she is determined not to add to the numbers of "Silly Novels by Lady Novelists." *Deerbrook* is written out of and against the tradition of romance, in the sense of both fantastic plots and idealized love stories.

All the romantic relationships in *Deerbrook* turn sour at some point or another, and many stay that way to the end. In the case of one of the main women characters—one of the two Ibbotson sisters, around whose lives in Deerbrook the story turns—married happiness is finally achieved, but only at the expense of another woman who had also hoped to marry the same man. The novel's central male character marries the older Ibbotson sister out of a sense of duty—she was not the sister he really loved—only to find that their marriage becomes a painful and depressing trap. Such problems develop when (as is so often the case) love is known only through romantic fiction or other idealizing forms; when it is finally experienced, it is often too late. For the average woman (or the average man), love (as the wisest woman in the novel explains) is "a mere empty sound . . . till it becomes, suddenly, secretly, a voice which shakes her being to the very centre,—more awful, more tremendous, than the crack of doom. . . . Depend upon it, Margaret, there is nothing in death to compare with this change." Margaret Ibbotson, the sister who does manage to escape this curse, can only take her friend's point with a shudder: "how dreadful is the process, if it be as you say!"[38]

Martineau's main interest is with an even larger, and even more dangerous myth: the myth of the idyllic provincial world as a whole. She shows how provincial life produces intellectual and moral provinciality, exploring the negative implications that (according to the *Oxford English Dictionary)* had been attached to that word for less than a century. The close intimacy of this world is not so much picturesque as paralyzing, characterized by small-minded gossip and rigid economic limitations that only more completely trap the beings who find themselves compelled to live there. It is a kind of rural enslavement, and it is not accidental that Martineau wrote this book just after her travels in America, undertaken primarily to support the cause of abolition. Those who attempt to break out of this bondage, or to rise above it, become little better than martyrs to their own high aspirations, like Martineau's central male character and would-be hero, the aptly named Mr. Hope. Here, too, the parallel with America is clear; Martineau's 1838 essay in praise of the abolitionists was called "The Martyr Age of the United States." And there is still another contemporary parallel with Hope's frustrated heroics. As Martineau explains in her *Autobiography,* she nearly abandoned work on *Deerbrook*

in 1837 to write a novel about Toussaint L'Ouverture, finally completed
and published in 1841 as *The Hour and the Man*. The parallel in *Deerbrook* can be seen, but only barely. Mr. Hope's "hour" in Deerbrook comes
in a very limited way; his reputation improves after unselfish attendance
on the sick during a cholera epidemic, but this hardly transforms him into
the Liberator of the community. Robert Colby has suggested that Martineau sought "not to denigrate heroes so much as to celebrate the unsung
heroism of the hamlet."[39] Yet this is a heroism with radical limits, a heroism that cannot effect much real change.

Martineau's characters discover these limits for themselves, and the
novel begins and ends with sharply defined moments of recognition. Margaret and Hester Ibbotson are orphans, forced by poverty to leave Birmingham and invited to live in the country by cousins, whom they have
never met before. On their first day in Deerbrook they manage to escape
the hospitality of their relatives to make an exploratory tour on their own.
But curiosity about their new home leads to embarassment when they accidentally overhear the remarks of an as yet unseen and unknown neighbor
about themselves and their hosts. What they hear is both unmannerly and
hostile, and this only increases the awkwardness of their own position.
Should they repeat what they have heard? What if some of those nasty
characterizations of their relatives turn out to be true? Suddenly the sisters
have been caught up in a circle of intrusion and concealment, which is for
Martineau one of the distinguishing marks of provincial society. They
have become parties to gossip, albeit unwillingly; to some extent, they
have been brought down to its level. They have been trapped in the vice
(in both senses of the word) of provinciality, one that is only tightened by
the rules of propriety with which young ladies ordinarily would hope to
extricate themselves. In less than a day they have discovered how radically
provincial life threatens privacy, and threatens the integrity of any separate individual identity.

This threat is particularly grave for women. Martineau makes it clear
that far more than men they are subject to constraints on their independence, in both senses of the word—constraints, that is, on both their freedom of action and on the possibility of earning a living. This is true elsewhere, of course; and in this feminist sense the provinciality of Deerbrook
stands for the provinciality of the whole world. But within a small country
community, given an already narrowed range of choices, women are limited even further, and in other ways. This does not make them exempt
from criticism. Martineau makes a point of showing that women are both
the victims and the instruments of provincial narrowness. The Ibbotsons
suffer from the narrow prejudices of this little world, and the main vehicle

of those prejudices is the malicious gossip they overheard on their first day in Deerbrook, Mrs. Rowland. She too is a victim, though, as Mr. Hope explains. "In a city, Mrs. Rowland might have been an ordinary spiteful fine lady. In such a place as Deerbrook, and with a family of rivals' cousins incessantly before her eyes, to exercise their passions upon, she has ended in being. . . ." "What she is," Margaret concludes (III, xiii, 286–287). The Ibbotsons manage to rise above this pettiness partly because they are from the city; Maria Young, a lame, witty schoolteacher who becomes Margaret's closest friend, can do so because of her education. But most women, uneducated and exposed to few influences outside the narrow circle of a dull, self-absorbed society, remain undeveloped, dependent, and degraded, bound by the limits of the society in which they live. Domesticity for them becomes a species of damnation.

Given this grim vision of the world most women must inhabit, we cannot hope for any simple, melodramatic resolution at the end. And Martineau offers a mixed, measured conclusion, containing both gains and losses. The beginning of Margaret Ibbotson's new, happy, married life clearly suggests the conventional solutions of romance; the future foreseen by Maria Young does not. She has been frustrated in both love and life and can anticipate only a lonely spinsterhood. Yet this intelligent schoolteacher, who speaks for Martineau more than any other character in the novel, looks towards her limited prospects with a tough-minded optimism. Why, Maria asks, should any of us "demand that one lot should, in this exceedingly small section of our immortality, be as happy as another?" She insists that there are "glimpses of heaven for me in solitude, as for you in love; . . . it is almost as good to look forward without fear of chance or change, as with such a flutter of hope as is stirring in you now. So much for the solitaries of the earth." So much, indeed! And so much for finding any simple alternatives to the myths Martineau explodes. There is no room here for romanticism or heroics , and none for an idealization of the everyday, either. The ordinary world is all we have, but it is a complex and challenging world, one that often must be faced with the mature self-consciousness of Maria's stoic realism. Martineau insists that all the human models handed down by literary and social tradition must be reexamined. She also warns how difficult it will prove to construct genuinely new ones.

IV

Every generation reshapes tradition, for images of the past always provide a more or less covert definition of the present. In the months following

Victoria's accession the press was filled with surveys of earlier reigns, especially Elizabeth's. A year later, the Queen's coronation was treated as an occasion to dramatize historical continuity, although the question of what this meant became political. Was it appropriate to stage a lavish traditional ceremony in a progressive era? Was the expense too great for a strained public purse? The debate over what became known as the Penny Coronation turned into a debate over the symbolism of the monarchy, with Conservatives thundering that the drive for economy debased the emblematic coin of the realm, the Sovereign herself. Architecture, too, was treated as an exercise in historical allusion, as the Battle of the Styles over design proposals for the new Houses of Parliament illustrated dramatically. Members of the Reform Club agreed upon Charles Barry's classical palazzo design for their new building (completed in 1840), a monumental assertion that the new political values associated with their name had emerged from a much older tradition. It was probably for the same reason that the architect's initial calculation of fees came to the historically appealing figure (alluding to the beginning of William and Mary's reign, and the beginning of a new Reform era) of 1689 pounds.[40] Tractarians used theological history as a tool of church reform: Newman in 1837 published his *Lectures on the Prophetical Office of the Church,* and in 1838 the *Lectures on Justification.* He proposed a *via media* between Catholic tradition and modern Protestant practice, a reappraisal of history in the service of a new religious era.

> We have a vast inheritance, but no inventory of our treasures. All is given us in profusion; it remains for us to catalogue, sort, distribute, select, harmonize, and complete. We have more than we know how to use.[41]

Carlyle's *French Revolution* was written and read as a tract for the times. And his long essay-review of Lockhart's *Life of Scott* focused on the problem even more directly: what are the risks of acquiescing in the wrong kind of history? Donizetti's *Lucia,* an adaptation of Scott's *Bride of Lammermore,* had premiered in London in 1837, the year before Carlyle's essay appeared. Was such a transformation of historical fiction into opera, romance into forms even more grandiosely romantic, symptomatic of a more widespread decline? A golden age indeed! Perhaps what glitters is only gilt. For Carlyle it was a question of moral values rather than simply literary ones. We are what we applaud, and who we worship. His task, then, was revisionist—like Martineau's, and like Macaulay's in his celebrated attack on Plato and Platonism in "Lord Bacon" (1837). New models must be found appropriate to a new age, models in life as well as art.

It was a question (as the title of Carlyle's later lectures put it) of *Heroes and Hero-Worship,* and the problem was to choose the right models. That is why the venom of "Sir Walter Scott" is directed at the poet-novelist's son-in-law and biographer, who is guilty of admiring the wrong traits for the wrong reasons and in the wrong ways. "Scott is altogether lovely to him . . . Scott's greatness spreads out for him on all hands beyond the reach of eye . . ., of his worth there is no measure."[42] The attack is on the cult of Scott, on uncritical attitudes towards biography, on a misplaced, outdated romanticism that undermines the spiritual potential of a new age.

Could that potential be realized? Was it possible to convert the negative energy of Carlyle's attack, or Martineau's, into positive fictional forms, into a postromantic heroism (if such a word really can be used) appropriate to new conditions? Was domestic heroism necessarily self-contradictory? Two of the most interesting answers appear in novels of 1837, Disraeli's *Venetia* and Mary Shelley's *Falkner.* Both focus on a romantic outsider who sets himself above and apart from ordinary society. The problem of both is to return those free spirits to a larger world, not so much to vindicate as to domesticate them (or at least see if that is possible). As it turns out, neither Disraeli nor Shelley experiences much difficulty in bringing the wanderer home; both demonstrate that the Promethean hero is never so contented as when he has been given a new life by the side of a good woman. Marmion Herbert, Disraeli's Shelleyan idealistic poet (with added touches of Byron, and others: at one point he goes off to America to become a general in the revolutionary war!), sums this all up in an explanation of his new ideology at the end of *Venetia:* "Once I sacrificed my happiness to my philosophy, and now I have sacrificed my philosophy to my happiness."[43]

"Poets! look well to your lives, for the novelists are after you!"[44] The reviewer's reference is to Disraeli's fictionalization of the biographies of Shelley and Byron. But in a sense the plot of *Venetia* concerns another related transformation: poetic eccentricity mellowed into the more prosaic civility we associate with the heroes of Victorian fiction. The novel is sprinkled with sermons against the excesses of romantic individualism, as if the dandaical young author is attempting to prepare the way for his own transformation into a pillar of established society. "Self was the idol of Cadurcis," he sermonizes on the novel's most Byronic character, "self distorted into a phantom that seemed to Lady Annabel pregnant not only with terrible crimes, but with the basest and most humiliating vices."[45] She has reason to be alarmed. Lady Annabel Herbert has been abandoned by her poet-husband, and devotes herself to the care and education of their daughter, Venetia, based on Shelley's Allegra. Venetia has grown up ignorant of her father's identity, which she only discovers midway through the novel, after entering the locked sanctum where her mother preserves his poems, a portrait, and a flower-bedecked marriage bed. This leads to their first conversation about Marmion, and Lady Annabel uses the occasion for a passionate denunciation of all egotistical excess, lashing out at both her husband and Lord Cadurcis, Venetia's childhood companion. Now Cadurcis has returned from college (where he kept a bear) as a handsome, restless poet (later, to make the Byronic echo more complete, he will spend time writing revolutionary verse in Greece); of course, he also has fallen in love with Venetia. But he is altogether too much like Herbert for Lady Annabel not to be suspicious:

> He cannot have a heart. Spirits like him are heartless. It is another impulse that sways their existence. It is imagination; it is vanity; it is self, disguised with glittering qualities, that dazzle our weak senses, but selfishness, the most entire, the most concentrated.[46]

She will not remain unmoved by the charm of poets for long. Venetia herself initiates the reunion of her parents when she first comes upon her father in an Italian country inn. Recognizing him from his portrait, she faints in his arms. Herbert, feeling the ties of family pull him strongly, instantly comprehends the errors of his unconventional quest for ideal, Platonic love: "Dreaming of philanthropy, he had broken his wife's heart, and bruised, perhaps irreparably, the spirit of his child; he had rendered those miserable who depended on his love, and for whose affection his heart now yearned."[47] The reconciliation is delayed briefly by the almost comical discovery that Herbert has been living with another woman—in Petrarch's house, on (we are assured) poetic and philosophical grounds. But Venetia's own filial and familial instincts cannot be denied. "O mother!" she exclaims at the climax of that first meeting, "he is my father, love him!"[48] It is easy to foresee that Lady Annabel's obduracy will melt. Soon a repentant Herbert is restored to the role of paterfamilias, bent and gray, content to modify his idealism under the marital yoke he once found so oppressive. He even abandons vegetarianism for the sake of familial bliss: "to please Lady Annabel," he confesses to Lord Cadurcis as they sit down to a hearty breakfast, "I have relapsed into the heresy of cutlets."[49]

Yet even this homey, conventional diet seems too rich for Disraeli's taste. Apparently he doubts whether the socialization of such figures ever can be complete. As Donald D. Stone observes, Disraeli's own enthusiasm for Byron did not prevent him "from seeing an incompatibility between imaginative ambition and domestic virtues."[50] Thus, after metamorphosing the poet into a papa, he still finds it necessary to punish his main characters for their eccentricity. In one of the most direct allusions to Shelley's life in the novel, Herbert and Cadurcis are drowned together in a storm. And the manner of the deaths suggests that both remain romantic figures to the end. Marmion's body provides unmistakable evidence that he died as a philosopher contemplating truth rather than as a husband and father regretting his final separation from the world of those he loved:

> It would appear that he had made no struggle to save himself, for his hand was locked in his waistcoat, where, at the moment, he had thrust the Phaedo, showing that he had been reading to the last, and was meditating on immortality when he died.[51]

Cadurcis, less philosophical, had attempted to swim for shore. But after all, he had expected to be married to Venetia. By killing him off, Disraeli acknowledges that the marriage was never a very convincing possibility. Could a wife and family reconcile Cadurcis to the loss of fame and his freedom to travel? Can we imagine him settling into the role of the philosopher at the breakfast table? Venetia herself requires a more thoroughly socialized companion, and at the end Disraeli pairs her with the stolid, faithful, and thoroughly colorless Captain George Cadurcis, the naval officer who inherits his cousin's title and wealth. The second Lord Cadurcis is far better equipped than the first to assume a conventional family life. The marriage will not be poetic.

The conventional marriage conclusion thus serves to recast Marmion's Shelleyan-Platonic philosophy of sympathy into a new domestic mold, and to realize its social implications more fully than Marmion himself could have done. "We exist . . . because we sympathise," he had explained to Cadurcis; it "is sympathy that makes you a poet." Sympathy, that is, of the right sort. For there are different forms, extending throughout all of animated nature. "If we did not sympathize with the air, we should die. But, if we only sympathized with the air, we should be in the lowest order of brutes, baser than the sloth." "Mount," he urges the younger man, in language that forecasts the conclusion to Tennyson's *In Memoriam,* "Mount from the sloth to the poet." This moral evolution culminates in marriage of a special kind. It is not enough to find another human being to love; we must search for the one who corresponds to the Platonic "spiritual antitype of the soul." Love conceived in this way rises above sensual gratification into "an universal thirst for a communion . . . of our whole nature, intellectual, imaginative, and sensitive." And the communion finally extends to all humanity. This is how poets become the unacknowledged legislators of the world (as Marmion remarks, showing that Disraeli was aware of the Cambridge manuscript of Shelley's still-unpublished *Defence of Poetry*). Once education extends broadly enough, the discovery of this ideal, Platonic companionship will become easy, and with it will come "the perfection of civilization."[52] Or so the philosophic formula runs. What is significant about Disraeli's conclusion is that the beginnings of this new harmony are achieved not by the novel's poetic and philosophic figures but by more ordinary ones. Much as at the end of *Wuthering Heights,* but without any of its subtler ironies, *Venetia* closes with a vision of personal and social tranquillity achieved by a new generation, removed in age and temperament from the one that struggled with great passions. The marriage will be happy because both partners are rather unremarkable; it is an ideal that requires men and women to remain in their conventional places.

Falkner, Mary Shelley's last novel, resembles *Venetia* in a number of important respects: the story of a Byronic wanderer (midway through the novel we find him fighting on the side of revolutionaries in Greece) and his eventual rehabilitation, the focus on a new generation capable of domesticating excessive individualism, the figure of a pure young woman who subdues the destructive masculine energy of the protagonists, and the central relationship of father and child. Rupert Falkner is not the actual parent of Elizabeth Raby; but the *de facto* adoption—as much hers of him as the other way around—restores both of them to life dramatically enough to make their relationship real and binding. Early in the novel a deeply depressed Falkner arrives at the village where Elizabeth recently has been orphaned. Preparations for suicide bring him to the churchyard, where she is tending her mother's grave. She begs him not to disturb "mama"; she seizes his arm and causes the fatal bullet to miss its mark. Falkner's life is spared, and his human sympathies are awakened. Plucked back from the ultimate abyss of egotism, the handsome romantic hero (Shelley at one point compares his features to Prometheus) has taken—or been led to—the first step on the path of domestication. When he discovers that the girl has no known relations, he decides to take her with him to Europe. Shifting from place to place, avoiding contact with other English people, they have little society outside of one another. Travel deepens their attachment. Falkner's role becomes both paternal and maternal, as Anne Mellor has pointed out. And this miniaturized family becomes a model for all human relations in the novel: a voluntary, selfless attachment uncomplicated by any possibility of sexual love. The last issue is important because so many instances of romantic love in the story end in suffering. For the most part this is the consequence of abused masculine power. Even

Falkner's life has been blighted by a tyrannical father, and he himself, in Mary Poovey's words, is a "transgressor into what should be the domain of maternal love."[53] The novel moves to reestablish that domain, and its influence. Unlike Disraeli, Shelley directs her plot in search of a fictional solution that will moderate the excesses of individuality, passion, and patriarchal power at the same time.

The stories of Rupert Falkner and Elizabeth Raby are only two strands of a complicated plot that Shelley attempts to weave together. She doesn't entirely succeed. Even the details of Falkner's guilty romantic past can only find their way into the text in a long prose narrative he presents to Elizabeth and her love, Gerard Neville, halfway through the book. Neville is about to set sail for America in search of information that will vindicate the reputation of his mother, who disappeared when he was still a child, apparently to run off with another man. As it turns out, that man was Falkner himself, who was attempting to rescue Alithea Neville from a brutal husband. He abandoned the scheme when he recognized her selfless devotion to her son, but his resolution came too late: she drowned attempting to escape from the house where he had hidden her. Although Gerard had long sought revenge for what he insisted must have been a crime against his mother, it is his father—who had always accused his wife of willful desertion and is now doubly bitter over the revelation of his own domestic character—who brings Falkner to trial for murder. Gerard is deeply touched by Falkner's remorse and equally repelled by "the malicious pursuit of his vindictive father."[54] He refuses to enter the scheme of revenge. After his father dies, forgiving Falkner (who is acquitted), he is reconciled to Falkner and married to Elizabeth. At the conclusion of this melodrama, then, both heroes are domesticated together (domiciled together too, as we will see), substituting a civilized love and friendship for fiercer romantic passions. As the last sentence notes, Neville "never for a moment repented the irresistable impulse that led him to become the friend of him, whose act had rendered his childhood miserable, but who completed the happiness of his maturer years."

Before this resolution, there has been some doubt whether any marriage could take place. We have seen too much of the brutality and pain of conjugal life. Elizabeth is not prepared to abandon the childhood attachment to her "father." "I suppose indeed that I am something of a savage— unable to bend to the laws of civilization."[55] The language is significant, not just because her bond to Falkner is a primitive one, in the Freudian sense, but because a similar but literal savagery has been associated with Neville. He first enters the novel as a wild child, roaming the woods at Baden, reduced to a precivilized (and mute) existence by the shock of his mother's disappearance. In spite of his strange behavior, or because of it, Elizabeth feels an immediate and intense sympathy. In fact, their histories are closely related. Her mother also had been victimized by an impetuous lover's insistence on eloping, for her husband (Elizabeth's real father) died after marrying against the wishes of his family, which had promptly disowned the couple, and refused to help her after his death. No wonder Elizabeth is reluctant to enter into marriage. The clearest alternative to the misfortunes of romantic love would appear to be avoiding sexual relationships altogether.

In a sense, this is what happens in Mary Shelley's apparently conventional novelistic conclusion. Happiness is secured with the usual symbolic marriage; yet it is not a marriage of the usual sort. When the wedding of Gerard and Elizabeth is finally arranged, Falkner remains close by to make the marriage a *ménage*. It seems in some respects like the union of two children, who will remain insulated from adult reality by the continuing presence of an ideally moralized father, now living with them in a placid Platonic threesome. Or else, as Mary Poovey argues, it is Elizabeth herself who occupies the unifying, parental role: "Mary Shelley erects an apparently unassailable barrier between father and lover only to level it by female love, exemplary and compelling in its selflessness."[56] And powerful: if the men have risen above melodramatic bitterness and possessive love, they also have been subdued in the process. We see this most clearly in the image of Falkner himself. Shelley describes at length his pale, subdued countenance during the trial: any "necessary communications with the lawyers" are conducted "with a calm eye and unmoved voice," and the remainder of his time is spent reading and writing. "He might have served for a model of Prometheus," she explains, except that "the tenderness which was blended with his fiercer passions" had made him less able to bear his pain. This is a Prometheus as Barrett might have wished to depict him. The active hero has been transformed into a contemplative saint. He is now "doubly imprisoned," for this modern Prometheus has become "the cannibal of his own heart."[57]

"The Modern Prometheus" is the subtitle of Shelley's classic novel, *Frankenstein*. The allusion to that figure here suggests that to some extent that first novel remains the model for her last. As Sandra Gilbert and Susan Gubar have shown, *Frankenstein* can be read as a woman's story, a retelling of *Paradise Lost* in which all of the characters are Eve.[58] *Falkner*, in spite of its masculine title, invites a similar feminist reading (without the specific reference to Milton): a story of women expelled from bliss, a reconsideration of the covenant that is supposed to restore them. The primary victims in the novel are women, the aggressors men. But this suggests that the settled marital resolution towards which the story is directed has less satisfying implications for wives than for husbands or fathers. Too many other marriages have ended badly; too many women have become martyrs at the hands of husbands and lovers. We should not be surprised to find that the closing picture of the three protagonists banding together to form a "little society" (the phrase comes from Dickens) resembles a childhood dream more strongly than an adult reality. For the sufferers of this novel all have retreated to, and been solaced by, childhood, starting with Elizabeth's rescue of Falkner in the opening chapters. We should recall that he encountered her while she was playing by the side of her mother's grave—playing happily, as if she recognized that some women find relief only in death, or in the company of their children.

Those two possibilities for women's happiness in one sense come to the same thing: escape, and above all escape from the society of men. Gerard's mother had retreated from her husband's tyranny and redirected all her feeling onto her son: "she was his playmate and instructress. When he opened his eyes from sleep, his mother's face was the first he saw."[59] The relation was too intimate to make Falkner's romantic offer of "freedom" seem attractive to her. He attempted to appeal to the memory of her own mother, who once hoped that Falkner and Alithea would marry; she was raised, he urged, for happiness. But Alithea's response was fiery and feminist. "My mother . . . brought me up for a higher purpose than even conducting to your happiness." It is not just that she rebuffed his amorous advances: she refused to compromise her maternal role for any other, including that of wife. Her mother, she continued passionately,

> brought me up to fulfill my duties, to be a mother in my turn. I do not deny . . . that I share in some sort my mother's fate, and am more maternal than wife-like; and as I fondly wish to resemble her in all her virtues, I will not repine at the circumstances that lead me rather to devote my existence to my children, than to be that most blessed creature, a happy wife.[60]

That closing irony should be enough to make us suspicious of the marriage settlement at the end of the novel. It was a novelistic convention already; it would become the standard Victorian fictional conclusion, too. But as in *Deerbrook,* the conclusion, like the institution of marriage itself, is qualified. Alexander Welsh has suggested that the marriage conclusion of all English fiction contains a fundamental ambiguity, for the finality it confers on the prior events of the plot also suggests the finality of death.[61] There is something of this closing stillness in Shelley and Martineau, too, but also (as I have said) a more specific cause for uneasiness. Marriage in their novels has been a source of punishment rather than peace, at least for women; it is a dangerous institution, at best. At the end of their books, the possibilities for future happiness, especially the happiness of women, seem at best dubious. Domesticity has begun to ring hollow.

V

There are always exceptions: not everyone was fixated on the ordinary. But some of the alternatives only remind us how difficult it is to create heroic figures in an uncongenial atmosphere. Elizabeth Barrett's letter to Mary Russell Mitford (which I quoted earlier) first complains of the "want of . . . ideality" in contemporary painting and then ends with a hopeful question about a new young dramatist: "Do you observe that the author of Paracelsus is bringing out a tragedy at one of the theatres?" But in spite of Barrett's optimism about the poet she would marry in 1846, Robert Browning's *Strafford* displays fewer heroics than histrionics, a straining after the tragic in unconvincing, quasi-Elizabethan rhetoric. The title character himself doggedly seeks out appropriate opportunities for noble action. "I want a little strife," he declares to Lady Carlisle in the second act, "real strife; / This petty palace-warfare does me harm." As he comes to realize, such trivial skirmishes soon will become the order of the day. The victory of the Parliamentarians marks an end to the last heroic era in British history, or such is the view of the hero and his author. Strafford dies prophecying that England will become "A green and putrefying charnel," or else, what is almost worse, a bland mediocracy in which youthful energies and motives like his own can have no place:

> As well die now! Youth is the only time
> To think and to decide on a great course:
> Manhood with action follows; but 'tis dreary,
> To have to alter our whole life in age—
> The time past, the strength gone! As well die now.[62]

The tragedy concerns the decline of tragic figures, the waning opportunities for tragedy itself, in both literature and life. The most modern element of this play is Browning's uneasiness about modernism itself. At the same time, he strains to adapt historical materials to a modern context, *à la* Pugin's *Contrasts* and many less notable contemporary works. This suggests the odd affinity between Browning's weighty tragedy and Bayard's *The Youthful Queen,* the revival of which for the London season of 1837 must have had a good deal to do with the topicality of its story. This "comedy," which at that time would not have seemed wholly that, concerns the capriciousness and vulnerability of Christine of Sweden, whose erratic public behavior is largely the consequence of an unsettled marital state. The play ends, aptly for the audience of Victoria's Year, with the Queen pledging to devote herself to her people rather than to a husband:

> we will reign alone. Though still young, our resolution is irrevocable. The sceptre of *my* ancestors shall remain undivided. . . . The love and courage of a nation are a monarch's surest safeguard, the firmest bulwarks of the throne; and, with the blessings of heaven, they will be enough for me.[63]

As R. H. Horne remarked of Sheridan Knowles, even historical subjects can be transposed into a domestic key.[64]

The same double focus on past and present is visible in Thomas Noon Talfourd's *The Athenian Captive* (1838). Talfourd altered his original ending (on advice from the actor-director W. C. Macready) to adjust "the severe spirit of the Greek drama" to milder contemporary sensibilities (as his preface explains). In both versions, Creon's son Hyllus is accused wrongly of his father's murder. According to the first ending, Thoas, the Athenian captive who actually committed the crime, confesses to Hyllus and then presents him with a knife to carry out the necessary act of revenge. But Hyllus is to become the ruler of Corinth as the play closes, partly on the urging of Thoas himself; perhaps a modern audience would have been made uneasy by a ruler with blood so fresh on his hands. Thus the second version changes Thoas' execution to a suicide. Nevertheless, in spite of the alteration, he remains the more appealing figure, more complex and more principled, murderer or no. As if in palliation of his crime, the murder occurs almost by chance, without Thoas realizing who he stabs during an attempt to escape. The killing even may have been justified: Creon—as Thoas learns from his mother, another Athenian captive who reveals her identity as well as her son's during the course of the play—had killed Thoas' father, the former ruler of Athens. Yet Talfourd is no more concerned than Mary Shelley in *Falkner* to ennoble revenge. Such heroic acts, as in *Strafford,* belong to a disappearing world; *The Athenian Captive* ends looking forward to a more ordinary and more modern society.

Much like Browning, Talfourd constructs a double tragedy: about the death of a particular (and particularly attractive) hero and about the death of the heroic mode as such, which is identified above all with the city of Athens. In his most visionary speech, shortly before his death, Thoas prophecies a new Athens, surpassing its own classical greatness. It is a stir-

ring but ironic moment, since the vision is imparted to an assembly of
Corinthians, who are unlikely to understand, let alone inhabit, such a
world:

> 'Tis not a city crown'd
> With olive and enrich'd with peerless fanes
> Ye would dishonour, but an opening world
> Diviner than the soul of man hath yet
> Been gifted to imagine.[65]

As the title of the play suggests, his own identity is partly derived from this
"world." Not unlike Oliver Twist (the subject of a sonnet of praise Talfourd addressed to Dickens), he has been shaped by the city:

> Her groves; her halls; her temples; nay, her streets
> Have been my teachers. I had else been rude,
> For I was left an orphan. . . . Fatherless, I made
> The city and her skies my home; have watch'd
> Her various aspects with a child's fond love.[66]

But that city is far away, in both space and time. As in both *Oliver Twist*
and *Strafford,* the action here occurs at the margins of a new era, in a new
kind of city that embodies new values. Their precise character is never
given in much detail, but it seems to exist somewhere between the dod-
dering tyranny of a Creon and the more energetic but colorless efficiency
of his son. Corinth will not, then, produce new heroes; men like Thoas
belong to the past. The conflict between a developing order and the values
of the Athenian traditions among which Thoas grew up extends to the final
line of the play, where it becomes clear that his ideals can only be realized
in death:

> Convey me to the city of my love;
> Her future years of glory stream more clear
> Than ever on my soul. O Athens! Athens! *(Dies.)*

This poetic glance forward remains ambiguous, coming not only at his last
moment of life but at the start of what seems bound to be a more prosaic
reign. Talfourd ends his play asking the questions we have heard before: if
this is the way of the future, is it really the beginning of a new golden age?
What ideals will inform the new society? What sort of greatness will it
honor with high rank?

Rank and romance are the staples of British dramatic tradition, and they are the main subjects of most of the plays written in the late 1830s as well. If any contemporary slant is given to these familiar themes, it concerns the problem of their relation to one another: will new distinctions change human relations; will the preoccupation with class and wealth erode the possibilities for true love, or any genuine human feelings? That this is a modern question is evident in the setting of Edward Lytton Bulwer's *The Lady of Lyons* (1838) in France just after the revolution—after, that is, the stable, traditional distinctions of rank have been replaced by the new universal title of "citizen." The real consequence of this apparent democratization is a vague, unsteady class structure based entirely on wealth. Even more dangerous, the uncertainty of class becomes an uncertainty of identity: it is difficult to discover anyone's true character in a wholly bourgeois society. The point is made even more plainly in Bulwer's 1840 drama *Money.* Evelyn, the hero of that play, must construct an elaborate scheme to discover the real motives of his professed friends—to find, if it can be found, "A good heart—a tender disposition . . . an impulse towards something more divine than Mammon."[67] There may be a reference to Carlyle's use of the final word in this remark, just as there may be an allusion to the Carlylean idea of "natural" aristocracies in making the hero of *The Lady of Lyons* the son of the heroine's devoted gardener. The play concerns the obstacles to their eventual union, above all the obstacles of class and wealth. But if Bulwer's radical politics might lead us to expect a democratic engrafting of the classes, the story follows a more conventional course. At first Pauline Deschapelles belittles Claude Melnotte's written declaration of love (he cannot bring himself to approach her in person) because of his father's occupation. She, after all, sees herself as the "Lady" of Lyons, although the phrase actually refers to the position conferred by the wealth of her father, a merchant. This overvaluation of riches will place her at the mercy of an amoral society, which sounds less like post-revolutionary France than the contemporary capitalistic Britain described by a character in *Money:* "The Vices and Virtues are written in a language the world cannot construe; it reads them in a vile translation, and the translators are—FAILURE and SUCCESS."[68] The problem, then, is to restore these terms to a genuine translation, to redefine virtue in a language that still makes sense. Pauline has a lesson to learn, as Bulwer suggests in his subtitle, "Love and Pride."

Luckily, his heroine has enough common sense not to give herself over to the worship of the new social code, although to some extent this is also a consequence of her attachment to the old one. She refuses the proposal of the oily but highly respectable "Citizen" Beauseant, perhaps in hopes of making a "true" aristocratic match. Beauseant then schemes to punish her and revenge himself by introducing Claude to her as a foreign nobleman, the Count of Como. The plot succeeds too well: the couple fall in love, and even when Melnotte confesses the deception Pauline recognizes his intrinsic worth: "Claude, take me; thou canst not give me wealth, titles, station—but thou canst give me a true heart. I will work for thee, tend thee, and never, never shall these lips reproach thee for the past."[69] As it turns out, they will not need to. By the end of the play, Claude has achieved a position of his own. He turns out to be none other than the "mysterious Morier" who has distinguished himself in the Napoleonic wars and risen to the rank of colonel ("Promotion is quick in the French army," as a soldier observes at the start of Act V). In the role of Melnotte/Morier, he delivers the moral of the piece:

> I honor birth and ancestry when they are regarded as the incentives to exertion, not the title-deeds to sloth! I honor the laurels that overshadow the graves of our fathers;—it is our fathers I emulate when I desire that beneath the evergreen I myself have planted, my own ashes may repose![70]

It is an appropriate creed for this Carlylean natural aristocrat, especially in its delicate compromise between traditional social distinctions and the rank achieved by talent. Perhaps in this world of shifting relations, some meaningful class distinctions can be preserved. So, perhaps, can some meaningful form of love.

Love is the persistent topic of the plays of James Sheridan Knowles; the word recurs in many of his titles. He wrote *The Love Chase* in 1837, *Love's Disguises* in 1838, and, in 1839, a drama simply titled *Love*. Once again, the problem of love is related to the problem of money, as Catherine, the heroine of *Love*, makes clear at the start of the play.

> Far as the poles asunder are two things,
> Self-interest and undesigning love;
> Yet no two things more like, to see them smile.[71]

Her own lineage is ambiguous, although her financial position is secure. That only makes her affection for Sir Frederick, a poor aristocrat, the more troubling. Can she be certain that she is being courted for herself alone? Lest we miss the point, the situation is mirrored in others: a Countess is in love with her serf; it is rumored that Catherine is the "love-child" of the duke, the Countess's father; the empress of the kingdom seems to be Catherine's rival for Frederick. Finally, of course, love conquers all: the serf gains freedom, demonstrates intrinsic nobility, and marries the Countess; the Empress turns out to be furthering Catherine's love for Frederick and they are married too. The play ends with the Countess praising Catherine for showing others how to recognize genuine merit:

> O, thou has taught a lesson to all greatness
> Whether of rank or wealth, that 'tis the roof
> Stately and broad was never meant to house
> Equality alone—whose porch is ne'er
> So proud, as when it welcomes in desert,
> That comes in its own fair simplicity. *(Finis.)*

The sentiments echo Bulwer in *The Lady of Lyons,* only now the attempt to define a subtle balance between "equality" and "desert" results in verbal and social confusion—or else results from it, as in the blurring of "rank or wealth." It is difficult enough to be certain about who is worthy of love. The even greater difficulty comes in attempting to describe the nature of that worth, to recognize "its own fair simplicity." The problem of love becomes a problem of identity.

Knowles' plays are filled with disguises. Women especially must conceal their identities (sometimes as men) to test the character of others. At various points both Catherine and the Countess assume disguises, as do several characters in *Love's Disguises* (originally titled *Woman's Wit, or Love's Defiance*). Hero Sutton, the central character in that play, compromises her reputation by dancing with Lord Athunree, "a libertine! / A man of pleasure—in the animal / Ignoble sense of the term."[72] This is enough to offend her Puritan fiance, Sir Valentine. She then must diguise herself as a Puritan named Ruth to put Valentine in a similar situation and teach him how difficult it is to judge from appearances. Meanwhile another character, Helen, disguises herself as a man (Eustace) to redeem her reputation, also tarnished by a prior association with Athunree. It is not just that one rake can compromise many innocents, but that one man can embody a much more pervasive drift from morality. Amid such currents, no virtue, no one's character, is secure. This is the conclusion drawn by Hero herself, speaking to the still-disguised Helen about the circumstances that brought their former friendship to an end:

> *Eustace:*   Had'st not a friend
> Misfortune lost thee?—not that thou shunn'dst her,
> But that her heavy and most strange affliction
> To thee and all her sex forbade her access?

Hero: A friend? a sister! What a fate was hers!
Of all I valued, she the being was
I least could measure worth with. Of all grace
A pattern was she—person, features, mind,
Heart, everything, as nature had essay'd
To frame a work which none might find a flaw in!
And yet 'tis said she fell—and if she did
Let none be sure they'll stand![73]

We will see many more instances of the same uncertainty, particularly in stories about young women and children who are abducted from the world in which their social standing and good name has been established. It is an uncertainty about the nature of self as well as its stability: if virtue is so frail, what in reality is it? How is it nurtured? What are its origins?

I have used a word with Darwinian undertones to suggest how rapidly the anxiety over identity transforms itself into anxiety over its biological source. The source of instability in *Love's Disguises* was, after all, "A man of pleasure—in the animal/Ignoble sense of the term." The social dislocations in these dramas are caused in part by the power of money, in part by the pressure of deeper elements of human identity bursting through the categories of morality and class. There is, at least, a new transparency to those categories, a recognition that they may grow from pre-social roots. Perhaps this explains why Claude Melnotte must be portrayed as both a Napoleonic soldier and a gardener's son. Huon, Catherine's serf in *Love,* ponders these matters in terms of his own status. He even begins with an appropriately Darwinian term:

Descent,
You'll grant, is not alone nobility,
Will you not? Never was line so long,
But it beginning had: and that was found
In rarity of nature, giving one
Advantage over many; aptitude
For arms, for counsel, so superlative
As baffled all competitors, and made
The many glad to follow him as guide. . . .
Not in descent alone, then, lies degree,
Which from descent to nature may be traced,
Its proper fount! And that, which nature did,
You'll grant she may be like to do again.[74]

What species of excellence prospers? Which becomes the source of a new line? The social dramas I have been considering all deal in such questions, although obliquely. Some even claim to settle them. But they proved too difficult to settle—too persistent, too threatening—as the history of Darwin's own thought from the late 1830s to 1859 and after illustrates. The neat theatrical conclusions provided by Bulwer and Knowles and Talfourd emphatically deny this, but by doing so they only emphasize further the magnitude of the threat. That is the final point worth making about the best and worst of these plays, and particularly about their endings. The pat Victorian dramatic resolution (we find it equally often in Victorian fiction, and, as we have seen, in Victorian poetry) has a double-edged quality, for its very artificiality makes us aware of problems that cannot be solved in more satisfying ways. The marriage formula invoked for these theatrical conclusions seems unsatisfying, yet it alludes (in perhaps the only way many Victorian writers could) to the presence of powerful biological forces working beneath even the most superficial social relations. The images of marriage and family suggest images of fertility and biological change and death that locate the Victorian home within a wider and wilder natural world. The distance between the conceptions of love in the work of Sheridan Knowles and Darwin is not as great as we might first suspect.

3

Under the Volcano

There are some arguments which strike the mind with force.
Charles Darwin, *Red Notebook* (1836)

These Explosions and Revolts ripen, break forth like dumb dread Forces of
Nature; and yet they are men's forces; and yet we are part of them: the Dae-
monic that is in man's life has burst out on us, will sweep us too away!
Thomas Carlyle, *The French Revolution* (1837)

Science advances with gigantic strides;
But we are aught enriched in love and meekness?
William Wordsworth, "The Planet Venus" (1838)

Knowledge comes, but wisdom lingers. . . .
Alfred Tennyson, "Locksley Hall (1837–1838)[1]

I

"What hope is here for modern rhyme?" Tennyson asks this question in
the seventy-seventh lyric of *In Memoriam*, and it expresses one of the
deepest preoccupations of that poem, his career generally, and the verse he
wrote in the first year or so of Queen Victoria's reign. In his great elegy,
the motive behind the question—implied in the word "here"—is the death
of Arthur Hallam, and, by extension, Tennyson's new sense of the world
under the pressure of grief. Can one compose poetry adequate to this
death, or any death? Can one compose poetry at all after recognizing the
pervasiveness of death in the world, past as well as present? Tennyson in
the late 1830s was absorbed by the problem of change; Hallam's death had
become an emblem for his sense of the impermanence of all things. His
reading of Lyell's *Principles of Geology* in 1837 provided him with a
glimpse of the infinitude of time and the impersonality of nature. On such

a scale, no loss, even one as painful as his own, could be regarded as catastrophic; Lyell's uniformitarianism seemed to deny even the possibility
of personal tragedy. Tennyson's interest in current issues had drawn him
to Lyell's geological writings in the first place, as it would to equally topical
scientific writings by Babbage and Robert Chambers. His writing of this
period, as we have seen, explores the possiblity of creating a new kind of
poetry, drawn from and addressed to the special conditions of the age. But
the very nature of those conditions undermines the poet's assurance that
he can attain his goal. "Modern rhyme" may be a contradiction in terms.

What are the requirements for a genuinely contemporary literature? In
what ways is the modern artist affected by, or responsible to, new developments in science, social science, or technology? It is an issue that can be
explored in Tennyson, Dickens, Carlyle, and many others, one that takes
on a new urgency in the 1830s. We see symptoms of what Harold Bloom
calls the anxiety of influence, only here the anxiety is schizophrenic in its
most extreme form, since the influence being mediated comes from the
present as well as the past and from fields often considered inaccessible to
the creative arts. Fields, that is, in a literal as well as metaphoric sense, for
now writers could consider the problem of formulating descriptive language for fossil beds (a few years later Martin Tupper would compose a
poem on "A Cabinet of Fossils"), or of picturing distant worlds few Europeans had ever entered before. And in many cases those new geographical
fields become symbolic of new intellectual ones, for fossils require geologists, and jungles zoologists or cartographers. The most widely recognized
image of a new natural site that implied in turn a new theoretical discipline
was the volcano, a phenomenon depicted on stage, in panoramas, in paintings, and in print. The excitement for volcanoes intensified with the publication of Bulwer's *Last Days of Pompeii* in 1834, and intensified still further when Vesuvius erupted a few weeks after the novel's appearance.[2]
Under the influence of Lyell and others, the older conception of the age of
the earth was rapidly being supplanted, and in a large number of books
that appeared throughout the 1830s, the volcano came to represent modern scientific thought and the opposition to traditional Deluge geology.[3]
More than the fossil and even more than the mastodon, the volcano was
taken as a token of a new sense of the world: a new conception of the
ancient, mysterious power of the earth as well as the new, almost magical
power of the sciences that study it. In using the word magic I do not mean
to suggest that either volcanoes or geologists were regarded in the category
of entertainment, even if (as Parry's watercolor illustrates) eruptions could
be staged as "spectacles" nightly. The very need for such performances
suggests a deeper uneasiness, which also referred to those who made natural cataclysms their scientific subject. If geology could be fearful, geolo-

gists could be feared. Ruskin in 1851 was not the first or the only Victorian to hear the sound of geologists' hammers punctuating the cadences of Bible verses.

Eruptions were terrifying, then, but intellectual explosions were too, especially since they were the ones likely to occur on home soil. Perhaps they already had. The most important contemporary source of the volcanic metaphor was Lyell, who had modified the Huttonian conception of the earth's history by insisting that its geological features could be accounted for by the operation of known agencies, including especially volcanoes and earthquakes. It is not accidental that in his *Elements of Geology,* which appeared in 1838 and summed up the conclusions of the *Principles* for a more general audience, the frontispiece centers on a volcano; it is an "IDEAL SECTION of part of the Earth's crust explaining the theory of the contemporaneous origin of the four great classes of rock." It was no longer necessary to explain vast mountain chains or valleys by special acts of Divine intercession; perhaps, though Lyell denied the charge, it was no longer necessary to refer to God at all. A writer in *Blackwood's* in November 1837 makes no effort to mask his hostility; geology, "Of all the sciences . . . is the most presuming." Even the advocates of modern geology could become uneasy about this. Reviewing the first volume of Lyell's *Principles* in 1831 for the theological quarterly *The British Critic,* William Whewell emphasized the difference between this new form of "geological dynamics" and the older assumption of "a period of paroxysmal action—an extraordinary convulsion in the bowels of the earth." It involved a different kind of geologist, as well. Lyell, he explained, "throws away" all the "crutches" of such traditional views. He

> requires no paroxysms, no extraordinary periods; he is content to take burning mountains as he finds them; and, with the assistance of the stock of volcanoes and earthquakes now on hand, he undertakes to transform the earth from any one of its geological conditions to any other.[4]

Whewell is distinguishing between catastrophic and uniformitarian science (he coined these terms in a review of Lyell's second volume in 1832); the *Principles* stands for adherence to regular, observable, physical laws. But his language suggests something else: Lyell's direct, personal access to the forces of nature, as if the geologist possesses superhuman powers. We can find similar undertones in a *Quarterly* review a year before, which portrays the geologist calmly surveying the elements: "amidst the yet more exciting spectacles of the earthquake and the avalanche, the volcanoe and the flood," he observes natural powers "in their momentary operation, and multiplies them in his imagination by the effects of ages."[5] Is this freethinking? The geologist regards all these, we are quickly reassured, as "the sure marks of a First Cause." There is (as Whewell also insisted) no necessary antagonism between science and religion. But the disclaimer is not entirely convincing, especially in light of the controversies that surrounded Lyell and later Darwin. Even in this fragment we can detect the transformation of the geologist into a Promethean figure, a challenger (or perhaps equal) to the Divine. As Arnold's Empedocles teaches us two decades later, one cannot peer into that burning crater without risking a deep estrangement from the more timid souls who remain at home. And it is not just that the natural philosopher himself runs risks. Arnold's career after "Empedocles on Etna" reminds us that the writer does too. Certain subjects bring art face to face with its own limits.

My concern in this chapter is with these limits: the sorts of problems art cannot solve, the scope of the solutions it offers to the ones it can, or claims it can. Above all, I am interested in the ways in which different people approach, accept, or resist the findings and implications of what they perceive as the new intellectual currents of their day. It is an issue I will pursue throughout *Victoria's Year*, for it cannot be confined to any particular debate or group of writings, or even to writers alone. The sense of challenge was almost universal, even though the responses to it were radically different from one another. Many even insisted that these were challenges that should not be met, that faced with new approaches to the material world a moral person could do no better than turn his back. What makes Dickens, Tennyson, and Carlyle particularly interesting as starting points is that they attempted to address the questions they believed new knowledge raised. Their solutions, insofar as they do in fact arrive at solutions, are varied and, in different ways, flawed. But much of the excitement in their writing of this period derives from a determination to confront and grapple with the implications of new conceptions of the world. And often we can discover that confrontation where we are least prepared to recognize it.

The opening paragraph of *Oliver Twist* introduces us to both the pervasive brutality of the young hero's surroundings and the critical but humorous detachment with which Dickens portrays them. With ironic echoes of the language of official reports, the narrative describes how the boy—this "item of mortality"—is "ushered into this world of sorrow and trouble, by the parish surgeon."

> Although I am not disposed to maintain that the being born in a workhouse is in itself the most fortunate and enviable circumstance that can possibly befall a human being, I do mean to say that in this particular instance it was the best thing for Oliver Twist that could by possibility have occurred. The

fact is, that there was considerable difficulty in inducing Oliver to take upon himself the office of respiration,—a troublesome practice, but one which custom has rendered necessary to our easy existence,—and for some time he lay gasping on a little flock mattress, rather unequally poised between this world and the next, the balance being decidedly in favour of the latter. Now, if during this brief period, Oliver had been surrounded by careful grandmothers, anxious aunts, experienced nurses, and doctors of profound wisdom, he would most inevitably and indubitably have been killed in no time. There being nobody by, however, but a pauper old woman, who was rendered rather misty by an unwonted allowance of beer, and a parish surgeon who did such matters by contract, Oliver and Nature fought out the point between them. The result was, that, after a few struggles, Oliver breathed, sneezed, and proceeded to advertise to the inmates of the workhouse the fact of a new burden having been imposed upon the parish, by setting up as loud a cry as could reasonably have been expected from a male infant who had not been possessed of that very useful appendage, a voice, for a much longer space of time than three minutes and a quarter.[6]

In spite of the tone, this is a crisis paradigmatic of the many others Oliver finds himself in throughout the novel, especially in light of the metaphor of battle with which Dickens depicts it. Oliver's warfare with Nature is part of a mock-heroic inflation, but it also involves a serious attempt to represent social and biological reality. So frail a child never could have survived an assault of professional medicine; he lives through his birth because of the neglect of the workhouse, because he is abandoned by everyone around him to conduct his "struggles" on his own. It is a triumph of inner drive over external conditions, a triumph achieved not so much in spite of those obstacles as because of them. Oliver's survival is a sign of fitness, of the inner resources (voiced in those first cries) that will carry him through even fiercer battles later on. Dickens gives us an account of the perseverance of life curiously close to the one associated with the theory of evolution by natural selection later in the century.

This could not, of course, involve a reference to Darwin, although Darwin's writings at this time (recorded in the privacy of the so-called Transmutation Notebooks) bear a close relation to the concerns of *Oliver Twist*. Still, the most decisive leaps in Darwin's thought came in response to his readings of Malthus in 1838; and a profound distaste for Malthusian or post-Malthusians views of population and social organization lies behind Dickens' grim account of Oliver's birth. What excited Darwin about Malthus was the definition of patterns and limits in population growth, so orderly and strict that they could be formulated as mathematical laws. It was precisely that notion of fixed laws, and the urge to codify them in mathematical and statistical form, that repelled Dickens—not so much from Malthus himself as from his followers and those who adopted his principles in political economy. We have seen one example of this aversion in "The Last Cab Driver." *Oliver Twist* is more detailed in its criticism, attacking both the New Poor Law of 1834 and the quantifying frame of mind responsible for it, the "moral calculus" of nineteenth-century political and social theorists. The language of that opening paragraph satirizes the bureaucratized complacency of an entire school of political economy, responsible for most of the legislation and public administration of the day. By a school, I mean not a specific economic theory but a general way of regarding the "human material" with which social thought concerns itself. Dickens ridicules this perspective through the parodic exaggeration of its world view: he immerses us in what it defines as reality by dramatizing its grotesque implications in both his story and his narrative voice. As Steven Marcus puts it,

> Dickens's passionate aversion to the doctrines of the political economists took expression in a style which curiously corresponds to their notion of a man's relation to other men and to society. The exacerbation of his responses to Malthusian theory, like that of many of his contemporaries, was perhaps the consequence of a certain dread that society was in the process of becoming what Malthus maintained it had always been.[7]

That dread is enacted from the opening pages of the novel. We read on not simply to learn if Oliver will survive, but to discover what he will survive as, what form this deterministic environment will force him to assume.

Thus the first glimpse of Oliver's biological "success" at birth has a chilling as well as a cheerful aspect. If we join the narrator in congratulating ourselves on the vitality of the young, this may mean that we consider them impersonally, as so many "items of mortality," as creatures in a world regulated by strict material laws rather than humans inhabiting a moral universe. That Oliver can be perceived in this way—as an animal—is symptomatic of the problems Dickens uses the novel to explore, above all the problem of sustaining moral vision in a society increasingly brutalized by subhuman conditions. For the only characters identifiable without irony as animalistic are criminals: Bill Sikes—constantly accompanied by and identified with his dog—and Fagin. Sikes was cited by the *Quarterly* in 1838 as exemplifying the decline of humanity under Benthamite morals: "a great ruffian . . . beating, for his own amusement, a little delicate boy."[8] Fagin, as his final appearance in the condemned cell testifies, is reduced in the course of the novel to the level of an animal, his moral nature (or what there was of it) totally degraded. He is shown at the end seated on his bed, "rocking himself from side to side, with a countenance more like that of a snared beast than the face of a man." His mind wanders deliriously. The jailer tries to awaken him to his own condition and the fact of Oliver's presence by calling his name: "Fagin, Fagin! Are you a man?"

"I shan't be one long," he replied, looking up with a face retaining no human expression but rage and terror. "Strike them all dead! What right have they to butcher me?" (472)

It is in this spirit that he evades Oliver's attempts to kneel with him in prayer, just as he has earlier "driven . . . away with curses" the "venerable men of his own persuasion who had come to pray beside him" (469). At one point, Dickens says, Fagin "howled and tore his hair." The last sounds he utters are beneath the level of human speech—"cry upon cry that penetrated even those massive walls." No wonder "Oliver nearly swooned after this frightful scene, and was so weak that for an hour or more, he had not the strength to walk." He has witnessed the outer form of a "blighted soul," the novel's most extreme enactment of the potential of a human being to descend to bestiality (469, 474, 470).

In *The Structure of Scientific Revolutions*, Thomas Kuhn describes the crisis following a challenge to traditional world views by new paradigms of scientific thought. There are many traces of such a crisis in the language and events of *Oliver Twist*, and their presence indicates the intensity of Dickens' response to the Malthusian social engineering of his age. In fact, he is recoiling from something even larger than the figures of Malthus and his followers, larger even than the figure of Darwin would come to be when many of these same attitudes became associated with his name. The largest issue here is materialism, and how large it actually is can be measured by the fact that it is simultaneously present in a number of ways. The word itself has several distinct connotations: a scientific approach to a world conceived as wholly physical, a quantifying vision of experience understood in terms of size and number, an economic assessment (perhaps based on that second point of view) that treats things strictly in terms of monetary value. All these are alluded to by the Dickensian parody, the power of which depends on its ability to identify a fundamental assumption underlying all the varying forms of materialism—an assumption of the essential physicality of things, of what John Fowles (in his modern portrayal of this Victorian crisis in *The French Lieutenant's Woman*) calls "the universal parity of existence."[9] Dickens is attacking precisely what Carlyle before and Ruskin after him attacked, and with almost equal vehemence: an analysis of human life couched wholly in quantitative terms, an analysis implicitly based (as Ruskin would delcare in *Unto This Last*) on "the negation of a soul."[10] If *Oliver Twist* treats such issues melodramatically, it may be a sign that except to a few prescient minds like Carlyle's they remained obscure, in spite of their urgency. Ruskin's *Unto This Last* was written in 1860, a year after the *Origin* appeared; the young Ruskin, as I will argue later, was far from attaining real clarity of insight about these matters, although in 1837–1838 he alludes to them in some of the most fevered sections of *The Poetry of Architecture*. The passion in Dickens is of the same sort as Ruskin's: intense, and yet not wholly focused onto specific targets. Some institutions are at fault, and some individuals. But the novel's main energy is directed against a more generalized threat, more pervasive and yet more difficult to objectify because it is also a threat from within, a threat to undermine the very sanctity of the self.

Materialism threatens Oliver and his world in a number of distinct ways. There are, to begin with, the various forms or schools of materialist thought I have mentioned already: the Malthusian sense of the child as an "item of mortality," the laissez-faire indifference (demonstrated by the Poor Law administrators) to human suffering, the readiness of people on both sides of the law (such as Fagin and Sowerberry, the undertaker) to view Oliver solely in terms of his potential to bring in profits. All these display a total disregard for the individual subject; all assume that people are objects of external conditions that determine human lives without regard for human hopes. This is the sense in which Fagin's miserly materialism comes to imply something very much like the materialism of early Victorian science; certainly as far as Oliver is concerned it comes to much the same thing. The brutality of London's underworld operates like a harsh, Darwinian nature: in Fagin's "den," all the other boys are reduced to animalistic existence, to a savagery that we must conclude was potential in each of them from the first. The dangers in this novel thus are manifold—to outward behavior, to inner character—and the threats against its victims come from everywhere at once. Much of the force of *Oliver Twist* derives from the obscurity of the powers the hero is pitted against, an obscurity that suggests their omnipresence and multiplicity. Even in his most secluded retreat from reality Oliver is threatened, even in what seems to him a dream—for Fagin and Monks appear as he dozes by an arbor window in the Maylies' cottage: *et in arcadia ego*. The presence of Monks in the plot (the one against the boy as well as the plot of the novel) demonstrates the inescapability of the dangers to be faced in this world. This is not simple class warfare, but a moral corruption that can infect all classes, any individuals, and degrade them into something beneath their ordinary humanity. How firm is the separation between people and animals? If Oliver is not safe, who is? Even a gentleman can become a beast:

this possibility is suggested in the very name of Monks, with its pre-Darwinian anticipation of disturbing evolutionary links.

Human animals lurk in many forms throughout the arts of the 1830s, almost always surrounded by the same atmosphere of anxiety we find in Dickens. It is an uneasiness about the nature of human nature and about the general structure of the world. In *Oliver Twist* the bestiality of the London underworld is associated with a wide variety of threats to established order, and to order itself. And this threat, to order as such, rather than its embodiment in any particular forms, greatly intensifies the novel's dramatic pitch. In one sense, what is at stake is the possiblity of education, which is to say the power of the ideas we inherit and transmit and try to codify in books. That is the world of ideas Oliver tries to enter by learning to read, the world from which he is abducted on an errand to return a bundle of books. No wonder he begs so piteously that Mr. Brownlow's books and money be returned: "Keep me here all my life long; but pray, pray send them back. He'll think I stole them; the old lady, all of them who were so kind to me, will think I stole them . . . " (164). To some extent he wishes to preserve his reputation with his new friends; but he also hopes to protect them, to shelter the only humanitarian vision of things he has ever encountered, and by so doing to preserve the very possibility of such a conception of the world. For that idealism also sustains his own capacity to hope, and to hope in particular for a way out of the network of overwhelming forces embodied by Fagin. Oliver above all fears that he can be reduced to the brutal condition of his life before Mr. Brownlow's, returned to reliance on his own untutored instincts in a world without human order. His predicament thus tests the cultural codes by which we order things, and the very possibility of order itself. There are no volcanoes in the novel, yet it dramatizes the power of subterranean forces to burst their bounds and expose the fragility, the impermanence of the solid surface separating a known from an unknown world. That eruption forces upon us a consciousness of the way in which such limits are posited—the way in which we conceive barriers, or laws, or any of the ideals of "civilized" life. What we can observe in Dickens, then, and can observe far more generally in the cultural products of this period, is what Michel Foucault has termed the "experience of order," the discovery of the hitherto unacknowledged fact of ordering itself.

In the preface to *The Order of Things*, Foucault describes the ways in which we do and do not, can and cannot, acknowledge the existence of the checkerboard of classification that underlies our conceptions of reality. To do so he identifies the regions in which we encounter cultural codes. There is a realm of practice that establishes the "empirical orders" governing everyday life, the codes regulating such activities as speech or exchange. At another extreme is a realm of "scientific theories or the philosophical interpretations which explain why order exists in general, what universal law it obeys, what principle can account for it, and why this particular order has been established and not some other." Between them is a region "more confused, more obscure, and probably less easy to analyze," a region that is nonetheless fundamental. It is both a cultural and a personal zone of experience, located both in time and space, a collectively occupied vantage point which "makes manifest the modes of being of order" and "liberates order itself."

> It is here that a culture, imperceptibly deviating from the empirical orders prescribed for it by its primary codes, instituting an initial separation from them, causes them to lose their original transparency, relinquishes its immediate and invisible powers, frees itself sufficiently to discover that these orders are perhaps not the only possible ones or the best ones; this culture then finds itself faced with the stark fact that there exists, below the level of its spontaneous orders, things that are in themselves capable of being ordered, that belong to a certain unspoken order; the fact, in short, that order *exists*. As though emancipating itself to some extent from its linguistic, perceptual, and practical grids, the culture superimposed on them another kind of grid which neutralized them, which by this superimposition both revealed and excluded them at the same time, so that the culture, by this very process, came face to face with order in its primary state. It is on the basis of this newly perceived order that the codes of language, perception, and practice are criticized, and rendered partially invalid.[11]

Foucault offers this as an "archeological" rather than an historical analysis, a study of the conditions that make knowledge possible at all times and places. Yet there are periods when "the pure experience of order" emerges with particular force, periods of fundamental epistemological discontinuity that break radically from the prevailing sense of the order of things, and he argues that the early nineteenth century is one of them.

We will see evidence of this discontinuity, of the "experience of order," throughout this book, although not so much in the form of a radical break as a questioning of the sort I have described in respect to Dickens. The discovery Foucault speaks of is made over and over in the late 1830s, or rather, partially made: an idea tentatively proposed, or incompletely expressed, a question that is only half formed. The recognition is potentially revolutionary, but it need not express itself in a revolutionary form. More often than not, it is simultaneously invoked and suppressed, present most vividly when it is being denied. I would not wish to suggest, for instance, that Dickens tries to invalidate traditional codes in his novel. Quite the reverse: the book is deeply conservative in the ambition to recover a less bureaucratic system of local charity, to restore Oliver to his birthright, and (by so doing) to defend the possiblity of birthrights generally being upheld. As his preface explains, Dickens "wished to show, in little Oliver, the principle of Good surviving through every adverse circumstance, and triumphing at last" (33). Yet this is a triumph achieved only with difficulty, and on terms that do not fully restore our confidence in the possibility of reconstituting a society that has been explored so critically. Monks remains outside the province of law and official justice to the end, banished to a "new world" where he will finally, and fortuitously, die. And the central group of Oliver's friends withdraws as well, forming a "little society" in the countryside, "whose condition approached as nearly to one of perfect happiness as can ever be known in this changing world" (476). How perfect, we may wish to ask, is that? Oliver has been removed from the world of the Malthusians and the threats of human bestiality, but only through the dramatic (or melodramatic) imposition of a new order specifically created with those dangers in mind. The crisis of the novel has passed; but the sense of crisis is codified in the social structures that mark its suppression.

II

Little of the poetry Tennyson composed in 1837 and the years immediately after does not touch in some way upon the issues of change and order, and the new ideas that make both so conspicuous. "The Golden Year" questions whether the classical idea of its title can be attached to an uncertain and increasingly technological society; "The Epic" evaluates traditional poetic models against the background (or is it foreground?) of modern debates. And no poem of this period sets out to articulate the experience of contemporary life more fully than "Locksley Hall." Articulate, because as a dramatic monologue it literally gives voice to the consciousness of the age, assigns it to a single speaker. Yet (and this is another sense of the poem's articulation) what the poem exposes is the fragmentariness of such a being—the shifting set of goals, ideas, and feelings that are embraced and rejected and reconsidered as he is tossed about in the changing currents of the present. Tennyson is concerned with the tensions between the different possibilities of this consciousness, and the historical situation that provides the source of its disorder and potential order. His first experiments in the dramatic monologue—"Ulysses" and "St. Simeon Stylites"—represented characters and attitudes associated with the past. Now he shifts the focus of the genre to the present, as if to treat it as a distinct historical moment as well, and to discover the unique modes of consciousness and speech that make it so. How far, Tennyson seems to ask, has the modern consciousness moved from its origins? What does it mean for our whole culture to have grown up?

"Locksley Hall" concerns growing up, coming of age, in both a personal and cultural sense. The speaker's bitterness and alienation (which also help create the isolation of the dramatic monologue's scene) is the result of a series of losses not atypical of the passage out of youth in any age: an early love, an old home, and a variety of comforts associated with both. Not the least of these losses is a sense of confidence in the known world—a sense that it *is* known, and knowable. The speaker has returned to the scenes of his youth, the places where his young life was spent and where he framed his experience in a series of reassuring images. Both kinds of scenes, as he recognizes, are irrecoverably lost. The place is the same and yet different; and his sense of place, his confidence in the beauty, unity, and purposefulness of nature, is even more seriously damaged. The power of money and change has shattered a placid world view that once seemed to extend back in unbroken continuity to the world of myth.

The loss of that mythic world view is the primary fact disclosed in the poem. It is a loss connected with the emergence of all the new conditions the speaker declaims against in his long, ranting chronicle of dissatisfactions: greed, poverty, technological progress that cannot move quickly enough to provide answers to the most fundamental questions. What do such "developments" mean for the self?

> Knowledge comes, but wisdom lingers, and I linger on the shore,
> And the individual withers, and the world is more and more.
>
> (141–2)

All of this is measured against a conception of knowledge and identity formulated in the quiet harmony of the past, an ideal of unity imaged most clearly by the view from the windows of Locksley Hall itself. That image is telling: a view. For Tennyson—as for Carlyle, Dickens, Martineau, Ruskin, and others—the loss of old ways of seeing is the clearest measure of the novelty of this new age. As he looks up to those windows, the speaker recalls the lost horizons that used to be visible from them, horizons of both vision and thought.

> Many a night from yonder ivied casement, ere I went to rest,
> Did I look on great Orion sloping slowly to the west.
>
> Many nights I saw the Pleiads, rising through the mellow shade,
> Glitter like a swarm of fire-flies tangled in a silver braid.

Here about the beach I wandered, nourishing a youth sublime,
With the fairy tales of science, and the last result of Time;

When the centuries behind me like a fruitful land reposed;
When I clung to all the present for the promise that it closed:

When I dipt into the future far as human eye could see;
Saw the Vision of the world, and all the wonder that would be.

(7–16)

We are only eight stanzas into the poem here—it is the first recollection of a poem filled with recollections—and the tone will grow far more violent. Yet as much as the speaker passes on to other thoughts and other moods, and concentrates especially on his bitterness over the loss of his cousin Amy's love, this initial visionary passage introduces and frames everything else that follows. Frames it literally, as if in the process of remembering how the world appeared through the ordered perspective of that casement he also realizes with new force how radically everything has changed.

As I have suggested, this loss of perspective and tranquil vision is the most drastic loss recorded in the poem, even more than the betrayal by Amy. The two are not unrelated. It is true to a great extent, of course, that the speaker's bitterness derives from his rejection; that is how he explains it himself. But we can regard his failed romance as the analogue of that more general experience of abandonment and disappointment. A whole universe of love has been closed off, and not just by one woman's infidelity. The passage I have quoted describes a mythic sense of time, history, and nature, now undermined by new kinds of knowledge and experience—especially by modern science. Even that word has changed. Formerly "science" referred to knowledge generally; now it has begun to denote the specialized findings of experts. The *Oxford English Dictionary* dates the emergence of this connotation of the word somewhere between the eighteenth and nineteenth centuries; 1867 is the first example given of the "modern use" of science "as synonymous with 'Natural and Physical Science,' and thus restricted to those branches of study that relate to the phenomena of the material universe and their laws." We almost can detect this new usage emerging in this poem, and to the speaker's horror. Once (and recently!) science was composed of fairy tales. Once history seemed poetic too, extending from a fruitful past to a perfect future through a present experienced as a land of promise as well as a promised land. Once the whole world was structured into a framed, picturesque view. No more. How can any human relationships or any individual psyche withstand such change? This is the first memory of the poem because it is the one against which all the rest are measured. Even Amy's betrayal did not leave a deeper psychic scar than the loss of this real and spiritual home. And in an important sense its architecture, its material existence as a token of stability and continuity, is the central symbol of the order that the new world has lost.

Little is said in the poem about the actual building that gives it its name. It may be abandoned or in partial ruin, like the houses in "Walking to the Mail" and "Audley Court," *English Idyls* written at about the same time. Certainly by the closing lines the speaker is prepared to conceive of the hall as crumbling at some point in the immediate or distant future:

> Howsoever these things be, a long farewell to Locksley Hall!
> Now for me the woods may wither, now for me the roof-tree fall.
>
> (189–90)

It is not clear whether that second line is meant as description, prophecy, or curse, but the effect is much the same whichever is the case. And in a sense two contradictory possibilities are validated. We are asked to imagine both a standing and a falling building; stability and instability are played off against one another. There is corroboration of this double consciousness in the historical models for the hall. Some evidence suggests that the original was Harrington Hall, the home of Rosa Baring, who is often identified as the poem's "Amy." In the early part of the century, Harrington Hall had a chapel that was (in the words of "Locksley Hall Sixty Years After") "slowly sinking now into the ground."[12] Another architectural source is Charles Tennyson d'Eyncourt's newly medievalized mansion, Bayons Manor.[13] Robert Bernard Martin, who discounts Rosa Baring's importance in Tennyson's life, argues for the second source, insisting that the poet has "at least some aspects of his uncle in mind" whenever he "glances at the vulgar efforts of the newly rich to create tradition."[14] Those last words make what I think is the important point, whatever house Tennyson has in mind. Tradition is seen in this poem as impermanent, like a building, for it can be created or recreated or undone. In the end, we should not try to separate those two kinds of buildings, one falling to pieces and the other so finely restored; they are part of a continuum, two stages of architectural existence. Architectural renovation and collapse allude to one another; both remind us of the vulnerability inherent in the apparent stability of even the most impressive structures. By analogy, the one defined by the poem's wide range of social and cultural reference, this instability is connected with instabilities of other sorts. The orders of architecture image the orders of society, and the order of traditional thought. All conceal a deeper uncertainty, a deeper disorder.

Midway between its former stability and the possibility of future wreck, embodying both the memories of a settled world and its distance from the present, the hall is the central image in a compressed psychohistory of the age. Above all, it is a history of confusion, as the shifting moods and pace of the poetry themselves demonstrate. The rhythms of the verse grow more violent as the speaker wrenches himself between various contradictory stances: optimism and despair, social commitment and alienation, action and passivity. There is no satisfactory point of rest, no midpoint within all these circles of frenzied uncertainty. He has lost his own center of being, and, correspondingly, any sense that the world is centered, or can be conceived in a unitary way. He claims to know that "one increasing purpose runs" throughout history, yet quickly adds that this has no meaning for him:

What is it to him who reaps not harvest of his youthful joys . . . ?

(139)

These were the pleasures, we should recall, associated with that magical "Vision of the world, and all the wonders that would be," from the casement window of his childhood. With the collapse of that traditional architected order, the possibility of all other kinds of structure fades. Now, to the "jaundiced eye, . . . all order festers." This is also to say that order, in its decay, becomes visible. Here, then, is one of the moments Foucault refers to when he speaks of a sudden recognition that order exists, that cultural codes have lost their transparency, and that the orders known in the past "are perhaps not the only possible ones or the best ones." When the sense of order itself has been subjected to so much violence, is it possible to have confidence in any particular sort of order at all?

That is the problem we are confronted with at the end of the poem. "Locksley Hall" closes with one of the most famous evocations of Victorian optimism. But it is so hedged by the ambiguities of a dramatic situation that we cannot be sure whether to accept the affirmation of a new order or to treat it as the sort of parodic mimicry we have seen in Dickens. This is a characteristic issue in dramatic monologues, complicated even further in this one by the layering of the narrative between past and present and between so many conflicting moods. It is difficult to accept any of the speaker's many assertions as unqualified, somehow final within the poem's shifting points of view. If any mood seems to dominate over the others at the end it is the mood of changeability itself. The poem closes with the world in storm, and the rhetoric of the speaker heightens itself to match the violence all around him. It is a world wholly demythicized and correspondingly terrifying, in spite of the speaker's appeals to this stormy epoch to "help" him find himself.

Mother-Age (for mine I knew not) help me as when life begun:
Rift the hills, and roll the waters, flash the lightnings, weigh the sun.

(185–186)

How can anyone find a voice or make it audible—even to himself—in such conditions? The speaker claims to have recovered the optimism of his youth: "O, I see the crescent promise of my spirit hath not set." Nevertheless, the conclusion is a moment of disjunction, when both the self and the world around it are represented in terms of violent change.

Thus this closing scene, this particular storm, represents a broader category of social and intellectual events. Above all, I suspect that the imagery of flood, lightning and earthquake—volcanic imagery, without the volcano—alludes to the disruptions embodied in the discoveries of modern science. Paradoxically, this is partly a consequence of the poem's catastrophism. But there also is an allusion to scientific thought in the speaker's final stance. For here, more than at any other moment of the poem, he becomes passive, a creature wholly at the mercy of the elements that sweep him away in the last line:

For the mighty wind arises, roaring seaward, and I go.

(194)

I must go, he might have said; I have no choice. We will see how easily such resignation came to be associated with a modern, postscientific view of a world governed by impersonal forces. The hint of determinism here makes that last burst of manic exultation unconvincing. The speaker (and it is significant that he is unnamed, without any explicit identity) is powerless by the end. And he is as deluded as ever—trying to persuade himself that alienation can be cured by moving to an even greater distance. But he will not outrun this storm. The future he turns towards promises to be a perpetual series of violent presents. As he prepares to sail away, it seems clear that he is permanently displaced, unhoused.

The abruptness of this ending is characteristic of much of Tennyson's verse—the art of the penultimate, as Christopher Ricks has called it.[15] Even *In Memoriam*, which introduces a wedding to conclude its cycle of mourning in an epilogue, displays the same impulse. Again the poem moves outside itself to solve its largest questions. The marriage in question—between Tennyson's sister Cecilia and his friend Edmund Lushington—took place in October 1842; and the coherence of the epilogue depends on linking that ceremony with ideas from Robert Chambers' *Vestiges of the Natural History of Creation*, published anonymously in 1844.

The dates are important, especially because the poem's crises are associated with the 1830s. Completing the poem required a new perspective. Before the 1840s the process of grieving could not be terminated naturally, or by mere poetic assertion. Up to 1842 (as we can learn from the new Shatto and Shaw edition) *In Memoriam* would have concluded with lyric lvii, where, as in "Locksley Hall" and other verse of that period, the poet does not so much settle his own uncertainties as turn his back on them.

> Peace; come away: the song of woe
> Is after all an earthly song:
> Peace; come away: we do him wrong
> To sing so wildly: let us go. . . .

It is a superimposed ending, a termination rather than a conclusion. It suggests that a fuller and more satisfying ending required the existence of a new myth that simply wasn't available to Tennyson before.

The absence of such a myth, and the need for one, is apparent in the lyrics most clearly associated with the experience of the poem in the late 1830s, especially the "evolutionary" lyrics of sections lv and lvi. Written between 1837 and 1842 (Eleanor Mattes assigns them to the earliest of those years),[16] they are often taken to be the locus of the most important meditations on science in the poem, if not in the entire nineteenth century. They are clearly among the gloomiest, as well, containing echoes of the often-unsettling Lyell, in whose work Tennyson was "deeply immersed" in 1837,[17] in addition to traces of Babbage, Butler, Malthus, and "the anonymous author of *Immortality or Annihilation*."[18] But it is not so important to document specific intellectual borrowings as to recognize how much the modernity of these lyrics allies them with a more general uneasiness about the problem of concluding any poem, or making sense of the world, in the late 1830s. In fact, the largest question addressed in this dark midsection of the poem concerns order and purpose: "Oh yet we trust that somehow good / Will be the final goal of ill." (liv). "Final goal," with its deliberate allusion to final cause, raises a serious question the poet will continue to pursue in the next lyric, "considering everywhere / Her secret meaning in her deeds." By lyric lvi, it becomes clear that such a meaning cannot be found, at least in the old sense of the word.

Lyric lvi of *In Memoriam* is sometimes read as implying that the poet's horror arises from a sense of the malignity of nature. In fact the source of disturbance is deeper than that.

> 'So careful of the type?' but no.
> From scarped cliff and quarried stone

> She cries, 'A thousand types are gone:
> I care for nothing, all shall go.'

> 'Thou makest thine appeal to me;
>   I bring to life, I bring to death:
>   The spirit does but mean the breath:
> I know no more.'

It is not simply nature's unconcern that motivates despair: it is the lack of any deliberate object or method. "I know no more." Those words might have been spoken by the mourner himself, and this is part of what makes them so unsettling. His own lack of a center suddenly appears mirrored in the external world. Fossil evidence suggests that even species are impermanent; the cycle of destruction eventually could reach up to humanity itself. But this mass carnage grows more terrifying when seen as the result of blind agencies. Once again, then, the longest fear concerns materialism. Even a distinguished scientist like Sir Humphrey Davy felt compelled to express his "disgust" for this doctrine, as the *Saturday Magazine* of 23 June 1838 noted in printing a short extract from his writing. Materialism: a conception of life with no reference to spirit. For Tennyson it implies that humanity as it has been known is on the verge of becoming extinct for modern thought.

There is a second level of despair in this lyric. The insistence of nature on its own ignorance ("I know no more") has its corrollary in the necessary ignorance of human beings as well: nature without a purpose means a corresponding purposelessness in all thought. Lyric liv asserts that "we know not anything," and terms the poet's prior yearnings for an orderly vision of the world a mere dream. By lv, these are "evil dreams" that "Nature lends." "I falter where I firmly trod." The culmination of these three lyrics of self-doubt comes in a nightmare vision of the "futility" of life and the life of the mind in a world governed by such conditions:

> What hope of answer, or redress?
> Behind the veil, behind the veil. (lvi)

It is a vision of an end to knowledge, or an end to any form higher than the mere recognition of factual information, as in the new conception of "science" itself—an end to wisdom, which implies not only an end to faith but an end to poetry.

Tennyson's reading in Chambers' *Vestiges*, then, did more than provide a humanized view of evolutionary change, although that was part of the power it exerted over him. The book mythologized science within a com-

Figure 2.3. "The Rose of England," "Presented with #3 of *Novelty*" (2 September 1837), Trustees of the British Museum.

Figure 2.2. Henry Collen, "Victoria," Trustees of the British Museum.

Figure 2.1. James Henry Nixon, "Queen Victoria's Visit to the
City of London, November 9, 1837," Guildhall, London.

Figure 1.7. John Orlando Parry, "A London Street Scene" (1836 and after, dated 1835), Alfred Dunhill, Ltd.

Figure 1.6. Contrasting Towns, 1440 *(bottom)* and 1840 *(top),* from A. N. W. Pugin's *Contrasts* (second edition, 1841), University of Oregon Library.

Figure 1.5. Gérard F. Bragg, "The View from the Back of the Greenwich
Road," from *Six Views of the London and Greenwich Railway* (1836),
Trustees of the Science Museum (London).

Figure 1.4. "The London and Greenwich Viaduct and Railway," from *The Penny Magazine*, January 9, 1836.

Figures 1.1–1.3. Princess Victoria, Watercolors of gypsies (1836).
Copyright reserved.
Reproduced by gracious permission of Her Majesty Queen Elizabeth II.

Figure I.2. Map of London from Actual Survey, Comprehending the Various Improvements to 1839, Humbly Dedicated to Her Majesty Queen Victoria, by the Proprietors E. Ruff & Co., Courtesy of the Guildhall Library, London.

TRAINS ARE COMING IN.

Figure I.1. Thomas Hood, "Trains Are Coming In,"
from *The Comic Annual.*

Figure 2.4. Edmund Thomas Parris, "Victoria," Trustees of the British Museum.

Figure 2.5. Daniel Maclise, "An Interview Between Charles I and Oliver Cromwell" (1836), National Gallery of Ireland.

Figure 2.6. Edwin Landseer, "Windsor Castle in Modern Times"
(1841–1845). Copyright reserved.
Reproduced by gracious permission of Her Majesty Queen Elizabeth II.

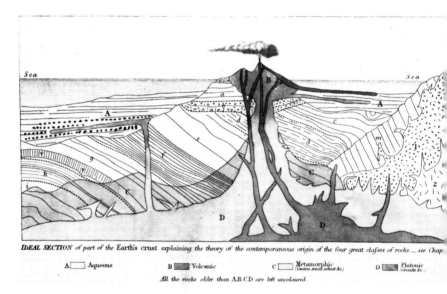

IDEAL SECTION of part of the Earth's crust explaining the theory of the contemporaneous origin of the four great classes of rocks.—see Chap.

A ☐ Aqueous   B ▨ Volcanic   C ☐ Metamorphic (Gneiss, mica-schist &c.)   D ▨ Plutonic (Granite &c.)

All the rocks older than A.B.C.D are left uncoloured.

Figure 3.1. Frontispiece to Charles Lyell's *The Elements of Geology* (1838), University of Virginia Library.

prehensive vision of all knowledge, a humanistic universe undisturbed by the assaults of new discoveries and new disciplines. John Killham has pointed out that many of the apparent echoes of Chambers in the epilogue are in fact echoes of a long and heavily quoted review of the *Vestiges* that appeared in the *Examiner* in late 1844; and that essay, perhaps more than Chambers' book itself, explores the humanistic implications of this new conception of the order of things. The reviewer notes, for instance, that Chambers appears to be unaware of the existence of similar theories among the Greek philosophers, "and it is the more strange to what an unconscious and large extent he corroborates many of their most striking views."[19] In supporting Chambers' defense of a benign, Divinely ordered evolutionary progress, his effort to define a common ground between traditional Christian belief and the findings of modern science, the review extends that argument even further: all truths are consistent with one another, as the Greeks themselves remind us.

> The Socratic idea of science is, that nothing can be known except together with the rest and along with its relation to all things beside. And it would be hazardous to say that a nobler definition of philosophy has been or could be given, than that which declares it to consist not in a partial cultivation of either morals or physics, but in the co-existence and intercommunion of both.[20]

"Let all be welcome," the reviewer declares early in the essay, "who bring new truths, if so they can be proved. Let the confident hope animate us, that these new truths will in time be found harmonious with the old."[21] This is the "benignant wisdom" of the *Vestiges*.[22] Traditional modes of thought, like the fossil remains of forgotten species, can have a living connection with our own world, even considered in the most up-to-date scientific terms.

The author of the review is anonymous, but the language and tone sound very much like that of William Whewell, whose *History of the Inductive Sciences* appeared in 1837. There, Whewell also urges us to have confidence in the ultimate reconcilability of all truths, even though the basis for that reconciliation may not yet be apparent given new discoveries and the present limits of knowledge. "The real philosopher, who knows that all the kinds of truth are intimately connected, and that all the best hopes and encouragements which are granted to our nature must be consistent with truth, will be satisfied and confirmed, rather than surprised and disturbed, thus to find the Natural Sciences leading him to the borders of a higher region."[23] For Whewell this means that all our researches should lead to the intuition of a Final Cause. His chapter on "The Doctrine of Final Causes" cites his own volume of the *Bridgewater Treatises* to explain how this intuition marks the distinction between lower and higher orders of mind:

> those who have been discoverers in science have generally had minds, the disposition of which was to believe in an intelligent Maker of the universe; and ... the scientific speculations which produced an opposite tendency, were generally those which, though they might deal familiarly with known physical truths, and conjecture boldly with regard to the unknown, did not add to the number of solid generalizations.[24]

Historians of science continue to debate whether the emergence of the conception of evolution by natural selection can be regarded as a radical shift from one fundamental scientific paradigm to another, according to Kuhn's model for scientific revolutions. Was there a specific biological orthodoxy that Darwin overthrew? Does it alter our view of his revolutionary status if it turns out that he only modified a series of related theories of origin that were too distinct to be regarded as a single paradigm?[25] Perhaps the best way out of this argument is to alter Kuhn's definition of paradigm by incorporating the extrascientific assumptions to which modern scientific theories posed so large a threat. What were the more general points of resistance from which the new knowledge was contested? What were the positions from which it was felt their radical implications could be resisted, or defused? Whewell suggests a fundamental one that helps us understand Tennyson's enthusiasm over Chambers as well. For Whewell almost seems to anticipate Kuhn's arguments about the progress of scientific revolutions, although only to deny their validity. The crisis of contemporary knowledge described in the pages of his *History* (or of its sequel, the *Philosophy of the Inductive Sciences*, published in 1840), stems, he claims, from the notion of revolutionary scientific discovery itself. Like Chambers and Tennyson and many others after them, Whewell disputes the assumption that new (especially scientific) knowledge inevitably need prove discontinuous with the old. Anomalies (Kuhn's term) suggested by modern geology need not represent a serious assault on theology. Whewell is minimizing the radicalism of contemporary thought, denying that any crisis, or any revolution, exists. It is a conservative notion of history, designed to keep history conservative. It is this embracing notion of the place of emerging scientific knowledge within a stable world view, as much as any specific idea of evolution, that Tennyson found in Chambers; this is the absent conception—the missing link—without which he could not complete his poem in the 1830s.

Poetic closure requires confidence that the world can be put in order, or confidence that it already has been. It requires what Frank Kermode has termed "the sense of an ending," which itself implies a sense of the distinctions by which endings are imposed and the world rationalized. But we must speak of ends along with beginnings; endings belong within a conception of sequence according to which some things come before others, time has natural or appropriate divisions. Endings belong to a universe of firsts and lasts, highers and lowers, structure, priority, rank. The idea of closure is hierarchical, precisely opposite to the parity of a uniformitarian approach to sequence. It is a difficult conception to break free from. "Never use the word higher and lower," Darwin reminded himself in a note pinned to his copy of the *Vestiges*.[26] If we wish to applaud the radical modernity of his vision, we should recognize that he needed a reminder, and needed to be reminded lest he fall under Chambers' spell. Tennyson found this radical perspective less reassuring, and less desirable; certainly it was less amenable to poetry. If one fully accepts Lyell's conception of time, is it possible to create structured literature of any sort? "What hope is here for modern rhyme?"

Lyell himself anticipated the problem. He offers several analogies to account for the mistaken interpretations for his own theories, several sympathetic explanations of those whose responses tended toward hysteria. A fixation on natural violence, he points out in the *Principles*, results from imagining that an immensely long sequence of events must have taken place in the narrow span of Mosaic chronology—as if (he explains, offering an analogy) the long history of a civilization were collapsed into a hundred years. No wonder such a distorted record "scarcely ever fails to excite a suspicion of the preternatural." And he offers a second analogy to explain the panic with which contemporaries viewed the geologic record, one even more directly applicable to *In Memoriam*. It is "as if the death of some individual in whose fate they are interested happens to be accompanied by the appearance of a luminous meteor, or a comet, or the shock of an earthquake. It would be only necessary to multiply such coincidences indefinitely, and the mind of every philosopher would be disturbed."[27] For Tennyson, who would have been struck by this passage, the earthquake was in part geology itself, encountered in the aftermath of Hallam's death. His first response is not to invoke the "preternatural" but to lose confidence that natural history can be charted against any pattern of orderly historic laws. "Are God and Nature then at strife?" (lv). In the generalized present tense of lyric lvi, the human race is conceived as potentially extinct: at least, this is the final implication of Tennyson's most fevered series of questions. Could Man, Nature's "last work, who seem'd so fair" (notice that anguished past tense),

> Who trusted God was love indeed
>   And love Creation's final law—
>   Though Nature, red in tooth and claw
> With ravine, shrieked against his creed
>
> Who loved, who suffer'd countless ills,
>   Who battled for the True, the Just,
>   Be blown about the desert dust,
> Or sealed within the iron hills?
>
> No more? . . .

The last phrase stands on its own as a complete thought, summing up much of the deepest anxiety in the elegy, much of what made it so difficult to complete. Before 1842, the words might have been taken to refer to the possibility of order, or even the possibility of human life. Under the pressure of modern scientific thought, humanity itself must be spoken of in the past tense, time (always measured by a human standard) viewed as disrupted, and the possibility of complete, continuous poetic discourse considered doubtful. Could any writing of the late 1830s ground itself more successfully in the new sense of the order of things?

III

1837–1838 was the central period of the most creative decade of Carlyle's life, and *The French Revolution* (published June 1, 1837, twenty days before Victoria became queen) the central work of that period. It is "of" that period in a double sense. Carlyle's history is both a study of events in France and an invitation to conceive them in new ways. It is in this sense partly about the consequences of political revolution for the modern temperament, about how to look back on certain events under their influence. Much like Tennyson in the *English Idyls* or "Locksley Hall," Carlyle is concerned with the relation between history and the age in which it is produced, the modern view of modern events. His basic premise is stated most succinctly in the opening sentence of his 1837 review of the "Parliamentary History of the French Revolution," an essay summarizing some of the research for his own history. "The event of these modern ages is the French Revolution," he declares, and either of the first two words might be italicized to express the weight of his emphasis.[28] The revolution is the thing that stands out above all others; it is the happening that embodies all the forces shaping the time. Then Carlyle moves to a longer metaphorical expansion of the same idea:

A huge explosion, bursting through all formulas and customs; confounding into wreck and chaos the ordered arrangements of earthly life; blotting-out, one may say, the very firmament and skyey loadstars,—though only for a season. Once in fifteen-hundred years such a thing was ordained to come. To those who stood present in the actual midst of that smoke and thunder, the effect might well be too violent: blinding and deafening, into confused exasperation, almost into madness. . . . And now, for us who have receded to the distance of some half-century, the explosion becomes a thing visible, surveyable: we see its flame and sulpher-smoke blend with the clear air (far *under* the stars); and hear its uproar as part of the sick noise of life,—loud, indeed, yet embosomed too, as all noise is, in the infinite of silence. It is an event which can be looked on; which may still be execrated, still be celebrated and psalmodied; but which it were better now to begin understanding.

Carlyle addresses a generation still under the volcano, as his imagery informs us. The metaphor as he uses it may come from Lyell, who, chronicling volcanic activity and other disruptive natural events, had spoken frequently of the "revolutions of the earth." Uniformitarian science made it necessary to speak of revolutions in the plural, as if no single example could be understood outside of the sequence in which it had a place. If this is disturbing to a settled conception of the earth, it is all the more so to a settled conception of society. It is almost as if the new findings of geology led inevitably to a vision of society in a state of continual, or at least potentially continual, ferment.

Darwin's *Beagle* journal moves toward the same conclusion in recording his first experience of an earthquake in 1835. "A bad earthquake at once destroys our oldest associations," he remarks at first: "the world, the very emblem of all that is solid, has moved beneath our feet like a crust over fluid;—one second of time has conveyed to the mind a strange idea of insecurity, which hours of reflection would never have created." By the time he surveys the damage in Concepción, this initial shock has been multiplied by hours of reflection, and his thoughts return from Chilean geology to English society:

Earthquakes alone are sufficient to destroy the prosperity of any country. If, for instance, beneath England, the now inert subterranean forces should exert those powers which most assuredly in former geological ages they have exerted, how completely would the entire condition of the country be changed! What would become of the lofty houses, thickly-packed cities, great manufactories, the beautiful public and private edifices? If the new period of disturbance were first to commence by some great earthquake in the dead of night, how terrific would be the carnage! England would at once be bankrupt;

all papers, records, accounts would from that moment be lost. Government being unable to collect the taxes, and failing to maintain its authority, the hand of violence and rapine would go uncontrolled. In every large town famine would be proclaimed, pestilence and death following in its train.[29]

It is far from clear which half of the comparison is dominant here, and perhaps that is the most striking point. Earthquake is as terrifying as political revolution, and political revolution as unsettling as earthquakes. The only way to explain unprecedented events is in terms of one another, and the only image adequate to suggest the fearfulness of the world surveyed by modern geology is drawn from the most potent nightmare of modern politics.

Wordsworth denounced this linkage of scientific and political thinking, along with other modern views, in a series of three sonnets "In Allusion to Various Recent Histories and Notices of the French Revolution," poems directly responding to Carlyle's book. Such analogies, he proclaims, are both false and impious:

> Who ponders National events shall find
> An awful balancing of loss and gain,
> Joy based on sorrow, good with ill combined,
> And proud deliverance issuing out of pain
> And direful throes; as if the All-ruling Mind,
> With whose perfection it consists to ordain
> Volcanic burst, earthquake, and hurricane,
> Dealt in like sort with feeble human kind
> By laws immutable.

"As if"—we must not delude ourselves, or move from deceptive appearances to false conclusions. "But woe for him / Who thus deceived shall lend an eager hand / To social havoc." The threat of revolution is no less fearsome than that posed by those who accept or propagate such "monstrous theories of alien growth." "Bend, ye Perverse!" the first sonnet concludes,

> to judgments from on High,
> Laws that lay under Heaven's perpetual ban
> All principles of action that transcend
> The sacred limits of humanity.[30]

Presumably that "ban" includes intellectual "principles" as well, books like *The French Revolution* and the vision of history on which they are based.

For all his hysteria, Wordsworth reads Carlyle accurately in at least one respect, as a revolutionary writer as well as the historian of a revolution. Carlyle's volcanic imagery dramatizes the legacy of the events in France: a continuing potential for violence in action and thought, a recognition that human events (still—always) are governed by material laws. The flamboyance of that imagery is a way of insisting that history in the old style will not do. Carlyle calls for a new Universal History (a quasi-scientific phrase itself) as distinguished from Local or Parish History,[31] the sorts of "Parliamentary" histories that were produced in the past. He returns to this subject (and to the book reviewed in the *Westminster* essay, Roux's *Histoire Parliamentaire*) in the final volume of *The French Revolution*, on the Terror. For it is in dealing with that last and most violent phase of the revolution that conventional history (including parliamentary history) has shown itself most unfit to confront or represent the truth. Somehow violence, like volcanic explosions, produces confusion and panic. The responses to the Terror range from hysteria to apologetics; even the most serious attempts to make sense of the period merely distort it by rationalizations according to "old Forms" that once had accounted for simpler events. It is like invoking Copernicus to explain a comet:

> so some accredited scientific Law of Nature might suffice for the unexpected Product of Nature, and History might get to speak of it articulately, and draw inferences and profit from it; in this new stage, History . . . babbles and flounders perhaps in a still painfuller manner. (iv, 203)

What if History were to "admit, for once, that all the Names and Theorems yet known to her fall short?"—to admit, that is, that "this grand Product of Nature was even grand, and new, in that it came not to range itself under old recorded Laws of Nature at all, but to disclose new ones?" (iv, 204).

Carlyle is proposing a new kind of history. His analysis of the failures of tradtional modes often invokes something like Kuhn's model of scientific revolution to suggest how dramatically we must break with tradition to account for phenomena history has never before explained. The problem is to rediscover "scientific historic fact" (iv, 55), including in part the most ordinary activities of daily life, the most apparently trivial things. *The French Revolution* teems with such ordinary, seemingly insignificant details, not only for dramatic effect but to give the historian's generalizations a material base. We are alerted to this historiographical technique, and its significance, from the start. The first volume opens with a description of the sick-room of Louis XV, "Louis the Well-Beloved," the king whose deathbed seems to contain the dying tradition of kingship itself:

"Sovereigns die and Sovereignties: how all dies, and is for a Time only" (ii, 7). Can we see the larger significance in such a specific human moment, the ideas concretized in the "natural supernaturalism" of the world?

> How such Ideals do realise themselves; and grow, wondrously, from amid the incongruous ever-fluctuating chaos of the Actual: this is what World-History, if it teach anything, has to teach us. (ii, 10)

We must be prepared to learn. In a characteristic trope, Carlyle shifts from "Ideals" back to the reality of the sick-room, urging us to gaze with a liberated, almost scientific "eye of History": "To Newton and Newton's Dog Diamond, what a different pair of Universes . . . ! Let the Reader here, in this sick-room of Louis, endeavour to look with the mind too" (ii, 15, 5).

Yet science no less than history can be entrapped by its own worst habits of misperception; even Newtonian science can arrive at limits, and perhaps has arrived at them already. This is certainly the case for the cause-and-effect quasi-Newtonian historical writing of Carlyle's predecessors, a literalistic form of pseudoscience he repudiates from the start. It is too simplistic, one-dimensional, rigid, confined too strictly to facts alone. "For ours is a most fictile world," he explains in "Realised Ideals," "and man is the most fingent plastic of creatures. A world not fixable; not fathomable!" Consider the problem of perception itself: "if the very Rocks and Rivers (as Metaphysic teaches) are, in strict language, *made* by those outward Senses of ours, how much more, by the Inward Sense, are all Phenomena of the spiritual kind: Dignities, Authorities, Holies, Unholies!" (ii, 6). Order becomes transparent as Carlyle searches for a new basis on which to establish historical analysis. Simple empiricism is not enough. Science cannot explain a king, unless it is a science of both inward and outward things, more than a strictly quantitative study. Carlyle is proposing a redefinition of science, to restore it (as Carlisle Moore has observed) "to its older eminence among the liberal arts."[32] He is redefining it in a form the speaker of "Locksley Hall" would understand, and approve, bringing it back from a specialized to a more generally humanistic discipline. The technical, modern forms of science have little value for explaining the complexities of human behavior. Carlyle illustrates the problem in relation to the National Assembly.

> Every reunion of men, is it not, as we often say, a reunion of incalculable Influences; every unit of it a microcosm of Influences;—of which how shall Science calculate or prophesy? Science, which cannot, with all its calculuses, differential, integral, and of variations, calculate the Problem of Three gravitating Bodies, ought to hold her peace here. (iv, 69–70)

It is not just that some phenomena never can be reduced to a single intellectual formula. Words themselves cannot do more than symbolize or approximate: "human language, unused to deal with these things, being contrived for the uses of common life, struggles to shadow out in figures" (iv, 122). No written history, then, can give a precise chronology or real causal explanation: "let no man ask History to explain by cause and effect how the business proceeded henceforth" (iv, 119). As Philip Rosenberg explains, "it was precisely the old historiography's commitment to a linear pattern of explanation that he singled out for attack." What Carlyle replaced it with was a more complex or (to use his own term) "solid" form of history, employing (quoting Rosenberg again) "nonlinear narrative techniques appropriate to his modern, somewhat Bergsonian sense of time."[33] It is clearly not so much a science as an art of history. Readers often call attention to its literary, even theatrical qualities. John Stuart Mill begins his laudatory *Westminster Review* essay by terming *The French Revolution* "not so much a history, as an epic poem."[34] Yet none of these terms does justice to the density of Carlyle's historical method, the illusion of presence created by the violent energy of his style, the chaotic sense of raw, perceived experience produced by "a mass of sociological detail in which the chain of causal relationships, if we can find one at all, is circular and continually turning in on itself."[35] It is less sociological, in other words, than dramatic, and the drama has the complexity and coherence of myth.

The mythology of *The French Revolution*, however, is radically new, and stamped indelibly with the marks of Carlyle's own vision—a personal mythology in the romantic tradition, a modern mythology (as Albert J. LaValley has argued)[36] that deliberately sets itself apart from the assumptions of traditional world views. Above all, it sets itself apart from their literalism, especially the literalism of explanatory categories. Categories, explanations, are always in some sense tentative, merely verbal constructions; the sheer exuberance of the language of the history makes us aware that all histories are made up of langauge, that what they present are not worlds but words. Carlyle thus remains visible as the self-conscious creator of this history. We never are allowed to forget that he is an artist in words, and in a sense only that: language can only approximate the actualities of experience; abstractions are that and nothing more. Traditional abstractions, especially when they are metaphysical, are introduced most cautiously of all. "The Gods are Athirst" declares the title of the first chapter in the penultimate book of the history. What does it mean? What can it mean, in 1795, or 1837? The phrase is quoted from the last volume of Camille Desmoulins' journal the *Vieux Cordelier*—a critique of the Jacobins that echoes the words of Montezuma: "les dieux ont soif" (iv, 253).

The primitive language seems appropriate to the demonic blood-lust of the Terror, yet Carlyle makes us aware of its oversimplifications: this is a demonism working wholly through human agency, an outpouring of genuine (if hateful) instincts. This is the sort of argument Wordsworth thunders against in his poems, for it suggests a conception of history with no room for God. Carlyle never asserts this directly, yet he invokes traditional theological categories only to insist on their inapplicability to the complexities of the situation in France.

> What then is this Thing, called *La Révolution*, which, like an Angel of Death, hangs over France, noyading, fusillading, fighting, gun-boring, tanning human skins? *La Révolution* is but so many Alphabetic Letters; a thing nowhere to be laid hands on, to be clapt under lock and key; where is it? what is it? It is the Madness that dwells in the hearts of men. In this man it is, and in that man; as a rage or as a terror, it is in all men. Invisible, impalpable; and yet no black Azrael, with wings spread over half a continent, with sword sweeping from sea to sea, could be a truer Reality. (iv, 248)

True reality? The phrase seems tautological until we recognize that Carlyle is exploding the categories of reality we normally rely on, above all our definitions of nature and humankind. "For Nature," he declares in the final volume, "as green as she looks, rests everywhere on dread foundations, were we farther down; and Pan, to whose music the Nymphs dance, has a cry in him that can drive all men distracted" (iv, 2). Even nature is an abstraction that distances us from human events: "These Explosions and Revolts ripen, break forth like dumb dread Forces of Nature; and yet they are Men's forces; and yet *we* are part of them: the Daemonic that is in man's life has burst out on us, will sweep us too away!" (iii, 249). That combination of images from geology and biology (for the forces "ripen" before they "burst") might suggest that Carlyle is searching for the language of a newer, human science, yet the point is the reverse. He moves among different sorts of vocabularies to remind us that all are merely systems of words, metaphors; it is precisely our bondage to such limited approximations that keeps us apart from Realities.

I have capitalized that last word because Carlyle so often does. It belongs to a semi-mystical vocabulary that alludes to unseen principles while keeping our focus on the known facts of the physical world, on the extreme conditions that motivate extreme deeds. "Hunger and nakedness, and nightmare oppression lying heavy on Twenty-five million hearts," we are told in a chapter titled "Cause and Effect," was the "prime mover in the French Revolution; as the like will be in all such Revolutions, in all countries" (iv, 115). That future tense is a crucial part of the argument. *The*

French Revolution is often described as a tract for the times, a warning to Carlyle's compatriots that a reenactment of the crisis of fifty years before remains a genuine threat to England in the late 1830s. The reason is the material determinants of human behavior. Men and women are as much subject to the power of natural laws and conditions as all the things in the world. "Our whole Universe is but an infinite Complex of Forces; thousandfold, from Gravitation up to Thought and Will; man's Freedom environed with Necessity of Nature: in all which nothing at any moment slumbers, but all is forever awake and busy" (iii, 102). This language draws partly on the theology of Carlyle's Calvinist upbringing, according to which freedom of the will coexists with Divine foreknowledge, yet the emphasis has shifted, perhaps as a result of the religious crises that led him to abandon the strict faith of his childhood. The God of *The French Revolution* operates wholly in nature, a term that includes human nature, rational and irrational, as well. Carlyle is insisting on the inescapable power of environment, a word he himself had coined in its modern usage in writings of the 1830s. Within such a vision of the world, the cherished concept of will becomes almost meaningless: "Volition bursts forth involuntary-voluntary; rapt along; the movement of free human minds becomes a raging tornado of fatalism, blind as the winds" (iv, 122). Humanity is at the mercy of large historical forces. It is not surprising that many of his contemporaries considered his history a determinist manifesto, or even associated it with the radical doctrines of modern science.

Some of those early responses sound pathological, but often they are alive to undertones in Carlyle we have forgotten to notice. "Men are treated as agents," complains an anonymous writer (Herman Merivale) in the *Edinburgh Review*—agents "who had a part to perform—a work to do—until we almost cease for a time to regard them as anything else."[37] Once we follow Carlyle in viewing the French Revolution as a "great hoard of volcanic matter . . . but one expression of the inarticulate and confused cry of these million struggling," "special causes sink into insignificance. . . . If so, the men who took part in it were less agents than patients:—men who may have conceived that they were forwarding or impeding it, but in reality the sport of the impulses they thought to control."[38] William Sewell, a Tractarian minister writing two months later in the *Quarterly*, responds in much the same way.

> He has treated the French Revolution, according to his metaphor, as the outbreak of a volcano, as a necessary result of certain combinations of circumstances, like the conjunction of certain gasses with certain metals, ending in a natural explosion; and in so doing, not only is his historical view miserably defective, but his morality is erroneous and pernicious.[39]

At best, Carlyle's philosophy amounts to pantheism, which for Sewell amounts to hopelessness. Like the geologist who "fancies in the earth a series of convulsions and explosions in which system after system was generated, and each grew up on the ruins of its predecessor, leaving no traces of that predecessor behind but broken skeletons, and empty shells, and shattered strata," the pantheist imagines that "the moral universe presents a series of successive revolutions." No matter that such thinkers "console themselves, in the face of falsehood, crime, and misery, by reflecting that all are parts of *one* system—all advancing under the eye of one God. . . . They have no conception of one immutable truth." Nothing, Sewell insists, could be more depressing.

> It were a miserable thought that the world of man's wisdom was nothing but a succession of wrecks and ruins, and that the temple of the very fairest philosophy, which the Pantheist clings to as his only hope, must soon perish likewise, and give way to some new delusion. It must end in the denial of all truth; and when truth is lost in the world, what, we ask again, is to become of man's intellect, or his heart, or even his body, amidst the ruins of a falling society?[40]

These writers (and there were others) exhibit two separate if closely related concerns. They are disturbed by the imagery of a crumbling society and even more by the spectacle of men and women reduced to their instincts within it. Even a much more sympathetic reader, Charles Dickens, would acknowledge this element of *The French Revolution* when he fictionalized it into *A Tale of Two Cities*: no character more fully embodies the revolution than Mme. DeFarge, and circumstances have "developed her into a tigress."[41] *Hard Times*, which Dickens dedicated to Carlyle, exposes the same potential: if you force people to live miserably for long enough, until "they and a bare existence stand face to face, Reality will take a wolfish turn and make an end of you."[42] But those conditional verbs soften the argument that other readers found more radical. Dickens wants to imagine a world in which people will have other motives and take other forms. *The French Revolution* warns that the animalistic dimension of humanity always will be there, perhaps starkly alone.

"Cruel is the panther of the woods, the she-bear bereaved of her whelps; but there is in man a hatred crueller than that" (iv, 222). Carlyle's remark on the Terror applies to the whole revolution, to the whole of history. The formalities of social behavior are merely clothing, superimposed to cover our inner nature. "Man is not what one calls a happy animal; his appetite for sweet victual is so enormous," we are told in "Contrat Social."

The lowest, least blessed fact one knows of, on which necessitous mortals have ever based themselves, seems to be the primitive one of Cannibalism: That *I* can devour *Thee*. What if such Primitive Fact were precisely the one we had (with our improved methods) to revert to, and begin anew from! (ii, 54–55)

According to this anthropological analysis, human institutions are simply legitimizations of primitive urges:

Fell Slaughter, one of the most authentic products of the Pit you would say, once give it Customs, becomes War, with Laws of War; and is Customary and Moral enough; and red individuals carry the tools of it girt round their haunches, not without an air of pride,—which do thou nowise blame. (iv, 47–48)

How can we blame it? The image of "red individuals" merges American Indians and British soldiers into a single representative form. Civilization coexists with the primitive. We can never outgrow our instincts.

The starkest example of this vision (for the post-Holocaust sensibility) appears in the brief account of the Meudon Tannery of Human Skins, where "perfectly good wash-leather" was made from "such of the Guillotined as seemed worth flaying." Looking from this incident back over all other forms of "terrestrial Cannibalism," History "will perhaps find none of the sort, on the whole, so detestable." Yet as Carlyle's language here suggests, it is an episode not wholly unique. "Alas, then," he asks, "is man's civilisation only a wrappage, through which the savage nature of him can still burst, infernal as ever? Nature still makes him: and has an Infernal in her as well as a Celestial" (iv, 247). Darwin also would refer to cannibalism (although he may have been mistaken about its existence)[43] in the chapter on Tierra de Fuego in the *Beagle* journal. But the connection between these books is not their interest in human savagery but the insistence that there is nothing extraordinary about it. Thus, the Terror collectively becomes a *Tigresse Nationale*, which "knows one law, that of self-preservation" (iv, 223). Like Darwin after him, Carlyle introduces us to a historical forebear who is far less dignified than we like to imagine ourselves. "Nature makes him still," and may make us the same way.

Of course *The French Revolution* is not grounded in evolutionary theory. In fact, for all its insistence on material agencies, it is not grounded in any particular historical mechanisms or any particular historical theory. As Rosenberg points out,[44] Carlyle refuses to deal in specific causes, and this helps explain further the contemporary response to his book. Perhaps its most radical element is a militant agnosticism, the resistance of the argument to allying itself with any "ism" at all. Carlyle rejects the possibility of historical certainty, and the possibility of finding any theoretical position from which he might approach it. This was the element of the book Mill objected to most strenuously:

> except by general principles, how do we bring the light of past experience to bear upon the new case? The essence of past experience lies embodied in those logical, abstract propositions, which our author makes so light of:— there, and no where else. . . . Without a hypothesis to commence with, we do not even know what end to begin at, what points to inquire into. Nearly every thing that has ever been ascertained by scientific observers, was brought to light in the attempt to test and verify some theory. To start from some theory, but not to see the object through the theory; to bring light with us, but also to receive other light from whencesoever it comes; such is the part of the philosopher, of the true practical *seer* or person of insight.[45]

Mill may be right; certainly he is nervous. Carlyle threatens some of the most basic assumptions of philosophical tradition. Mill strikes a surprisingly conservative note, not really so different from Sewell's objection to Carlyle's neglect of "abstract principles, general laws, all which lies deeper than sight." Sewell's ostensible targets are pantheism and the Calvinist preference of faith to reason. Yet like Mill he is aroused by Carlyle's disregard for any established definition of truth.

> There *are* realities [Sewell writes] wholly independent of our fancies and opinions. The laws of nature are truths, whatever be our conceptions of them; the laws of morals are immutable, however corrupt may be our conscience: the eternal attributes of God continue the same, though our rationalising theology vacillates and wanders. Thus physical science would test our conceptions of the phenomena of matter by the experience of general laws: thus ethical science would lay deep the distinctions of right and wrong.[46]

Principles for Mill mean rational principles, arguable articulated principles. They are designed to advance speculations towards some conclusive result, towards the truth; this is why he (like Sewell) introduces the example of science. What makes Carlyle's historical mysticism so radical is its refusal to move towards such conclusiveness. For him the Nature of Things is in its deepest sense unknowable, at least given the current state of human knowledge. Mill joins Carlyle in describing the present as a time of transition; but he is unprepared to follow the next step and insist that this requires a radical break from the intellectual conventions of the past. That is the real challenge of *The French Revolution*. It is not just that old paradigms have lost their potency: there are no new ones available—or at least none visible to modern eyes—to take their place. The revolution is continuing, in action and in thought. We must abandon our claims of certainty.

> All things are in revolution; in change from moment to moment, which becomes sensible from epoch to epoch: in this Time-World of ours there is properly nothing else but revolution and mutation, and even nothing else conceivable. (ii, 211)

Revolution "can never stop till Time itself stops." How, then, can a history of it be finished? Carlyle raises the question himself, and half answers it. Homer's epos "does not conclude, but merely ceases. Such indeed, is the Epos of Universal History itself" (iv, 321). *The French Revolution* similarly closes describing the "whiff of grapeshot" with which Napoleon dispersed the last of the revolutionary mobs. It is less a conclusion than an anticlimax, and a self-conscious one. Since change is continuous, the terminations we assign in history books are artificial, fictive. Our sense of an ending is only that—and if this seems to anticipate poststructural views of narrative Carlyle would add that it is a postrevolutionary view above all. The French Revolution altered our sense of everything else: why not our sense of an ending? Can we even maintain a sense of an ending in a postrevolutionary epoch? Perhaps the French Revolution never ended, or never ended fully; what form will it take next? A few pages from the end of the book he returns to the imagery of volcanic history to remind us that natural cycles are endlessly continuing into an unknown future: "The World is black ashes;—which, ah, when will they grow green?" (iv, 323).

Most readers of Carlyle would look for answers to such questions in the lectures of 1840, *On Heroes and Hero-Worship*. But heroism in *The French Revolution* is as problematic as everything else. The figure of Napoleon is only half-drawn at the end of the history. Mirabeau, who comes closer to appearing in heroic form, struggles for a stature he never achieves: "This brother man, if not Epic for us, is Tragic" (iii, 147). Had he lived, "the history of France and of all the World had been different" (iii, 138). But he did not, it was not. "Whereby indeed, it comes that these same *would-have-beens* are mostly a vanity; and the World's History could never in the least be what it would, or might, or should, by any manner of potentiality, but simply and altogether what it *is*" (iii, 139). At first this sounds like a simple assertion of fact. But it is Carlyle himself who juxtaposes "is" with "would, or might, or should." And this is where his determinism, his rigorous insistence on the operation of historical/natural laws, gives way to another sort of vision, a sense of historical potential. In the process his writing of history becomes a rewriting that imposes a new form on the solidity of facts—projecting an ideal future, dreaming of a past that did not exist. "The Night of Spurs," for instance, tells the story of the king's indecisive, abortive attempt to escape to Austrian territory in late June 1791; Louis' vacillation at Varennes not only prevents his own escape but reconfirms the leaderless confusion of the whole nation, reenacting the failures of leadership that helped produce the revolution in the first place. In describing these, Carlyle tantalizes us with possibilities that were not to be: a brave king, resisting capture, stirring soldiers into action, riding back into France—"and the whole course of French History different!" (iii, 181). The negation that took place in reality implies its opposite, evokes it in an instant of heroic daydreaming. The glare of determinism casts shadows that remind us of the possiblity of freedom. Heroism in *The French Revolution* is defined by its absence.

The most dramatic example appears in one of the first episodes of the revolution, the storming of the Bastille. Storming is the crucial term to keep in mind in reading this chapter, since Carlyle is writing about a mob that gathers into itself much of the natural energy that produced the revolution as a whole. It is, as the imagery of "Storm and Victory" continually illustrates, a human fire-storm, a living volcano. The man in its midst is the commander of the Bastille, the "Old Marquis" De Launay, a minor character, historically and within the epic structure of the narrative, figuring only in these few brief chapters, and here only to ponder and then be frightfully dismembered by the revolutionary storm. Yet this very marginality is what makes him important in Carlyle's treatment of the scene, or potentially important. For he alone at the height of mob frenzy embodies the possiblity of detachment from that confusion, and from the dissolution of self that it implies. "Paris wholly has got to the acme of its frenzy," Carlyle declares; "whirled, all ways, by panic madness" (ii, 191). The imagery of storm and flood portrays a force destroying any individuals in its path. "At every street-barricade, there whirls a minor whirlpool—strengthening the barricade, since God knows what is coming; and all minor whirlpools play distractedly into that grand Fire-Mahlstrom which is lashing round the Bastille." De Launay resists the tide momentarily, isolated and alone, fixed at the still point around which it surges. "Motionless," the governor of the prison meditates on his response to Thuriot de la Rosière, the mob's representative, sent to demand surrender. It is a moment symbolic of inwardness: De Launay pulled up the Bastille's drawbridge and "retired into his interior." The conclusion of the whole incident is known: the building will fall. But Carlyle creates dramatic suspense over a historic impossibility: "let the curtains of the Future hang." De Launay is presented as the last man in Paris, perhaps the last in France, capable of asserting individuality of any sort outside of the mainstream of that deterministic revolutionary tidal wave—the only man in a position to resist effectively, to be a man at all.

"What shall De Launay do?" (ii, 194). His choice is represented in a melodramatic iconographic tableau. The marquis has pledged to blow up the Bastille sooner than surrender his keys. Carlyle portrays him frozen in a statuesque heroic posture, holding a torch beside the powder magazine of the fortress. This pictorialism takes De Launay briefly out of time; the historical narration stops while Carlyle examines the unachieved would-have-been, and we are momentarily removed from the flux of historical process. Like Louis during his abortive flight, the marquis is trying to decide, and the speculations on the embryonic future suggest what might have been, perhaps should have been, going through his mind.

> What shall De Launay do? One thing only De Launay could have done: what he said he would do. Fancy him sitting, from the first, with lighted taper, within arm's length of the Powder-Magazine; motionless, like the old Roman Senator, or Bronze Lamp-holder; coldly apprising Thuriot, and all men, by a slight motion of his eye, what his resolution was:—Harmless, he sat there, while unharmed; but the King's Fortress, meanwhile, could, might, would or should in nowise be surrendered, save to the King's Messenger: one old man's life is worthless, so it be lost with honour; but think, ye brawling *canaille*, how will it be when a whole Bastille springs skyward!—In such statuesque, taper-holding attitude, one fancies De Launay might have left Thuriot, the red Clerks of the Bassoche, Curé of Staint-Stephen and all the tagrag-and-bobtail of the world, to work their will. (ii, 194)

The closing word emphasizes the fundamental issue underlying the scene. It is a test of freedom, as we see in the iconography of the torch held aloft, the comparisons with classical figures, the marquis' statuesque posture, the reminders of his venerable age. This is a tableau of heroism—potential heroism, if we recall what will happen when the suspended narration resumes. For the vision must dissolve, and does so barely a paragraph after it was introduced: "And yet, withal, he could not do it." The torch is lowered. The Bastille is razed. The revolution continues.

How could it have been otherwise? De Launay, at the center of the whirlpool, represents the possibility of freedom throughout history, "environed by necessity" like the Calvinist will. Yet even as Carlyle describes the forces to which the marquis finally yielded, he suggests what it would have taken to resist them—what it would have taken for another sort of man.

> Hast thou considered how each man's heart is so tremulously responsive to the hearts of all men; hast thou noted how omnipotent is the very sound of many men? How their shriek of indignation palsies the strong soul; their howl of contumely withers with unfelt pangs? ... Great is the combined voice of men; the utterance of their *instincts*, which are truer than their *thoughts*; it is the greatest a man encounters, among the sounds and shadows which make up this World of Time. He who can resist that, has his footing somewhere *beyond* Time. De Launay could not do it. (ii, 194–195)

Bound by the constraints of mass psychology and the habitual force of social identity, De Launay is simply a man of his time. But in declaring this much, Carlyle also indicates that an alternative exists.

We are reminded of the alternative more grotesquely when the marquis is butchered by the crowd at the doors of the Hôtel de Ville. "He shall never enter," Carlyle writes: "only his 'bloody hair-queue, held up in a bloody-hand;' that shall enter, for a sign" (ii, 196–197). De Launay's head is carried through the streets on a pike, another "sign" that his death, like his failure of nerve, entailed a literal dissolution of self—human potential disembodied. Beginning with his failure of self-consciousness in the "interior" of the Bastille, he failed to conceive himself heroically, or to conceive himself as subject at all. Emerging to the ramparts from the world of spirit into the world of matter and external events, De Launay surrendered to a wholly material history that treated him as, reduced him to, a wholly material being; in his death he becomes wholly an object, a plaything of the mob. It is as if the self-consciousness he nearly achieved in the powder magazine could have given him not only great destructive power but a measure of humanity no one caught up in the revolutionary process can maintain. The same loss of humanity underlines the events at Varennes: the "King can give no order, form no opinion; but sits there, as he has ever done, like clay on potter's wheel; perhaps the absurdest of all pitiable and pardonable clay-figures that now circle under the Moon" (iii, 182–183). The ironic reference is to the Divine Creation of life from earth and dust: none of the historical figures in the revolution can reanimate this clay with genuine life.

How is such vitality achieved? How can any historical being find a foothold "*beyond* Time"? The implied presence of such questions in the text suggests that Carlyle, too, felt uneasy about the new historical consciousness he urged others to embrace. *The French Revolution* is a book about the limits of material historical conditions, yet it seeks to transcend those limits in its dreams of an unachieved historic potential. Or in the act of recording them. Writing history becomes a kind of heroic action, and occasionally one has the sense that Carlyle attempts to achieve the ideals lacking in the revolution through a sort of verbal sleight of hand. The impulse surfaces first in that seminal essay of the 1820s, "Signs of the Times." The essay concerns reality, and the possibility of human freedom; by the end, the relation of the two becomes a function of the power of imagination alone. "We are but fettered by chains of our own forging," Carlyle declares, echoing Blake; and they are chains "which ourselves also can rend asunder."[47] Our "deep, paralysed subjection to physical objects comes not from Nature, but from our own unwise mode of *viewing* Nature." Thus we are trapped not by a determined world but by our conviction that it exists—not by necessity but our sense of necessity, our worship of it. Religion itself has been replaced by determinism, and above all, by the "mechanical" forms of thought associated with modern science. The argument is familiar. To make its implications clearer, Carlyle translates it into an image:

> If Mechanism, like some glass bell, encircles and imprisons us; if the soul looks forth on a fair heavenly country which it cannot reach, and pines, and in its scanty atmosphere is ready to perish,—yet the bell is but of glass; "one bold stroke to break the bell in pieces, and thou art delivered!" Not the invisible world is wanting, for it dwells in man's soul, and this last is still here.[48]

This is at first an image of the self as object, regarded as a specimen for analysis and definition by some external scientific point of view. That bell is a common apparatus for scientists and gardeners; the first us of the word in this sense recorded in the *Oxford English Dictionary* is Evelyn's reference to "large Glasses . . . to clap over tender plants or such as are to be forced." As that last word shows, the bell requires both a particular kind of investigator and a particular way of regarding the thing being studied: isolating and defining it in terms of its biological properties. To examine humans in this way is to trap them in a structure of their own making (or ours), for they/we are both the investigators and the creatures being studied, subjects and objects who abandon their/our very subjectivity in the act of objectifying existence. Such modes of perception constitute us as wholly material beings. But this also means that we can escape from our material confines at the moment we learn to regard them, and ourselves, differently. "The bell is but of glass." The illusion of confinement shatters the moment its transparency—the transparency of order—is named. In the beginning is the word.

Carlyle's authorial presence reasserts itself in the final paragraph of *The French Revolution*. The historical narration has ended; the revolution has been dissipated in "the whiff of grapeshot." Now little remains except to bid the reader farewell. Yet this simple flourish comes as close as any other moment in the book to defining the sort of human possibility we have observed frustrated, over and over, in actual revolutionary events. It also reminds us how fully that possibility is bound up in the potential of language. Not that Carlyle suddenly discloses himself as the heroic artist he would go on to describe in *On Heroes and Hero-Worship*. But he reminds us of something equally precious, the "sacred" relation of writer and reader.

> And so here, O Reader, has the time come for us two to part. Toilsome was our journeying together; not without offence; but it is done. To me thou wert as a beloved shade, the disembodied or not yet embodied spirit of a Brother. To thee I was but as a Voice. Yet was our relation a kind of sacred one; doubt not that! For whatsoever once sacred things become hollow jargons, yet while the Voice of Man speaks with Man, hast thou not there the living fountain out of which all sacrednesses sprang, and will yet spring? Man, by the nature of him is definable as "an incarnated Word." Ill stands it with me if I have spoken falsely: thine also it was to hear truly. Farewell. (iv, 323)

If Carlyle has spoken truly, and we heard truly, the "incarnated Word" of his history may possess power, commensurate to the power that shattered the glass bell of Mechanism in "Signs of the Times." It may possess, that is, the power to liberate, to restore us to an identity that in revolutionary times is both close at hand and constantly in danger of being lost. A great deal lies concealed in the modesty of this conclusion, above all a tribute to the function of writing to name or misname, to free or to imprison, to resist or accede to illusory forms of order, to constitute humanity in more or less human forms. This may be the most revolutionary declaration in the book, for it leaves us to inhabit a world created by language. In the end, too, is the word. In the end is a new beginning.

4

The Stolen Child

Then sink not oh! my dear soul nor
Yeald to sad dispair, thy cause is
Great that calls thy Lord away
A great sinking spiriet and a silint
Tear but ill becomes the child
Who from the bonds of Satan
May go free.

Poem found on the body of "Sir William Courtenay,"
written in a woman's hand (1838)

within

Wan Childhood's squalid haunts, where basest needs
Make tyranny more bitter, at thy call
An angel face with patient sweetness pleads
For infant suffering to the heart of all.

T. N. Talfourd, "To Charles Dickens—on His 'Oliver Twist'"

let us pray

That thou, in this exceeding glory maskt,
Be not to loss of thy true self beguiled;
Still be able at thy Maker's feet to lay
The living, loving, nature of a child!

Richard Monckton Milnes, "To Queen Victoria, On a Public Celebration" (1838)[1]

I

One of the most memorable Dickensian scenes centers around the figure
of young Oliver Twist asking for more gruel in the workhouse. It is memorable partly because it is composed as a scene, a literary set-piece, much
in the manner of the images of contemporary life in *Sketches by Boz*.

Action is suspended, arresting our attention on a variety of physical details, heightening the sense of expectation; the moment is deliberately overdone, a piece of written melodrama, another instance of The Dickens Theater. But it is all the more memorable as a consequence of George Cruikshank's celebrated illustration of the incident, which seizes upon all these dramatic qualities and translates them into pictorial form. After *Oliver Twist*, "asking for more" has become a standard motif of political cartooning, a staple of satiric language; this has as much to do with Cruikshank as with Dickens, for the phrase in that particular form appears only in the caption to the illustration (Figure 4.1), not in the text itself, as Richard Vogler has pointed out.[2] The illustration achieves even more than this. As much as it depends on hints in the text, its power derives from Cruikshank's ability to move beyond a literal representation of details and actions in the narrative and suggest, picture, their nuances, along with the undertones that would continue to sound throughout the novel. It is a remarkable achievement: not simply because it even captures aural qualities of the story in pictorial imagery, but because it makes the particular incident evocative of a wider set of dramatic implications. Cruikshank's illustration helps us understand this moment as a representative one, perhaps *the* representative one, of both the novel and a larger context of issues out of which it has grown. Reading Dickens through Cruikshank, we can rediscover *Oliver Twist* as a Theater of 1837, a nightmarish melodrama that enacts some of the deepest fears and uncertainties of the age.

After detailing the ritual of mealtime starvation in the workhouse over a period of months, Dickens mentions some of its most visible results: the "wasted, shrunken forms" of the boys, bowls polished until they shone, the "eager eyes" with which these young inmates stare at the "copper" where their gruel is cooked, "as if they could have devoured the very bricks of which it was composed." They hold spoons that are "nearly as large as the bowls." Finally lots are cast, and Oliver is chosen to approach the master. This is the moment when drama becomes melodrama. The action stops, so the latent contrasts can be recognized more clearly.

> Child as he was, he was desperate with hunger, and reckless with misery. He rose from the table, and advancing to the master, basin and spoon in hand, said, somewhat alarmed at his own temerity:
> "Please sir, I want some more."
> The master was a fat, healthy man; but he turned very pale. He gazed in stupefied astonishment on the small rebel for some seconds, then clung for support to the copper. The assistants were paralysed with wonder; the boys with fear.
> "What!" said the master at length, in a faint voice.[3]

It is precisely this instant of suspended activity that Cruikshank illustrates, the scene between actions. The master, resting on the bricks, is open-mouthed with amazement, not yet sufficiently recovered (and his posture suggests that Oliver's words actually have driven him backwards, so that before moving forward again he must wait to regain his physical strength, and his voice along with it) to respond. His wide-eyed assistant gapes, one hand upheld in a conventional gesture of astonishment. All the boys but one (still draining his bowl) stare, in various attitudes of uneasy expectation. And expectation is the dominant quality in the illustration, the one to which viewers must respond. Like Oliver, we wait, with enough time between events to allow us to imagine the worst.

The illustration makes it even clearer than the associated moment in the text that only horror can follow. We await a blow that is awaited over and over in the nightmare of continual threat that is Oliver's childhood. This does follow in the narration, but only after the action has speeded up once again: Oliver repeats his request, the master "aimed a blow at Oliver's head with the ladle, pinioned him in his arms, and shrieked aloud for the beadle," who immediately takes him before the Board; the chapter ends with various expressions of official disgust, and the universal conviction that the boy "will come to be hung." Oppression continues, then, but violence is postponed. The illustration, on the other hand, suggests that savagery is more imminent. The master himself looms grotesquely over the frail boy. The very gloom of the hall, represented in the grey areas circling (almost seeming to move towards) the central figures, contains a related suggestion of threat. J. Hillis Miller points this out: "It seems that it might be impossible to escape or even to see beyond the confined place in which the inhabitants are trapped."[4] In "Oliver asking for More" the shadows seem to threaten something even more terrible than this. Oliver will be imprisoned; the Board thinks he will be hung. In the illustration we can imagine that he will be torn apart. The master's face is almost bestial. There is even something strangely inhuman about the faces of the other children, too. They are skeletal, faces we can think of as real only after seeing photographs from concentration camps. They have been reduced to primal needs and emotions: hunger and fear, the instinct of self-preservation. That is why we know that the only face we do not see (the boy draining his bowl) mirrors those we do—for they are all feeding, either by continuing to eat a few last drops of gruel, or by "taking in" every detail of what is going on across the room in order to be ready to act and save themselves. These are children starved down to their most fundamental reflexes, reduced (not unlike their master) to a condition of animal life. There is one hint of this in those grimly enclosing shadows, too. On the brick wall behind the head of the one standing boy, the most emaciated of the group, we see a form that may be his shadow, although it is not the shadow of a human form: the face is still rounded, but it is topped by pointed ears, and the mouth opens wide enough that we can imagine both jaws are hinged. In this world, humans cast animal shadows, suggesting a potential for savagery that is already being realized. The greatest horror in this image is not the hint of what might be done to Oliver but the hint of what he might become.

There are precedents for this in the Dickensian text, although they are not represented directly by Cruikshank. The boys

> got so voracious and wild with hunger, that one boy, who was tall for his age, and hadn't been used to that sort of thing (for his father had kept a small cookshop), hinted darkly to his companions, that unless he had another basin of gruel *per diem*, he was afraid he might some night happen to eat the boy who slept next to him, who happened to be a weakly youth of tender age. (56)

Both Dickens and the young speaker are indulging in comedy here, but the humor is based on a deeper fear, which we have encountered in Carlyle and Darwin. Is this what happens to children in the workhouse? Could Oliver descend to such a level of bestiality? After his fight with Noah Claypool, one of the board members terms him an "audacious young savage." And Mr. Bumble explains the outburst of violence even more simply. "It's not Madness, ma'am," he tells Mrs. Sowerberry: "It's Meat" (92, 93). What can be made of this boy? What can he be made into? These questions grow all the more unsettling as Oliver is taken in (in both senses) by Fagin's gang, and more unsettling still when he is recaptured after his apparent escape. When he is assigned to the custody of Bill Sikes and his dog what endangers him is not mere lawlessness but a descent into savagery, a moral degradation so extreme that it involves a total dehumanization. And even if Oliver can, eventually, magically, emerge unscathed from a world of such beings, it is difficult for the reader to feel confident that others will prove so lucky.

This is not the only aspect of the illustration that seems to look ahead and represent a particular incident in terms of its place in the still-developing narrative. The best visual evidence for this anticipation is found in the eyes of almost all the characters in the scene. They all stare—tensely, intently, as if seeing were the most all-consuming activity of their lives. This is precisely what seeing becomes for Oliver. The need to observe clearly, to interpret visual evidence, is one of the most recurrent motifs in the novel, from Oliver's increasingly well-informed appraisals of Fagin and the gang to Bill's final desperate fall from the rooftops while attempting to escape "the eyes" of the crowd, his dog, and a remembered Nancy. Of course we cannot know any of this as we read the novel for the first time; and it is important to remember that the workhouse scene comes in the second chapter, part of the first serialized number, so that "Oliver asking for more" is the first published illustration. But this only stresses how Cruikshank's imagery—and especially the pervasive staring—begins to establish an independent iconography within the structure of the narrative itself, a set of visual motifs that take on a prominence, an urgency, beyond their role in simply picturing the written story. It is as if elements of the Dickensian material take on an independent life of their own—or what seems to be an independent life, since ultimately many of these will be thematized in the novel. At this stage of the telling we can simply anticipate, a process Cruikshank helps structure. His illustrations alert us to the aspects of Dickens that require most intense thought.

I have concentrated on the two groups of figures positioned roughly at the two sides of "Oliver asking for More": master and assistant on the left, and the rows of boys along both sides of the table, stretching from the middle of the image to the right edge. Oliver stands between. His position suggests the nature of his plight here, and in much of the remainder of the novel: between worlds, between roles. There is a suggestion of the same condition in his outgrown clothing (a detail from the text), all the more noticeable as a reflection of his personal status because he is the only one of the boys we can see at full length. How will he be outfitted next? What is his proper appearance, his real costume? This is not so much a metaphysical question (*à la Sartor Resartus*) as it is a social one, in the spirit of Dickens' investigations into costumes and metropolitan types in *Sketches by Boz*. We see enough of the "healthy" master behind his apron to recognize that he represents "vested" authority, that he is clothed for his position. We see so little of the clothing of the boys in the background that we suspect their dehumanization entails an "unfitness" for any clearly defined places in society. Oliver is not simply caught between the worlds of power and the powerless; he is balanced on the precarious division between two sorts of appearances, two sorts of identities, only one of which can "suit" him for the world. Immediately after this scene, he narrowly escapes being apprenticed to a vicious, blackened chimney sweep; at the Sowerberrys' he is costumed as a mute to walk at the head of mourning processions. Later, his transition back into Fagin's world will be marked by the appropriation of his new expensive clothing: "Look at his togs! Superfine cloth, and the heavy swell cut! Oh, my eye, what a game! And his books, too! Nothing but a gentleman, Fagin!" (163). Little wonder that Cruikshank's phrase took on a life independent of the scene being illustrated in the first number of the novel: asking for more. In the story Oliver simply demands food. In the picture he seems to be waiting for much more than that: clothing, security, a better "place," a sense of self. From the look of things, it would take very little to thrust him irretrievably back into the world from which he is trying to emerge: back to the bench of hungry boys, back to their condition of sheer creatural existence, back to the even more obscure darkness behind. He is close to being lost. What little he has is all too easy to take away, including his self. The illustration hints that abduction cannot be too far in Oliver's future.

II

In 1837 Harrison Ainsworth, Mrs. S. C. Hall, Edward Bulwer, Charlotte Adams, and Captain Marryat published novels that center around abductions, and there are metaphoric abductions in books by the Countess of Blessington, Mrs. Trollope and G. P. R. James that appear at the same time.[5] We also can read about real kidnappings, or real examples of these metaphoric abductions (a phrase I will explain shortly), in the newspapers of the day. Kidnapping was topical, a serious business, no less serious than it is now, when ransoms can run into the millions and some children are abducted for deprogramming by their own parents. Still, a mood of romance clung to these stories, one Yeats would enlarge on in his poem "The Stolen Child." Oliver himself is lured into Fagin's den by the charming blandishments of the Dodger, and apparently a similar spell has been cast over the other boys in the gang. The curious attraction of this unusual "home" was exploited by the modern musical *Oliver!*, especially as it enlarged upon the Dodger's reference to Fagin as "a 'spectable old genelman" (102). Children often dream of new homes, and different parents; perhaps this is one reason adults take kidnapping stories so seriously. The romanticized myth is contained within the horrified fixation on kidnapping, as if that more apparently realistic view is at least in part a reaction against the other impulse. But the prevalence of the motif suggests another dimension of its threat: kidnapping endangers not only particular victims but groups: families, the community as a whole. The title of Lady Blessington's novel about gossip and social intrigue suggests that we all can become what she calls *The Victims of Society*. She and Dickens are not the only writers of the 1830s who warn us to reconsider our assumptions about social stability—the security of the shelters in which we live, the security and stability of the identities we think of an inalienably our own.

I have mentioned that the title of this chapter refers to Yeats. *The Stolen Child* also was the title of two novels published in the 1830s, one of which appeared in Victoria's Year. The first, John Galt's last book, appeared in 1833; the second, a children's book by Charlotte Adams (who is identified in the British Library catalogue only as a "Writer of Tales") was published in 1838.[6] Both, like *Oliver Twist*, concern the abduction of middle-class children by members of the "lower orders." And both writers enlarge on the motif of kidnapping to explore a more pervasive instability of personal and social identity, an instability that threatens the structure of the family as well. In Galt's case, the actual circumstances of the abduction play only a small role in the plot; the question of family takes over. Shortly after the kidnapping, within the first pages of the novel, we learn of the death of the young hero's parents, his adoption by a benevolent gentleman in the rural district where his kidnappers almost immediately abandoned him, and of his admirable progress to manhood. Several chapters later Edward Troven (as the foundling appropriately has been named) has passed through a distinguished career at Oxford and is beginning to make his name in London as a young lawyer at the Inns of Court. Here the main story begins. Galt's real interest is not the loss of self (as in Dickens) but the process necessary to find it again. Especially given Troven's chosen profession, it is not surprising to find much of the novel preoccupied with legal inquiries, especially the laborious efforts of the hero to establish his identity and regain his birthright.

Adams' subtitle suggests a similar concern: "Laura's Adventures with the Travelling Showman and His Family." Perhaps because she writes with a different audience in mind, she focuses our attention on the predicament of the young heroine during her captivity, and on the family she is forced to join. What is threatened is not simply her life but her identity: she is made an accomplice in the unsavory lives of her captors; they try to make her one of them, one of the gang. Which sort of family will prevail? Laura Clarence is first noticed by her abductors while she gaily "exhibits" her skill at dancing and leaping in her parents' garden; gypsies seize her and force her to perform as a rope-dancer in various country fairs. Again as in Dickens (and perhaps Laura's story was written to exploit Oliver's popularity), the greatest fear is that the young victim will eventually adapt to a degrading new way of life (a possibility made all the more threatening by the fact that Laura takes great pride in her dancing), that she will learn the ropes too well.

This situation in Galt's novel is radically reversed—not simply because Troven (as his name suggests) is quickly found (and made at home in an equally secure upper-middle-class environment) but because the unfolding plot confronts him with a final change of fortune opposite to Laura's, that of being dragged down from the genteel way of life to which he has become accustomed. The proof that he is who we know he is, the lost heir to the Mordant family fortune, the real Lord Buyborough, remains equivocal even at the end; the "Conclusion" begins with a reference to the "*virtual* restoration of Troven to his birthright" (my italics). In the course of the last few chapters, some characters suspect that Troven really is the son of the madwoman who was guilty of the kidnapping many years before (so that the man she claimed as her son, a pickpocket later reformed into a sailor, may turn out to be the real heir to the fortune); Troven is for some time not entirely sure himself. It appears at first that the only way to estab- lish his claim will be through a lengthy Chancery suit. Fortunately, the Mordant family acknowledges his identity as the long-lost (and mostly for- gotten) eldest brother before such steps are necessary, even though Troven has been preparing for this possibility with extensive legal groundwork. The novel ends conventionally enough: reconciliation, a birthright rees- tablished, a marriage of love and convenience in the offing. But what makes it curious is the abruptness with which Galt turns away from the legal mechanisms he seemed to be setting up to make that conclusion pos- sible. If he is concerned about the danger that identity can be stolen and the rights of class and property lost, he seems no less uneasy that the only way to escape from this state of affairs is through official judical processes.

This anxiety is reflected in the fact that Troven is involved in a second potential lawsuit just before the novel ends. The small fortune he lives on during his legal apprenticeship has been provided in the will of Mr. Pearl, the gentleman who adopted him early in the story; the validity of that set- tlement is being challenged by Mr. Pearl's cousin, a lawyer (of the same name) who attempted to seize Troven's inheritance by concealing a codicil from the will he had prepared. But this lawsuit, like the other one, seems to be forgotten as the novel closes, as if the law itself is part of the problem rather than part of the solution. The status of the law is ambiguous; it is at least potentially corrupt (as the other Mr. Pearl, the lawyer, demon- strates), not wholly to be trusted, and too easily employed in the restruc- turing of social identity with which Galt is preoccupied. Does family iden- tity depend on a complex set of rules? Troven himself is a lawyer too, and makes his name by successfully defending in the House of Lords a case much like his own: a claim to property and title, which he explodes by showing that the "claimant . . . had not so good a claim as a third unknown party."[7] This underscores the danger posed by reliance on legal machinery: there are, apparently, many other such third parties. The woman who abducted Troven in the first place also turns out to be an aristocrat, disowned by her family after she ran off with a servant. Almost everyone's "fortune" is precarious in this novel; each rise involves a corresponding fall. Troven's younger brother fears he will lose both rank and money if the claims of the long-lost heir are validated. The novel hints that such instability could become even more pervasive if society were reduced to a wholly impersonal legal structure of relations. I suspect this is the reason Galt forgets to return to those pending lawsuits. Troven's plight can be settled more amicably, more traditionally, by the aristocratic graciousness of the "natural" family that finally admits the unavoidable "evidence" of bearing, appearance, and noble nature. If there is a moral in the novel it is, quite simply, that blood will tell. But this reassurance is too heavy-handed; we have seen too much evidence that families are merely a legal fiction, to be manipulated by those in the know. Is society itself up for sale? The possibility is latent in the odd aristocratic name of Buyburough. And the same possibility helps explain Galt's somewhat inappropriate subtitle, "A Tale of the Town." These are the dangers confronted in an increasingly urban, legalistic, even democratic society, one based increasingly on the power of money. Troven's good fortune finally allows him to pass, magically, out of this uncertain world of individual achievement and back into the more stable, closed world of an eighteenth-century squirearchy, which retains absolute control over its own affairs. Galt, writing in the year after passage of the Reform Bill, suggests that such control could be stolen by representatives of the wrong class.

Both versions of *The Stolen Child* attempt to validate a level of identity deeper than the accidents of social and class interaction, an ideal of family and self immune from the pressure of change. The only refuge from the degradation of her captivity Laura finds is in a book of letters between a mother and her daughter, who was "compelled by circumstances to reside in a situation and among people every way [*sic*] uncongenial to her." Laura is "particularly struck" with the mother's main moral argument:

> that though her child was the constant witness of what was wrong, there was not the slightest necessity for her copying what she saw. She told her that, young as she was, her life had hitherto been passed among virtuous people; that good principles had been inculcated in her mind, and that she perfectly knew right from wrong.[8]

This sounds like an argument for education, as does the account of Troven's career—at first. But Laura soon discovers that such examples must be presented very early to be effective. She attempts to serve as the instructress of the most sympathetic member of the gypsy family, a girl of her own age. But although she has some improving effect on Lydia's character, and teaches her "to stitch and to mark," she cannot persuade her to read with much success or pleasure: "Laura became aware how hard it is to overcome habits of indolence, and to substitute rational employment for frivolity and idleness."[9] And are these merely habits? Adams is touching on the same questions of nature and nurture that Dickens examines throughout *Oliver Twist*: how far is genuine character embedded within the self; is virtue only skin deep? Adams' answers emerge when Laura manages to escape and return to her family mansion (a scene depicted in the novel's frontispiece [Figure 4.2]). At first she has difficulty getting past the servants at the gate; they are suspicious of ragged clothing and a complexion stained with berry juice to increase the captive's isolation from the genteel world. "They dyed my skin," Laura cries piteously to her nurse, trying to gain recognition.[10] The servants are unconvinced, but it takes only an instant to reconcile the child to her parents. She races past her nurse, up the stairs, into her parents' room, and into their arms. "No explanation was necessary to the father and mother, no proof was wanted of her identity; they knew their child though all disguises, and in an ecstasy of joy they welcomed their lost one back."[11]

Laura's trials do not end with her return. In the closing chapter we learn how much the question of inner character is opposed to the uncertainties of outward social position. Even after she is welcomed back, her home is faced with a crisis, or, rather, with two, although they are closely related to one another and to the story of Laura's loss of identity as well. The family fortune is threatened by "a man who had arrived from the East Indies, and who laid claim to my estates, and consequently all property that has accumulated upon them. You would hardly understand," Laura's father adds, in the spirit of Galt's novel, "the technicalities of the law" involved in this claim.[12] But it is easy for him to explain his own difficulty in refuting it. The family house recently has been robbed; little of value was carried away, but the "booty" included a strongbox containing deeds and papers establishing the family's title. Those robbers turn out to be none other than Laura's gypsy captors, who are seized moments later. But their arrest would have had little effect on the family fortune were it not for the fact that Laura, after fleeing from their house, had returned at her own peril to warn the sleeping inhabitants about a fire started during her escape; the villains rushed from the burning house, with the stolen papers. Laura is not only restored herself but becomes the means for restoring her family to its proper place in the world. Her father emphasizes this in announcing the book's first moral: "it is to you, my dear good child, that we owe this happy event; your right conduct in returning to save the lives of your fellow-creatures was at the same time the means of preserving to us our fortune."[13]

This settles only the question of conduct—external or social identity; the novel also concerns the more elusive internal conception of self. This is explained in proper moral form (after all, it is a children's book) in the last pages of the story, appropriately by Laura's father. He announces first that all these misfortunes serve a purpose: "Yours, my dear Laura, has been a severe lesson, and I feel assured that you will never again let your efforts to excell be at the instigation of—Vanity." For Laura, this can be interpreted in only one way. She vows never to dance again; this, she hopes, will chasten the "foolish love of admiration" that led to her kidnapping in the first place. But her father takes a more balanced view, and this leads to the second moral (actually it is presented first). "Yes, yes, my little girl . . . you must dance again; for be assured that nature has given us no powers which it is not wisely intended we should, according to circumstances, cultivate to the best of our ability."[14] It is a measured and even complex conclusion; no wonder Laura at first was confused. In spite of the doubts raised earlier about the stability of those inner resources, Adams returns to validate them at the end. As in Galt and Dickens, there must be a compromise between nature and nurture. Laura Clarence, like Edward Troven and Oliver Twist, can be restored to a proper home only after she has learned that her identity depends on a combination of both.

Kidnapping was a fact of life, documented in police reports and the daily press. *Chambers' Edinburgh Journal* of October 14, 1837 reprints a "story of romance in real life" (taken from the Hereford *Times*) about the reunion of a mother with a child who had been abducted many years before. As in the stories by Galt and Adams, the boy was kidnapped near his home as he walked from the house of playmates; when he cried, he was threatened with beheading; eventually he was taken to Jamaica, where a friendly shopkeeper saw to his education. The more typical victim of abduction was a young woman, and the most common objects of the crime were social and financial advancement through marriage. The *Times* of February 26, 1836 reprints a story of this sort from the Limerick *Chronicle*, which terms it "another of those outrages so frequent in this country." A report of 18 November in the same year tells of a foiled attempt, this time in London but also involving an Irishman, who claimed that the woman he tried to seize had met and married him on a recent visit to Ireland. In nineteenth-century Ireland, as in twentieth-century Sicily, the victim was assumed to have no choice but to marry her captor after being compromised by confinement with him for some period of time. (The report from

Limerick added that an earlier incident of the same sort had ended with a wedding.) But this is not to suggest that the motives of these assaults were strictly sexual: rape often proved to be the means to financial ends. The attempt in London was against an heiress (Mary Ann McCulloch), a ward in Chancery; the girl's stepmother insisted that the accused was interested only in her money.

What I am concerned with here is not so much the "truth" of such episodes as the proportions they assumed in the contemporary imagination. The *Times* of January 17, 1837, reports two attempts in separate parts of London, probably related or else the work of the same person. In the first, an episode in the style of *Moll Flanders*, "A fine little fellow of about three years of age," accompanied by his older sister, was first followed, and then taken, by a "genteely dressed woman." She would have escaped with him but for the fact that her behavior had aroused the suspicions of a passerby, who followed and freed the boy. The writer agrees that "there can be little doubt of this attempt having been made with a view to claim the reward which would probably have been offered by the distracted parents." But speculation doesn't stop here. If the reward offered

> had not met with the brutal and mercenary approbation of those engaged in such dreadful traffic, the poor child would in all probability have been stripped, and thrown naked into the world, and probably perished from the inclemency of the weather before the helping hand of charity could be extended in its relief.

These are the possibilities Dickens expands upon in *Oliver Twist*, both in his analysis of criminal behavior and in his exposé of the administration of justice and charitable relief. Yet the imagination of the *Times* article almost goes beyond that of the novel in speculating on whether "this outrage" is "part of an organized system" rather than "the mere incipient attempt of an abandoned few." "Amid the varied shapes which guilt and crime take in this metropolis, it is impossible to say. . . . At all events, it holds out a caution to parents and gurdians," as well as to the police. Perhaps all children are at risk.

Were they really? Is all this "evidence" a sign of rational concern or pathological obsession? The examples I have cited represent most of the entries in the *Times* dealing with this subject in the late 1830s; and it should be recalled that some of this material has been reprinted from other sources. The fictional examples are more numerous by far. There is a reality, actual crime, yet some psychosocial mechanism amplifies it, appropriates isolated cases into the service of compelling popular myths. J. R. McCulloch's *Statistical Account of the British Empire* (1837) lists only one case of "child-stealing" for 1835, and two other cases of "abduction." In the ten previous years, fifty cases of "child-stealing" are listed in all, and two abductions.[15] Of course, the very act of printing such figures, and calling attention to such categories of crime, heightens the mythology I have been discussing, even if it isn't corroborated by the numbers. An even more inflated example of this mythologizing appears two decades later in Henry Mayhew's encyclopedic survey of poverty and crime in *London Labour and the London Poor*. The appendices to the final volume include a map and a table "Showing the number of persons committed for ABDUCTION in every 10,000,000 of the male population in the several counties of England and Wales."[16] Yet Mayhew is surveying a total population in all of England and Wales that comes to well under nine million; the largest county (Middlesex) contains under nine hundred thousand people, according to his figures. And in all of England and Wales, the total of reported abductions for this ten-year period is only twenty-three! There is a moral as well as a statistical imperative operating here, a fascination with this kind of crime as well as with the potentialities of numbers themselves. Abduction had to be magnified into such gross disproportions; nothing else could indicate the quality of the offense as it was registered in the contemporary imagination.

We can observe a similar imaginative disproportion in one more report of an actual kidnapping, this one taking place in October 1837. In this case, the victim was seized from the family of a baker named Gilson and then recovered almost by chance. After a sweep of prostitutes in St. James's Park one night, the police are tipped off that one of the women is holding a child in her lodgings; a Sergeant Otway visits the address and there discovers "the stolen child, whom he immediately recognized" from other reports. Yet the story does not end here. In spite of her child's fortunate escape, the mother is inconsolable, for she cannot be persuaded "but that the child had been carried off to be smothered or otherwise destroyed with a view to its dissection by the surgeons." Imagination has detached itself from reality and transformed it into several myths at once. Abduction becomes body-snatching, and suddenly we seem to be close to one of the post-*Frankenstein* roots of science fiction in the popular consciousness. The closest fictional approximation to such fantasies in Victoria's Year may be in Ainsworth's *Crichton*, where a Venetian maiden is kidnapped by an astrologer in the pay of Catherine de Medici who seems capable of all sorts of unnamed experiments on human subjects; it is not irrelevant to add that the Venetian girl is disguised as a boy, so that her real identity is unknown to the astrologer, who later turns out to be her father! That a parent should be involved in such a venture is not so much a sign of the unique perversity of this man as it is a reminder of the precariousness of all childhood, and the middle-class family.

Nina Auerbach has argued that the fictional orphan is a latter-day version of the picaresque hero, endowed with a "religious and revolutionary energy" that can "transform at a touch the decaying houses he enters." Perhaps this is true in the fiction of the 1840s, when "the strange cunning power of the orphan is yoked to forces of social evolution."[17] But a decade earlier the status of the orphan, like that of those social forces themselves, is far more ambiguous, just as the orphan's experience is far more bleak. In the 1830s the focus is on the experience of being orphaned, being alienated from any original or final home, on separation and suffering rather than reunion and success. Even when some traces of magical power cling to this figure, as in Oliver's case, the predicament remains grim; even when the story ends happily we recognize how close it came to not ending at all. There is something convincing in all these versions of the abduction plot, even in their most fabulous or didactic forms, for they stubbornly resist their own resolutions and close with a mixture of reassurance and lingering dread. This is because so much is at stake: not simply social success or personal advancement but the dignity and autonomy of the self, the reality of the family unit, the very possibility of remaining human in a world that makes contradictory claims on everyone. How much of our selves can we preserve, even in our fondest dreams of recognition and reward? The enormity of the problem is suggested in the "real stories" I mentioned earlier. When a young woman is raped and forced to marry, it is not just her name and virginity but an essential part of her identity that is being compromised. The fixation on kidnapping stories suggests a need to decide, or discover, whether such a change is (as Mrs. Gilson feared) irreversible.

III

The novel that explores these possibilities at most length in 1837 is not *Oliver Twist* but *Uncle Horace*, by Anna Maria Hall. As the title implies, it concerns family ties, which are examined against the background of the shifting relations between social classes. The girl who is abducted is the daughter of a rising middle-class father, and the structure of narration suggests that the two changes in status may be related to one another. What are the consequences when a successful merchant attempts to move into (and in) aristocratic circles to which he has access by wealth alone? The kidnapping story suggests how seriously such attempts are regarded. The melodramatic overcomplexity of the plot locates abduction at the center of a concentric series of related issues, the most serious of which is the final problem of the heroine's acceptance back into the society she had become a part of, or believed she had. It isn't easy to enter a new level of society or to resist the forces that are constantly tending to pull one back. Mary Brown's father has left his Liverpool business in the care of his down-to-earth brother, Horace, and come to London to assume a higher rank. He changes his name from plain, honest, British Brown to Lorton-Brown; he takes a carriage; he entertains high hopes for his daughter's marital possibilities. But no one is fooled by his pretensions, or impressed. While Mary's beauty and charm secure her admission to aristocratic homes, her father is expressly excluded; the novel opens as she struggles over the decision whether to accept such an invitation. She is not eager to assume a new identity; she remains loyal to her parents, and to her Uncle Horace. As we might expect, these family loyalties eventually preserve her, but not until her happiness, position, and sense of self have been threatened by a crime that underscores the precariousness we have observed from the first.

Mary is abducted on the eve of her marriage to Harry Mortimer, her childhood sweetheart, and the timing of the event is the key to the widening circle of consequences that nearly destroys her. Although the motive of the kidnappers (the ruined Count d'Oraine and his villainous companion Moskito) is strictly financial, the crime seems to alter Mary herself, in the eyes of her father-in-law-to-be and then in her own. Mortimer had been adopted as heir by the affected Lord Norley, who had urged his protege to sever all ties with the middle class. Norley originally opposed the marriage on these grounds, for it might have affected his own standing in the world. He changes his mind only when his high-minded daughter, Lady Ellen Bevis, persuades him that Mary's intrinsic dignity had already received the approbation of "society." But it seems inevitable that Lord Norley's vanity will be wounded again by the kidnapping, which is reported in various society journals. Mary knows this, and knows the bizarre logic of social acceptability in the world she has been taken from. She has been compromised, even though never actually assaulted by the count. As it turns out, she resists even his demands to write her friends for ransom—and resists so forcefully that she wins his respect. But in spite of this resistance, she despairs. Unlike Clarissa Harlowe, she cannot think of writing, because the identity which would make this possible has been destroyed. Her social identity, that is: in regarding this loss as catastrophic and absolute, she shows herself to be her father's daughter. Taken violently from the world where her being is defined, Mary is separated from her self, and separated from the possibility of recovering it. She is unable to conceive any tolerable future for herself; in a sense she has given herself up for dead. *The*

Victims of Society warns that such a conclusion is inevitable: "The woman who has lost her honour should live to atone for her crime; but for her who has lost her reptuation, there is no refuge but death."[18]

There are many parallel situations in *Uncle Horace* supporting this grim view. The count has had other victims, all middle-class girls like Mary, and they parade through the last half of the novel to define some of the dark possibilities facing her. The first case we learn about, and the most devastating for Mary's sense of her own predicament, is that of her own mother! Margaret Lorton-Brown (*née* Linden) had eloped with d'Oraine as a girl on Jersey twenty years before. He has returned to blackmail her. The shock of his reappearance deranges her, so much so that she is unable to arrange the payments he requires; and it is this failure that drives the count to kidnap Mary. We later learn that Margaret Linden is legally, if not morally, innocent of any wrongdoing. The count had abandoned her immediately after their "marriage," and in fact he previously had married and abandoned another woman (invalidating the second marriage), who also turns up to attack her husband in a rage of jealousy that has only increased through the years. An early version of *Jane Eyre?* There are even clearer anticipations: this first, real, wife has been reduced to an almost animal ferocity by the twenty years of ill treatment initiated by d'Oraine, and there are signs that Mrs. Lorton-Brown has begun to move along the same path. After her daughter is abducted, Margaret leaves her home and wanders insanely through the Dorset countryside; somehow, her instincts lead her to the house where Mary has been taken, and she gains access to Mary's room by climbing a tree. This is not simply madness, then, but a kind of primitive cunning, a resurgence of animal instincts that overpower both women's higher identities. Will Mary fall victim to the same sort of change? Will she lose both her social identity and her humanity?

These issues are closely connected. Identity in the world of this novel largely is a function of family and class; it is undermined most seriously when people like Mary's father try to pretend that it is not. Even Count d'Oraine, in spite of the European and aristocratic connotations of his name, turns out to have firm, British, middle-class roots; eventually he rediscovers them. First, though, even more than the women he has seduced, the count descends to a bestial level of existence; but he also makes a stunningly theatrical recovery, a return to civilized "human" behavior precipitated by a chance reminder of his proper place and origins. His accomplice, Moskito, ignores d'Oraine's mysterious warnings and puts a kettle on the hob at their hideout. The action reminds the count of his English mother and restores his nearly extinguished sense of home, hearth, and honesty. Of course, no aristocratic mother would have been associated with a whistling, steaming kettle; apparently then, the count himself is of mixed class origins, as well as being only half foreign. No wonder he descended to this life of crime in the first place; no wonder he recovers. Shortly after this scene, he takes his own life in a fit of remorse. It is, of course, a moral suicide, one more testimony to the power of middle-class British values. Yet at the same time it heightens the problem of Mary's future. Perhaps she can remain sane and honorable: but can she do so and still remain alive, or return from this predicament into a normal social setting?

Mrs. Hall, as we might expect, insists that she can, although "normal" society seems less aristocratic than bourgeois. In keeping with her method throughout the novel, she illustrates the possiblity through another pointed family history. Magdalen Marsden, Mary's devoted maid, was one more of the count's victims, although she has recovered from the experience and regained her self-possession. But one of her brothers died defending her honor against the count, and the other brother, the talented sculptor Philip Marsden, has vowed to take revenge. The act would mean misery for his sister and the end of a promising artistic career, as well as his own execution, and it is those first factors that keep him from committing it. He rejects the false aristocratic code of blood and honor for the middle-class values of love and labor. At the end of the novel he and Magdalen depart for Italy, where he will continue his artistic studies. But this is a triumph of ethics rather than aesthetics, a new dedication to the same virtue of hard work his sister has adhered to in long years of domestic service.

The bourgeois virtues of patience and steady labor are exemplified above all by Uncle Horace. There are moments when Mrs. Hall almost treats him as the sort of divided being we see in Dickens' mercantile characters: compulsively routinized in daily working tasks, all heart and good humor at home. But where the separated household and business worlds of a character like Wemmick in *Great Expectations* may be evidence of a deeper, damaging split, *Uncle Horace* urges us to accept the contradictions between complete gentility and the habits that produce bourgeois prosperity. Such distinctions are necessary, Mrs. Hall suggests, and even a sign of psychological health. She tells the story of a proud young Irishman who solicits employment from an old friend of his family, then nearly abandons the project in disgust over the shabby appearance of the man at his counting house; dining with the same man at his home, however, the youth is astonished at the "magnificent . . . arrangements." "I am now convinced," he exclaims, "that it is not impossible to be both a trader and a gentleman."[19] Yet apparently it is impossible to be both at the same time. Uncle Horace disdains polished manners and polite speech as species of false pride. "Ambition," he declares to Lady Ellen, whether it be called spurious or otherwise, appears to me the moral curse of England. Our schools are "academies," our servants seek not service but "situations;" our dancers are artists; our attorneys (the rascals!) are grown lawyers; our mantuamakers are fashionists; our milliners, *modistes*; our butchers, purveyors; each village must have its square, and every farmer would be a squire! The ignorant might imagine that to be *distinguished*, was synonymous to being respectable.[20]

Clearly enough, this is the fault of his brother, and leads to his ruin. Mary's father, attempting to divorce himself completely from the world of business, leaves his money under the supervision of city financiers, and "fails." But his real failure is personal rather than financial: a failure in assuming false identity, a failure to be himself.

Horace believes in self-knowledge. "I am a plain man, madam," he tells Lady Ellen; "an English merchant—nothing more." But as he also adds, this means a great deal, not just in social terms but morally as well. "An honest British trader can stand unabashed before the greatest monarch in the world; and, more than that, he can hope to meet his God face to face at the last day!"[21] His function in the novel is to return us to such basic moral considerations, to bring us back out of a world of superficial valuations to a sense of family loyalty, to insist upon the distinction between mere social acceptability and a deeper sense of self. Such a clear conception of self is what distinguishes him from every other character in the book. To some extent he appears as a stock figure, a jolly, slightly eccentric, old-fashioned merchant taken straight from eighteenth-century drama: a stereotype of the middle class. But that same personal narrowness is presented as a species of psychic strength: whatever Horace may be, he knows who he is. This explains why the novel, which mainly centers around Mary and the Lorton-Browns, is named after him. He is the principle of order, internal and external, that is required as an antidote to the social instability in which Mary and her family come so close to being displaced. His name is the last phrase of the text—uttered as a reminder that such figures will continue to be needed in the future—printed in capital letters so we cannot miss the point: UNCLE HORACE!

Still, there is a great deal that cannot be subsumed under his name: as we have observed in other works of this period, the ending does not fully account for the rest of the narrative. Mrs. Hall introduces Horace to humanize the tensions of modern bourgeois society, to contain them within a traditional familial stability and a reassuring comic character. But Mary's experience demonstrates that the world is growing too complex for this, class relations too tense and potentially violent, individual identity too difficult to secure or maintain. Or else, to put this another way, the identity that came so naturally to an older generation requires much more self-consciousness in a new one. Now a sense of self will always be hard-won, and as a result always somewhat precarious. Of course, Mary does achieve her father's ambition by rising out of the middle class, but only after she has been made aware (as he never could have been) of the dangers latent in the process. Painfully aware: as it was originally planned, Mary's marriage to Harry and into the world of Lord Norley might have seemed too easy. Now her identity never will be taken for granted. That is why Mrs. Hall places the abduction so close to the original wedding date: there is an analogy between kidnapping and Mary's impending change in social status, one she is forced to experience, and understand, before the marriage is allowed to take place. Changing places involves grave risks. Mary must understand them if she is to understand herself, or understand how to search for it. And Mrs. Hall suggests that such searches will be necessary, for Mary and others like her.

The victims are individuals but the threats against them are collective. The very unsteadiness of the family in many of these stories is related to the ambiguous status of all authoritative social structures and the figures entrusted with their power. Mary, like Oliver, was close to being lost before she was abducted (although she was unaware of it at the time), due to the nature of the aristocratic world she was preparing to enter and that of the middle-class world her father was trying to help her leave. Lord Norley and Mr. Lorton-Brown share some of Count d'Oraine's guilt for placing her in an impossible situation. It is difficult to have confidence in many of those serving *in loco parentis*. In *Oliver Twist* the risk of the hero's corruption at Fagin's hands is only one step removed from the threats posed by the official institutions that were supposed to have been educating him up to that time. Alice Darvil, the now-you-see-her-now-you-don't heroine of Bulwer's *Ernest Maltravers* (1837) and its sequel *Alice, or the Mysteries* (1838), is stolen back from Maltravers by her own father, a thieving gypsy. Maltravers himself becomes a surrogate father, teacher, and (illicit) husband to Alice. As we are left to wonder about the identity of her illegitimate child in the second novel, Bulwer raises the question of whether her instruction in genteel refinements at the hands of this aristocratic intellectual was entirely in her own best interests. Similarly, the kidnapper in *The Dog Fiend, or Snarleyyow* (1837), by Captain Marryat, is a Dutch sea captain who plots against his cabin boy, a twenty-year-old child-man named Philip Smallbones. Abduction displays parental authority, or all authority, gone wrong, exerting its influence malevolently, or assuming it falsely. The most dangerous criminal in G. P. R. James' *The Robber* is not the outlaw chief named in the title but a former associate whose control of various familial records falsely establishes him as the Earl of Danemore. And what

may be the most chilling example involves a kidnapping in only a metaphoric sense, one that is prophetic of the stories associated with religious
cultists in the 1980s. In Frances Trollope's *The Vicar of Wrexhill* (1837),
the villain is an evangelical clergyman named Cartwright who effectively
captures the souls, and affections, of nearly all the women with whom he
comes in contact.

As a hypocritical evangelical clergyman, Cartwright is an almost direct
ancestor of Mr. Slope, created by Mrs. Trollope's son Anthony in *Bar-
chester Towers* twenty years later. But the villain of 1837 is much more
disturbing than the one of 1857 because of the depth of evil revealed
beneath his schemes. One character refers to him as a "black tarantula,"
and by the end of the novel his period of ascendency in the village is spoken of as a time of "serious epidemic."[22] Like the outbreak of plague in
Deerbrook, this moral illness is an occasion for the release of the lowest
human instincts, although it also presents an opportunity for the uncontaminated few to exhibit their virtues. As we might expect, those are old
virtues, strengthened under the tutelage of the former vicar in times when
there was less confusion about moral standards because there were fewer
shifts in ecclesiastical (and social) style. Cartwright is presented as a product of new ideas, as part of a disturbing breakdown in the barriers between
religious classes. But what the novel stresses above all is his potential to
release dark forces latent in almost all of the characters, almost all of his
parishioners. Without the stability of traditional religious guidance, the
people of Wrexhill are in danger of losing their Christian virtues, and even
their Christianity.

The magnitude of this risk is illustrated in Cartwright's gloomy, intellectual daughter, Henrietta. Perceptive enough to see through her father's
pretensions, she still has no other model to turn towards as a source of
faith. This plunges her into the darkest despair, leaving her no capacity for
warmth, friendship, or even self-respect. This is the real core of Mr. Cartwright's ministry, as Henrietta explains to the novel's heroine, Rosalind
Torrington, who has befriended her in spite of her grim demeanor. But
Henrietta cannot trust Rosalind, for the same reason she can trust no one:
"Because you are a woman;—no, no, because you are a human being."
Knowledge of her father has led her to conclude that all people are false.
She even wonders whether it isn't better so. "Were I one of those who
fancy that pincushions are often made by the merciful decrees of an all-
wise Providence, I should say that we were ordained to be false, in order
to prevent our being straightforward, undisguised demons."[23] Of course
she does not believe in Providential pincushions, or anything else. Thanks
to her father's influence, all religion seems hollow. After much hesitation,
Henrietta admits to Rosalind her most horrifying secret: she has wandered

too close to the "hideous abyss of Atheism."[24] The only reality in her life is the villainy she finds incarnate in her father, and which, therefore, she fears in everyone, including herself. Her pathological terror of her own bestial impulses emerges in actions as apparently innocent as the construction of net purses, a task she performs as if (Mrs. Trollope comments) she had no nails on her fingers or scissors in her work-box. She rarely trusts herself to use sharp implements. Without a continuous vigilance and restraint—without, in other words, what she considers consummate hypocrisy—she fears she would be "stabbing and scratching half-a-dozen times a day."[25]

Cartwright's deepest impulses are sexual rather than murderous, although his capacity to disrupt the lives of the women he influences suggests that this may be closely related to the violence that preoccupies Henrietta. We see him at his worst in two climactic seduction scenes at the end of the first volume, inviting first Fanny Mowbray and then her mother to indulge in passionate, private prayers which Mrs. Trollope describes as not only impious but highly sensual. His particularly erotic form of evangelical piety emerges first when he "instructs" Fanny in her prayers beneath a secluded lime tree (one of the scenes depicted in the novel's illustrations) (Figure 4.3). There is little doubt that we are expected to regard this place (like the whole pastoral setting of the novel that it mirrors) as a demiparadise threatened by a clerical serpent. The lime tree itself is "the tree of trees . . . the bower of paradise," as Henrietta remarks later on.[26] But even without her interpretation, we cannot fail to recognize that Cartwright's behavior with this young zealot is "perfectly indecent and profane."[27] Rosalind, who has tried to force Cartwright to put an end to these sessions, happens on the furtive, outdoor service and watches in horror for as long as she can: "Heartsick, indignant, disgusted, and almost terrified by what she saw and heard, she retreated hastily."[28]

The exaggeration of Cartwright's fleshliness disturbed others. A reviewer in the *Times*, hardly a voice of the evangelical party, protested against what he termed a "bigoted, rancorous, indecent book," a treatment so "dangerous, vulgar, unjust" that extracts could not be printed.[29] It is not simply that Cartwright is a minister, although clearly that is part of the problem. Mrs. Trollope has introduced him as a "capital clerical Whig,"[30] and stressed his peculiarly "sectarian" manner of prayer.[31] According to the *Times* reviewer, this is too generalized an attack. "Thank God," the writer declares, "there is no such thing as a *sect* of hypocrites." But he seems even more uneasy about the nature of the abberations the novel depicts and the view of human nature they imply. Perhaps Mrs. Trollope, like Henrietta Cartwright, is at heart contemptuous of all people. The *Times* writer refers, only half-humorously, to the frequent appearance of "*paw-paw* work" in the novel; this, I think, suggests the problem that disturbs him most. The pun refers to sensuality, but it also implies an eroticism that links human passions with animal instincts—instincts not confined to the villain alone. Mr. Cartwright's presence, after all, precipitates the fall of many of the women of Wrexhill, who, even if they do not express their animal passions directly, do become detached from their normal civilized selves. They become, at the very least, un-British. When Fanny uncurls her hair to make herself more visibly evangelical, she looks "more like a Chinese beauty on a japan screen than like herself."[32] The implication is clear: Fanny has descended to a "lower" racial type. It is a moment of devolution, a reminder of Cartwright's power to undermine civilization.

A minister should be a pillar of family and community. Cartwright disrupts both. He unleashes primitive impulses, subverting the social structures created to keep those energies under control in the first place. Mrs. Trollope had ridiculed the crude habits she observed in the United States in *Domestic Manners of the Americans* (1832); here she seems to be speculating on whether a more advanced culture could be returned to such a primitive state. Under Cartwright's influence, sexuality becomes more open and free. The village schoolmaster, Mr. Marsh, warns Cartwright about his nighttime prayer meetings, which young people of both sexes attend together. Marsh insists that these are only popular because they provide an opportunity for unchaperoned flirtations—especially for servants, who are taken out of the stabilizing atmosphere of their masters' homes. But it is not only the lower classes that are threatened. The aristocratic Mowbray family at the center of the story is also divided against itself, nearly forever; and we are made to feel that their plight could represent that of the British class system generally.

The novel opens as the village of Wrexhill gathers to celebrate Charles Mowbray's coming of age. It is a portrait of harmonious communal and class relations: the young man is about to inherit a placid, well-ordered world. But that order is disrupted when his father dies suddenly the same night, leaving a will that deeds all his property to his widow rather than his son. This is the opportunity the new vicar seizes upon. He attempts to inflame Charles' resentments over the will and then reports those feelings in the most damaging way to his mother. Soon he is advising Mrs. Mowbray on familial and financial matters, including her son's allowance (reduced). Eventually he marries the widow and changes the name of Mowbray Park to his own. It is not simply that he is vain or greedy: he uses his power to unsettle traditional social structures, and by so doing throws individual lives and family units into confusion. When Fanny and her mother first fall under Cartwright's influence, Charles becomes alienated from them; when Mrs. Mowbray marries the vicar, Fanny becomes distanced from her mother too. The same pattern shatters the Richards family, where pious daughters reject their mother when she refuses to join Cartwright's fanatical following. For Mrs. Trollope this is the clearest proof of the dangers posed by his presence.

> If all other circumstances left it a matter of doubt whether evangelical influence (as it is impiously called) were productive of good or evil, the terrible power which it is so constantly seen to have of destroying family union must be quite sufficient to settle the question. Any person who will take the trouble to inquire into the fact, will find that family affection has been more blighted and destroyed by the working of this fearful superstition than by any other cause of which the history of man bears record.[33]

Henrietta reveals on her deathbed that Cartwright had a previous wife and child, invalidating his marriage to Mrs. Mowbray and disinheriting their child. And his assault on home virtues brings some of the Mowbrays' former aristocratic circle to their aid, to participate in his final undoing.

The Mowbrays are rescued by their long-time family friend (the association had broken off with Cartwright's ascendency) Sir Gilbert Harrington, an old-fashioned landed aristocrat who speaks like a character from a Fielding novel. Sir Gilbert had recognized Cartwright from the first for what he was and fumed over the clause in the will leaving the Mowbray monies under the control of the widow. He secretly arranges for the familial properties to be transferred back to the son by the mother (now Mrs. Cartwright), who, having realized the enormity of her mistake, is grieving to death; the final retrieval of property is announced, fittingly enough, at the reading of her will. These aspects of the ending are curiously parallel to the end of *Oliver Twist*, where legal control is also reasserted by a representative of the old order of things. Much as in Moliere (the novel's epigraph is from *Tartuffe*), Cartwright finally is banished (into "the Fens"). The threat of change has been averted but, as in Dickens, only barely.

Steven Marcus observes that the "fable" of *Oliver Twist* reflects "a society which, while still fixed in traditional attitudes, was becoming increasingly aware of its fluidity."[34] This fluidity is embodied above all in a fluidity of character, evident in kidnappers as well as their victims. Cartwright is both clergyman and ordinary man, the latter all the more dangerous because he is concealed within the former's costume. This helps explain why Dickens in *Sketches by Boz* looks back so fondly on all those varied antique types who are gradually disappearing from the London scene. It also helps explain why he so insistently refers, over and over, to the chief villain of *Oliver Twist* simply as "the Jew." The world would be more manageable if people simply behaved in accordance with established stereotypes, if all they were was plainly visible from their exteriors. But as the very persistence of the kidnapping theme suggests, the same body can house many very different forms of being. None of us is really safe within a fixed, visible character, and we are not safe to assume that anyone else really is what he or she appears to be. This is one reason why so many of these fictions are settled by legal rulings, which stabilize fluidity in fixed forms. It is also a reason why illustration often plays so important a role and assumes a clarifying function.

IV

Oliver's first genuinely urban experience (which actually happens just outside London) is an attempt to decipher the identity of a type of being he has never seen or imagined before. At the same instant, that other is surveying and trying to decipher him, and that scrutiny first draws Oliver into the task of intensive observation. As much as he had started, terror-stricken, at the form of the workhouse master, he had never been impelled to engage in such an extended and deliberate act of perception before. Oliver first only notices "a boy, who had passed him carelessly." Later, the same boy returns, "and was now surveying him most earnestly from the opposite side of the way." Survey: the Dickensian verb is important here. Soon Oliver will be plunged into the dizzying confusion of London's streets and backstreets, where survival depends on one's ability to construct at least a mental map. The Dodger, as we sense from the first, has mastered this art. Oliver never does, although he is continually on the alert for clues throughout his time in Fagin's world. Even in his first encounter with the Dodger, he only imitates the other's far more accomplished analytic techniques: "the boy remained in the same attitude of close observation so long, that Oliver raised his head, and returned his steady look" (100).

Cruikshank did not illustrate this scene, but it helps account for the pervasive imagery of the ones he did. *Oliver Twist* is a novel about seeing, seeing that becomes a vital necessity when Oliver enters the puzzling, dangerous world of London. Oliver does not always recognize that danger, but his puzzlement is there from the first, an outgrowth of the desire for knowledge that proves to be his most fundamental reflex. We see as much in the first illustrated encounter with London's underworld, "Oliver introduced to the Respectable Old Gentleman" (Figure 4.4). Here everyone is surveying everyone else, yet Oliver still stands out. For his expression is blank— just as in the text he is left speechless, never responding to any of the words of "polite" welcome until he falls into a deep, drugged sleep. He is not yet afraid, and what we can see of his expression in profile is very different from the terror of his approach to the workhouse master when he asked for more gruel. Above all, he is confused, confused enough to remain even more immobilized than he was then, or when he first met, watched, and conversed with the Dodger on the London road. The subject here is what the Dodger would call Oliver's greenness, a sense of which is beginning to dawn on him. He is beginning to realize that the world he has entered is unknown, perhaps unknowable. Cruikshank represents this quality too in the smoke-darkened walls and ceiling of the room, and the bizarrely suggestive forms of handkerchiefs (a detail borrowed from the Monmouth Street "scene" in *Sketches by Boz*), which almost seem to have human features as they hang in a group on the rear wall. We will see many more of these suggestive shadows, both in the narrative and in Cruikshank's illustrations. In both, they threaten to absorb Oliver himself.

The growing threat against Oliver can be seen in a comparison of the illustrations of his first and second arrivals in Fagin's lair. The second, which takes place after his abduction by Sikes and Nancy while on an errand for Mr. Brownlow, explicitly develops motifs from the first. Cruikshank labels it "Oliver's Reception by Fagin and the Boys" (Figure 4.5), and the ironic reference to formality in that title is expressed visually in the mock presentation by Master Bates, who displays Oliver to Fagin with hilarity, while the Dodger grips him tightly by one arm and rifles his pockets. In the first illustration the gray of the room was relieved by the bunches of pocket handkerchiefs hanging on the wall and by the white poster showing a bunch of hanging men. Now the grayness is uniform, except for a looming black shadow rising up the wall behind the horrific figure of Sikes. Sikes is more frightening here than in the illustration to the previous serial number, "Oliver claimed by his Affectionate Friends" (Figure 4.6), and in this picture we have a much clearer glimpse of his ferocious dog, too. Sikes himself now appears vaguely animalistic, and the shadowed form behind him on the wall has no visible features except for one light area which could represent (as in the shadow of the boy at the workhouse) an open mouth. The title of the illustration mentions "the Boys," but only Master Bates seems even remotely youthful; apparently that term is meant to include Sikes, his dog, and Nancy as well. It is not surprising, then, to see Oliver himself still questioning but far less uncertain about the nature of the world he is entering than in his initial visit. His eyes are widening, and his trunk is pulling instinctively back and away from Charley, Fagin, and Sikes. Dickens twice refers to Oliver's confusion—"as if he were bewildered, and could scarcely understand what passed" (164). But he is roused to an attempted escape when Sikes remarks that the "soft-hearted psalm-singers" who had been caring for Oliver are unlikely to inquire into his disappearance, since that might require them to prosecute him for theft. He is roused, that is, when he recognizes the possible lasting effects of his capture. This is Oliver's second abduction (or perhaps, his third, since Mr. Brownlow's authority over the boy, though exercised benevolently, has no apparent foundation in law). What is so terrifying about it is the suggestion that Oliver can be wholly reclaimed by the dark world Fagin inhabits, retransformed, in spite of the efforts of his friends and himself.

The possibility that Oliver might be claimed by the darkness that surrounds him is closely linked to the character, or the figure, of Sikes. Character almost seems too subtle a label for someone who is seen so insistently from the outside, in the starkest two-dimensional form. This is not to say that he is a well-defined stereotype, for much of his power has to do with a generalized sense of threat: he is not, as we will see, represented in clear or complete detail; he can strike at any time, any place, for any (or no) reason, against anyone. And at some points his grotesque size and power seem to be associated with the fearfulness of London itself. Leading Oliver out of town, towards a burglary that will implicate the boy even further in the criminal world, Sikes "threaded the streets between Shoreditch and Smithfield" along a route so twisting, and at a pace so swift, that it seems he alone possesses the key to what J. Hillis Miller has termed the daedal labyrinth of the city.[35] Once at Smithfield, Sikes "bestowed very little attention on the numerous sites and sounds, which so astonished the boy." Clearly Bill is in his element here, at the center of the area of London called the City, yet that element seems to partake less of civilized life than of the bestiality of a primitive world.

It was market-morning. The ground was covered, nearly ankle-deep, with filth and mire; and a thick steam, perpetually rising from the reeking bodies of the cattle, and mingling with the fog, which seemed to rest upon the chimney-tops, hung heavily above. All the pens in the centre of the large area, and as many temporary pens as could be crowded into the vacant space, were filled with sheep; tied up to posts by the gutter side were long lines of beasts and oxen, three or four deep. Country-men, butchers, drovers, hawkers, boys, thieves, idlers, and vagabonds of every low grade, were mingled together in a mass; the whistling of drovers, the barking of dogs, the bellowing and plunging of oxen, the bleating of sheep, the grunting and squeaking of pigs; the cries of hawkers, the shouts, oaths, and quarrelling on all sides; the ringing of bells and the roars of voices, that issued from every public house; the crowding, pushing, driving, beating, whooping, and yelling; the hideous and discordant din that resounded from every corner of the market; and the unwashed, unshaven, squalid, and dirty figures constantly running to and fro, and bursting in and out of the throng; rendered it a stunning and bewildering scene, which quite confounded the senses. (203)

Oliver's senses, that is: Sikes is impervious to it all. In an important respect, the bestiality of Sikes and the disorder of the city are versions of one another, images of a prerational meaninglessness that continually threatens to claim Oliver, to swallow him up (quite literally, in the cannibal savagery of the meat market scene) in a world of random sound and fury. Here and through much of the first part of the novel, Sikes and London blend together, not only as the instruments of Oliver's torture but as the puzzle he must solve, the maze from which he must try to escape. And what makes them so overwhelming is the constant suggestion that they cannot be escaped or overcome because they cannot be fully known.

There is a contemporary account of Smithfield curiously parallel to Dickens' in John Hogg's *London As it Is . . . a Series of Observations on the Health, Habits, and Amusements of the People* (1837). Hogg, a medical doctor, is primarily concerned with public health, and he does not conceal his aversion to the same stimuli that assault Oliver's senses:

> the scene of filth . . . the overpowering miasmata, the savage conduct and exclamations of the drovers, the cursing and swearing of their men, the lowing and bleating of the affrighted, parched, and exhausted animals, goaded into narrow folds, and panting even for air; the incessant recurrence of drunkenness, confusion, and riot among the hosts of butchers and salesmen's attendants, in the adjoining public houses and in the streets; and all this occurring for the most part in the night, baffles even an attempt at description.[36]

Or, to be more precise about that last remark, it baffles all attempts at description from within. This is the implication of the Dickensian passage as well. The authorial voice guides us, at Smithfield or through London generally: naming streets, labelling various figures according to their occupations, assembling the lists of verbs that reduce the formless energy of the scene to order. But Oliver is in constant danger of being lost. He cannot separate the different aspects of that "mingled . . . mass" of the "stunning and bewildering scene." He is as lost on the journey with Sikes as he was entering London for the first time with the Dodger. And of course he lacks the experience to label individuals as "butchers, drovers, hawkers, boys, thieves," and the like. But even if Oliver had such knowledge, Sikes would remain a problem and a threat. Bill is of this world, at home in its very center; yet even the Dickensian narrative voice avoids assigning him a neat, descriptive label in the way such terms are attached to others. He is part of this confusion, one of those "thieves, idlers, and vagabonds," yet something more, something different. And just as he is difficult to reduce to a single descriptive name, he cannot be identified in any well-known pictorial form.

This does not mean that Cruikshank avoids depicting him. Sikes is shown in six of the twenty-four illustrations (twice with Fagin, who also appears four times without Sikes); other than Oliver, no character is shown more frequently. But it does mean that the figure of Sikes is qualitatively different from those other Londoners in the novel. He is always recognizable as himself, yet he does not conform to any familiar urban type. Other characters are also recognizable and distinct, but they are versions of figures we might see in other books, or in the streets. Fagin especially seems very much like the stereotypical Jew, just as in the text he seems at times to be a parody of himself. This is what makes Sikes so formidable, not only to Oliver but to any reader or viewer of the illustrations. John Bayley has commented that all villains in Dickens "have the unexpungeable nature of our own nightmares and our own consciences." In Sikes this reaches a special intensity. Although the author's preface promises realism in the treatment of character, a depiction of "things as they really are," these, as Bayley observes, "turn out to be things as the fantasy fears, and feared in childhood, that they may be."[37] Sikes, then, is a creation of surrealist rather than realist art, just as his great final scene on the rooftops is above and apart from the actual city and city dwellers Dickens represents with so much sociological accuracy.

That surreal uniqueness is represented from Bill's first introduction in the text. First we only hear a voice, swearing. Then Dickens describes him.

> The man who growled out these words, was a stoutly-built fellow of about five-and-thirty, in a black velveteen coat, very soiled drab breeches, lace-up half-boots, and grey cotton stockings, which inclosed a bulky pair of legs, with large swelling calves;—the kind of legs, which in such costume, always look in an unfinished and incomplete state without a set of fetters to garnish them. (136)

The passage goes on to list some of the most prominent details visible in Cruikshank's illustrations: a three-days' growth of beard, "scowling eyes," a brown hat, a "dirty belcher handkerchief round his neck; with the long frayed ends of which he smeared the beer from his face as he spoke." Details of this sort belong to the caricatured ruffian, the sort one might find in other literary treatments of street life, or in Cruikshank's early drawings of London types. Years later, in fact, Cruikshank claimed to have been the creator of Bill and many other characters in *Oliver Twist*—the creator, that is, in the sense that they are types to be found in his own early work. Richard Vogler has pointed out that this claim is truer in the case of Sikes than for any other figure in the story.[38] But can we speak accurately of a prototype for a character like this? My point in quoting these descriptions is that the details of Bill's appearance don't quite add up. He is a patchwork figure, a combination of suggestions from many different "sources" and sources of many different sorts; something always is missing from what we would regard as the "completed" image.

It is true enough that we can see parts of this bizarre conglomeration in earlier work by Cruikshank. The illustration of "The Last Cab Driver" in *Sketches by Boz* shows a man wearing a hat very much like the one we later see on Sikes. Similarly, there is a version of that dirty, omnipresent belcher scarf in the volume titled *London Characters* (1829), a sociological picture gallery of street types that anticipates Mayhew's *London Labour and the London Poor*. Cruikshank anticipates Mayhew, that is, in the effort to construct a sociological catalogue, in trying to explain London by representing its colorful, typical figures. In a sense this is also what Cruikshank was doing in the years he was illustrating Dickens. As Guilland Sutherland remarks, the illustrations of both *Oliver Twist* and Ainsworth's *Tower of London* (1840) constitute an "explication of London" for readers. This is in a sense the master project of Cruikshank's career, to create "a panorama of London, sometimes individually and certainly *en bloc*."[39] Thus in *The Comic Almanack* (which began to appear in 1835) caricature blends with the calendrical format to present a month-by-month humorous catalogue of familiar urban habits and scenes. It is as if every variety of city dweller and city habit can be represented and identified within an appropriate time and place. We laugh because we recognize what we see, because even within the exaggeration there is a solid element of truth. That is precisely why it is impossible to laugh at Sikes, or at Cruikshank's pictures of him. He is anomalous, fearfully unique. There can be no complete models. In Cruikshank's own work we can find partial versions, anticipations, but no one who is wholly Sikes himself. This is not simply to restate the truism that no fictional character exists until an author creates him. I am suggesting that the sociological impulse, visible through most of Cruikshank's career and through much of the text of *Oliver Twist* as well, is fundamentally different from the artistry that creates Sikes.

Dickens calls our attention to the difference between these two conceptions of character at the end of that first piecemeal description of Sikes. We expect to find fetters on his legs; without them, the image remains somehow "incomplete." We want such details to be present to make such figures conform to our notions of their "real" identities, our notions of how and where we would find them (or like to find them) in life. This can only be the captured criminal, we want to say, someone who has not only broken the law (and violently: not every criminal requires fetters) but has been identified, convicted, and imprisoned by it. But Dickens reminds us of these expectations to make us realize that they are being violated. It is not just that Bill Sikes is physically free, on the loose, but that he is epistemologically and sociologically unbound as well. He is unknown, uncatalogued, outside of all rationalizing systems. We are being forewarned, in fact, that he can never be captured, or brought to justice by the system. He is already, as he will be in that last scene on the rooftops, apart from the structured sociological density of the urban world as we usually know it, as we (like Mayhew) would like it to be known. He belongs to the species of the Freudian uncanny, recognizable and at the same time unfamiliar, terrifyingly out of place.

Cruikshank's work in the decade before *Oliver Twist*, as epitomized in a volume like *London Characters*, attempted to create a city that could be classified and known. It is a catalogue of familiar and beloved types, composed in part because Cruikshank recognizes (as does Dickens in *Sketches by Boz*) that some of those "characters" are beginning to disappear from the urban scene. Dustmen, hackney coachmen, watchmen, parish beadles: part of our pleasure in looking at their portraits is in confirming our own abilities to identify them by their external appearances, by the consistency with which they conform to the ideal types of their own professions. The beadle in *London Characters*, for instance, is very close to the representations of Mr. Bumble in the illustrations to *Oliver Twist*. And even within the novel it is clear that Bumble is a caricature to those who encounter him:

> "You *are* a beadle, are you not?" inquired Mr. Grimwig.
> "I am a porochial [*sic*] beadle, gentlemen," rejoined Mr. Bumble, proudly.
> "Of course," observed Mr. Grimwig aside to his friend, "I knew he was. A beadle all over!" (175)

An even earlier version of Cruikshank's beadle appears in the *Gentleman's Pocket Magazine* for 1827. There, as Sutherland has observed, he is recognizable not simply because of his own appearance but because of his place "within the pattern of local society"—"a remarkable animal," as an essay on "Dustmen" (illustrated by Cruikshank) from the same magazine puts it, "in a gallery of specimens of the natural history of the creatures which inhabit London."[40] The impulse to classify is thus in part a scientific, or pseudo-scientific, one, although it is also a characteristically middle-class approach to reality. Walter Benjamin observes an identical phenomenon in the literature of Paris at the same time, a "petit-bourgeois

genre" of descriptive writings dealing with familiar human types and providing the assurance "that everyone was, unencumbered by any factual
knowledge, able to make out the profession, the character, the background,
and the life-style of passers-by."[41]

At times *Oliver Twist* presents familiar types, or London itself, as if
nothing is easier than to gain a thorough knowledge of the world through
its appearances. But it returns again and again to the limits of such external
knowledge, to the uncanny, to the unknown. Fagin's world, especially, is
filled with examples of these limits—although by the end of the book Mr.
Brownlow is able to gather the necessary information to remove Monks,
so that Fagin and his gang (with the conspicuous exception of Sikes) are
captured and punished. Yet until the end it is a story of labyrinths and
darkness, an impenetrable, inescapable world, the real terror of which lies
in the fact that it cannot be wholly seen or wholly described. This is what
makes Cruikshank's achievement as illustrator so remarkable. The first
indication of his sensitivity to the epistemological obscurity of *Oliver
Twist* is the pervasive darkness of his illustrations. Fagin's is a gray world,
in which the known merges with the unknown, the seen with the unseen.
Yet I think there is an even more impressive achievement in his handling
of the anomalous, unchartable form of Sikes, who begins to merge with
those shadows in the scene of "Oliver's Reception by Fagin and the Boys"
and seems wholly absorbed by them in the rooftop scene Cruikshank calls
"The Last Chance." The only picture in which we see him clearly is the
one where he is the only human figure. Yet in that illustration, "Sikes
attempting to destroy his Dog," it is the equivalency of man and beast that
interests the artist most; and with the distant church steeple separating
them into the left and right halves of the image, respectively, it is Bull's-
eye, on the right, rather than his master, who seems understandable and
sympathetic.

The most complex pictorial exploration of the mysterious nature of
Sikes comes in the illustration of Oliver's second kidnapping, his recapture
by the gang as he goes through the streets on his errands (Figure 4.6). The
main undertones of the scene are implicit in the Cruikshankian title,
"Oliver claimed by his Affectionate Friends." This is, to begin with, a grim
caricature of the impersonality of urban life, a "street scene," like Parry's
watercolor, where criminals are able to operate without interference. Most
of the figures in the illustration are taken directly from the text: a "sleepy-
faced carpenter," several female onlookers, and a "butcher's boy with a
shiny head of hair annointed with suet" (157). The carpenter and butcher's
boy are identified as they would have been in *London Characters*, by their
clothing and tools-of-the-trade: the first wears a square paper dust hat, the

second carries a meat board. Cruikshank adds a barman from the neighboring beer parlour, and he is labeled by a characteristic apron. This deliberate stereotyping of all the urban figures contributes to the mood of lifelessness in the picture: aside from those three main characters struggling at the center of the image, we see a group portrait of urban indifference. The text makes it clear that Nancy has taken advantage of this, exploiting the familiarity of urban costuming to blend in with the crowds on the streets. The disguise she has borrowed from Fagin (who has a considerable supply of such protective clothing), including the ridiculous domestic basket and key (which Cruikshank enlarges to remind us of the inappropriateness of this role), mimics the code of appearance by which people identify themselves and others. Yet if the artificiality of her costume seems to us grotesquely humorous, it convinces (or doesn't unconvince) the other passersby of her claims on Oliver. He, to his misfortune, also appears in a stereotypical London outfit, that of the schoolboy, and is therefore assumed to be up to no good.

All of these familiar urban exteriors only set apart further the looming figure of Sikes. Dickens suggests his villain's extraordinary appearance by introducing him to the scene anonymously:

> "What the devil's this?" said a man, bursting out of a beer-shop, with a white dog at his heels. (157)

At the opening of this chapter, Sikes was shown slumped within the same beer shop, an object for careful visual scrutiny:

> there sat, brooding over a little pewter measure and a small glass, strongly impregnated with the smell of liquor, a man in a velveteen coat, drab shorts, half-boots, and stockings, who even by that dim light no experienced agent of police would have hesitated to recognize as Mr. William Sikes. (152)

Here we are seeing and not seeing at once, recognizing Sikes and discovering how easy it is for him to escape recognition. Dickens describes what is at first only a collection of details, adding afterwards that only the practised observer (the police agent) can make sense of them. Even then their meaning cannot be summarized by any role or label beyond the man's name. Sikes is Sikes: irreducible, uniquely, and terrifyingly himself. Such a figure becomes doubly dangerous in a world where everything is assumed to be known (and knowable) by its appearance, where everyone is supposed to be identifiable in a quick visual survey. Little wonder that in Cruikshank's illustration Oliver stares so intently at the rough features of his captor. His fright is emphasized further by the circle of blank faces around him. They also comprise one source of the threat: no one notices Sikes, a fact of which he is aware, and takes advantage; this makes him all the more formidable. It is as if Oliver is recognizing, for the first time, the unknown dimensions of the known—how horrifyingly, qualitatively different this danger is. And Cruikshank's placement of Sikes with his animated savagery in the midst of so much workaday immobility makes explicit another hint latent in the text. Sikes embodies a dark potential of the city itself, concealed beneath its surface of apparent legibility and order. If *Oliver Twist* describes London as a daedal labyrinth, this is its human respresentative—or else the beast at its center.

Dickens, of course, is both attracted and repelled by the complexity of London; some of the same ambivalence extends to his portrayal of Sikes. He even grants him a species of heroism at the end of his life. Sikes escapes to the country and risks his life fighting a fire. Returning to the city, he is pursued by a crowd of outraged citizens to a final defiant stand on the rooftops. "'Damn you!' cried the desperate ruffian, throwing up the sash and menacing the crowd. 'Do your worst! I'll cheat you yet!'" (449). In a sense he does cheat justice; Dickens allows him to tie his own hangman's noose (which the illustration shows) and, in a bizarrely heroic way, die in action. The animal has been humanized, or else (as R. H. Horne commented) we have come to sympathize with the victim of people no less bestial than he.

> Perhaps, in reality, no retribution, on earth, could very well be too heavy for such a destable wretch as Sikes to suffer; but we cannot bear to see so much. The author hunts down the victim, like a wild beast, through mud and mire, and darkness, and squalid ways, with crowds upon crowds, like hell-hounds gnashing and baying at his heels.[42]

Cruikshank's "The Last Chance" shows some of this, but not all; it is as if the final dramatization of evil in Dickens involved moral complexity he was not prepared to represent (Figure 4.7). Sikes is nearly absorbed in the nighttime darkness of the image; practically the only traces of light are on the faces of the people peering from windows below, and there is little suggestion of savagery in them. Bull's-eye crouches just above his master, prepared to spring. The noose hangs inertly, as if the death that is about to come is the token of something fixed, preordained. Cruikshank's picture, like its title, alludes to the heavy hand of fate. In effect, he kills Sikes before Dickens does, refusing to grant him a final moment of humanity.

This tendency to dehumanize evil is even more apparent in the final illustration of Fagin (Figure 4.8), although it seems to correspond more closely to the character of the Dickensian text:

The condemned criminal was seated on his bed, rocking himself from side
to side, with a countenance more like that of a snared beast than the face of
a man. (471–472)

Cruikshank's illustration portrays a Fagin no less brutish than this. The
stress is on his disorientation rather than his rage, yet he remains creatural,
at the center of a darkness that fills the picture more fully than in any other
illustration to the novel. The darkness associated with Fagin's world
throughout the story seems to have absorbed him and permeated the
whole image. As G. K. Chesterton remarked, the "baseness of the subject"
is evoked by a "kind of baseness in the very technique of it."

> It is not drawn with the free lines of a free man; it has the half-witted secrecies
> of a hunted thief. It does not look merely like a picture of Fagin; it looks like
> a picture by Fagin.[43]

The remark is perceptive in more ways than Chesterton knew, for Cruikshank's Fagin is partly a self-portrait. One story has it that he chanced to
catch sight of his own reflection in a mirror, his features distorted by the
strain of trying to create a picture of Fagin! Cruikshank himself quibbled
with this account, insisting that he was trying to enact Fagin's desperate
facial expressions when he suddenly happened on the one that seemed
right.[44] Either way, the story of the drawing is related to the way Dickens
treats Fagin and his world. Evil, like the Freudian uncanny, is both familiar and unfamiliar, of the self and other, a form of existence that both can
and cannot be portrayed or known. Fagin, in his last night alive, is moving
across the boundary that separates these delicately balanced conditions,
becoming dehumanized even before his death, turning into a beast as we
read. Cruikshank shows him experiencing the same process, although in a
slightly different form.

It is not surprising that the portrayal of Fagin has brought charges of
anti-Semitism against Dickens (and perhaps by implication against Cruikshank as well), for anti-Semitism is a quintessential form of characterization through dehumanization, an attempt to render the otherness of a self
absolute and impenetrable. To some extent the charge against the novelist
is merited, if only for the frequency with which he refers to this villain
merely as "the Jew." But the point of this last scene is precisely the reverse.
As a "Jew," Fagin is known, a familiar stereotype from daily life or a volume like *London Characters.* By the end of his life, when the depth of his
villainy is disclosed, he passes into something less precise and far more
dangerous, something far more difficult to name or depict or explain away.
Dickens explains that Fagin refuses to pray with the "venerable men of his

own persuasion," and drives them away with curses" (469); now he is identified with no one else in the world. For him there will be no final moment of redemption, not even by the daring of Bill Sikes' last days. This is not a man at all but a thing, a creature of the darkness, satanic;[45] in Cruikshank's picture the ends of his two manacled legs on the floor seem to come together into one huge cloven foot. And perhaps that detail begins to suggest how this illustration falls short of the Dickensian text in this practice of identification. Cruikshank's Fagin is the more grotesque of the two conceptions, almost comic as he peers into empty space and gnaws at his fingertips. Dickens could acknowledge his power along with his bestiality, in the very reference to "a face retaining no human expression but rage and terror." This is still a man, in spite of those snarls. Cruikshank's image moves closer to ridicule, as if the uncanny proximity of evil to our normal selves is finally too threatening, too dark, to be taken seriously.

V

I have moved from actual to metaphoric kidnappings, from stories of women and children to images of villains and beasts. The shape of this chapter up to now ought to suggest that the preoccupation with stolen children is bound up with fears about those who might abduct them, with images of savagery and extraordinary physical and psychological power. The magnitude of these fears is most fully illustrated in an actual event and the responses to it. It was (depending upon which account we read) a riot or an abortive rebellion—E. P. Thompson calls it "the last peasants' revolt"[46]—leading to a skirmish between a group of peasants in Kent and the local militia. By the time it ended, eleven people had been killed. The story of the encounter surfaces in the press on the first day of June 1838 and dwindles out by the end of that month, buried under the growing preoccupation with Victoria's impending coronation. As it turns out, the two events are not entirely unrelated, since the leader of the brief uprising, claiming noble descent, had promised that he would sit at the Queen's right hand during her coronation and obtain special dispensation for his followers. It is upon that bizarre leader above all that the interest of the event—a real example of metaphoric abduction—depends.

The first appearance of this strange character had been six years earlier, at Canterbury in late 1832, under the name of Count Moses Rostopchein Rothschild. Within several days, after distributing largesse and making promises of more, he disappeared, only to return several weeks later with the new and equally fanciful name of Sir William Percy Honeywood Courtenay, Knight of Malta, Rightful Heir to the Earldom of Devon, King of the Gypsies, and King of Jerusalem. These were the same titles he laid claim to on his reappearance in 1838, with special stress on his putative divinity. Courtenay—a huge, muscular man with "a great mass of hair"[47] who dressed in bizarre, colorful costumes—sometimes claimed to be a supernatural messenger, and sometimes represented himself as "the Saviour of the World" while displaying stigmata. As we can see in the poetical fragment in the headnote to this chapter, it proved difficult to persuade his followers of his mortality even after his death (he had left instructions on preparing his body for resurrection), when he was identified as one John Nicholls Thom (or Tom), "late of Truro, in Cornwall."[48] Thom, or Courtenay (as I will continue to call him), stood for Parliament (and was defeated) in 1832, during "the excitement following the First Reform Act" (as J. F. C. Harrison puts it).[49] Later he appeared at the trial of some fishermen for smuggling and was found guilty of perjury on account of the improbable stories he told in their supposed defense. Instead of prison, he was confined in a local lunatic asylum until his release (obtained under unusual circumstances that became the subject of heated parliamentary discussion). By early 1838 Courtenay had begun to renew contact with the local peasantry. One report[50] describes him marching through the countryside under a flag of blue and white and a broken loaf of bread on a pike, promising "not only redress, but plenty and affluence," and declaring that the people "were oppressed by the laws in general, but more particularly by the New Poor Law."

Such revolutionary gestures did not pass unnoticed. In May 1838 magistrates issued a warrant for his arrest, concerned that he was "enticing laborers from their work and inciting them to violence."[51] This seemed to offer Courtenay the opportunity he had been seeking. He killed the magistrate who attempted to serve the warrant—first shooting him with a pistol and then stabbing the body with his sword. Troops were called, 100–150 men from two companies of the Forty-fifth Infantry, "conveyed by two fish vans and a coach to the place where it was said the party had formed a kind of intrenchment."[52] Again seizing the initiative, Courtenay led his band of about forty people in a charge ("Boys, come forward, and do not behave like dastardly cowards") against the much larger and better-trained force of soldiers; he and seven of his followers were killed, but only after he had shot and killed an officer leading one section of the troops. Later the father of this officer, Lieutenant Henry Boswell Bennett, claimed recompense for the death of his son, noting that he was "the first officer of the armed forces of the Crown to be killed in the service of the new queen."[53]

Here, for the most part, the incident ends—excepting, that is, what we might term the epilogues, added almost compulsively in various official responses to the melee: the summations presented in the courts, the press, and Parliament. His followers only wanted to forget what had happened. Others, outside the class Courtenay appealed to, wanted to give his story elaborate formal closure, to attach a strong moral lest anyone should misunderstand its significance. To some extent this is a normal response: crimes must be punished, the law reasserted, parliamentary questions asked. Yet it is the manner of these concluding gestures that remains striking, even granting that something like them could have been expected. It is surprising to discover, for instance, that the survivors of Courtenay's little army were not treated as harshly as they might have been. Even Lieutenant Bennett's family pled for mercy: "it would be the greatest aggravation of their sufferings for the loss of their son if any more blood was to be spilled in consequence of this unhappy affair."[54] The judge in the case, Lord Denman, put on the black cap and pronounced sentence of death, only to revoke it immediately thereafter. Two prisoners shown to have been most directly inculpated in the violence were transported for life, a third for ten years. These were apparently meant as deterrent sentences, in spite of Lord Denman's concern that clemency only "prevents the last example from being given to the ignorant people at large, of what they must expect if they encourage courses like these."[55] Perhaps, then, such messages to the lower classes were less important than the image of the event an established society constructed for itself, an image alluded to in that apparently casual reference to "the ignorant people."

Ignorance was the most common explanation produced for the affair in the weeks after it had concluded, one that treated all the actors (except, oddly enough, the chief one) as irresponsible, in effect as children.[56] There are many other versions of this condescension. Most of the subsequent responses to the brief revolt, including the sentences meted out to Courtenay's accomplices, display a compulsive urge to minimize the significance of the episode, not simply to explain it but to explain it away, in tones of contempt and satirical smugness. The full-page *Times* report of June 4, after the inquests on the deaths of Courtenay, Bennett, and the others, reiterates (as the writer emphasizes) whichever details of the encounter might seem to bear a political interpretation, in order to show that in fact they do not. Prior accounts of the event were fairly accurate, we are told, but certain facts must be examined again "for the purpose of positively denying that the New Poor Law was one of the subjects on which Thoms [*sic*] excited his deluded followers." We might have expected a different response given the usually vocal antipathy of the

Times to the New Poor Law (the radical *Morning Chronicle* suggests that Tory rhetoric helped to inflame Courtenay's supporters).[57] But apparently party politics are less threatening here than the notion of a politicized popular revolution, the possibility of class warfare. Whatever else may have happened, this must not be construed as genuine political action. Even the *Morning Chronicle* agrees: "these unhappy murders were all the result of wild and furious fanaticism, completely unconnected with politics."[58] Nor are we permitted to regard this as a form of authentic religious fervor: it was madness, pure and simple. J. F. C. Harrison suggests that "polite" society almost always regarded millenarian movements this way, discounting the supposed evidence of Divine inspiration as mere insanity.[59]

The condescension of official culture becomes particularly evident when the *Times* correspondent tries to treat the bizarre events as humorous, as if they can be laughed away. This "unfortunate day . . . will form a new chapter in the history of fanaticism," he explains, "and will present a picture of human nature which would be most ridiculous were it not for the fearful and tragical incidents mixed up with it." This tone resurfaces conspicuously in the account of an interview with one of Courtenay's band, emphasizing the stupidity of both the man and his son—another child "stolen" by a persuasive religious leader.

> Again I put my wonted interrogatory, how his lad could have been such a noodle as to believe in this man's incomprehensible mysteries, and again I was told, "Lord, Sir, my lad is an *unlarned* man like myself; he can neither read nor write, and how was I or my lad to go for to gainsay such a great scholar as Sir William! He showed us his wounds, and how could we dare to disobey him!"[60]

Another former Thomite makes the same point even more forcefully: no simple person who heard Courtenay speak could resist his charisma. "Oh, Sir," he responds to the "wonted interrogatory," "you did not know Sir William. He had too much 'larning.' No one could stand before him. When he went to Canterbury nobody could stand before him." The dispatch translates the episode as an outburst of mass hysteria, the sort of fanaticism that particularly threatens those mired in ignorance—a quality Courtenay's former disciples seem deferentially eager to acknowledge now that their leader has been killed and discredited. "Oh! Sir," that second "informant" continues, "he was an awful man. He had a tongue which an *unlarned* person could not get over."

Learning was the main issue addressed by commentators on the right and the left. To some extent it divided them, yet the same note of paternalism is sounded from both sides. The radical Joseph Hume declared in

Commons on June 6 that the riot revealed a "state of brutal ignorance, in which Englishmen ought not to be." Had such an event taken place in Ireland, "members would perhaps not be surprised." Yet here is astonishing ignorance within fifty miles of London, surrounded by wealthy homes. Doesn't this demonstrate (he asks, rhetorically) the failure of the Church to educate? Shouldn't "measures" be taken "for extending to all classes that information and instruction which would prevent such lamentable occurences."[61] Lord Brougham, speaking the next day in the House of Lords, expressed the hope that this appalling display of ignorance would persuade Lord Melbourne and his government to support the education bill he (Brougham) was about to introduce. But such remarks were controversial: identifying specific social causes of the disturbance, they implied that social and institutional solutions could be found. This is what the *Times* objected to in Brougham's speech. If only ignorance *were* the sole cause of such behavior, a leading article laments. Isn't this rather a problem of superstition (not so easily suppressed), such as that exhibited by the "Confusion of Useful Knowledge Society" when they profess belief in animal magnetism, or by the pope when he uses relics to try to cure cholera? What about such educated fanatics as the followers of Edward Irving? What about Irving himself—or Swedenborg, or Bentham, or Cobbett? At least the ignorant rabble who followed Courtenay had an excuse. A dispatch of the same day (June 9) reports that Courtenay was aided by some women who could read, and whose knowledge helped him "distort" scripture in support of his messianic claims. "Better that they had not been taught to read than to read so unwisely and for such dangerous and fanatical purposes."

What is needed now, the *Times* urges, is greater moral superintendence, which Brougham's bill would not guarantee. And yet this is what Brougham himself was arguing for, education in the service of social order; even Hume, favoring different means, looked to the same ends. The only real question is whether the popular mind is amenable to guidance, and (if so) of what sort. It is the nature-nurture problem again. Perhaps this is why Courtenay's adventure aroused as much concern as it did. For in dramatizing the susceptibility of the masses to charismatic leadership it raised the spectre of their possibly irremediable primal instincts. Charles Buller, who had been educated in such matters by no less a tutor than Thomas Carlyle, addressed this question a year later, during the extended parliamentary debates on education.

> Whenever I contemplate the condition of the working classes, the deep and
> dark gulf that separates them from the knowledge and the sympathies of their

superiors in fortune, the utter ignorance in which we are of their feelings and wants, the little influence which we have over their conduct, and the little hold which we appear to have on their affections, I shrink with terror from the wild passions and dense ignorance that appear to be fermenting in that mass of physical force. We see vast portions of them utterly neglected, utterly uninstructed, and plunged into debauchery during the intervals of toil. . . . Sometimes the murmur of their discontent and ignorance assumes an artic-ulate form, and speaks in the accents of the disciples of Tom."[62]

Supporting the same position a year earlier, the *Morning Chronicle* con-cluded that the events in Kent demonstrated "how dangerous it is to neglect altogether the moral culture of the labouring classes. Throughout the greater part of England," it continued, "the agricultural labourers may be said to be in the condition of the brutes that perish."[63] Tories and the *Times* would not have argued with that final characterization, only with the claim that such brutality can be altered. For them, the important thing was to keep it under control, to place every human creature and every human instinct under the sway of law and order. In some cases, this required force of arms; some impulses only can be suppressed by death.

The education bill was passed, not simply as a way of improving the lot of the masses but to insure that they would not continue to exist outside the boundaries of authority. In this sense, the moral of the whole affair was drawn most clearly by Dr. Poore, the magistrate conducting the prelimi-nary hearing on the violence (June 2). Addressing his remarks especially to the spectators in the Kent courtroom (who included some survivors of Courtenay's band), he declared: "The kindest act that a man can do to his family is to abstain from opposition to law, which, if put in motion against him, must crush him."[64] We have seen the same conclusion, enforced more subtly, in the abduction stories of 1837 and 1838. No wonder all those young heroes and heroines felt so vulnerable. The greatest threat of all is not merely to find oneself cast adrift amid the shifting boundaries of a fluid society but to feel that the final boundary remains impassable, that one must remain radically and unalterably outside.

If that is the fate of a Fagin or a Sikes or a Courtenay, most civilized beings find ways of avoiding it, ways to return or compromise. This is illus-trated in the most amusing aftershock of the Kent eruption, a series of exchanges in Commons near the end of June involving a radical member who also happened to be a popular romantic novelist—Edward Lytton Bulwer, later Bulwer-Lytton. Questions about the episode were still being raised, and Bulwer became impatient enough with the display of establish-mentarian morality to venture a sally of wit. He begged to remind one of his colleagues on the other side of the House, Mr. Praed, of radical leanings he might have felt in his own youth, and in particular of a "calf's-head dinner" held at Cambridge to celebrate the death of Charles I. Praed was incensed; the exchange became heated. Bulwer was compelled to retract, to promise to have no further hostile communications with Praed, and to remain in the House for fear words would lead to open battle! (They nearly did: Praed reported several days later that he had, in fact, placed "his honour and his character in the hands of a friend"—but upon hearing of the House's action felt he had no need to carry on.) At last Bulwer explained, "in a remarkably low voice" according to the *Times,* that he had not intended to injure anyone's feelings by his remarks, and expressed regret. The apology was accepted; peace was quickly reimposed, as in Kent. Drawing the same parallel, the *Times* of June 28 terms this the "not very sane debate relative to the insane man." So much for dramatic gestures by romantic novelists! So much for even purely verbal assaults! Here is one more lesson of the Courtenay affair: heroic stances are better left to fiction; it is dangerous to confuse literature and life.

Courtenay aroused so much concern and discussion because he was partly a figure from a book—in those "learned" speeches, in his physical appearance (riding a white horse, to correspond to the prophecy in Revelation), in his vague program of radical cliches. In fact, he actually did step into real life (or back into it) from the pages of popular fiction. The *Morning Chronicle* of June 2 recalled that William Harrison Ainsworth's 1834 novel *Rookwood* introduced a character based on Sir William Courtenay, among a band of gypsies. He appears entertaining his companions with a "ditty" he composed and named after himself, "THE KNIGHT OF MALTA: A Canterbury Tale." The first stanza of the song illustrates Ainsworth's impression of the "the Knight."

> Come list to me, and you shall have, without a hem or haw, sirs,
> A Canterbury pilgrimage, much better than old Chaucer's.
> 'Tis of a hoax I once played off, upon that city clever,
> The memory of which, I hope, will stick to it for ever.
> *With my coal-black beard, and purple cloak,*
> *Jack-boots, and broad-brimmed castor.*
> *Hey-ho! for the Knight of Malta!*[65]

The memory had stuck at least until 1838, for Courtenay's opponents as well as his supporters responded overdramatically to his overdramatized role. *Rookwood,* with gypsies, kidnappings, and confusion over birthrights, helped link this flamboyant figure to all those other abduction stories, helped make him even more topical though not necessarily more real.

Ainsworth, however, denied that the mad knight properly should be regarded as a topical figure of the 1830s. A note in the novel explains his motives in adapting Courtenay's activities at Canterbury in 1832 for a historical romance: "The anachronism of his character in a tale (the date of which is nearly a century back), will perhaps be overlooked when it is considered of how much value, in the illustration of 'wise saws,' are '*modern instances*.'" Ainsworth urges us to regard such an "extra-ordinary individual ... of a half-crazed understanding," as an "instance" of universal behavior, outside history. "Imposture and credulity," he adds, "are of all ages."[66] He, too, wants to explain such acts away; even in 1834 Courtenay seemed too clichéd, too melodramatic. By 1838, as I have been suggesting, the uncanny resemblances of fiction and reality were even more discomforting. It was not as easy to muster Ainsworth's secure good humor in dismissing someone who might have seemed comic if only he did not represent so serious a threat—psychological as well as social. Courtenay looms so large in the consciousness of Victoria's Year because he reminds readers of a story they already knew too well: a story of shifting classes, families shattered, titles falsely claimed and innocent people tricked into dangerous courses of action; a story in which the confusions of identity endanger the stability of society and of all the individuals within it. It is a story all the more disturbing because it does not seem wholly real, one that calls for rationalization because its facts seem to arise out of nightmares.

5

How To Observe

I want a History of Looking.

Roland Barthes, Camera Lucida

A child does not catch gold fish in water at the first trial ... knowledge and method are necessary to enable him to take what is actually before his eyes and under his hand. So it is with all who fish in a strange element for the truth which is living and moving there: the powers of observation must be trained. ...

Harriet Martineau, How To Observe

For there are wonders, wondrous strange,
To those who will through nature range,
And use the mind, and clear the eye,
And let instruction not pass by:
There are deep thoughts of tranquil joy
For those who thus their hearts employ,
And trace the wise design that lurks
In holy nature's meanest works,
And by the torch of truth discern
The happy lessons good men learn. ...

Martin Tupper, "A Cabinet of Fossils"

... what can be more different than the feelings of the barbarian about to display to his fellows the benefits with which civilisation has clothed him; and those of the civilised man voluntarily descending to herd with savages?

Edinburgh Review (1839)

not people but species, not flowers but specimens,
not fragrances but descriptions. ...

Adam Zagajewski, "Franz Schubert: A Press Conference"

Observations are never perfect.

William Whewell, Philosophy of the Inductive Sciences (1840)[1]

I

Recalling her visit to America forty years before, Harriet Martineau's *Autobiography* mentions only one fact concerning the Atlantic crossing. "The first steam voyage to the United States took place in 1838: and I set forth in 1834: so there was no thought of a quicker passage than a month. I did not wish a shorter one."[2] She is not simply reminding us of a change in nautical technology, although that is part of the point. She was going in order to prepare a progressive account of a progressive society, to compose a piece of distinctively modern history. America in the 1830s was still a political and social experiment, close enough to its own beginnings for its direction to seem uncertain, and exciting; it was a world wholly apart from Europe. A long, slow Atlantic crossing almost necessitated contemplation of that difference—as if the same breezes that powered the ship inspired its occupants to a higher level of cultural self-consciousness. The excitement of the first steam journeys might distract travellers from the novelty of the New World they were approaching; but voyagers before 1838 could think of themselves as adventurers, exploring the unknown. Andrew Bell, who made the crossing in August 1835, points out that his trip was the same length as that of Columbus, thirty-three days. And Bell adds that he used that time for meditation—trying (in Peter Conrad's phrase) to imagine America, clarifying his own expectations to contrast them more accurately with reality.[3] Martineau reports an almost identical experience. It is as if she needed a month on the Atlantic to keep herself from being at sea in the New World, to prepare herself to confront an unprecedented set of political and social conditions. And she prepared herself by writing. Disobeying her own resolution to make the sea journey a period of complete rest, she began "reluctant toil" on a different sort of book from any she had written, a book of the sort that might be conceivable only in the passage to an unfamiliar world. And it was not just conceived in that space of self-consciousness between the Old and New Worlds, it was about it, a *rite de passage* (or perhaps a write of passage) enacting in advance the struggle of a stranger to understand a foreign people and place. A recent biographer has termed this a "primitive sociological methodology."[4] Martineau called it, more ostentatiously, *How to Observe.*

This chapter will examine Martineau's writings of 1837 and 1838, her writings on America, in the context of books by two very different sorts of travellers: John Ruskin and Charles Darwin. But in spite of the obvious dissimilarities of their concerns—above all, the dissimilarities between political and aesthetic and scientific forms of travel writing—their books share Martineau's self-consciousness about the issue of perception. All of

their books from this period might be titled *How to Observe,* for all three
authors are writing to persuade us of the value of seeing in a certain way.
Yet if each has a kind of epistemological program to advance, each also
discovers the difficulties of carrying it out. How to observe—the phrase at
first suggests a set of practical instructions, a kind of traveller's guidebook,
and then gradually transforms itself into an inescapable question, one difficult to answer in any simple, final way. Almost in spite of themselves,
Martineau, Ruskin, and Darwin confront the problem of seeing accurately:
the barriers to understanding aspects of reality that fall outside the limits
of a particular set of intellectual categories; the dangers of acknowledging
that which is not supposed to be there in the first place. Is it possible to
observe correctly in a world wholly different from the one we have known,
or one that reveals aspects of the known world our culture has systemati-
cally tried to suppress?

The importance of these issues is apparent from the very beginning of
Society in America. It is, as we will see, a highly politicized survey of
American life and institutions. Yet the first principles discussed are not
the abstract notions of liberty or justice, or the tenets of the American Constitution that the rest of the book sets out to test. Instead, Martineau begins
by considering the problem of knowing and interpreting the world, making
us aware of the difficulties facing anyone who undertakes this apparently
straightforward task. Her introduction quotes a recent number of the *Edinburgh Review* to summarize the epistemological pitfalls in the path of
sociological accuracy:

> How shall a man, to whom all characters or individual men are like sealed
> books, of which he sees only the title and the covers, decipher from his four-
> wheeled vehicle, and depict to us, the character of a nation? He courageously
> depicts his own optical delusions; notes this to be incomprehensible, that
> other to be insignificant; much to be good, much to be bad, and most of all
> indifferent; and so, with a few flowing strokes, completes a picture, which,
> though it may not resemble any possible object, his countrymen are to take
> for a national portrait. Nor is the fraud so readily detected: for the character
> of a people has such a complexity of aspect, that even the honest observer
> knows not always, not perhaps after long inspection, what to determine
> regarding it. From his, only accidental, point of view, the figure stands before
> him like the tracings on veined marble,—a mass of mere random lines, and
> tints, and entangled strokes, out of which a lively fancy may shape almost
> *any* image.[5]

This account of the visual "reading" of national character like a Rorschach
test anticipates E. H. Gombrich's sense of "the beholder's share" in con-

stituting what is seen. And in spite of the warning about "optical delu-sions," the passage also voices a modern, relativistic recognition that sub-jectivity is finally inescapable. Aren't we all trapped by personal prejudices or the assumptions of our own cultures? The image of that "four-wheeled vehicle" suggests how easy it is for all of us (in Martineau's phrase) to be "boxed up in a carriage of Long Acre origin."[6] If a gentleman wishes to become "a citizen of the world," she adds, he would do well to travel on foot (*HO,* 57). There is a theoretical point here as well as a practical one: we must attempt to travel outside our normal cultural limits, to escape the familiar confinements of class and habit, to ground ourselves (literally) in any world we wish to understand.

The same epistemological self-consciousness echoes through Marti-neau's books of the late 1830s, particularly those about her visit to Amer-ica. *How to Observe: Morals and Manners* was published in 1838, the same year as the second of her two accounts of that visit, the *Retrospect of West-ern Travel. Society in America,* a longer and more densely analytic book, had appeared a year earlier; the *Retrospect* is more like a conventional travel narrative and is easily the more readable of the two. But neither really should be considered a travel book in the usual sense. Both are writ-ten to serve specific philosophical goals: to compare the theory and prac-tice of American government, to measure the country's contributions to modern (and especially republican) political thought, to carry back word of its achievements to England. It is quite clearly a political project, but this also poses a distinct epistemological challenge. For in one sense Mar-tineau's conclusions are implicit before any investigation has begun. Her *Autobiography* recalls that the philanthropic Lord Henley begged her to make the journey and report on the Americans' "principles of justice and mercy in their treatment of the least happy classes of society" (*A,* i, 270). He told her, in other words, to see and to see through America, to record data and to discover a set of abstract "principles" located somewhere beneath the surface of ordinary reality. Her task, then, is to chart a path between particular facts and general ideas, to teach her readers not simply how to observe but how to observe for a purpose—how to carry on a detailed sociopolitical analysis of a particular society, an analysis that will never lose contact with large moral principles. Observation for Martineau is both a fundamentally philosophical and a fundamentally human activ-ity, not so much a neutral record of impersonal facts as a passionate search for truths essential to individual and social improvement.

In the American books, this commitment to a political conception of truth also defines a special narrative technique: we shift between detail and generality, between an observed, external world and the perspective of the enlightened visitor observing it. Martineau constantly makes us aware of her own presence as an observer in America, as if to allow us to test the extent to which she moves outside the barriers of custom and class, the extent to which her own personality filters the data of experience. Thus, the question of whether anyone can see clearly is focused specifically on her: what sort of information is she equipped to gather? how trustworthy an account is she able to provide?

The preface to *Society in America* disarmingly admits that three sorts of objections are likely to be levelled against her own claims of epistemological liberation, or against any conclusions from her pen: her own views are too well known for people to confide in her; she is a woman; and she is deaf. But in fact, she explains, these apparent liabilities may be assets. An observer possessing her special qualities has a privileged access to truths that otherwise would be undiscoverable. Consider the "problem" of her reputation. Any outsider is kept at a distance: isn't it better that the basis of that distance be apparent from the start, to make honest conversation possible? Martineau found, for instance, that slave-owners were all the more anxious to explain their own views to a known opponent of slavery. By not visiting as a "spy," she penetrated the disguises of conventional manners, avoided the avoidances of polite talk. Her biases unveiled truths normally hidden from the supposedly neutral visitor. And Martineau insists that her gender functioned in much the same way:

> I have seen much more of domestic life than could possibly have been exhibited to any gentleman travelling through the country. The nursery, the boudoir, the kitchen, are all excellent schools in which to learn the morals and manners of a people: and, as for public and professional affairs,—those may always gain full information upon such matters, who really feel an interest in them,—be they men or women. (SA, i, xvi–xvii)

Her point, of course, is not just that men often fail to move beyond such "public and professional affairs," but that the world of official culture is deceptive or even propagandistic. Once again, the echo of her other book is revealing: *How to Observe: Morals and Manners.* What better place to get a clear glimpse of these facts than the home? Who has better understanding of the home than a woman?

Paradoxically, then, Martineau argues for a kind of subjective objectivity, an observation that gains access to the truth as a consequence of displaying openly its inescapably personal character. Thus her own most obvious handicap, which some might regard as a barrier to a full apprehension of reality, actually brings her closer to it. Her deafness, she explains, forces everyone she meets to address her with an intimacy and directness that cuts through the superficiality of polite conversation.

> I carry a trumpet of remarkable fidelity; an instrument, moreover, which seems to exert some winning power, by which I gain more in tete-a-tete than is given to people who hear general conversation. Probably its charm consists in the new feeling which it imparts of ease and privacy in conversing with a deaf person. However this may be, I can hardly imagine fuller revelations to be made in household intercourse than my trumpet brought to me. (*SA*, i, xvii–xviii)

It is important to notice the irony with which she refers to the traditionally separated spheres of masculine and feminine discourse: "general conversation . . . household intercourse." She admits that perhaps something is lost in her inability to attend to that "general conversation." Yet as that phrase suggests, what is lost is something diffuse, whereas the "philosophic" traveller (Martineau's term in *How to Observe*) seeks precise knowledge. The proximity created by a trumpet requires "fidelity" in the way she listens, an attention to detail that extends to her observation everywhere. Deafness, then, imposes on her a strict and inescapable adherence to induction, the method *How to Observe* urges all travellers to adopt.

From politics to personality, from injustice to induction—the first pages of *Society in America* have taken us a long way quickly, and the argument already has begun to turn back upon itself. If the observer is always in danger of being confused by flaws in her own vision, a fuller consciousness of self can lead to a fuller and more intimate contact with the real world. The paradox, which we will encounter again, may partly reflect self-centeredness, but it is also a sign of some of the most modern elements of Martineau's thought. The pursuit of truth in the American books follows a kind of hermeneutic circle, and we are never allowed to forget her presence as interpreter of the data from which she will draw conclusions. We are confronted with the relativity and contingency of truth, confronted with a problem of epistemology not so much because it is solved as because it is inevitable, recurring, to be acknowledged and grappled with perpetually. To read the American books and *How to Observe* in conjunction with one another is to understand that travel is always partly a metaphor for the search for an adequate epistemology. We must move far enough away from our normal cultural preconceptions to see things as they are; yet in travelling to a new world we encounter a reality that at least partly stands outside any analytic structures we have been prepared to impose in the past. That is why such a journey is attractive in the first place—it takes us to a new epistemological frontier. In America nothing can be taken for granted, Martineau explains; it is like being on another planet (*SA,* i, 209, 210). It is the situation described at almost the same time by John Stuart Mill in "Civilization," where it is also associated with an observer of contemporary American life: "'Il faut,' as M. de Tocqueville has said, 'une science politique nouvelle à un monde tout nouveau.'"[7]

What would it mean to construct a genuinely new, genuinely modern mode of observation and analysis? In addressing this question Martineau takes her place in a debate on method that extends from the 1830s until well past midcentury (at least through publication of the *Origin of Species* in 1859). At the center of the controversy is T. B. Macaulay's self-confident empiricism, represented especially in the 1837 *Edinburgh Review* essay on Bacon. That essay proposed a kind of inductive purism as the model for modern philosophy, or rather as a replacement for philosophy, since everything traditionally known by that name (associated above all with Plato) was misguided, irrelevant, and (to use the primary metaphor of the essay) fruitless. The claim was threatening for reasons we have already encountered in some of the conservative responses to Carlyle, for it implies the possibility of a value-free methodology, with no obligations except to the observable facts of a material world. Thus William Whewell, in his highly moralized *Philosophy of the Inductive Sciences,* argued that Bacon himself would have disputed this version of induction. All reasoning, Whewell insists, must begin somewhere; without clear first principles to help us interpret information gathered through the senses, "facts are collected in vain."[8] Mill was equally hostile, although from a very different political-moral position; objections to Macaulay's inductive model recur throughout his writing. His most overt rejoinder to "Lord Bacon" appears in the first sentence of the essay on Bentham (1838); it does not mention Macaulay by name, but it is clear enough what sort of mind is being attacked. "Speculative philosophy, which to the superficial appears a thing so remote from the business of life and the outward interests of men, is in reality the thing on earth which most influences them."[9] Speculation also requires (as Mill objected in his review of *The French Revolution*) that one begin with principles, hypotheses that can be tested in reality; one cannot gather facts in a vacuum. Martineau's position is similar. Induction cannot be divorced from principles—especially if we are to move beyond merely "superficial" insights, to produce arguments of real value to the real world. "A traveller may do better without eyes, or without ears, than without such principles" (*HO,* 15). The reference to her own handicap is not accidental. In part she proposes an abstract method, combining induction and deduction (much like what Mill, following Comte, termed the "inverse deductive method).[10] But the method is constructed around an image of herself.

Martineau's conspicuous presence in her studies of America may reveal (as critics argued) egotism, but it also reveals a more general analytic procedure. There is a joint commitment to detailed observation and philosophic reflection, and this produces a focus shifting between specifics and generalities, invariably returning to the figure of the author herself. She certainly is the most lively character in her own narrative: visiting twenty-three states, entering homes from very different social and economic classes, speaking with notables and ordinary people; all of this is narrated specifically and at length. We see her fording rivers and riding mules, testing the hardness of hickory by chopping wood, demonstrating her educational theories about the transmission of sound by placing music boxes on the heads of deaf children. She delights in the variety of the American landscape and visits the most extraordinary natural sites; she is thrilled with the opportunity for thrills—only regretting that after so many months she never arranged a ride on a flatboat (*SA*, ii, 200). And Martineau illustrates the character of the new nation in telling details: the pig driver wearing spectacles, the factory child with its umbrella (*SA*, i, 16; ii, 246). She concludes, in fact, that there is an unusually "strong predilection for Umbrellas in the United States" that even burglars share. One convict explains that he returned to a house he had robbed in order to carry away an umbrella that later led to his identification and capture: "What English burglar," she quips, "would have thought of minding rain?" (*SA*, ii, 247). From these details Martineau shifts to discussions of institutions of all sorts and at all levels: marriage and money, infants and immigrants, religion and recreation (to name a few of the general issues that interest her). Her greatest disappointments concern moral conditions: the provinciality of intellectual life in the West, the fever of speculation in Chicago, the pressure of public opinion, the continuing subjugation of women and slaves. Her greatest enthusiasm (aside from her love of landscape) is reserved for those who share her political sympathies, above all the Abolitionists, "the clear-eyed and fiery-hearted few who began and are achieving the virtuous revolution" (*SA*, ii, 170). As this language suggests, the narrative of experience invariably leads back to a narrative of ideas.

This movement is part of the philosophical structure of her argument: particular observations never should be separated from broader questions, especially questions of social justice. The first of the Philosophic Requisites for the ideal traveller in *How to Observe* is the commitment to return to such questions: to recognize that the only measure of social conditions is their effect on "the general happiness of the section of the race among whom they exist" (*HO,* 13). All theory, and all material evidence, must be tested by a human standard. In America this means that the ideal of republican justice must be compared to the actual experience of the citizens of the country, especially those who seem to benefit from it least. Thus Martineau turns again and again to the group she calls (in one of the final chapters of *Society in America*) "Sufferers." It is the most important subject of all her American writing, the one by which all the rest of her observations is judged. Sufferers: the word refers to all the members of a varied underclass, all those who are excluded (*de jure* or *de facto*) from the normal rights and privileges of citizenship; the class includes women and slaves, prisoners and those confined in various other official institutions. Sufferers are the victims of state power, and their condition reveals something essential about the nature of that power and the true moral status of the nation that wields it. The issue, then, has intrinsic epistemological significance. Sufferers are the mirror of a nation, for the character of any society can be measured most precisely by an analysis of those it excludes, and of how those exclusions are made. Martineau anticipates the Marxist sense of the constitutive function served by the creation of marginal classes, although it is her admitted object to undermine that marginalization and reconstitute the society she examines on a juster basis. As she comments in reference to the political and social status of women (who, along with slaves, are for her the most important members of this class of victims), "No test of civilization can be so sure as the condition of that half of society over which the other half has power" (*SA,* iii, 105).

Yet as we move into Martineau's chapters on the American underclasses, an odd contradiction appears. Her books, and her journey, are directed above all towards an examination of slavery, the ultimate "test" of justice in the New World. Almost inexplicably, she seems to fear this test, or the most extreme form she is likely to encounter. The climax of her visit seems destined to occur with what the *Retrospect* terms the "First Sight of Slavery." But she confesses to having experienced increasing uneasiness about how that sight would be met, how slavery would be sighted, how observation will live up to her expectations. The admission is surprising in light of her courageous behavior in similar or even more threatening situations. She never conceals her anti-slavery views; after all, these were known before her arrival through *Demerara,* the anti-slavery fable in the *Illustrations of Political Economy* (published starting in 1834). And she helps keep that reputation alive by announcing her convictions everywhere, even in the homes of slave-owners in the deep South. The *Retrospect* tells how, after making her views well-known to her fellow passengers on the voyage from England, Martineau was discouraged by the ship's captain from landing in New York, the scene of recent antiabolitionist riots. But she showed no signs of faint-heartedness and was allowed to disembark after reassuring the captain that she had come to America "to learn and not to teach."[11] This was not the complete truth, of course. But why would anyone so eager to face such risks claim to have "dreaded inexpressibly the first sight of a slave"?

The *Retrospect* identifies one source of her anxiety: she fears that the brutality of slavery might prove too overwhelming to bear. But there is no admission of similar hesitations before visiting prisoners or the sick. She comments elsewhere that she had looked forward to this "first sight" as a "time of awakening" (*R*, i, 139). It is as if she begins to wonder what sort of awakening it will be. There are hints that she is less fearful of horror than of insufficient indignation on her part, even a weakening of moral convictions if the reality should be less dramatic than her expectations. The basis for that concern is suggested in her remarks on arriving in Baltimore, the first slave city she visited:

> I dreaded inexpressibly the first sight of a slave, and could not help speculating on the lot of every person of colour I saw from the windows on the first few days. The servants in the house where I was were free blacks. (*R*, i, 140).

Apparently some blacks are taken for granted, since they provide the daily comforts of her visit. Or does she mention those servants here to deny that she has taken them for granted, to prove that she only accepts their services in the knowledge that they are free? As a genteel visitor, waited on by some sort of servant wherever she goes, and some sort of black servant wherever she goes in the South, she is in danger of being implicated in the institution of slavery unintentionally, or against her will. No wonder Martineau is uneasy and inconsistent. How long will she be able to avoid direct contact with slaves, accepting or demanding their services? Is it possible to enter a slave society and remain neutral, a mere observer? If not, what are the consequences? The hero of *Demerara,* an English abolitionist named Alfred, admits a similar concern. He may not be able to live in a slave society and maintain his ideals: "the very sight of slavery is corrupting, he declares."[12] Of course, Alfred does survive this "test," and remains a reformer. But *Demerara* is fiction.

Reality turns out to be far less dramatic. Martineau discovers that the "first sight" already had taken place without her being aware of it at the time. A New England woman she meets in Baltimore explains:

I told her I dreaded seeing a slave. "You have seen one," said she. "You were waited on by a slave yesterday evening." She told me of a gentleman who let out and lent his slaves to wait at gentlemen's houses, and that the tall handsome mulatto who handed the tea at a party the evening before was one of these. I was glad it was over for once; but I never lost the painful feeling caused to a stranger by intercourse with slaves. No familiarity with them, no mirth and contentment on their part, ever soothed the miserable restlessness caused by the presence of a deeply-injured fellow-being. No wonder or ridicule on the spot avails anything to the stranger. He suffers, and must suffer from this, deeply and long, as surely as he is human and hates oppression. (*R,* i, 141–2).

Of course, there had been, no "painful feeling" at the first encounter, nor could there have been, since she didn't know the encounter was taking place; it is not necessarily possible for a stranger, even a philosophical traveller, to recognize slavery when she sees it. Martineau is adding a corollary to the arguments of *How to Observe* and almost totally inverting those of *Demerara:* "To see slaves," she remarks a page after this passage, "is not to be reconciled to slavery" (*R,* i, 142), The "sight" of slavery is not necessarily corrupting—because to a mind grounded in the right principles no sight ever is, or can be. The real issue is not seeing but understanding, interpreting. To put this another way, the philosophic traveller possesses the knack of not seeing certain things as well as the knack of seeing others. Martineau's initial ignorance was oddly appropriate, or even prescient.

What, finally, is the significance of this "first sight of slavery"? In part to remind us of the contingency of all sight, the limits of visible evidence as such. The experience took place in a marginal situation, existing somewhere in a shadowy middle ground between slavery and ordinary household service; the slave in question was either "let out" or "lent," and we never learn which; he is himself a "tall handsome mulatto," between distinct racial types. Precisely who or what *is* he? What does he "illustrate"? We never are told for certain, nor is it necessary that we should be. Facts by themselves are ambiguous. There are even certain situations in which they must be ignored. Martineau makes it clear that no observer should place any confidence in the testimony to the humaneness of the slave system given by slaves in the presence of their masters; "no mirth and contentment" of slaves should be regarded as evidence at all. For the "philosophic observer," then, philosophy is more important than observation, if and when he must make a choice. She had objected to the writings of Basil Hall and Mrs. Trollope (*Travels in North America,* 1829, and *Domestic Manners of the Americans,* 1832, respectively) for losing sight of principles in a welter of detail. Her own American books not only treat all details in terms of principles, they recognize only those details that can be so treated. The task of philosophic observation is learning to see *as* (to use a phrase from modern epistemology), learning that there never can be a "first sight" by an innocent or unsuspecting eye uncolored by the assumptions of the observer. All appearances, all "sights," are subordinate to general truths; perceptions that potentially could conflict with or modify those principles are simply screened out.

This incident also helps explain why Martineau does not choose to describe her American travels more journalistically, in the form of a diary organized chronologically or according to her route. Both of the American books are conceived in the form which is named in the title of the second one: a "Retrospect," a reassessment in the light of mature reflection. These are books of memory, in which the presentness of particular occurrences is less important than their aptness as illustrations of larger questions. Illustrations: the term recalls the *Illustrations of Political Economy,* where a not-very-convincing fiction is mustered in support of fundamental issues of social and economic theory; the method of *Deerbrook* is very much the same, in spite of her own claims for the novel's realism (made in the *Autobiography*). The *Quarterly* had ridiculed the *Illustrations* in 1833 for its succession of "dull didactic dialogues."[13] The same moralizing tendencies make the American books read more like fables than accounts of an actual visit, transforming many of the people encountered into dramatic (or melodramatic) types.

This didacticism is most evident in the accounts of those "sufferers." They stand at the center of her political and moral arguments, so perhaps this should not surprise us. Yet the purpose of the American books is to acknowledge their claims to humanity and equal treatment—to recognize them, to allow them to speak in their own voices. And that is precisely what Martineau's retrospective technique does not allow. Sufferers are not so much known as invented for ideological purposes, reconstituted by Martineau into figures of her own imagination.

A fine slave was walking about in Columbia, South Carolina, when I was there, nearly helpless from the following causes. His master was fond of him, and the slave enjoyed the rare distinction of never having been flogged. One day, his master's child, supposed to be under his care at the time, fell down and hurt itself. The master flew into a passion, ordered the slave to be instantly flogged, and would not hear a single word the man had to say. As soon as the flogging was over, the slave went into the back yard, where there was an axe and a block, and struck off the upper half of his right hand. He went and held up the bleeding hand before his master, saying, "You have mortified me, so I have made myself useless. Now you must maintain me as long as I live." It came out that the child had been under the charge of another person. (*SA*, ii, 321).

That final, unnecessary sentence typifies her method. The enormity of the crime would not have been diminished if the slave actually had been taking care of the injured child. But Martineau must keep her moral contrasts stark.

Equally important, she must give every incident a voice, and one familiar to an intelligent English audience. It is not enough for the accumulated details spread over a book, or even a chapter, to supply evidence for her views: each event must articulate a clear and present moral: suffering must be linked to eloquence. Hence that slave-owner is left speechless, so passionate that he "would not hear a single word the man had to say"—in effect, beyond reason, beyond words; his slave, correspondingly, is represented as speaking with a weighty and articulate formality. Does Martineau fear that colloquial speech would distract us from the point, or even undermine it? The preface to *Demerara* explains that slave dialects have been "normalized" because of her own distaste for idiomatic, ungrammatical speech: "Their jargon would be intolerable to writer and readers, if carried through a volume."[14] Lest this be dismissed as racist censorship, I should add that she makes the same adjustments in the language of most of the sufferers she represents. The most dangerous convict at the Weathersfield Prison eloquently bursts into tears when the humane warden gives him a key that would allow him to carry out a secret plan to escape. "Sir. . . . I have been a very devil these seventeen years; but you treat me like a man" (*R*, i, 126). Obviously, he chooses to serve out his sentence. But he is being "sentenced" by Martineau as well, who distances his identity as a real person in the melodramatic language she uses to "represent" him as a literary creation. The American books become most unsettling when they reveal this same distancing representation—or misrepresentation—passing out of narration into actual experience. For Martineau is writing about people she actually met, proposing analyses of their conditions she proposed in reality, recommending solutions she was prepared to introduce on the spot. She did not simply visit America to observe. She carried principles with her and urged others to adopt (or impose) them, even if doing so made heavy demands on her "subjects." In schools for the deaf and blind, for instance, Martineau quickly drops the premise of surveying conditions impartially in order to expound her own educational theories; in one case her "realism" about the condition of a deaf child requires her to disabuse its mother of any hope for great intellectual improvement ("The mother laid her hand on mine, and thanked me for pleading the cause of the depressed against those who expected too much from them" *R,* ii, 130–131).

The certainty with which Martineau imposes her own views is most apparent in her visits to prisons; and it is important to recognize that it is the prisons themselves rather than the prisoners alone, the sufferers within them, that interest her. Even more than in schools for the deaf, she is in her element visiting prisons—in her element as a deaf person, in fact. For the most important feature of American prisons, especially those in Pennsylvania and New York, was the "silent system" that had made them models of modern reforming principles. They stressed moral improvement rather than the physical punishment of prisoners: the first penitentiaries, in the precise sense of that word. Silence, and the total isolation of prisoners from each other, was imposed to focus the attention of the inmates on a process of self-examination and self-transformation. David Rothman has pointed out that this made Pennsylvania prisons world-famous by the 1830s. Travellers like Martineau, Basil Hall, or Captain Marryat "would no more have omitted this stop from their itinerary than they would have a southern plantation, a Lowell textile mill, or a frontier town."[15] This is not to deny that there is something impressive in Martineau's visit: how many other women would have done as much? how many deaf persons of either sex? *How to Observe* urges travellers to visit prisons as a way of moving beyond the experience of a single class. Yet there also must have been a kind of genteel thrill associated with such touring, even if Martineau does not behave like those proper eighteenth-century visitors to madhouses Michel Foucault and Max Byrd have described.[16] And there is another contradiction implicit in her visits. Conversation with prisoners may, as Martineau claims, reveal the way society constitutes itself through exclusions and punishments. But at the same time the visitor, the tourist on this brief excursion across the boundaries of civil society, may help legitimize those borders and exclusions, perhaps by the very act of treating prisoners as objects of study. Observation, even when intended to bridge the gap of otherness, may help widen it.

There was considerable debate in the 1830s over the effects and value of solitary confinement: would it, for instance, drive prisoners mad? Martineau acknowledges the problem but endorses the Pennsylvania system strongly. A less strict alternative, the combination of solitary sleeping facilities and common workrooms she found in New York pentitentiaries, is, she concludes, both unhealthy and inconsistent: prisoners not only exchange germs, they share one another's moral infection as well; even innocent conversation must be conducted with the guilty awareness that it is in violation of the rules, so that all prisoners inevitably must continue to break the law during their confinement. Prisoners in Philadelphia are exposed to no such temptations, and the benefits are obvious. They look healthier than any other convicts she has seen on her travels; a number even commend the superiority of their present treatment to what they have experienced in other kinds of jails. But the mental and moral health of prisoners is the crucial issue, and this evokes her warmest enthusiasm. The solitary rule promotes genuine improvement. Contacts with others are limited to approved visitors, like Martineau herself, and they are required to limit conversation to the state of the prisoners' minds. Theoretically, no prisoner is aware of any other, or of events in his own family or anywhere else in the outside world. He becomes exclusively a moral being—moral, that is, in terms defined by his keepers and the State.

Throughout the American books Martineau urges her readers to acknowledge the humanity of the sufferers in their midst, to look beneath socially imposed masks of otherness. She explains in the *Retrospect* that this is the standard by which she judges the solitary system. "The first principle in the management of the guilty seems to me to be to treat them as men and women. . . . Their humanity is the principal thing about them; their guilt is a temporary state" (*R*, i, 125). Yet here she endorses another sort of treatment, one that redefines the identities of the people being observed, imposing new categories of being upon them from the outside; in a sense, it is a way of dividing them within and against themselves. "The greatest advantage of solitary confinement," she notes, "is that it presents the best part of a prisoner's mind to be acted upon by his guardians" (*R*, i, 127). Humanity is acknowledged only in certain carefully controlled contexts—that "best self" is defined for the prisoner. Michel Foucault argues in *Discipline and Punish* that the solitary system, especially when enforced as thoroughly as it was in Pennsylvania, supports a structure of surveillance designed to impose uniformity externally and internally. The isolation of prisoners is an invasion and manipulation of identity: even the privacy of the self is subjugated to official inspection and control—is, indeed, its ultimate object.[17] It is curious, and chilling, that a social commentator as suspicious of institutions and authority as Martineau not only approves but enters into this system. Enters literally: for by visiting prisoners and conversing on approved topics, she becomes an agent in this process. It is a dehumanizing process, too, although conducted in the name of humanity. And her participation seems all the more ironic because she comes close to recognizing this contradiction.

Martineau remarks on how often the theories of prison officials are echoed by prisoners. The convicts she interviews are not merely docile but well-schooled, and she comments on the similarities in their responses. The claim that solitary confinement preserves the individual's self-respect is repeated with particular frequency. Furthermore, each of the "prisoners, (none of them being aware of the existence of any other), told me that he was under obligations to those who had charge of him for treating him 'with respect.' The expression struck me much as being universally used by them" (*SA*, iii, 181). But she does not inquire where or how it might have been learned. Nor does she consider how her own presence might have evoked it (even though she had raised precisely this question about slaves interrogated in the presence of their masters, or by any whites): what the implications of her visit might have been for the prisoners she spoke with, or how they might have understood her relation to themselves. She recognizes their readiness to supply desired "cant" responses to religious visitors without perceiving that her own questions imply their own set of "correct" answers. "Sooner or later," she explains "they told me their stories in full: and I found that in every case some domestic misery had been the poison of their lives. . . . The stories, infinitely varied in their circumstances, were all alike in their moral" (*SA*, iii, 185). It is not simply that the prisoners are performing here, but that Martineau herself plays a part in the drama. She allows herself to become an official observer, to fill an assigned role (besides those melodramatic prisoners) in the theater of penitentiary life. Apparently the spectacle of silent moral reform is too appealing for her to achieve any detachment. And her engagement in this setting may reveal something of the fundamental character of her behavior elsewhere, a basic element of the role of philosophic observer in a New World.

Martineau began *Society in America* with a frank admission of her handicaps, and a suggestion that these may have proved to be advantages in helping her observe more clearly; by the end of the books she makes larger claims, in a far less humble tone. In a sense, her own limitations become models, for individuals, for America, and even for the world. For she ends by imagining America as it ought to be, its revolution fulfilled, America as the beginning of a New World everywhere. But it is a New World of the imagination, based not on an America she saw but on the one she projected from her own philosophic models. It is oddly close, in fact, to the image of herself she presents at the beginning of *Society in America,* and no less oddly close to the one that emerges from her enthusiastic account of American prisons: a world of close conversation and silent, self-conscious reflection. It is not a prison she has in mind, of course, but a society governed by definite principles, freed from the materialism and conformist pressures that already marked the United States in the 1830s. It is a world of self-conscious thought and observation. Like Tocqueville, who had made his visit a few years before her, she is concerned about the effects of a mass democracy, above all about the loss of inwardness that seems to occur in the most apparently flourishing American communities. A crowded New England factory town, for instance, atrophies even the "inclination" for solitude, "that need of it which every healthy mind must feel, in a greater or less degree." "Man's own silent thoughts," she adds, "are his best safeguard and highest privilege." If we are to have any hope for the future, the "innocent and industrious youth of a new country" must not be deprived of the benefits of quiet isolation (*SA*, ii, 258–359). The headnote to the chapter on prisons in the *Retrospect of Western Travel* cites *Sartor Resartus* on the restorative effects of "silence and secrecy." "Do thyself but hold thy tongue for one day; on the morrow how much clearer are thy purposes and duties!" America has much to learn from England, it seems, and much to learn from Martineau herself. The final volume of *Society in America* warns that the country may become paralyzed by that "low state of civilization which presupposes specified outward aims, and relies with such confidence on the mechanical means of attaining them" (*SA*, iii, 4). Yet at the same time we see traces of her own mechanical formulas for improvement. Although she made this journey to discover new truths about political theory and practice, it has in a sense brought her back to an image of herself projected onto the American landscape—not so much philosophic observation as a kind of poetry.

How to Observe is divided into two parts: "How to Observe" and "What to Observe." It is as if the philosophic traveller is not to be given too much freedom in the choice of subjects. Perhaps Martineau herself had begun to frame both the form and contents of her observations before she set foot on American soil. Benjamin Disraeli, reviewing *Society in America* for the *Times* in 1837 (and thus without the benefit of the account of its writing in the *Autobiography*) comes to much the same conclusion. She describes morals, he complains, "not as they appear to her or to any other chance speculator, but as they ought to figure according to the principles which she imbibed before her visit, and the crude meditation of which probably amused her outward voyage."[18] R. K. Webb, Martineau's best modern biographer, notes the extraordinary perspicacity of the remark: Disraeli had "hit on the core of her intellectual method." Martineau, Webb concludes, was "not really interested in America at all. She was interested in certain abstract propositions which America could prove."[19] But still this is only half of the truth, even if we grant Martineau's tendency to search for confirmation of her own theories and personal ideals. For to some extent this could be done only in a New World, a place unknown and uncertain enough to give full reign to her idealism, to allow the philosophic observer to hold fast to principles while also seeing. She travelled to find a land of possibility; where else could one imagine the eventual unification of theory and practice? Early in the final volume of *Society in America* Martineau compares the united states to a caterpillar in the midst of a mysterious but beautiful metamorphosis. Then the metaphor shifts as she suggests what the change might lead to, "when the idea, which now burns like a taper in scattered minds shall have caught, and spread and lighted up all into an illumination sufficient to do the work by" (*SA,* iii, 53). The changing image suggests the changing terms of her epistemology: from observation to illumination, from science to a kind of Shelleyan vision capable of changing the world. In the end, we might say, the philosophic traveller sees things according to her own lights. It is the poetic rather than the empirical traveller who has learned best how to observe.

II

Travel books can be of several kinds. Some accounts move through the various stages of a journey, narrating chronologically or place-by-place. Others proceed according to a logic of the things seen or considered—mental travels, to paraphrase Blake. Martineau's books, of the second sort, are organized around the main institutions and issues she encountered in America and the principles she found illustrated there; yet even there we are aware of the traveller as protagonist, aware that travel produces her socio-philosophical meditations. But there are works even closer to the margins of this genre, in which travel is a central but nevertheless only an implicit activity, in which the traveller seems to vanish beside the things being observed. Seems to vanish: this impersonality, I am suggesting, can be an illusion, as can the impersonality of the language with which such a surreptitious travel book represents the world encountered by this invisible observer. It is worth paying close attention, then, to arguments that clothe what we take to be personal responses in deliberately neutral language, that invite us to accompany them into matters of feeling with the assurance that everything will be reduced to the certainty of science. Such science, such impersonality, such certainty, often conceals something very different.

J. C. Loudon's *Architectural Magazine,* which began publication in 1834, refers on the opening page of its opening issue to the "science of architecture," and the phrase recurs in the first sentence of a series of essays that appear in the journal between 1837 and 1838 under the name of *"Kata Phusin."* Yet science, as we will see, is an extremely ambiguous word in these essays, especially in connection with the views of architecture they propose. For the author turns out to be John Ruskin, still an Oxford undergraduate; these essays constitute his first book-length publication and in many ways anticipate the concerns of his later and more famous works. Already for Ruskin architecture refers to appearance as well as structure, to the suggestions of buildings as well as their shapes; the study of construction is also in part a study of morals, but morals that can be seen in substantial form. Once again the underlying subject is how to observe. And if there are scientific possibilities in such a project, they are subject to many of the tensions visible in Martineau's search for a modern epistemology. We can sense this from the very title of the series: *The Poetry of Architecture.* Evidently mere science (mere prosaic science, we might say) is not enough. The opening paragraph elaborates on this distinction, and on the meaning of Ruskin's title, at some length:

> The Science of Architecture, followed out to its full extent, is one of the noblest of those which have reference only to the creations of human minds. It is not merely a science of the rule and compass, it does not consist only in the observation of just rule, or of fair proportion: it is, or ought to be, a science of feeling more than of rule, a ministry to the mind, more than to the eye. If we consider how much less the beauty and majesty of a building depend upon its pleasing certain prejudices of the eye, than upon its rousing certain trains of meditation in the mind, it will show in a moment how many intricate questions of feeling are involved in the raising of an edifice; it will convince us of the truth of a proposition, which might at first have appeared startling, that no man can be an architect, who is not a metaphysician.[20]

From architecture to poetry, from science to metaphysics: the peculiarity of the argument is not a function of any of the terms in themselves but of the way Ruskin links them together, as if they mean one and the same thing—or as if they might, for the right observer. The passage moves from architecture as such to the "intricate questions of feeling" required to understand it, from buildings to the minds of those who study them. It is clear from the start, in other words, that Ruskin has his own special kind of philosophic observer in mind, his own special kind of traveller, and that the way such a person regards architecture has a great deal to do with its—and thus his —"nobility."

I mean to emphasize the social connotations of that last word. The initial paragraph moves us rapidly from science to metaphysics and implies an equally swift connection between construction and class. Poetry requires readers. Architecture, in this high Ruskinian sense, is defined in relation to a viewing audience, the right kind of audience; this is how travel first finds its way into the argument. Soon Ruskin's poetic prose will carry us on a literary journey among various examples of greater and lesser architectural achievements; Elizabeth Helsinger terms it an extended exercise in "excursive sight."[21] But we must not forget the social condition such a perceptual grand tour implies. Ruskin writes for a genteel tourist, who requires both the leisure and the capital to sustain his researches; it even may turn out that those researches offer ways to increase that capital, if only in the form of poetic gems. To some extent, any collection of touristic views implies such a process of appropriation; even cameras, as Susan Sontag has pointed out, enable us to "take" pictures.[22] This acquisitiveness is all the more prominent in the tradition of picturesque view-hunting, in which a living world is reduced to a series of portable, dead scenes. Ruskin later would attack this practice in the final volume of *Modern Painters,* and some of his vehemence may derive (as John Rosenberg has observed) from the fact that much of his early writing engages in the same excesses.[23] *The Poetry of Architecture* in particular is studded with brilliant passages of poetic prose in which rhetorical elegance seems more important than descriptive accuracy. And it is not simply the lack of specificity that is at fault in these purple patches. The elegance of this early Ruskinian picturesque depends upon the operation of a special kind of social myth, which distances and effectively dehumanizes its subject. We are, after all, seeing buildings by themselves; their charm derives partly from the absence of human figures. Yet this way of seeing also makes it possible to imagine a special sort of human activity, a set of ideal relationships—a mythology—against which the picturesque beauty of any architectural site must be measured. The poetry of architecture is also a poetry of social relations, a poetry of class.

We can observe these assumptions in the first description of a specific building, an English lowland cottage. Ruskin stresses its "finished neatness." The thatch is pegged down firmly, the whitewash is stainless, and "the luxuriant rose is trained gracefully over the window." A glance among the sweetbriar leaves reveals a diamond-latticed window opened to admit the breeze "that, as it passes over the flowers, becomes full of their fragrance."

> A few square feet of garden, and a latched wicket, persuading the weary and dusty pedestrian, with expressive eloquence, to lean upon it for an instant, and request a drink of water or milk, complete a picture, which, if it be far enough from London to be unspoiled by town sophistications, is a very perfect thing in its way. The ideas it awakens are agreeable, and the architecture is all that we want in such a situation. It is pretty and appropriate; and if it boasted of any other perfection, it would be at the expense of its propriety. (12)

Ruskin is speaking in a class idiom[24] that appropriates the visual details of a particular setting in the service of a traditional social myth. The charm, the neatness, above all the drink of milk suggest a harmonious feudal world. The "picture" is completed, according to Ruskin, only when we imagine the viewer incorporated into it, receiving both refreshment and reassurance that his presence is normal and welcome.

The contemporary vogue for such images is suggested by the popularity of two paintings by William Collins, *Rustic Civility* (1832) and *Cottage Hospitality* (1834), the latter of which depicts a child taking broth to a poor traveller.[25] Ruskin's essay on Swiss mountain cottages refers to an even older tradition, inviting us to indulge in "Sweet ideas . . . of such passages of peasant life as the gentle Walton so loved; of the full milkpail, and the mantling cream-bowl" (38). It is difficult not to love such pictures, unless one happens to be a peasant. Picturesque translates the real life of the countryside into the formal structure of pastoral, idealizing class relations to disguise the tensions of actual experience. No wonder Ruskin closes the paragraph by acknowledging that these objects and this scene might take other less satisfying forms. The perfection of the picture could be spoiled by London sophistications; further improvements would only lessen its propriety. This means, in part, that the scene (to be a scene) must remain fixed as it is, and the clearest threat to such fixity comes from the real, varied, changing world of the city. A perfect cottage is picturesque only insofar as it exists apart from history, subtly persuading the spectator that he can view the world and himself outside any specific social context.

The Ruskinian traveller, then, is conducted on a journey towards a new vision of the world. Learning how to observe architecture is a disguised lesson in how to observe people, or how not to. We hear very little about the inhabitants of cottages in these essays, or, when we hear of them, it is with reference to their "ideal character" rather than their actual conditions of life. When the discussion of lowland Italian cottages forces Ruskin to confront the question of poverty, he at first dismisses, then excuses, and finally praises the architectural dilapidation that is its external sign. After all, we are told, "the filthy habits of the Italian prevent him from suffering from the state to which he is reduced." If this creates "a picture which, seen too near, is sometimes revolting to the eye, always melancholy to the mind . . . even this many would not wish to be otherwise." For the observer, the tokens of human misery comprise of a moral tableau, an instructive spectacle of mortality:

> Who would substitute the rush of a new nation, the struggle of an awakening power, for the dreamy sleep of Italy's desolation, for her sweet silence of melancholy thought, her twilight time of everlasting memories? (28)

That last question is better left unanswered; certainly Ruskin's British reader feels no need to answer it. No change is needed, or possible. To the practiced eye of this genteel spectator, poverty will seem as permanent, as inevitable, and perhaps even as moving, as the landscape itself. Martineau's philosophic observer learns to discern injustice, the discrepancy between theory and practice, and the fundamental failings in things as they are. Ruskin's architectural tourist recomposes those flaws into a lofty, complacent poetry, which naturalizes broken lives as effortlessly as broken buildings.

The subtitle of these essays promises to treat "The Architecture of the Nations of Europe Considered in its Association with Natural Scenery and National Character." It could be taken as the subtitle for most of Ruskin's later socio-architectural writings, yet the examination of these terms in 1837–1838 has little of the complexity or critical sophistication of *The Stones of Venice,* fifteen years later. Ruskin is not prepared to stand apart from and criticize the institutions of his own society; this is probably what he had in mind in writing later that the essays are "deformed by assumption."[26] Yet in another sense the problem is that he stands too far outside, not so much outside his society as outside all human relations, ignoring them as if they did not exist. Architecture is integrated into a dead landscape, unmoving and uninhabited by anyone except the spectator and the occasional figure of a statuesque peasant, who helps compose the countryside into a picture. The most beautiful places Ruskin describes are distinguished by the nearly total absence of any signs of human activity. In Italy, for instance,

> the pale cities, temple and tower, lie gleaming along the champaign; but how calmly! no hum of men; no motion of multitude in the midst of them: they are voiceless as the city of ashes. (19–20)

Italy becomes "but one wide supulchre, and all her present life is like a shadow or a memory" (19). Ruskin teaches his ideal traveller to observe the world not just through but as architecture, to superimpose a vision of aesthetic order on all the conditions of individual and social life.

This explains why the project begins with cottages. Rural poverty is the chief obstacle in sustaining such a vision. We must learn how to see it, or how not to. In the English countryside, where some might see nothing but hovels, the Ruskinian traveller finds "humility and gentleness" (52). Cottage architecture is "as peaceful as silence itself"(12). Poverty will not intrude into this picture either, once we have learned to see its Ruskinian poetry. The cottage represents an architecture, and a social class, that is happy in its place and keeps its distance, respectfully: "it can never lie too humbly in the pastures of the valley, nor shrink too submissively into the hollows of the hills" (44). Architecture and nature are enlisted together to reassert the ideology of traditional pastoral, to create poetry out of the prosiac realities of cottage life.

Such pastoralism took on a new importance in England in the years following passage of the Reform Bill, but it was not always introduced uncritically. Another book of 1838, William Howitt's *The Rural Life of England,* simultaneously invokes and criticizes this myth: the illustrations (Figure 5.1) show both poverty and the picturesque; the prose warns us not to let pastoral beauty distract us from the actualities of cottage life:

> I say, let every man gratefully rejoice, who has the means of commanding the full blessings of English life,—for alas! there are thousands and millions of our countrymen who possess but a scanty portion of these; whose lives are too long and continuous a course of toil and anxiety to permit them even to look round them and see how vast are the powers of enjoyment in this country, and how few of those sources of ease, comfort, and refined pleasure are within their reach.

"Reflect," he adds, "poetical as our poets have made the shepherd and his life,—what must be the monotony of that life in lowland counties—day after day, and month after month, and year after year." The comments could be written directly in response to Ruskin. Howitt's chapter on cottage life conducts us on an anti-picturesque tour to a Highland hut, isolated amid "patches of cultivation" that produce little food for the inhabitants or their animals. The house itself is cramped, cold, dark, and smokey, crowded with animals and people, who "are fixing their eyes on the stranger." And Howitt makes the identity of that visitor far clearer than Ruskin ever does, describing how in 1836 he and his wife "passed the night in such a dwelling." They were reluctant visitors, only asking for shelter when it was discovered that the nearest inn was miles away. Nor did the peasants respond in the genteel-pastoral fashion described in Ruskin's prose: "What shall I do for the like of you? What shall I find for the like of you?" When oatmeal cakes and tea are provided for a meagre supper, the woman adds the obvious social commentary: "'There was,' said our hostess, 'a great cry in the country for food.'" "Ah cottage life!" Howitt exclaims later: "There is much more hidden under that name than ever inspired the wish to build *cottages ornées,* or to inhabit them."[27]

The *Westminster Review* applauded both "the appearance and success" of such books "as proving the increase of humanizing pursuits, which must spread downwards, from the hall of the squire to the cottage of the hind."[28] Such humanizing had to spread upwards, too, if a monied class was to discover social reality hidden behind its favorite mythologies. That is what makes Ruskin's so remarkable a text: the signs that a more complex vision of things is developing from within Ruskin's genteel complacency. There is no evidence that he actually read Howitt in 1838, yet some of the humanizing tendencies of *The Rural Life of England* begin to find their way into *The Poetry of Architecture.* Howitt's popular sympathies are to some extent a function of a traditional genteel outlook which can afford to gaze humanely on those of lower ranks. "Is it not in these noble ancestral houses, amid their ancestral woods and lands," he asks rhetorically, "that the spirit of our gentry is most likely to acquire its right tone?"[29] Ruskin also engages in the most traditional form of self-criticism by the wealthy, raising the classical question of the proper use of riches. But he is also beginning to subject the platitudes of *noblesse oblige* to scrutiny. His poetic descriptions of cottages display signs of strain, as if the pastoral myth has been stretched too thin. In the second half of his essays, as he shifts focus from cottages to villas, strains are even more apparent, as if he senses for the first time what his subject really involves.[30]

Ruskin's critical task begins in the definition of the villa itself—"the ruralized domicile of the gentleman" (74)—or rather in the ambiguities of that phrase. "Ruralized" suggests the artifice of naturalness consequent on the attempt of an urban patron to construct an appropriate country seat. It is a "domicile" (as distinguished from the "rural dwelling of the peasant"), a term that in legal usage refers to the mobility of its owner; the *Oxford English Dictionary* describes it as "the place where one has his home or permanent residence, to which, it absent, he has the intention of returning." One might argue that this is the country residence of the cultured traveller whose cottage contemplation was the subject of the first group of essays. But the possibility of absence implies not only travel but absenteeism, so that the very existence of this domicile determines some of the most essential conditions of the lives of those who are left behind. It is a holiday home, to which the mobile, middle-class villa-builder retreats from "the business of his life" (76). And as such a remark suggests, this gentleman is himself a divided being, occupying different roles as well as different homes. Ruskin's strictures on villa architecture become a vehicle for examining the contradictions between those roles.

The most fundamental contradiction is rooted in the mythology of the villa itself, in the claim that there can be a structure associated only with leisure and recreation, that it is possible to build a house uncontaminated by any associations with work. To some extent Ruskin is referring to this ideal only to defend it from abuse (and exposure) by a tasteless *nouveau riche*. The last essay ends citing Juvenal and Moliere's *Bourgeois Gentil-homme,* and chides those "who are setting all English feeling and all nat-ural principles at defiance" (187–188). But Ruskin is addressing a larger issue. If a villa is intended to be associated with leisure, how can it be built at all—built, that is, without reminding us of the physical labor it is some-how supposed to transcend? It is almost as if he is trying to imagine an idealized dwelling in a prelapsarian world, "where it has committed no injury" (162), where idleness can be universal and wholly natural. That is what he depicts in his illustrations of such buildings as the Villa Serbelloni, on Lake Como (Figure 5.2): "although the eye falls suddenly from the crags above to the promontory below, yet all the sublime and severe features of the scene are kept in the distance, and the villa itself is mingled with grace-ful lines, and embosomed in rich vegetation" (82). There are no human figures in the drawing to distract us from the naturalness of the "scene." The villa is put "exactly into the place where it ought to be" (82), and we almost are persuaded to forget the work required to construct it there.

> For the very chiefest part of the character of the edifice of pleasure is, and must be, its perfect ease, its appearance of felicitious repose. This it can never have where the nature and expression of the land near it reminds us of the necessity of labour, and where the earth is niggardly of all that constitutes its beauty and our pleasure; this it can only have, where the presence of man seems the natural consequence of an ample provision for his enjoyment, not the continuous struggle of suffering existence with a rude heaven and rugged soil. There is nobility in such a struggle, but not when it is maintained by the inhabitant of the villa, in whom it is unnatural. (162–163)

Above all, we are not to be reminded that this proprietor works, causes this or some other piece of land to be worked, or employs others to work for him. His intellectual cultivation can be imagined only in an unculti-vated landscape. Only an unproductive setting can persuade us that the villa itself has not been produced.

It is a difficult fiction to maintain, and Ruskin senses that it would break down under certain conditions. Since villas are "the dwelling of wealth and power" (80), their existence is dependent upon a particular set of social, economic, and historical conditions. They could not have existed under other conditions, in (for instance) the instability of warring Greece. They appeared in Rome because the power of the state "secured tranquility, and . . . distributed its authority among a great number of individuals," but still did not give anyone the more extensive power required to build palaces or fortresses (102). Creation of villas thus presupposes a delicate balance

ance between centralization and distribution of wealth—presupposes, that is, a powerful class that is still subject to limits. The arrangement sounds vaguely like the bourgeois capitalism of the early nineteenth century, but only vaguely. Historically, the traditional ideal of balanced, stable power was increasingly threatened, not only by popular discontent but by the very expansion of bourgeois wealth; those balances, those limits, were breaking down. It is almost as if Ruskin grasps the Marxist conception of capitalism as class warfare, although his model is strictly classical. Might the modern villa extend its power beyond those Roman limits? Is the British villa thus a contradiction in terms? Does the very existence of such monied houses imply a threat to pastoral harmony?

Ruskin in fact senses two kinds of threats. To some extent he fears a modern version of those warring classical city-states in the emergence of powerful capitalists asserting their individual power. But such violence is particularly dangerous because it is directed against nature. The chief crime of capitalism, as Ruskin understands it here, is to appropriate a landscape that must remain a "national possession."

> The nobler scenery of the earth is the inheritance of all her inhabitants: it is not merely for the few to whom it temporarily belongs, to feed from like swine, or to stable upon like horses, but it has been appointed to be the school of the minds which are kingly among their fellows, to excite the highest energies of humanity, to furnish strength to the lordliest intellect, and food for the holiest emotions of the human soul. (132)

Landscape has a privileged status as a symbolic embodiment of wealth. But it also symbolizes a certain conception of human nature, one that is disrupted and degraded as soon as new classes of builders invade the countryside. Greed and money are part of the problem, but only part. These new proprietors are repulsive creatures, with their basest motives, their "petty interests and grovelling imaginations," left undisguised; they invade the countryside "to build baby fortifications upon the bones of the world" (132). That last phrase suggests a poverty of the modern mind (far more serious than the poverty of the modern body) that is little short of blasphemy. Those who regard the earth as a place "to feed from like swine, or to stable upon like horses," have betrayed their own humanity. They are no longer living "according to nature" (and that is what "Kata Phusin," Ruskin's *nom de plume,* means), or else they are calling into question the nature of that nature itself.

Poetic architecture pays homage to the spirituality of the landscape and by so doing erects monuments to the spirituality of human beings. "Nature has set aside her sublime bits for us to feel and think in; she has pointed out her productive bits for us to sleep and eat in; and, if we sleep and eat amongst the sublimity, we are brutal; if we poetise amongst the cultivation, we are absurd" (182). These are, in effect, the landscapes of poetry and prose. Ruskin is writing to enforce the distinctions between them but also, as the tone of urgency suggests, writing out of a sense that the rigid separation has begun to break down. It is not simply that architectural decorum has been neglected; there have been violations of the rules of nature, including human nature. The introduction of the word "brutality" suggests how easy it is for him to turn an argument about architectural practice—including the economic values expressed in it—into one about our status as members of a species. Brutality in its literal sense refers to "the state or condition of the brutes," which is to say of animals. The first definition listed in the *Oxford English Dictionary* adds, "Wanting in reason or understanding; chiefly in phrases *brute beasts, the brute creation, the* 'lower animals.'" Thus it is a term bound up in other issues: the problem of the relations between lower and higher forms of life, ultimately the question of the relations of different species. While writing about "The Science of Architecture," then, Ruskin is aware of other sciences, and some of the most burning issues they were addressing. In exploring the nature of architectural poetry, he is led to question the most poetic claims about the nature of men and women: to what extent are people to be defined by their own "highest" faculties? To what extent are they merely "prosaic," merely creatures, another biological species building functional shelters dressed up as "architecture"?

Such questions emerge only tentatively, even furtively, within the ostensible architectural argument. This is one of the least-developed dimensions of Ruskin's theory, and similarly one of the least conscious. Yet the problem of biology appears, if in oblique or unexpected ways; and it is necessary to examine the conditions under which it does if we are to understand Ruskin's passion. For there is passion here, although it also surfaces unexpectedly. One example occurs after Ruskin restates his Wordsworthian insistence on the inherent relation between human feelings and certain fundamental "forms" in nature:[31]

> ... it is evident that the chief feeling induced by woody country is one of reverence for its antiquity. There is a quiet melancholy about the decay of the patriarchal trunks, which is enhanced by the green and elastic vigour of the young saplings; the noble form of the forest aisles, and the subdued light which penetrates their entangled boughs, combine to add to the impression; and the whole character of the scene is calculated to excite a conservative

feeling. The man who could remain a radical in a wood country is a disgrace to his species. (69).

What makes the remark so curious is that the final biological term merges into a political argument. Somehow Ruskin finds a connection between several apparently disparate categories: the perception of landscape, architectural taste, political sympathies, and one's dignity as a member of a biological or social group. And the ambiguity of his final word is especially revealing: it may refer to class rather than to species in the scientific sense; but what matters is that one word serves for the other, as if social position is somehow caught up in biological identity. The failure to venerate nature is partly social and political, partly a failure to rise above our own potentially animal nature. Ruskin is warning us to regard landscape in one way and not another; certain qualities in such scenes must not be dwelt upon. Architecture has led him to questions of life and death: the succession of generations, the decay of the body, the fundamentally physical character of existence. It is a vision he almost presents, and then resists violently. What does he want us not to see? Buried at the base of those venerable trunks is a reality so simple that it cannot be avoided, and yet so unpleasant—so dirty—that it cannot be named: it is mud.

I am introducing this word partly because Ruskin defines his various architectural countries in terms of their soils, but more particularly because it suggests so many of the issues underlying, literally beneath, the architectural argument. In the passage I have been discussing, Ruskin's language makes us aware of these unpleasant, buried elements, almost compulsively returns to them. In this case, he alludes to that mud in both a geological and psychoanalytical sense. Psychoanalytical, because those decaying patriarchal trunks, like his analysis of the use of riches generally, bring Ruskin dangerously close to the middle-class world of his father. If his tentative argument about wealth were developed further it might begin to dismantle the very architecture of bourgeois ideology to reveal the ground on which class relations, like villas and cottages, are built. This was the object in his major economic writings of the 1860s, *Unto This Last* and *Munera Pulveris*—and it is worth noting here that the second of those books, which refers in its title to the "gifts of the dust," closes exhorting readers not to "take dust for deity, spectre for possession."[32] His arguments then were radical enough to lead his father, who regularly scrutinized and sometimes censored his son's work, to attempt to modify and even suppress the most alarming sections. In 1838, though, I believe that the argument is truncated for other reasons. I have called them geological because that term, in the 1830s, included the study of both the earth and what was found within it. It included, that is, both rocks and fossils, and hence became a science of origins, especially a science of the origins of life. This is what made geology so dangerous for theologians. For a believer in Genesis, to speak of life originating in mud might mean no more than to reaffirm that God created men and women from the earth. For a geologist to say the same thing might imply a belief in the evolution of human beings from lower forms, a wholly material architecture of the organic world—perhaps even an architecture without an architect. Ruskin could not have moved in the scientific circles he moved in at this time and remained unaware of such views, or their implications for the study of structures of all kinds. William Whewell's *History of the Inductive Sciences* observes that "it is not always easy to know where the task of the geologist ends and that of the antiquary begins."[33] Ruskin, similarly, has difficulty in speaking of architecture without alluding to geology at the same time.

It is an allusion with which he is ill at ease, for it carries his argument into a doubly dangerous region of political and scientific thought. "The man who could remain a radical in wood country is a disgrace to his species." Ruskin is on the verge of unmasking, in the same stroke, two fundamental truths concealed beneath prevailing contemporary ideologies: the existence of *homo economicus* and that of *homo biologicus,* the latter all the more formidable insofar as he is a wholly physical being divested of economic and social identity altogether. What is disturbing in this, then, is materialism: not just a recognition that people have bodies, or economic motives, but the possibility that this may be all they have, or all they are. This is not something Ruskin wishes to see, not the sort of being projected by the mythology I have discussed earlier. Indeed, he wishes not to see it, and the tone with which the word "species" intrudes so suddenly suggests how much the issue of biology is felt to be out of place. One should not experience such thoughts in the country, he is saying; to do so is to be less than human, to become a mere animal. In beautiful buildings, however, aesthetics keep such possibilities at bay. The architectural argument is designed (like architecture itself) as a mode of elevation: poetry serves both to distance and to raise. Ruskin implies as much as he shifts the focus of his essays to the "nobler" subject of villas: "not that we have any idea of living in a cottage, as a comfortable thing; not that we prefer mud to marble, or deal to mahogany. . . . But we are going into higher walks of architecture" (73). It is as if that loftier subject rises out of the simpler, more humble one, just as every "ideal" form is defined by contrast to some reality, or "abomination" (to use another word that pops up at odd moments). The wish to ennoble, as Freud would add, always depends upon its opposite, the potential for (perhaps secretly a desire for) degradation. The beautiful harmony of ideal human architecture in the landscape is thus at best a precarious one, always implying the possibility of other, less perfect relations.

Ruskin would persuade us, and himself, that this is not the case. He takes pains to show that those dwelling in the "higher walks of architecture" are in no way soiled by the earth, by their physical surroundings, and that those "higher walks" carrry us away from a conception of architecture as "merely" the physical structure of a building designed in terms of a particular use. There is an apparent exception in the "Chapter on Chimneys," which anticipates some of Ruskin's later functionalist strictures: "what is most adapted to its purpose is most beautiful" (64). Yet we must not be made aware of this function by chimneys that obtrude, "interrupting all repose, annihilating all dignity." The distinction is clarified further by an illustration of more and less pleasing chimneys (Figure 5.3): the Venetian chimney marked "o" is singled out for special abuse—"it is too tall, and attracts by far too much attention" (63)—but Ruskin is more generally ridiculing the sort of mock picturesque that appeals "to the mind of master-sweeps" (65). And if undue emphasis on function links us to the wrong social class, it can bring us into a disturbing proximity with the wrong biological class as well. The chapter on Italian villas considers the implications of building houses "*merely* to be lived in" (the italics are Ruskin's own), so that "the whole bent of our invention, in raising the edifice, is to be directed to the provision of comfort for the life to be spent therein" (104). After describing such a project at length, he asks what it represents: in using "great knowledge and various skill" in this way, what have we done?

> Exactly as much as brute animals can do by mere instinct; nothing more than as bees and beavers, moles and magpies, ants and earwigs, do every day of their lives, without the slightest effort of reason; we have made ourselves superior as architects to the most degraded animation of the universe, only insomuch as we have lavished the highest efforts of intellect, to do what they have done with the most limited sensations that can constitute life. (105)

The passage fuses biological and social categories again as Ruskin lashes out in defense of distinction as such. William Howitt commented on such views ironically in *The Rural Life of England:* "If the peasant can be satisfied with his establishment, and the gentleman could not tell how to live without his, one would be almost persuaded that they could not be of the same class of animals."[34] For Ruskin such divisions are real and inevitable: without a separation into classes, into higher and lower forms, all architectural, social, and biological dignity would be lost. Architecture enshrines these differences. No wonder the traveller should learn to observe it in the correct spirit.

It is equally important that genteel readers (real or aspiring) who stay at home should learn how to build, that everything we build should testify to our dignity. The issue would become increasingly important in the Victorian building boom: what rules apply to modern cities or factories, to the use of new materials or the use of old ones in new ways? Can one, for instance, employ brick (an imperial material but ordinary, composed of mud) in important public architecture? The young critic has predictably violent opinions, although he also grants that there are conditions in which brick does belong. Ruskin endorses its use in what he calls the Simple Blue Country; but, like that phrase itself, his description of this region is partly (perhaps unconsciously) ironic. It is productive countryside, including agricultural lands and manufacturing districts, a world of "temporary wealth" and "matter-of-fact business-like activity," dizzying in its instability. A shifting, ambiguous world—and the ambiguity of his tone matches the ambiguous approval of brick itself: a lower form of architecture fits a lower form of life. Brick is

> admirably suited for that country where all is change, and all activity; where the working and money-making members of the community are perpetually succeeding and overpowering each other; enjoying, each in his turn, the reward of his industry; yielding up the field, the pasture, and the mine, to his successor, and leaving no more memory behind him, no farther evidence of his individual existence, than is left by a working bee, in the honey for which we thank his class, forgetting the individual. (141)

This reads like a post-Darwinian nightmare vision of industrial competition. In fact the imagery derives from some of the same sources Darwin knew, and ultimately from Malthus. It is as close as Ruskin comes to fully amalgamating *homo economicus* and biological man, or to acknowledging openly what makes their presence so foreboding. The figure of that drone, caught up in an endless Malthusian struggle, incorporates them both, suggesting that our membership in a class—whether social or a scientific classification—robs us of individuality, which is to say of identity itself. Suddenly all the latent anxieties of the essays are articulated together. Ruskin projects a landscape dominated by graceless, uniform industrial buildings; a community (if that word really applies at all) based on universal unchecked competition; human behavior reduced to elemental struggle; thought and moral life replaced by the instinctive bustle of insects.

Ruskin mentions bees in response to the conventional association of hives and human architecture. But he also senses—rightly, I think—how easily such an analogy could lend itself to a more extended comparison between "higher" and "lower" forms of life. The seventh edition of the *Encyclopedia Britannica* (still being issued in the late 1830s) terms bees a "remarkable tribe of insects," paying particular attention to their "curious processes of architecture."[35] The point—at least the one someone like Ruskin would be apt to take—is made more directly in the discussion of Ants, "a tribe of insects so long celebrated for their industry and frugality, and for the display of that sagacity which characterizes some of the higher orders of animals."[36] An even more important contemporary example of this sort of thought can be found in Dr. John Macculloch's three-volume *Proofs and Illustrations of the Attributes of God, from the Facts and Laws of the Physical Universe: Being the Foundation of Natural and Revealed Religion* (1837). In spite of the apparent conservatism of this title, or his desire to found "a system of animal metaphysics,"[37] his speculations "On the Mental Faculties of the Lower Animals" lead to a radical acceptance of the links between all forms of life. "Is it," he asks, "because the bee is small in size that we refuse it reasoning powers?"[38] While granting that hive-building results from instinct, he still insists that it displays a surprisingly human form of "reason," and "profound geometrical knowledge."[39] "Such proceedings as this," he adds, "are those of an artist." Macculloch, as his title suggests, sets out to reconcile natural history and theology. Yet the farthest-reaching implications of his argument can be measured by the fact that one of his most attentive readers was Charles Darwin, just returned from his work as the naturalist aboard H.M.S. *Beagle,* and revising his journals for publication—while also theorizing privately about evolution, natural selection, and the structural affinities between species. Ruskin could not have read those speculations, of course. But he was more than a casual student of modern scientific thought. As he prepared to enter Oxford in December 1836, he described his "light reading" as consisting of "Saussure—Humboldt—and other works of natural philosophy, geological works, &c, &c."[40] A month later he attended a meeting of the Geological Society at which Darwin read a paper on "Recent Elevations on the Coast of Chile." In October 1837 he dined with "two celebrated geologists" and Darwin, with whom he "talked all evening."[41] The word "species" turns up unexpectedly in the "Concluding Remarks" on cottages published in May 1838, and hence probably written shortly after that dinner. Ruskin had more than architecture on his mind.

   The Poetry of Architecture was concluded when the *Architectural Magazine* ceased publication in 1839. But Ruskin already was moving towards the limits of his own argument. His most fundamental impulse had been to naturalize architecture, yet in attempting to do so he was forced to confront his own uneasiness about the nature of nature itself. The case he wanted to make required another sort of book, one that would allow him to deal with nature, and its poetry, more directly. *Modern Painters,* which began to appear in 1843, and which grew out of an attempt in 1836 to rebut hostile reviews of J. M. W. Turner in *Blackwood's,* became the vehicle he needed—a survey of landscape painting in which Ruskin could devote most of his energy to landscape alone, to the "poetic" nature of the physical world. And only when we regard the later book in light of the questions raised in *The Poetry of Architecture* can we explain the choice of the first picture *Modern Painters* considers at any length. It is not a Turner landscape but an interior scene by the great animal painter Edwin Landseer, a picture of a dog resting his head on a coffin. In fact, *The Old Shepherd's Chief Mourner* (Figure 5.4) is itself a product of 1837, related to the mounting uncertainties about the nature of nature and humanity.

Landseer had been treating animal subjects throughout the 1830s and was widely admired for his ability to associate them "with human thoughts and passions" (as a *Times* reviewer in 1829 commented about *The Poor Dog,* a scene much like the *Mourner* that would be engraved as a companion piece to it).[42] In some pictures, such as *Dignity and Impudence* (1829), the human resemblance of the animals is comic; in some it is heroic, as *Deer and Deerhounds in a Mountain Torrent* (1833); the most famous example of the latter mode, *The Monarch of the Glen* (1851), may allude to Victoria or Albert. But the immediate popular appeal of this genre is not inconsistent with a more subtle reference to the moral questions raised by contemporary science: what are the intrinsic relationships between human and animals? do animals modify our vision of ourselves? Many of Landseer's animal pictures are double-edged: ennobling animals by reference to people while at the same time suggesting an animal element in even the most noble human beings. They express what a recent historian of science has termed "that most haunting of Victorian fears, the bestialization of men."[43] It is especially in the comic versions of this genre that we can find the issue acknowledged, and then laughingly dismissed. Landseer's *A Distinguished Member of the Humane Society* (1839, Figure 5.5) makes the same joke as George Cruikshank's *Fellows of the Zoological Society* (1851, Figure 5.6), the former depicting a Newfoundland dog, the latter a group of hippopotami in coats and hats. (Charles Knight's *Penny Magazine* for February 3, 1838 begins with an article on the new orangutan at the Zoological Gardens, and the accompanying illustration (Figure 5.7) shows it seated in a chair, dressed in a child's play outfit, holding a ball.) The point of the humor is simple: the formal, scientific approach to such creatures is ridiculous; they are what they are, as anyone can see. Animal pictures contain another lesson in how to observe, and how not to. That is also Ruskin's point.

The long description of *The Old Shepherd's Chief Mourner* in the first volume of *Modern Painters* praises the "clear and expressive" language of the painting, moving from detail to detail, and guiding us in the process of reading pictorial imagery: "the exquisite execution of the glossy and crisp hair of the dog, the bright sharp touching of the green bough beside it, the clear painting of the wood of the coffin and the folds of the blanket"—all this, Ruskin emphasizes, using the word twice, is language; he might have said poetry. What does it express?

> The close pressure of the dog's breast against the wood, the convulsive clinging of the paws, which has dragged the blanket off the trestle, the total powerlessness of the head laid, close and motionless, upon its folds, the fixity and tearful fall of the eye in its utter hopelessness, the rigidity of repose which marks that there has been no motion nor change in the trance of agony since the last blow was struck on the coffin-lid, the quietness and gloom of the chamber, the spectacles marking the place where the Bible was last closed, indicating how lonely has been the life, how unwatched the departure, of him, who is now laid solitary in his sleep;—these are all thoughts—thoughts by which the picture is separated at once from hundreds of equal merit, as far as mere painting goes, by which it ranks as a work of high art, and stamps its author, not as the neat imitator of the texture of a skin, or the fold of a drapery, but as the Man of Mind.[44]

"Mind" suggests first that the artist himself is an intellectual, a deep thinker in spite of the apparent triviality of his subject. But it also implies that Landseer has depicted the mind of his subject. We "all know," Macculloch writes, "what a shepherd's dog can learn."[45] What gives this painting its real importance for Ruskin is, finally, that faithful, all-too-human dog. Perhaps I should say more than human: the other mourners have left, after performing a purely ceremonial tribute. The collie has been loyal for a lifetime, and beyond. This is an image of faith, a doggy anticipation of *In Memoriam* answering in simple pictorial form that poem's darkest doubts. For here there is natural dignity instead of nature "red in tooth and claw," a dignity that links animals and humans across the barrier of death, a dignity that requires no science to be comprehended, if it is accessible to science at all. In a later volume of *Modern Painters* Ruskin proposes a special name for such scientifically profound aesthetic responses to nature, "the science of the *aspects* of things."[46] In 1843—certainly in

Figure 4.1. George Cruikshank, "Oliver asking for More,"
illustration to *Oliver Twist* (1837), University of Virginia Library.

Figure 4.2. "Laura's return to her Father's house." Frontispiece to Charlotte Adams' *The Stolen Child* (1838), Trustees of the British Museum.

Figure 4.3 (below). August Herview, "The Lime Tree," illustration to Frances Trollope's *The Vicar of Wrexhill* (1837), University of Oregon Library.

Figure 4.4. George Cruikshank, "Oliver introduced to the Respectable Old Gentleman," illustration to *Oliver Twist* (1837), University of Virginia Library.

Figure 4.5. George Cruikshank, "Oliver's Reception by Fagin and the Boys," illustration to *Oliver Twist* (1837), University of Virginia Library.

Figure 4.6. George Cruikshank, "Oliver claimed by his Affectionate Friends," illustration to *Oliver Twist* (1837), University of Virginia Library.

Figure 4.7. George Cruikshank, "The Last Chance," illustration to *Oliver Twist* (1837), University of Virginia Library.

Figure 4.8. George Cruikshank, "Fagin in the Condemned Cell," illustration to *Oliver Twist* (1837), University of Virginia Library.

Figure 5.1. "Oxen Plowing," vignette from William Howitt's *The Rural Life of England* (1838).

Figure 5.2. John Ruskin, "Villa Serbelloni, Bellagio," from *The Poetry of Architecture* (1836–1839).

Figure 5.3. John Ruskin, "Chimneys,"
from *The Poetry of Architecture* (1836–1839).

Figure 5.4. Edwin Landseer, "The Old Shepherd's Chief Mourner" (1837), Victoria and Albert Museum.

Figure 5.5. Thomas Landseer after Edwin Landseer
(with extensive retouching by Edwin Landseer),
"A Distinguished Member of the Humane Society"
(painting 1838, print 1839), Trustees of the British Museum.

Figure 5.6. George Cruikshank, "Fellows of the Zoological Society," from *The Comic Almanack* (1851), Library of the University of California at Los Angeles.

THE ORANG-OUTAN.

[The Orang-Outan of the Zoological Society.—From an original drawing.]

Figure 5.7. "Orang-Outan of the Zoological Society," from *The Penny Magazine,* 3 February 1838.

Figure 5.8. "Fuegian," illustration from *Narrative of the Surveying Voyages of His Majesty's Ships Adventure and Beagle, between the years 1826 and 1836, describing their examination of the Southern Shores of South America, and the Beagle's Circumnavigation of the Globe,* University of Virginia Library.

Figure 6.1. J. M. W. Turner, *The Fighting "Temeraire" Being Towed to Her Last Berth to be Broken Up* 1838 (1839). The Tate Gallery, London.

Figure 6.2. J. M. W. Turner, *The Battle of Trafalgar* (1823–1824),
The National Maritime Museum, Greenwich.

Figure 6.3. J. M. W. Turner, *Peace—Burial at Sea* (1842), The Tate Gallery, London.

Figure 6.4. J. M. W. Turner, *War—the exile and the rock limpet* (1842), The Tate Gallery, London.

Figure 6.5. J. M. W. Turner, *Yarmouth Sands* (1830), The Fitzwilliam Museum, Cambridge.

Figure 6.6. J. M. W. Turner, *The new moon, or 'I've lost my boat you shan't have your hoop'* (1840), The Tate Gallery, London.

Figure C.1. "Exhibition of the Nelson Statue at Charing Cross,"
from *The Illustrated London News,* 4 November 1843.

Figure C.2. William Henry Fox Talbot, "The Open Door,"
from *The Pencil of Nature* (1844), International Museum
of Photography, George Eastman House, Rochester, N.Y.

Figure C.3. William Henry Fox Talbot, "Shelves of Books,"
from *The Pencil of Nature* (1844), International Museum
of Photography, George Eastman House, Rochester, N.Y.

1837 and 1838—he would have used a simpler label, one that contains no reference to science at all. For the only way to see this mode of existence, and the only thing to see it as, is poetry. Otherwise we would be in danger of observing too much.

III

We would expect a different sort of travel journal, and a different sort of narrative, from the pen of Charles Darwin. What we find are both similarities and differences, some of which are evident in his titles. The record of his long journey aboard the *Beagle* was published in 1839 as the third and final volume of the *Narrative of the Surveying Voyages of His Majesty's Ships Adventure and Beagle, between the years 1826 and 1836, describing their examination of the Southern Shores of South America, and the Beagle's Circumnavigation of the Globe.* Darwin's volume had its own separate title, *Journal and Remarks, 1832–1836* and was quickly reissued on its own, as the *Journal of Researches into the Geology and Natural History of the Countries visited during the Voyage of H.M.S. Beagle round the world under the Command of Capt. Fitz Roy, R.N.* By the second edition, *Natural History* was listed before *Geology*: the definition of the project had begun to shift. Later it would reappear as *A Naturalist's Voyage Round the World,* and, finally, as *The Voyage of the Beagle.* Under that final title, it has become a classic of what is sometimes called "naturalist" literature, in part because it is considered an ancestor of Darwin's most celebrated and revolutionary scientific work, *The Origin of Species.* Yet what we find in the *Beagle* journal is less purely scientific than its reputation suggests. Darwin's "remarks" are more casual than systematic, a series of fragmentary observations rather than an orderly account in support of a developed theory—a phenomenology, not unlike *Sketches by Boz.* As in Dickens, or Martineau, the persona of the author as observer becomes an integral part of the record. Gillian Beer has observed that the "tone of a single man speaking, the presenter of the evidence," is a "necessary counterpoise" to the theoretical scope of the *Origin.*[47] In the *Beagle* journal, that voice, that man, is not so much counterpoise as a central fact of the narrative itself. It is the story of a voyage, a journey of discovery—as a research *journal,* part science and part autobiography. From the opening sentences of *The Journal of Researches* (as I will refer to it) we encounter the naturalist in the process of observing, describing both external conditions and their effect on him.

The first short entry in the first edition (dated January 16, 1832) moves from a remark on the "desolate aspect" of Porto Praya, to mention of its heat and sterility, to a sentence on its topography, and then quickly returns to the perspective of the traveller himself.

> The scene, as beheld through the hazy atmosphere of this climate, is one of great interest; if, indeed, a person, fresh from sea, and who has just walked, for the first time, in a grove of cocoa-nut trees, can be a judge of any thing but his own happiness. The island would generally be considered as very uninteresting; but to any one accustomed only to an English landscape, the novel prospect of an utterly sterile land possesses a grandeur which more vegatation might spoil.[48]

There is a level of self-consciousness here that surpasses almost anything we have seen in Martineau or Ruskin, and a remarkable level of epistemological self-consciousness as well. Darwin recognizes that another observer, perhaps even himself under a slightly altered set of conditions, might react in a different way; yet the point is that he did not, or rather (given the dramatic present tense of the *Journal of Researches*) cannot. The choice is made clear if we compare the parallel remarks in the journal of Darwin's commanding officer, Robert Fitz Roy (in the second volume of the three-volume series): "The vicinity of Porto Praya offers little that is agreeable to the eye of an ordinary visitor, though interesting enough to a geologist."[49] Fitz Roy seems to refer to Darwin here, but in doing so he misses the point of his naturalist's text. For Darwin's perspective is that of a stranger, not a scientist, or at least not a scientist as he is usually defined. Darwin allows himself to be carried away by novelty, to abandon his ordinary standards. He is finding himself in the landscape, and finding in the landscape a new kind of self.

This is not to suggest that Darwin's voice, or persona, as narrator of his *Beagle* record is not that of a naturalist, but to say something about what sort of person that naturalist is. He experiences a heightened sense of life by virtue of his training: both the inner self and the external world are perceived with a new intensity, opening new sources and new levels of pleasure. Here is another early entry (from 1832):

> BAHIA, OR SAN SALVADOR, BRAZIL. Feb. 29th.—The day has passed delightfully. Delight itself, however, is a weak term to express the feelings of a naturalist who, for the first time, has been wandering by himself in a Brazilian forest. Among the multitude of striking objects, the general luxuriance of the vegetation bears away the victory. The elegance of the grasses, the novelty of the parasitical plants, the beauty of the flowers, the glossy green of the

foliage, all tend to this end. A most paradoxical mixture of sound and silence
pervades the shady parts of the wood. The noise from the insects is so loud,
that it may be heard even in a vessel anchored several hundred yards from
the shore; yet within the recesses of the forest a universal silence appears to
reign. To a person fond of natural history, such a day as this, brings with it
a deeper pleasure than he ever can hope again to experience. (11)

Sound and sight—elegance, novelty, beauty: it is not the sort of writing we
expect to find in scientific literature. The very struggle to arrive at a precise
terminology for such exquisite pleasure reminds us that this is an aesthetic
experience, outside the naturalist's normal expertise. It is worth noting
here that in September 1838, when he was revising these journals for publication, and at almost the same time his reading of Malthus led him to
the germ of his new evolutionary theory, Darwin was reading Reynolds'
Discourses.[50] Yet this passage, and the *Journal of Researches* generally, recommends something more than a painter's approach to nature. It is a
response made possible by the trained discriminations of science itself;
how else could he remark on "the novelty of the parasitical plants"? In the
closing pages of the book Darwin distinguishes the "growing pleasure in
comparing the character of scenery in different countries . . . from merely
admiring its beauty." The difference has to do with the observer's familiarity with a specific scene's "individual parts"; it is related to what Carol
Christ calls the Victorian "aesthetic of particularity."[51] "He who examines
each part of a fine view, may also thoroughly comprehend the full and
combined effect." Thus, he concludes, summing up his experience over the
full voyage, "a traveller should be a botanist, for in all views plants form
the chief embellishment" (604).

Still, this is botany from a distance, surveying a view in which vegetation is an "embellishment," observing with feeling. The identity of the
Darwinian naturalist is a function of that distance, of his ability to remain
at once engaged and detached enough to sense what he terms elsewhere
the "excitement from the novelty of objects." The point is not simply to
be alert but to be human, to preserve and even sharpen "that want and
craving, which, as Sir J. Herschel remarks, a man experiences although
every corporeal sense is fully satisfied" (607). A more impersonal, systematic, professionalized observer might lose contact with the novelty of this
new world and the imaginative activity it ought to evoke. His own procedures would become more regular, and so would his image of nature.
"The limit of man's knowledge in any subject possesses a high interest,"
he remarks in connection with the geology of Chile, adding that his interest
"is perhaps increased by its close neighbourhood to the realms of imagi-

nation" (345). In his *Autobiography,* written many years later, Darwin confessed to the "curious and lamentable loss of the higher aesthetic tastes" of his youth: "My mind seems to have become a kind of machine for grinding general laws out of a large collection of facts."[52] But this, of course, was after his own theoretical conclusions were clearly formed, after moving beyond what he earlier regarded as the "limit" of his own knowledge near "the realms of imagination." As long as he can continute his observations in this borderland, at the edge of the charted regions of his own knowledge, he can retain the excitement that enables him to look at the external world and his own conceptions of it critically. Sandra Herbert has remarked that Darwin's interests and theoretical leanings carried him outside the boundaries of "fields" defined by contemporary scientific practice.[53] In the *Journal of Researches* there is a continual sense of limits being crossed, unknown territories being entered—territories of thought as well as geography. Darwin in South America finds himself suddenly and dramatically on his own: literally alone, when he enters forests or deserts few if any Europeans had ever visited; on his own as a young Cambridge graduate faced for the first time with a demanding adult task; on his own intellectually as he attempts to account in any way he can for phenomena that cannot be explained satisfactorily by the mental equipment he has carried with him. It is not surprising that he experiences many moments of uncertainty. What makes the *Journal of Researches* so impressive as a scientific and literary text is the fact that he admits them. Thus perhaps the most telling gesture of the young aesthete-cum-naturalist-cum-explorer is the question; perhaps more than anything else questions account for the character of his first book.

Questions: even while he must record, the writer-naturalist is dealing with facts he is not yet prepared to explain, facts that may fall outside previous explanatory systems. At times, Darwin's questions seem to exist in the space between other, prior categories of aesthetic and scientific response; at other times they suggest the transformation of imaginative insights into scientific discourse, into a new mode of discourse being created while the questions are being asked. They also identify the element of Darwin's role others found it hardest to comprehend. An English member of the party named Harris attempted to account for Darwin's activities to a group of suspicious Argentine solders. As Fitz Roy's *Proceedings* explains:

> "Un naturalista" was a term unherd of by any person in the settlement, and being unluckily explained by Harris as meaning "a man that knows every thing," any further attempt to quiet anxiety was useless.[54]

To Harris, the naturalist is someone who provides answers, to all questions. The difference between this and Darwin's own sense of his task emerges in a parallel episode, which he narrates. Here, too, scientific study must be explained to an unsympathetic and uncomprehending audience. A group of Chileans have become suspicious of his investigations and are convinced that science is a cover under which he hunts for mining sites.

> I found the most ready way of explaining my employment, was to ask them how it was that they themselves were not curious concerning earthquakes and volcanoes?—why some springs were hot and others cold?—why there were mountains in Chile, and not a hill in La Plata? These bare questions at once satisfied and silenced the greater number. (435–436)

He is not only explaining himself as a questioner—he is doing so by asking questions: why don't others raise the same questions he does? He is not only asking questions about nature, then, but questioning the human response to it. What sets him apart is a "normal" curiosity that others, somehow, do not share, a "human" response that is oddly uncommon among the people he visits and among his compatriots as well. That final irony is unveiled as the passage continues, with Darwin admitting that although the "greater number" accepted his description, it didn't satisfy everyone. "Some (like a few in England who are a century behindhand), thought that all such inquiries were useless and impious; and that it was quite sufficient that God had thus made the mountains" (436). The questioner sets himself apart from orthodoxy, from the "normal science" (Kuhn's term) of the day.

On board the *Beagle* Darwin debated his views almost continually with Captain Fitz Roy, who insisted on turning every observation of South America into a new confirmation of the Biblical history of the earth. Stephen Jay Gould suggests that Darwin may have been "led to his philosophical outlook partly as a response to Fitzroy's dogmatic insistence upon the argument from design."[55] In any case, the debate is extended into the pages of both of their books, although it is often concealed within a genteel prose that seems only to argue against unknown or hypothetical opponents. It is natural for us to read this as an argument between evolutionary and creationist science, given our own awareness of the outcome of Darwin's researches and the modern battles concerning them. But such an interpretation ignores the more complex character of the disagreement, and of Darwin's position within it. He is not actively confuting religion, simply following the logic of his own uncertainties. This is why his disagreement over a traditional Christian understanding of the natural evi-

dence in South America takes the form of questions—is an extended questioning, we might say. Darwin is not so much advancing a clear position
as admitting to facts that cannot be reconciled to any clear position that
he knows. Fitz Roy might have been less troubled by a less flexible
antagonist.

Fitz Roy concludes his *Proceedings* with several chapters that attempt
to link his observations on the voyage with a complete theory of natural
history. His "Very Few Remarks with Reference to the Deluge" analyzes
the fossil findings made during the voyage, mostly by Darwin, in an effort
to reconcile their apparent anomalies with the Biblical record. Darwin
responds (without referring to this argument directly) by asking how such
conventional conclusions are generated. Where did Fitz Roy's evidence
come from? What other explanations might account for it? Darwin reports
eyewitness accounts of a series of Argentine droughts so severe that thousands of animals crawled to riverbeds and marshes to die, leaving a set of
modern "fossils" littering the mud, It is hardly surprising that Fitz Roy (or
anyone else) would interpret the resulting evidence as he did.

> What would be the opinion of a geologist, viewing such an enormous collec-
> tion of bones, of all kinds of animals and of all ages, thus embedded in one
> thick earthy mass? Would he not attribute it to a flood having swept over the
> surface of the land, rather than to the common order of things? (157)

The sceptical methodology used here anticipates the combination of
inductive and deductive reasoning in the *Origin,* where hypotheses are
measured by comparing their predicted consequences with conditions
actually observed in nature.[56] In both cases the assumption is that truth is
elusive, to be discovered through an endless series of hypotheses, attempts
at verification, modifications, and (of course) more questions. Darwin
assumes, in other words, that the truth evolves, and he assumes this long
before he has reached even tentative conclusions about the place of evolution in natural history.

His own views are tentative and often necessarily uncertain. Some of
Darwin's most open admissions of this appear in the chapters on the Galapagos Islands, that *locus classicus* of evolutionary theory. In 1839 the possibility of substantiating that theory is only glimpsed for the first time, so
that he simply must apologize for the investigations he did not carry out—
biogeographical investigations, for instance, into different species of tor-
toise, or vegetation.

> Unfortunately, I was not aware of these facts till my collection was nearly
> completed: it never occurred to me, that the productions of islands only a

few miles apart, and placed under the same physical conditions, would be dissimilar. I therefore did not attempt to make a series of specimens from the separate islands. (474)

Even the 1845 edition (revised to hint at his still-developing evolutionary theory), continues to stress errors of judgment and perception: "I never dreamed that islands, about fifty or sixty miles apart, and most of them in sight of each other, formed of precisely the same rocks, . . . would have been differently tenanted; but we shall soon see that this is the case."[57] Even when recognizing the inadequacies of a theologically based science to account for his data, Darwin is often unprepared to offer any alternative of his own. Thus, the similarity of the Galapagos birds with those of Chile or La Plata "would be explained," he tells us, "according to the views of some authors, by saying that the creative power had acted according to the same law over a wide area" (474). His own explanation does not appear.

It is worth focusing on the Galapagos chapter for a while longer, both to illustrate Darwin's emerging sense of his own project and to distinguish more sharply his view of the naturalist's task from that of a more orthodox investigator like Captain Fitz Roy. Both are struck by the uniqueness of the site, and both are inspired by it to even greater detail than usual. In the Galapagos chapters more than anywhere else in their respective journals, we have a strong sense of the two travellers comparing notes, both on the spot and while making the final revisions in their manuscripts; the accounts speak in chorus, and on the same themes. But although at times their conclusions seem strikingly similar, everywhere there are differences in tone. Darwin, for instance, remarks that the Chatham Island hillocks give "the country a *workshop* appearance, which strongly reminded me of those parts of Staffordshire where the great iron-foundaries are most numerous" (455). Fitz Roy makes the same point in reference to Albemarle Island, only in more theatrical language:

> our eyes and imagination were engrossed by the strange wildness of the view; for in such a place Vulcan might have worked. Amidst the most confusedly heaped masses of lava, black and barren, as if hardly yet cooled, innumerable craters (or fumeroles) showed their very regular, even artificial looking heaps. It was like immense iron works, on a Cyclopean scale![58]

Not to be outdone, Darwin invokes the Homeric giant too. But his use of mythology is different:

> The day, on which I visited the little craters, was glowing hot, and the scrambling over the rough surface, and through the intricate thickets, was very fati-

guing; but I was well repaid by the Cyclopean scene. In my walk I met two large tortoises, each of which must have weighed at least two hundred pounds.... These huge reptiles, surrounded by the black lava, the leafless shrubs, and large cacti, appeared to my fancy like some antediluvian animals. (456)

It is not just the tone that has changed. He introduces the flood reference more tentatively than Fitz Roy ever would, with an admission that "fancy" is at work. We are reminded of the barriers to accurate observation and description, of the way language shapes what it describes.

Given this high level of self-consciousness, Darwin is particularly wary of the danger of imposing a European vision on this alien landscape—aware of himself as intruder, outsider; this moderates the sort of moral intensity we find in Fitz Roy. Both of them admit to being disturbed by their first sight of those "hideous" creatures, iguanas, and that adjective appears in both accounts. But within a few pages Darwin's treatment becomes not only sympathetic but playful. He tells of pulling the tail of a burrowing iguana, which "was greatly astonished, and soon shuffled up to see what was the matter; and then stared me in the face, as much as to say, 'What made you pull my tail?'" (470). Fitz Roy never alters his grim view that "Few animals are uglier than these iguanas; . . . of a dirty black colour; with a great mouth, and a pouch hanging under it; a kind of horn mane upon the neck and back; and long claws and tail." At first landing he concludes that the shore is "fit for Pandemonium." Departing, his response does not seem to have changed: "This first excursion had no tendency to raise our ideas of the Galapagos Islands."[59]

Darwin has not yet arrived at the sophisticated biogeographical analysis of the Galapagos he would present in the *Origin*. But there are signs that it is forming. He identifies thirteen species and four new subgenera of finches. "These birds are the most singular of any in the archipelago. They all agree in many points; namely, in a peculiar structure of their bill, short tails, general form, and in their plumage. . . . It is very remarkable that a nearly perfect gradation of structure in this one group can be traced in the form of the beak" (461–62). As Howard Gruber has shown, this is one of the portions of the *Journal of Researches* most drastically changed for the 1845 edition. And if, as in the treatment of Galapagos natural history generally, it is not always clear "just where he is at any given point in the development of his ideas," "the changes in what he wrote do suggest the direction of movement of his thought".[60] The detailed account of finches suggests the same thing, even before Darwin knows where it will lead. He speculates at the end of the Galapagos chapter that the information he has gathered may "directly bear upon that most mysterious question,—

whether the series of organized beings peculiar to some isolated points, are the last remnants of a former population, or the first creatures of a new one springing into existence" (569). It is, in other words, the question of the origin of species, in an embryonic, hypothetical form, at least. Darwin raises it cautiously, not wholly sure of its significance or of his own views. Fitz Roy, by contrast, is certain about the conclusions to be drawn. It is one of the moments where his implied rebuttal of Darwin is strongest, as if he senses (perhaps more acutely than Darwin himself) that crucial scientific-theological issues are at stake. For him, the Galapagos finches must be seen as a single group, and they illustrate a single point. "All the small birds that live on these lava-covered islands have short beaks, very thick at the base, like that of a bull-finch. This appears to be one of those admirable provisions of Infinite Wisdom by which each created thing is adapted to the place for which it was intended."[61]

The point is not that one of these views is more accurate than the other according to the standards of our own contemporary science, but that one is presented so much more dogmatically (and defensively). We see the same contrast in another covert debate, on the Falklands fox. Darwin concludes that these animals form a distinct species, and marvels at the fact: "As far as I am aware, there is no other instance in any part of the world, of so small a mass of broken land, distant from a continent, possessing so large a quadruped peculiar to itself" (250). Fitz Roy is not impressed.

> Naturalists say these foxes are peculiar to this archipelago, and they find difficulty in accounting for their presence in that quarter only. That they are now peculiar cannot be doubted; but how long they have been so is a very different question. . . . I can see nothing extraordinary in foxes carried from Tierra del Fuego to Falkland Island becoming longer-legged, more bulky, and differently coated.[62]

Fitz Roy had insisted on the importance of having a naturalist on the *Beagle,* yet here he belittles scientific findings. His first words are uttered with intense irony. Natural history can be grasped by anyone as well as by a naturalist—perhaps better! It is not surprising to find the captain, at an earlier point in his *Proceedings,* almost openly contemptuous of Darwin himself:

> My friend's attention was soon attracted to some low cliffs near Point Alta, where he found some of those huge fossil bones, described in his work; and notwithstanding our smiles at the cargoes of apparent rubbish which he frequently brought on board, he and his servant used their pick-axes in earnest, and brought away what have since proved to be most interesting and valuable remains of extinct animals.[63]

The condescension could not be laid on much thicker. Once again, it is less remarkable as an expression of Fitz Roy's dogmatism than of his nervousness about the implications of Darwin's research. Or its potential implications. His ironies constitute one last effort at persuasion, or conversion. For Fitz Roy seems to sense both the radicalism of Darwin's thought, and its internal contradictions.

Darwin is not always the forward-looking, liberated chronicler of a new world. At times he sounds, no less than Fitz Roy, like a European gentleman on tour for his amusement. He is not above pulling iguanas' tails, or "experimenting" with the tameness of boobies and noddies of St. Paul's rocks by walking up to those birds and killing them with his geological hammer (9)! It is true, of course, that this last episode comes early in a journey that was to see the young naturalist abandon his old pastime of hunting in favor of geology (as Gertrude Himmelfarb has observed).[64] But other traces of what we might term a colonialist's mentality remain, particularly in Darwin's comments on the "natives" he encounters in various parts of South America. That he comments at all is important: clearly he understands his task as naturalist to include anthropology (although that modern sense of the word did not become current until about 1860). He discusses tribal customs, languages, dress, characteristic gestures, herding and hunting techniques, and even the politics of both native tribes and the various representatives of European governments he encounters. The very range of subjects suggests the beginning of the researches that would lead to *The Descent of Man*. Yet as Himmelfarb notes in connection with that book, the detached rationalism that makes it possible to study humans as scientific subjects also can produce failures of human feeling in the observer. "His sensibility was of that inverted order that is unable to extend to human beings the same sympathy and respect it has for animals."[65] In the *Journal of Researches* we can see some signs of this distance beginning to emerge, most notably in his accounts of those beings to whom he, like Fitz Roy, refers simply as "savages."

The word itself should give us pause, as did Ruskin's use of the word "brutes." The perception of humans as animals imposes a radical otherness upon them, a distance across which it is nearly impossible to conceive them as akin to ourselves. Even as sympathetic and humane an observer as Harriet Martineau could fall victim to this impulse.

> We visited the negro quarter; a part of the estate which filled me with disgust, wherever I went. It is something between a haunt of monkeys and a dwelling-place of human beings. The natural good taste, so remarkable in free negroes, is here extinguished. Their small, dingy, untidy houses, their cribs, the children crouching round the fire, the animal deportment of the grown-up, the

brutish chagrins and enjoyments of the old, were all loathsome. . . . a walk through a lunatic asylum is far less painful than a visit to the slave quarter of an estate. (*SA,* i, 302)

Of course Martineau recognizes that this is a reduction of humanity, that nobler qualities have been "extinguished." It is the sort of insight we expect from the future evolutionist as well, yet at times that sense of distance, and superiority, grows so strong as to leave Darwin's own view in some doubt. Even when he recalls that Europeanized Fuegian, Jemmy Button—who had been brought back to England and educated by Fitz Roy to return as a missionary to his people—Darwin seems to forget how easily the line between cultures could be erased by a brief period of training:

> It seems yet wonderful to me, when I think over all his many good qualities, that he should have been of the same race, and doubtless partaken of the same character, with the miserable, degraded savages whom we first met here.[66]

Some people are more human than others, some simply beyond the possibility of sympathy or fellow feeling. His comments are not unlike the responses of Jemmy Button himself, who is ashamed at the behavior and appearance of his own people when he first lands at home. Darwin describes the responses of the Fuegians on that occasion with cultivated amusement. Their attempts to imitate European gestures are "ludicrous" (230). Their astonishment at the bared white arms of the *Beagle* party remind him of orangutans at the Zoological Gardens.

Yet it is not simply race but power that is being asserted in these encounters, power that reconstitutes itself through just such descriptions. "Savages" become pawns in a game of self-definition, the dark distant figures against which the enlightened images of modern European visitors can be distinguished (in both senses of that word). We laugh at primitive behavior to preclude sympathy, to remind ourselves of the distance necessarily implied in our superiority to the "objects" of our study. I am mixing metaphors from early anthropology and Joseph Conrad's *Heart of Darkness* in speaking of the motives that led people to gaze into these dark mirrors; but in fact similar images, and similar ideas, were current in the 1830s. Mill's essay on "Civilization" defines the main term of its title by contrasting advanced and primitive peoples. Civilization "stands for that kind of improvement . . . which distinguishes a wealthy and populous nation from savages and barbarians."[67] Perhaps civilization requires such primitive others to define itself against, just as the colonialist requires colonial subjects. Is there any relation between subjugation of that sort and the scientist's search for appropriate subjects for analysis?

Darwin at times seems fully prepared to regard the people he encounters in places like Tierra del Fuego as representatives of a "lower" state of existence wholly different from his own. The Fuegians are the natives for whom he has the least tolerance or sympathy: "the most abject and miserable creatures I any where beheld" (235). His response to them suggests moral shock rather than rational or scientific analysis, as if fundamental cultural assumptions are being reversed or challenged too openly. These are the moments when he sounds most like Fitz Roy, Fitz Roy at his worst. Both men are made particularly uncomfortable by the Fuegians' nakedness. Darwin tries to objectify his feelings about this by remarking on the bitter winter conditions (it is December 1832) these unclothed creatures must endure. But his language indicates that he is fascinated by the very nakedness he deplores. Six Fuegians approach his boat during heavy rain. All, he explains, are "quite naked, and even one full-grown woman absolutely so" (235). The phrase "full-grown" is a polite way of describing something that cannot be mentioned in print, but the word "absolutely" is even more curious. The distinction ("absolutely" as opposed to what?) makes little sense except as a comparison of his own levels of attentiveness: Darwin must acknowledge, "absolutely," something he does not, or should not, wish to see. The language is trying to cover moral uncertainty, and failing to do so. Similarly, he reports how in a nearby harbor another naked woman rows close to the visitors, remaining to stare out of curiosity ("mere curiosity," he would say in one of the revised versions of this passage),[68] "whilst the sleet fell and thawed on her naked bosom, and on the skin of her naked baby!" His exclamation does show concern—over her hardiness, or her self-neglect—but it arises also out of a profound sense of difference. The subsequent comments make this clearer.

> These poor wretches were stunted in their growth, their hideous faces bedaubed with white paint, their skins filthy and greasy, their hair entangled, their voices discordant, and their gestures violent, and without dignity. Viewing such men, one can hardly make oneself believe that they are fellow creatures, and inhabitants of the same world. (235)

But that final remark is more complex than it first appears to be. One can hardly make oneself believe this, Darwin says, yet it is something we know to be true. Even as he is detaching himself in this way, Darwin begins to recognize that the separation is a false one, his own moral withdrawal unjustified. As inhabitants of the same world we live in, these "creatures" are, no less than we, subject to physical conditions, shaped and limited by environment. A question is beginning to form, undercutting Darwin's own position as representative of a superior culture and class. He is beginning to recognize how strongly his perception of the Fuegians is a function of that position, of that class and culture. To some extent, then, Darwin's reassessment of the Fuegians involves a reassessment of himself. On a return voyage to Tierra del Fuego in 1834, he notices how sailing into native waters aboard the *Beagle,* rather than on the smaller boats Fitz Roy's party had used on most of their earlier visits, alters his relation to these human subjects.

> I was amused in finding what a difference the circumstance of being quite superior in force made, in the interest of beholding these savages. While in the boats I got to hate the very sound of their voices, so much trouble did they give us. (241)

The naturalist must analyze his own response, as well as the actions of "natives." There is still reference to two classes of beings, and Darwin's tone is more than a little condescending. But there is the beginning of another kind of approach. Once everyone is subject to this scrutiny, there can be no absolute distinction between savages and civilized beings.

Darwin is moving towards this position. But in the *Journal of Researches* it is still only a possibility. The fundamental relationship between these apparently disparate beings is presented tentatively, as a question.

> Whilst beholding these savages, one asks, whence have they come? What could have tempted, or what change compelled a tribe of men to leave the fine regions of the north, to travel down the Cordillera or backbone of America, to invent and build canoes, and then to enter on one of the most inhospitable countries within the limits of the globe? (236–237)

The answer is all around us. "Nature, by making habit omnipotent, and its effects hereditary, has fitted the Fuegian to the climate and the productions of his country" (237). Clearly we are reading one of the early speculations that led Darwin on the path towards the *Origin* and later the *Descent;* but even recognizing that does not remove the sense of uneasiness throughout this section of the text. In 1839 this is a matter for speculation only, and not wholly welcome speculation at that. Perhaps the possibility of common origins only adds to Darwin's sense of shock here; perhaps the real horror of these "savages" is in their resemblance to ourselves, not simply to what we are now but to what we might have been or might become. They tell us something fundamental about our nature and origin, or at least raise fundamental questions. And it is as a question that Darwin returns to this issue in his conclusion.

> Of individual objects, perhaps no one is more certain to create astonishment that the first sight in his native haunt of a real barbarian,—of man in his lowest and most savage state. One's mind hurries back over past centuries, and then asks, could our progenitors have been such as these? (605)

The 1845 edition is more confident of an answer, for Darwin removes the phrase "without dignity" from the description of the Fuegians I quoted earlier. Once he was committed to the notion of evolution, the primitive took on a new importance and assumed a clearer relation to his own world. As Sandra Herbert puts it, "Darwin's work and the nascent science of anthropology now appear parallel and related developments."[69] Like Conrad's Kurtz, he discovers the artificiality of the contrasts he carried as part of his cultural baggage into a new world. He is beginning to experience, with some of Kurtz's "horror" but a far greater measure of pure fascination, that the savage Other is in reality his own double.

Once again, it is useful to compare Darwin's responses to Fitz Roy's, both to recognize their kinship on certain issues and also to see how serious even their small differences could prove. Fitz Roy is in some respects the better ethnographer, and a reader interested in early anthropology (as well as early data on primitive tribes) might find his account of South American natives the more rewarding of the two. Fitz Roy's interest in primitive peoples must have determined many of the *Beagle's* stops and led to the inclusion of so many drawings of South American natives in the illustrations to the *Narrative:* his frontispiece, in fact, shows a Fuegian (Figure 5.8). Yet as I have noted before, Fitz Roy shares little of Darwin's openness to these peoples, little of his curiosity about the possibility of their kinship to himself. There are signs that he recognizes the radical implications of Darwin's ambivalence about the Fuegians and other primitive groups quite as fully as does Darwin himself. But this leads to very different conclusions, and to a very different tone. The second supplementary chapter in the *Proceedings,* "Remarks on the early migration of the human race," pauses to dismiss Darwin's views on human origins.

> That man could have been first created in an infant, or savage state, appears to my apprehension impossible.... Have we a shadow of ground for thinking that wild animals or plants have improved since their creation? Can any reasonable man believe that the first of a race, species, or kind, was the most inferior? Then how for a moment could false philosophers, and those who have been led by their writings, imagine that there were separate beginnings of savage races, at different times, and in different places?[70]

Darwin regards the Fuegians' "abjectness" as proof of a low degree of development; at times he hints that these conditions may show us the evolutionary starting point for any advanced society. As he remarks in a footnote on Tierra del Fuego, humanity in the southern tip of South America "exists in a lower state of improvement than in any other part of the world" (235n). Fitz Roy devotes at least as much space as Darwin to accounts of various "savages" in South America, yet he reminds us everywhere that they exemplify a condition of "degradation" from some originally perfect form. His anthropology is designed to constitute a body of evidence for the Fall.

Both Darwin and Fitz Roy refer to the "brutality" of those "savages," implying in both words the resemblance of the Fuegians to animals. But Darwin's sense of this is the more complex, the more ambivalent of the two. The animal nature of these beings both separates us from them and defines an essential kinship. It is as if Darwin tries to preserve his civilized superiority at the same time he recognizes the much greater significance of a biological identity between himself and his "subjects." In the concluding section of the *Journal of Researches,* this double response emerges when he attempts to answer his own question: "could our progenitors have been such as these?"

> Men, whose very signs and expressions are less intelligible to us than those of the domesticated animals; men, who do not possess the instinct of those animals, nor yet appear to boast of human reason, or at least of arts consequent on that reason. I do not believe it is possible to describe or paint the difference between savage and civilized man. It is the difference between a wild and tame animal: and part of the interest in beholding a savage, is the same which would lead every one to desire to see the lion in his desert, the tiger tearing his prey in the jungle, the rhinoceros on the wide plain, or the hippopotamus wallowing in the mud of some African river. (605–606)

At first savages are treated as beneath animals, then suddenly they stand beside us as animals of similar though still different types. Wild or tame: the very words suggest the shifting values underlying this brief exercise in comparative anthropology. Even the word "savage" has shifted, imperceptibly, into adjectival use, one which finally gives the South Americans a new dignity that Europeans, suddenly viewed as only tame (or tamed), seem to lack. Darwin is looking across a cultural chasm at beings wholly removed from his prior experience of humanity: the distance is both disturbing and attractive. By the end of the passage he has begun to romanticize wild animals in their native haunts and to admit his fascination with them. Gillian Beer suggests that this response can be traced throughout Darwin's notebooks of this period, which record "the exultant pleasure which Darwin felt in restoring man to an equality with other forms of life and in undermining that hubristic separation which man had accorded himself in all previous natural history."[71] We see the same response in a more compact form when Darwin praises the horsemanship of gauchos in the Banda Orientale, a people and place midway between European civilization and Fuegian primitiveness: "A naked man, on a naked horse, is a fine spectacle; I had no idea how well the two animals suited each other" (168).

Part of our interest in these passages derives from their self-consciousness: the naturalist aware of his own surprise, prepared to make his own fascination an object for study. He understands that such encounters reveal something important about the civilized European spectator as well as the natives he observes, something that further closes the distance between them.

> It has been said, that the love of the chase is an inherent delight in man—a relic of an instinctive passion. If so, I am sure the pleasure of living in the open air, with the sky for a roof, and the ground for a table, is part of the same feeling: it is the savage returning to his wild and native habits. I always look back to our boat cruises, and my land journeys, when through unfrequented countries, with a kind of extreme delight, which no scenes of civilization could have created. (606)

There is a direct echo here of those earlier passages on the intense pleasure reserved for the naturalist in this lush new world; in a sense, Darwin is modifying the description of himself given there. In experiencing this delight, the scientist has returned to the primitive sources of aesthetic pleasure. Just as he studies fossil remains of early forms of organic life, or primitive tribes that exist close to the structural roots of his own culture, he learns to respond to simple stimuli with a directness that many civilized beings have lost. We are expected to grant the universality of that "love of the chase," and modern readers are even better prepared than those of the 1830s to admit to a fondness for camping out. Darwin has managed to distance himself from many of the values and feelings we would expect from someone of his education and class.

In one sense, the achievement of that distance is the most important journey recorded in this book—a voyage within the voyage, although in fact it is the element of Darwin's narrative to which most readers most readily respond. The continuing popularity of the *Journal of Researches* (as *The Voyage of the Beagle,* for most readers) is largely a function of its success as an adventure story and the appeal of its all-too-human but exceptionally brave protagonist. In this we may be reminded of Martineau's American books; and if we compare them on these terms, even taking her gender and handicaps into account, Darwin scores high marks for sheer pluck. Riding bareback, camping out without roof or blankets, exposing his arm to swarms of mosquitos to examine their habits, venturing into dangerous jungles with only a few native guides, facing armed and hostile tribes whose suspicions were only increased by his peculiar role as a naturalist, Don Carlos (as he is known in this new world) moves a long way from his normal British identity indeed. There are, of course, traces of a special form of that identity, the figure of the Hearty Colonialist who would become more familiar later in the century. But Darwin is never wholly at ease in that civilized traveller's costume. Those repeated acts of physical daring seem to make him aware above all of his own physical being, the body beneath the clothes. It is as if for the first time the Gentleman discovers his identity as Man, the gender and corporeality that link him with all the varied groups of "natives" he seems at times to observe with so much detachment. Perhaps this explains why his concluding remarks begin by stressing the apparently trivial facts of the physical discomforts of his journey before moving towards such weighty matters as the relation between civilized and primitive forms of life. Darwin's experience of his own physical being was a necessary ingredient of that more abstract conception of the fundamental linkage of all organic existence. The very conditions of the voyage helped stimulate that other journey towards a radical, evolutionary conception of the world that included all humanity, and the naturalist himself.

Of course, it is a long distance to travel; but the journey has begun. Even if Darwin is not prepared to insist upon absolute biological kinship, he does warn his reader not to assume that such primitive peoples are necessarily too distant, too different, from ourselves. At times they seem sub-human, yet we have no basis for concluding that they are so far degraded as to be beneath the possibilities of experiencing normal human emotion, such as pleasure. At first it seems as if Darwin images the Fuegians this way:

> It is a common subject of conjecture what pleasure in life some of the less gifted animals can enjoy: how much more reasonably the same question may be asked with respect to these barbarians. (235–236)

He goes on to offer many reasons for believing that Fuegians cannot possibly enjoy life at all: as nomads they can have no feeling of home or domestic affection; their surroundings offer no stimulus for reason, judgment, or imagination; even their skills are limited, little better than instincts in animals. Yet he introduces this evidence only to refute it later on, to rebut the sort of response we have come to expect from an ethnocentric observer like Fitz Roy. "Although such reflections must at first occupy one's mind, yet we may feel sure that many of them are quite erroneous" (237). The problem lies in how we observe: the sort of evidence we have come to accept, and that we have not—in what we have not even chosen to recognize as evidence. He mentions one prominent example of this, and it is a crucial one: there is no reason to believe that the Fuegian population has decreased. Clearly, then, these is sexual activity, and thus both pleasure and a desire to produce offspring: "We must suppose that they enjoy a sufficient share of happiness . . . to render life worth having" (237).

Aside from the phrase in ellipsis (to which I will return shortly), it is a remarkable moment in the history of naturalistic thought, and even of modern psychology. The insight anticipates Darwin's revolutionary reading of Malthus, from which the fundamental hypotheses of the *Origin* took form. A. Dwight Culler has argued that that reading, really an inspired misreading, fundamentally reversed the sardonic vision of the original text, transforming the Malthusian conception of human nature's tragic demands into comedy—a comedy that celebrates, among other things, the sexual drive.[72] We can see the beginnings of the reversal here, or perhaps one of the products of it, since Darwin's "Malthus insight" (as Gruber calls it) came in late 1838, when he still may have been making final revisions in the text of the *Journal of Researches.* Chronology aside, the two perceptions are very much of a piece. The Fuegians are redeemed by their biology, for it links them in a chain of life stretching from the most primitive sexual organisms to the most civilized efforts "to render life worth having." We can sense the beginnings of a Freudian insight into our own behavior too: all human efforts to ennoble or beautify existence are only more elaborate (sublimated) versions of a fundamental reproductive instinct. The argument alerts us to a view of those primitive Others precluded by our normal intellectual perspectives, a view according to which that otherness begins to vanish. Their inner life remains closed to us, but there is enough evidence for us to judge, to "suppose," that it exists. This conclusion is related to that Malthusian insight too, for we are being warned of the self-imposed limits of "normal science," the values it necessarily projects onto the world it claims to observe dispassionately. But Darwin is not yet prepared to repudiate that norm, or to stand wholly beyond the barriers of his own culture. The limits of his vision are apparent in the phrase I have omitted in citing this passage so far. "We must suppose," the full text reads, "they enjoy a sufficient share of happiness (of whatever kind it may be) to render life worth living." Of whatever kind? It is one of the most condescending moments in the book. Apparently all pleasures are not equal, or not equally comprehensible. Some humans are more human than others; some remain radically beyond our full sympathy. If this is so, a fundamental inequity between different ways of life, between different peoples, remains, even in the most radically modern sections of the *Journal of Researches.*

To what extent does that contradiction persist into Darwin's mature thought? Answering such a question fully is beyond the scope of *Victoria's Year,* but in the concluding pages of this chapter I do wish to suggest one direction in which a search for an answer might proceed. The issue I have in mind concerns Darwin's language, and one image in particular—a simile that can be traced back from the closing pages of the *Origin* to the *Journal of Researches,* through the intermediate step of a work composed around 1842, a preliminary "Sketch" of his still-developing theory of evolution by natural selection. That work was reissued by his son in 1909 under the title of *The Foundations of the Origin of Species.*[73] It contains "foundations" of several sorts: for the general arguments of the later book and, as we will see, for the first versions of some of its most important passages. One of those passages, in the versions of both 1842 and 1859, indicates the extent to which the experience of the *Beagle* voyage structures Darwin's mature view of nature, and the place of the naturalist within it. The very emphasis on that figure, on the observer, increases the importance of the "Sketch" as a transition between the work of the late 1830s and the *Origin.* For it is not just the "Sketch" of a theory, but of the impact of that theory on one who embraces it. It is a "Sketch" in the sociology—or the psychology, or aesthetics—of knowledge. It reminds us that the origin of the *Origin* is bound up in the question of how to observe.

The concluding sentence of the "Sketch," which would be adopted into the much more elaborate conclusion of the *Origin,* begins by declaring that "There is a simple grandeur in the view of life with its powers of growth, assimilation, and reproduction, being originally breathed into matter under one or a few forms."[74] It is still the language of the 1830s, the language of the naturalist-cum-aesthete. Lyell had written to Herschel in 1836 of the "grandeur" he felt when he "first came to the notion, which I never saw expressed elsewhere . . . of a succession of extinction of species, and creation of new ones, going on perpetually."[75] Darwin came across the same term in a similar context in the July 1838 *Edinburgh Review,* in a discussion of Comte's theories of "the origin and destiny" of the universe.

Appealing to our imagination by this grandeur, and to our reason by the severe principles of science on which they rest, the mind feels as if a revelation had been vouchsafed to it of the past and future history of the universe.[76]

Darwin uses the word with little of this quasi-theological rapture, but with an even closer connection between imaginative and reasoned response.

This is a "grandeur" uniquely available to the evolutionist. As the adjacent remarks in both the *Origin* and the 1842 "Sketch" make clear, the word does not refer to a generalized sublimity, to be regarded with the sort of stupefied admiration displayed by that Fuegian woman who remained to stare at Darwin's party in driving rain despite her own nakedness— remained, as later editions of the *Journal of Researches* put it, "out of mere curiosity." It is true, of course, that Darwin had chided those Chileans for their lack of curiosity about volcanoes and earthquakes. Yet curiosity alone, mere curiosity, is somehow still suspect, characteristic of primitive peoples and primitive imaginative responses. The evolutionary world view begins with curiosity, but still differs sharply from such untutored, undiscriminating fascination.

Another passage from the 1842 "Sketch" makes the distinction clearer (I will cite the longer, revised version from the *Origin*):

> When we no longer look at an organic being as a savage looks at a ship, as something wholly beyond his comprehension; when we regard every production of nature as one which has had a long history; when we contemplate every complex structure and instinct as the summing up of many contrivances, each useful to the possessor, in the same way as any great mechanical invention is the summing up of the labour, the experience, the reason, and even the blunders of numerous workmen; when we thus view each organic being, how far more interesting—I speak from experience—does the study of natural history become![77]

The 1842 version had referred to "a ship, or other great work of art," but by removing that phrase Darwin preserves the more complex sense of an aesthetic "grandeur" that is reserved for the naturalist's eye. We may overcome the primitive view of nature as magical and inexplicable, yet this only makes the world "more interesting." "I speak from experience," Darwin adds; and to a great extent the "Sketch" concerns that experience, and the identity of the naturalist defined in the process of observing his subject.

Yet it is in the relation of those two beings that this simile of natural history becomes paradoxical, and as in the *Journal of Researches* the paradox centers on the figure of the savage. In one sense Darwin argues for an inclusive category of organic beings that seems to encompass people and animals together, linked in a shiplike unity. But somehow the savage remains, different, set apart. There is first a sense of connection with nature, a broad sympathy that breaks cultural and ethnocentric barriers. But at the same time there is a distinctly civilized voice, speaking to us from the decks of an intruding ship. It was from those decks that Darwin managed to look upon the Fuegians with a newly achieved sympathetic

detachment, on his return to Ponsony Sound in 1834. Yet he was still looking down upon them, and his detachment resulted (as he explains) from
the fact that instead of paddling alongside them in one of the smaller vessels he now could observe from the safety of the more formidable *Beagle.*
This is the moment when he begins to see them as humans, rather than
distant Others; and yet it is a moment determined by the fact that he is set
apart, no longer in the same boat.

The 1859 account of the modern naturalist's unified vision of the world
thus is undercut by what can be termed the politics of Darwin's experience
in the 1830s. It is worth recalling here that the *Beagle* and *Adventure* (Captain King's ship) were commissioned on what the full title of the three-
volume offical report calls "surveying voyages." Darwin's work was autho-
rized within this mission too. The instructions from the Lord High Admiral's Commissioners to Captain King in 1826 (they were signed by no less
a figure than John Wilson Croker) confer official status on the naturalist.

> You are to avail yourself of every opportunity of collecting and preserving
> Specimens of such objects of Natural History as may be new, rare, or inter-
> esting; and you are to instruct Captain Stokes, and all the other Officers, to
> use their best diligence in increasing the collection in each ship: the whole of
> which must be understood as belonging to the public.[78]

Darwin's own task was vague and undefined. But this does not preclude
an official conception of it as an arm of government authority, or a conception of his collections as possessions of the state. Europeans, after all,
survey the new world to make it rational, known, accessible for orderly
government control and the development of markets. A map, as Brian
Friel's play *Translations* reminds us, is itself an instrument of power. Darwin's activity on this surveying mission also becomes an expression of
power—the power of modern technology, for one thing, embodied in the
Beagle itself. It is clear enough from the *Journal of Researches* that his
work is perceived in this way by some natives of the lands where the incur-
sion takes place. And Darwin's language suggests that at times he perceives
the voyage in these terms as well.

Beginning with that image of the ship, Darwin's simile associates nature
with use, purpose, value, and ultimately, power. The "mystery of mysteries" referred to in the first paragraph of the *Origin*[79] has been supplanted
by a vision of the world as explicable in terms usually applied to modern
industrial processes: "production . . . contrivances . . . mechanical invention . . . workmen." The early version of the passage, with its reference to
a "great work of art," reminds us that this account of nature as a "great
mechanical invention" goes back to the eighteenth-century view of the

universe as magnificent Divine clockwork. The longer version in the *Origin* contains a more modern allusion to collective labor on a mass scale (there are now "numerous workmen"), what Tennyson calls, in a curiously parallel reference to the unity of natural processes, "toil cooperant to an end" (*In Memoriam,* cxxviii). And the allusion to labor suggests something else about the nature of nature. Darwin's Notebook account of his insight into natural selection after reading Malthus refers to the "economy of nature" (the same language reappears in his account of this insight in the *Autobiography*).[80] The phrase reminds us that even nature's ecology, its system of checks and balances, can be understood as a form of politics, governed by laws intimately related to those regulating human populations and their markets. To some extent this analogy is inherited from Malthus himself, although, as Gertrude Himmelfarb has observed, the theory of his *Essay on Population* is "itself derived from natural history."[81] Similarly, it often has been pointed out that the notions of natural struggle in both Darwin and Malthus are metaphors taken from economic and social competition. Stephen J. Gould suggests that the "theory of natural selection should be viewed as an extended analogy—whether conscious or unconscious on Darwin's part I do not know—to the laissez-faire economics of Adam Smith."[82] That argument has been extended further in the best recent writing on Darwin, most notably in the work of Robert M. Young and Gillian Beer. We are learning that it is mistaken, and indeed impossible, to separate Darwin's scientific arguments from the allusions of his metaphors to larger contexts. As Young puts it in the title of one essay, "Darwinism *is* social."[83]

Social analogies helped Darwin recognize the inescapability of natural change, for better or for worse. Earlier I cited Darwin's speculations on the effects of an earthquake of major proportions on English economic and social life, and Lyell's similarly political metaphor of the "revolutions of the earth." It is as if natural change, especially change of the greatest magnitude, can be understood only by reference to social disruption. Surely these connections were partly illuminated for Darwin by the unstable political conditions he observed in South America alongside the effects of geological instability. Similarly, specualtions about evolutionary success may have seemed all the more inescapable on a journey that carried the naturalist first from Argentina "down" to Tierra del Fuego and the most "abject" tribes on the continent, and then West and North, "up" to the colonized communities of New Zealand, where Darwin confesses his pride in viewing evidence of the "progress" that British influence could produce. Human nature, it would seem, can be improved. And, of course, Darwin (like any English country gentleman) would have had prior experience with the possibility of improving animals. John Cornell and others have argued that the idea of natural selection emerges from Darwin's investigations into the technology of animal breeding, one of the most significant forms of nineteenth-century argricultural capitalism.[84] All of these insights help us understand more fully that image of the ship. It is based, after all, on the *Beagle*—and the very name reminds us that nature can become part of an agricultural technology strongly influenced by the requirements of social class. Darwin's *Beagle* is the official vehicle of a governmental surveying mission and it is named after a popular breed of hunting dog. What better vantage point from which to pursue and control wild nature without losing one's identity as a member of a particular society? We must disavow the attitude of a savage towards this ship because its very presence is predicated on a commitment to bringing order to uncharted regions, a commitment to a "natural" potential for improvement, for cultivation. A writer in the *Edinburgh Review,* discussing the volumes by King, Fitz Roy, and Darwin, notes that those surveying voyages were probably motivated by the opening of South America to British trade following a series of revolutions against Spain.[85]

Thus, as Darwin's image of nature, that ship also comes to stand for civilization, a Macaulayesque conception of progress. He was, in fact, reading Macaulay's essay on Bacon at the time he was revising the *Journal of Researches* for publication, and mentions it in a letter to Lyell at almost the same time he arrived at the "Malthus insight."[86] He might have been reviewing it for methodological reasons. Macaulay's essay is a classic defense of pure empiricism, and Darwin's *Autobiography* explains that the conclusions of 1838 were derived "on true Baconian principles and without any theory."[87] Macaulay's essay also invokes the image of a ship entering a new world, to illustrate his disdain for generalized Platonic wisdom: disciples of Epictetus and Bacon arrive in distant lands to offer their respective philosophical services to the benighted natives; we are expected to compare those philosophies in terms of their practical applications. But there is an even more specific literary source for Darwin's ship, one his reading notes indicate he saw some time before beginning work on the "Sketch"; it is from *How to Observe.*[88] The passage makes it even clearer how much his new, inductive grasp of natural law is bound up in questions of power. A group of Plains Indians, Martineau tells us, were visiting some major Eastern cities during the course of peace negotiations. They were trying to learn something about the government they were treating with, and their American guides were trying to create an impression of their own power to emphasize the need for a speedy settlement. Martineau had cautioned, earlier in the book, that no traveller should trust verbal explanations of the lands or peoples he set out to observe; these Indians are wise enough to seek out firmer evidence. Yet they do finally come to accept their hosts' claims to superior power and technology, not because of what they are told but because of what they see—Baconian (or Macaulayesque) material evidence: the "exhibition of a ship." They come upon it by chance, but study it in awe.

> The warriors of the prairies were too proud to utter their astonishment,— too noble to hint, even to one another, their fear; but the perspiration stood on their brows as they dumbly gazed, and no word of war passed their lips from that hour.[89]

Martineau presents this as a fable of insight: these noble travellers have used "the evidence of things" to learn something essential, and something essential for their own survival. The ship embodies the power of the American state and the extent of its technology; war would be futile against a government capable of producing such things. The construction of warships is intended to express this, in a grim architectural poetry that warns would-be enemies. Ships like H.M.S. *Beagle* (itself a military vessel, after all) can be charged with threatening messages regardless of their particular missions. The governor of New South Wales recognized this in authorizing the use of the ship to help the British resident in New Zealand restore order among the local tribes: "by the skilful use of those powers which educated man possesses over the wild or half-civilized savage, an influence may be gained."[90] Martineau's Plains Indians are confronted with the same sort of "influence" and seem to understand it quite well.

This suggests that there are in fact two representations of naturalistic knowledge in the scene Darwin adopts from Martineau. We must imagine ourselves belonging to that civilizing ship, but also to the world that learns how to observe it. And the point, of course, is that we haven't fully learned yet. It is only in the future that "we *no longer* look at an organic being as a savage looks at a ship." The primitive response to nature is one we all have been guilty of, are guilty of still. Civilization loses its privilege, then, its exclusive access to the truth, its distance from nature. In one sense, civilization *is* nature, we are the savages we observe. Evolutionary nature, after all, is often associated with that world of violence, "red in tooth and claw," from which so many moral Victorians turn in dread. Yet in this simile it is the civilized ship that bears the most lethal power to destroy its own kind. Standing momentarily alongside that savage, we are forced to recognize this—forced to recognize, that is, the ambiguous and potentially deadly knowledge possessed by the natural scientist himself. Michel Foucault argues that it is with Darwin that a new figure begins to appear in the history of Western thought. Instead of the universal moral speculator we find the "specific intellectual," a savant, an expert: "no longer he who bears the values of all," but rather he "who, with a handful of others, has at his disposal, whether in the service of the State or against it, powers which can either benefit or irrevocably destroy life. He is no longer the rhapsodist of the eternal, but the strategist of life and death."[91] It is an ambiguous figure, whose knowledge might be put to very different uses. By the end of the *Origin,* in the simile that grows out of his experience aboard the *Beagle* and his reading of Martineau, Darwin presents his reader with a hint of these possibilities. It embodies a kind of ultimate choice. It is his last, and most complex, question.

The naturalist who emerges at the end of the *Origin* has gained access to the "mystery of mysteries" only to discover that an infinite regress of further mysteries lies hidden beyond. It is not just that his own role has become endlessly complex, but that his sense of the natural world has too. He is at once on and off that ship: empowered with a new sense of the order of things, but also charged with the necessity of perpetually questioning that order, and the forms it takes. "Certainty, in Darwin's world," George Levine remarks, "is valuable only as it opens on uncertainty."[92] All the naturalist knows for sure is that his knowledge must be modified endlessly, that there will always be new data and new problems, that he must never stop asking questions. As Darwin comments at the end of the introduction to the *Origin,* "Much remains obscure, and will long remain obscure." Little remains, then, except observation, an endless process of observation leading only to hypotheses that can be refined endlessly but never conclusively proved, leading in many cases only to images. If Darwin manages to imagine himself—and asks us to imagine ourselves—on board that ship rather than simply peering at it nervously from a distance, it is because everything in our world, including ourselves, must become subject to this heroic epistemological task. The whole world, that is to say, becomes subject and object at once, "known and unknown" (as Tennyson says of Hallam at the end of *In Memoriam*), the source and the topic for an endless cycle of questions and answers. By 1837 the *Beagle* had returned to home port. But Darwin's great intellectual voyage was only beginning.

III

EPILOGUE—1839

6

Remember the *Téméraire!*

There is a circle between life and death, and between death and life again, far more wide, far more intricate, and far more wonderful, than the great chemical circle of the atmosphere. . . .

        John Macculloch, M.D., *Proofs and Illustrations of the Attributes of God* (1837)

According to the constitution of things dissolution is no less necessary than production and preservation; for the earth would soon cease to afford habitation and sustenance to the animal and vegetable tribes, if life and death were not the prelude to each other. Decay then is necessary, and organized forms having fulfilled one part of their destination, are abandoned to that destructive principle in order to accomplish the other.

        Penny Magazine (May 21, 1836)

Thro' great memorials wande'ring to and fro,
Waves of old Time about me seem to roll,
Most like a tune heard somewhere long ago,
Whose sepa'rate notes have left upon my soul
Some footmarks as they past, and though I know
That memory's hardest toil can raise the whole
Into continuous being, nev'er again,
I still strive on as one in love with pain.

        Richard Monckton Milnes, "Written at Rome" (1838)

Memorial Pillar! 'mid the wrecks of Time
Preserve thy charge with confidence sublime—
The exultations, pomps, and cares of Rome,
Whence half the breathing world received its doom;
Things that recoil from language; that, if shown
By apter pencil, from the light had flown.

        William Wordsworth, "The Pillar of Trajan" (1825)

Fast flashing, like the phosphor gleam
Upon the southern seas,
Shine, rippling o'er his waking dream,
The wavelike memories.

        Edward Lytton Bulwer, "The Death of Nelson" (1839)[1]

I

In its final number of October 1839, *Nicholas Nickleby* ends, as so much
Victorian fiction does, looking forward: we learn of the futures of the Link-
inwaters, Newman Noggs, Mrs. Sliderskew, Gride, Squeers, and Sir Mul-
berry Hawk; the success of the firm of Cheeryble and Nickleby is described
in a few sentences, and a few paragraphs glance ahead to the happiness of
their children. Dickens closes in what would become a characteristic bit-
tersweet tone, telling of the loving care with which those children (of Nicholas and Madeline, Frank and Kate) tended "the dead boy's grave." Only
now that "boy," Smike, is part of their family history, "and they spoke low
and softly of their poor dead cousin." Curiously, this briefly imaged future
is narrated in the past, and the events of the rest of the novel are transformed into memories that inform the pious good nature of those who
survive and thrive. Wealth and success cannot be purchased without suffering, and can be ennobled only if the sufferers remain conscious of that
price. The recent Royal Shakespeare Company production of *Nickleby*
added a last tableau to dramatize this self-consciousness: Nicholas moves
apart from the group of glad wedding couples at the curtain to raise in his
arms the huddled figure of a beggar boy at the front of the stage. It is an
anonymous figure, representing (as the narrator explains) a world of suffering outside these miraculously blessed households; it is played by the
same actor who until then has filled the role of Smike. Nicholas is applying
the lesson of his recent experience to the rest of the world. Even more dramatically than in the novel, and in a scene it does not contain, we see
memory at work.

This change in the modern *Nickleby* is linked to another, more strictly
adapted from the final pages of the book. The last of Dickens' words spoken on stage, shifted from their position five paragraphs before the end of
the story in the text to fit the compulsive charity of that closing tableau,
emphasize that the hero, as well as the generation after him, ends his quest
preoccupied by the conditions out of which it began—preoccupied, that is,
by memory, and by the past.

> The first act of Nicholas, when he became a rich and prosperous merchant,
> was to buy his father's old house. As time crept on, and there came gradually
> about him a group of lovely children, it was altered and enlarged, but none
> of the old rooms were ever pulled down, no old tree was rooted up, nothing
> with which there was any association of bygone times was ever removed or
> changed.[2]

We are expected to think of his uncle Ralph at this moment, and the moral corruption associated with a denial of family origins. But the references of this passage are wider than that, and extend beyond the novel. Alteration, enlargement, rooting up: by 1839 those terms were beginning to take on the currency they would maintain for most of the century as descriptions of the physical condition of England, and London especially. Pugin's warnings about the future went unheeded: his nightmare rapidly became a reality.

The great age of Victorian architecture was dawning, and to many, including Dickens, Pugin, and even the young Ruskin, its light was both brilliant and fearful. Little wonder Ruskin's first book should have been an effort to define, and preserve, *The Poetry of Architecture.* In actual experience, building seemed a long way from that—to some extent, not architectural at all. Ruskin's near-hysterical response to a wholly material, wholly practical program for building can be explained, in the simplest possible terms, as a recognition of the realities of urban design. Was there any poetry in Victorian London? Was it really composed of what we call architecture? By the late 1830s London was beginning to assume the varied, sprawling, unplanned character that is associated with it still. "The Rejection and Destruction of Georgian London," as Donald J. Olsen terms it, involved a turn away from a more formally architected urban landscape, away from the symmetries and order we usually think of in connection with the idea of urban design. Olsen cites what he calls the example of Paris, the model of "antiquity, permanence, and solidity," against which contemporaries measured the unique qualities of an emerging, modern London.[3] Flora Tristan, a French visitor writing in 1840, complains of "modern edifices" disfigured by "borrowings from every architecture, a bizarre mixture of all possible forms, totally without harmony and without thought."[4] The same cultural contrast is implicit in the remark I cited earlier from an 1840 number of the Dublin *Evening Post,* where it is observed that "the *air* of Paris is that of an old city; while London looks . . . neither new nor old, a sort of *Provisional City,* a multitudinous congregation of houses that are constantly . . . in a state of transition of being run up or run down." Tristan reduces all this to a single phrase, the title of the first chapter of her *Promenades dans Londres:* London is "The Monster City."[5] She has glimpsed in reality that sprawling Horizontal City Pugin is haunted by. Clearly, Nicholas is not the only one with preservationist impulses, nor the only one made uneasy by change.

Had the bustle and restlessness we now associate with the Victorian period as a whole already been set in motion? Moods of that sort are difficult to document, and perhaps impossible to fix so precisely in time as in a single year. But there are some events of 1839 that confirm the contemporary intuition that Britain was becoming a rootless, timeless, "provisional" culture—events staged to halt that drift. Perhaps the most widely known is the Eglinton Tournament, and it is the fact that it is so widely known that makes it significant. As Mark Girouard recently has observed, it was almost immediately—even from the moment of the first public announcements of the project—taken as a symbol, by enthusiasts and critics alike. "Whigs insulted Tories, Utilitarians made fun of romantics. As the excitement grew the tournament grew with it, until it became not only a full-scale re-enactment of a medieval event, but even more a symbol of Tory defiance, of aristocratic virility, of hatred of the Reform Bill, of protest against 'the sordid, heartless, sensual doctrines of Utilitarianism.' "[6] It was, in other words, a self-conscious retreat from the present, a ritual memorializing a better world in the past. Girouard mentions several events ("One, to be exact, was a non-event")[7] that led up to the tournament itself. All three took place in 1838. The production of an opera called *The Tournament* by Lord Burghersh; the opening of Samuel Pratt's armor showrooms in Lower Grosvenor Street; and, perhaps most important, the controversial refusal of Lord Melbourne to stage Victoria's coronation with the traditional banquet and accompanying medieval display (Queen's Champion throwing down a gauntlet, presentation of two falcons, etc.).[8] The symbolism of Eglinton grew out of that of the Penny Coronation—or rather, grew out of the failure of symbolism at the start of the new reign, a failure regarded by many as nothing short of sacrilegious. Remembering history was a serious matter, indeed. Obeisance to the past in 1839 was not simply a fad; for some, it was an urgent need.

J. M. W. Turner was one of those. His paintings had always been deeply steeped in the classical tradition, and 1839 turned out to be a year with particularly strong classical emphasis: *Cicero at his Villa; Pluto Carrying Off Proserpine;* or, finally, the paired set of ancient and modern paintings that both refer to the classical past—*Ancient Rome: Agrippina landing with the ashes of Germanicus; The Triumphal Bridge and Palace of the Caesars restored,* and *Modern Rome—Campo Vaccino.* Another painting of 1839, the *Fountain of Fallacy,* has been lost, although if it is, as believed, similar to or identical with the *Fountain of Indolence* (1835) it has a classical subject too, even if it is not disclosed in the title. But the most famous painting of 1839 is historical in another way, an evocation of the British rather than the heroic classical past. The reference in the title suggests a recent event, as if Turner has set out to create a visual image of the historical significance of the contemporary world. Apparently the painting—*The Fighting*

"Temeraire" tugged to her last berth to be broken up. 1838 (Figure 6.1)—has a personal significance as well. Subsequent legend has associated it with Turner's remark about his "darling" picture, with which he would not part for any "consideration of money."[9] But whatever it meant to the painter, it also meant a great deal to its first audiences. The *Temeraire* provides a rare instance of a Turner masterpiece that struck a clearly sympathetic chord from the time of its first exhibition, and it is worth considering why. How did the first viewers see the *Temeraire?* What did they (to use E. H. Gombrich's phrase) see it *as?*

To answer such questions, we must first try to rephrase them a bit. The problem of how contemporary viewers saw Turner's painting is not strictly a problem of what they thought it meant: we must also be clear about what kind of a painting they thought it was. The most basic answer can be given in the words with which Courbet described his *Atelier* just over fifteen years later: an *"allégorie réelle,"* a real or modern allegorical picture. Those words, or even similar ones, do not enter the first interpretations of the *Temeraire;* but the notion can be recognized everywhere. The *Morning Chronicle* of May 7, 1839, reviewing the Royal Academy exhibition in which the *Temeraire* was hung, speaks of it as representing "the decay of a noble human being." Behind the ship, "the gorgeous horizon poetically intimates that the sun of the Temeraire is setting in glory." These terms echo in the comments of the *Literary Gazette,* which appeared four days later: the reviewer refers to "the sun of the glorious vessel . . . setting in a flood of light . . . typifying the departing glories of the old Temeraire." The *Athenaeum* joins in (on May 11) to give an admiring account of this picture of the "doomed vessel."[10] Within a few years, Ruskin was to give this sort of reading a far wider circulation. And it is still maintained. Modern critics devote much of their attention to that sense of "doom," stressing the picture's reference beyond a particular warship to the whole navy, and to Britain generally—even to the predicament of modern history, or to the situation of the artist. Louis Hawes, in the most extended discussion of the painting, treats it as a double allegory of the predicament of England and the fate of Turner himself. As Jack Lindsay puts it elsewhere, "Turner's sense of mortality is merged with his definition of history."[11]

Mortality and the definition of history: those issues are not unique to this picture, but for once they meet with critical acclaim, as if Turner's methods are understood. The change is in part a matter of style. In other works of the last dozen or so years of his life, the same concerns emerge in complex, allusive imagery—an allegory that puzzles the most determined interpreters, a dense pictorial surface from which it often isn't possible to separate all or even many of the represented details with certainty. But what sets the *Temeraire* apart above all is its subject; that is what makes it possible for this deeply felt personal vision to find expression in so clear and legible a form, and for its viewers to feel so confident in explaining what they see. I have spoken of the painting as a modern or real allegory, in the mode of Courbet, and yet we can lose sight of that modernity, that contemporary sense of fact, if we do not recall that the *Téméraire* was well known to Turner's audience, that the scene represented in the painting was one many of them would have heard about or even witnessed.[12] Those reviewers can allegorize a picture they have never seen before because they recognize the material treated in it. And their interpretations are bolstered further by the fact that the *Téméraire* had been the object of other symbolic and even allegorical interpretations well before Turner painted his picture. Entirely apart from this painting, the ship was caught up in popular lore as an image of greatness—both national and personal greatness, although the person in question was of course not Turner himself. The *Téméraire* was associated in a rich and complex way with Trafalgar and Nelson; all of the earliest descriptions of Turner's painting are informed by this fact. We must investigate that lore in some detail to understand the way in which the painting was understood, to understand what it was seen as, to determine its relation to the task of preserving and remembering and its relation to the sense of the past that was emerging at the end of Victoria's Year.

II

The *Téméraire*, one of the most celebrated of all Nelson's fighting ships, was towed up the Thames on September 6, 1838, to be deposited in the wrecking dock. Turner's title refers to the specific event and its ultimate object, and there is evidence that he was there to witness it at the time. Thomas Woolner reports the account of W. F. Woodington, who was with Turner returning by steam packet from Margate when they saw the *Téméraire* appear in "a great blazing sunset." Turner was "also noticing and busy making little sketches on cards."[13] Some of this story may have been colored by hindsight, from a later awareness of the eventual use of those preparatory drawings. But we can find some confirmation of this version in a report on the towing in the *Times*. A week after the *Téméraire* came up river, a brief article on the event notes some of the qualities that caught the painter's attention: "The majestic appearance of this fine ship excited much interest and curiosity; every vessel she passed appeared like a pigmy. . . . She was a noble specimen of the wooden walls of old

England."[14] The report differs from Turner's visual description in one significant respect: it mentions that the *Téméraire* was being pulled by two steam tugs; Turner includes only one. I will return to this discrepancy later. For now what is interesting to notice is how much of the public record of this event seems related to the painting executed in the next year, the record of both that initial towing and the ship's last days.

During the month after its trip up the Thames, the *Téméraire* was being dismantled by its purchaser, a Mr. J. Beatson. The process was observed by a number of visitors to the demolition site. The *Times* of October 12 mentions the presence of "several naval officers and seamen who fought and bled for their country, under the immortal Nelson on board the Temeraire; and many a brave fellow has displayed considerable emotion at the recollection of that glorious battle, which the sight of the Temeraire was so well calculated to awaken; and her present dismantled and helpless condition, contrasted with honourable appearance when her broadsides were thundering over the vast ocean . . . drew forth many a sigh from the veterans." One "jolly old tar" who lost his "larboard leg" at Trafalgar exclaimed that he "couldn't have believed they would have served her so." "Howsorndever," [*sic*] he added, shifting his attention to practical matters, "I hope I shall have timber enough for a new leg out of her." He begged and received a stout piece of oak from the ship to fashion a new limb. Others made similar requests, and Beatson seems to have been generous enought to grant them. He was more possessive about Nelson's "celebrated signal" from Trafalgar, the set of flags declaring "England expects that every man shall do his duty." In spite of numerous offers to purchase this relic, Beatson "refused to part with" it, as the *Times* report explains, "at any price."

At least three aspects of this account are immediately relevant to the examination of Turner's painting: the language of Beatson's refusal, which seems to anticipate Turner's reported insistence on keeping his picture from would-be buyers; the gaiety of that otherwise sober tar as he carries away a piece of broken ship; and a word introduced casually by the *Times* correspondent to describe what it was people came to see and to experience—a "sight . . . calculated to awaken" deep emotion. *Calculated* seems an inappropriate word, at least in its literal sense. The ship is not a work of art; and, although it is being visited and observed, it is not really on exhibit, not intended for the contemplation of spectators. Yet this is how the writer instinctively responded to the circumstances of the demolition dock. The ship has become an object for contemplation of the most serious kind, as if it has been displayed for the purpose of moral instruction. As we have seen in *The Poetry of Architecture,* structures can become sights whose significance is realized in the responses of viewers. Ruskin, of course, is addressing genteel Continental tourists, creating a sort of modern courtesy-book of observation. But his point of view helps us to understand the motives of those unnamed (and not always genteel) visitors at Beatson's as well, and to sympathize with the impulse of a well-known artist, supposedly returning from holiday, to notice and sketch the old ship as it passed. Images of a certain kind were welcomed as an occasion for emotional release, and not just welcomed when they happened to appear but actually sought out. Ruskin does not simply write for those who may be travelling, he encourages travel as a form of moral education; Martineau does much the same thing in *How to Observe*.

In this case, the object of so much interest is an extraordinary one: a ship steeped in historical associations, venerable enough by virtue of its own past that even outside of Turner's painting we can imagine it suggesting (to cite the *Morning Chronicle* again) "the decay of a noble human being." Those first *Times* articles show that the ship was seen initially as a magnificent, moving ruin, an image of greatness in decline; this is why so many spectators came to see it. There is something attractive in such gloom, something sublime. Turner's painting depicts both the gloom and the attraction at once in an eerie image so powerful that it almost seems to detach itself from its context. This is not to pretend that the rest of the painting disappears, above all not that dark, disturbing tugboat. But somehow the *Téméraire* is qualitatively more important than its surroundings. It is a separateness Turner expressed verbally in a revised version of the title, attached to the prospectus for the 1845 engraving: "The (fighting) Temeraire (tugged to her last berth to be broken up   1838)."[15] Even the date is contained within those brackets. It is as if the ship is detached from time, in an eternal contemplative and symbolic space. The revised title refers to the ship's past (when it fought) and future (its impending destruction), but for an instant we are forced to see it as timeless. It is apprehended in a specific historical moment, yet it embodies the possibility of transcending historical change.

The urge for such transcendence may seem to exist at an opposite extreme from that drive to remember I spoke of before. But these fantasies of timelessness grow out of a clear sense of time and history. The towing of this ship to its "last berth" bespeaks above all the economic and political realities of a particular historical moment. The one-legged souvenir-hunter recognized this, as did the *Times* correspondent who referred to "the wooden walls of old England." As Louis Hawes has demonstrated, that phrase alludes to an ongoing debate over the state of the Royal Navy, which was being altered by an increasing tendency to scrap the huge old ships of the line like the *Téméraire* and replace them with smaller steam frigates.[16] By 1838 the *Téméraire* was one of only nine surviving veterans (the word suggests how closely linked were the personification and sentimentalization of ships) of the Trafalgar fleet (twenty-seven ships in all), and the number was shrinking. It was a question of naval tactics, economics, and technological imperatives as well as a matter of sentiment and memory, and the intensity of the debate suggests that even larger issues were at stake: not just the state of the navy but what Carlyle would call the Condition of England, both the future of naval warfare and the future of the whole British tradition of the sea. In a sense, the largest issue was the problem of the future itself, the threats of time and change, but this only meant that envisioning the future became another exercise in memory, born out of conceptions of the present and the past. Thus Sir John Barrow's biography of the great eighteenth-century admiral Lord Anson, published in 1838 (but dated 1839), ends with a glance forward in a long polemical "Supplemental Chapter" answering the "oft-repeated charges of the neglected and *reduced* condition of the British navy."[17] The future of the "wooden walls of old England" was a matter of contemporary policy and history; the present and the future had to be judged in terms of the past. Fighting ships became an image of this comparison, and a controversial one.

So did fighting men, particularly Nelson. Alongside the debate over England's ships of the line, a lively public discussion arose over a suitable memorial to the nation's greatest naval hero. A Nelson Memorial Committee began to meet in February 1838 to organize the effort. The timing had something to do with Victoria's accession to the throne: earlier plans for a monument to the "achievements of the British navy throughout the late wars" (as an 1816 resolution of the House of Commons put it) had been complicated in the early 1830s by the previous monarch, William IV, the Sailor King; when a statue of William was proposed as the central image of this memorial, the project was dropped.[18] In addition to this, there was a sense of rivalry occasioned by the activities of the Wellington Memorial Committee, which in 1837 had begun its planning to erect a statue in honor of the duke. Carlyle might have observed that a people defines itself by its choice of heroes. In this case the choice involved a range of other issues: the army versus the navy, the living versus the dead. Clearly the two heroes were very different sorts of men, exemplifying different virtues. Of course, there were already other monuments to each. But the Nelson committee was attempting to establish the first national monument to the admiral, as distinguished from the tributes by various cities or private institutions. As it was stated at a meeting on August 1st, there was a need to demonstrate "that this country is not unmindful or regardless of such services—that she will celebrate them however great the distance of time, and enduce [*sic*] others to emulate such brave and noble examples."[19] The committee earlier had announced an open competition for memorial designs, which provoked public debate through the next year. It was curiously parallel to the controversy over the fate of those great men-of-war: is Britain properly preserving the images of its past greatness? When Turner sketched the *Téméraire* being towed up the Thames, he could not have been unaware of the increasingly heated discussions of these issues, and especially those about the proper form of a national tribute to the Great Admiral, the man he venerated as "the True Briton."[20]

The issue of form is not incidental: a good deal of the controversy concerns how any suitable memorial should look. By 1839, when Turner would have been hard at work on the nearly finished painting, the *Times* printed a number of letters challenging what then seemed to be (as it was) the committee's choice of William Railton's design (the basis of the statue in Trafalgar Square today). A correspondent calling himself "Fiat Justitia" ridiculed it in February as a "jack on a bean-stalk, a pillar with a man upon it." In early March, just before the public exhibition of all the entries was to open, an article in the *Times* supported this view, declaring that it must be "mortifying . . . to the national character to reflect, that its artists are . . . incompetent to do justice to the merits of the very best of its heroes." Railton's entry might make sense in another context, as for the interior of St. Paul's, we are told, but it hardly achieves the nobility the committee had sought. Even granted that his sketch of the project may be "very cleverly coloured and drawn," it is nothing more than that. Trafalgar Square in his design assumes a misleadingly "smiling face," with a few spectators and redcoated grenadiers thrown in for effect—"all help to make a very pretty picture."[21] It is almost as if the alternative is not only another sort of monument, but another sort of picture showing it—as if monumental sculpture must be tested by the more clearly understood requirements of painting. In a letter to the *Times* on February 18 "A Traveller" urges the committee not to bind itself to awarding any commission at this time. Why not wait to determine the response of the public to the collection of all the submitted designs? "What exhibition has ever taken place at the Royal Academy," he asks, "at the conclusion of which, some one, or two, or three general favourites have not been proclaimed by a common accord and the general voice?" Once again, painting is the model by which such designs should be judged. And, since a national monument is in question, what is needed is a genuinely popular image, one that reflects both the general veneration for Nelson and the general taste in art.

What sort of image is that? Turner's own earlier efforts at memorializing Trafalgar had not met with general approval; even his representation of ships proved controversial. James' *Naval History of Great Britain* (1822–1826) ends a lengthy account of Trafalgar discussing various extant representations of that battle: diagrams, written records, and paintings, including Turner's own *Battle of Trafalgar* (Figure 6.2), commissioned by the crown and painted in 1823–1824 "as a national memento of the naval victory to which it relates."[22] Or so it was intended. James adds his voice to the chorus of critics who attacked the picture when it first was shown, and he focuses above all on inaccuracies that diminish its value as a memorial to the facts. It is impossible "to say what time of the day, or what particular incident in the Victory's proceedings, is meant to be referred to." Wouldn't it have been possible, he asks, to remain faithful to such facts, and still produce the desired "pictorial effect"?

> Here is a ship, shattered in her hull, and stripped of the best part of her sails, pushing into a cluster of enemy's ships without a grazed plank or a torn piece of canvas to fire her first gun. Here is symbolized the first of naval heroes, with chivalric valour, devoting himself to his country's cause; and yet, says an artist of high repute, "there is a lack of pictorial materials." We hope some public-spirited individual, if not the State itself, will show whether this is really the case; for it is almost a national disgrace that there should yet be wanted a picture which, in accuracy of representation, no less than in strength and brilliancy of execution, is calculated to illustrate, and to stand as a lasting memorial of one of the greatest sea-battles that ever has been, or that perhaps ever will be fought; a battle to the success of which England at this time owes, if not her political existence, her prosperity, happiness, and exalted station.[23]

In spite of the literalism of his approach, James recognizes one of Turner's primary objectives (while denying that it has been achieved): the creation of an appropriate symbolic memorial "calculated to illustrate" Nelson and Trafalgar. In effect he challenges the artist to produce one, in language anticipating the critics of 1839 who found such failures "mortifying . . . to the national character." It is the sort of rhetoric, and the sort of challenge, Turner would have been unlikely to ignore.

An equally insistent challenge appeared in the work of other painters. The figure of Nelson was becoming increasingly prominent in the late 1830s. In the Royal Academy's annual summer exhibition of 1835 a "Design for a National Naval Monument proposed to be erected in Trafalgar-Square, Charing-Cross" was submitted by Thomas Bellamy. The emphasis is on honoring the navy rather than Nelson alone, but the connection is implicit. The same exhibition contained two portraits and one portrait bust of Wellington; heroism was in the air. But Nelson was beginning to attain equal status with the great general. In 1836, with Wellington represented in the same number of entries, Clarkson Stanfield exhibited his *Battle of Trafalgar,* showing a scene several hours after Nelson received his death wound: the *Redoubtable* is lashed to the *Téméraire,* which is in the act of capturing the seventy-four-gun *Fougueux.* By 1838 two Trafalgar pictures were shown, by John Christian Schetky and Charles Henry Seaforth, the latter with a catalogue citation of James' *Naval History* describing the *Téméraire* receiving fire along with the *Victory.* In this year Wellington was still more frequently depicted than Nelson, with four entries containing his image in all, including one John Turner's pedestal for a memorial statue, John Francis' "colossal bust in marble," and R. E. Phillips' design for a Trafalgar Square memorial containing tributes to both Wellington and Nelson flanking an equestrian statue of the new Queen. Finally, with the exhibitions of 1839 and 1840, the pieces on Nelson (for the most part entries in the design competition) outnumberd those representing Wellington; and that former group included, in 1839, W. B. S. Taylor's painting of the *Vanguard* (Nelson's flagship in 1798) as well as Turner's *Temeraire.*

Before 1838 the most familiar form of "lasting memorial" to Nelson had been in biography. Matthew Henry Barker, writing under the pseudonym of "The Old Sailor," had issued his *Life of Nelson* in 1836 and described it in a dedicatory preface to the Sailor King as a kind of verbal monument: "To add another trophy to the memory of Nelson, by commemorating his acts, is praiseworthy, and therefore merits patronage."[24] Southey's *Life of Nelson* was far more celebrated and more than any other single account made Nelson into a figure of popular legend. Appearing first in 1813, it ran to a second edition a year later, reappeared in several new editions (including a single-volume version) in the 1820s, and several more in 1830 and 1831; by 1842, a sixth edition would be released; by 1853, a thirteenth! It was, clearly, a book of tremendous popularity, and Southey treated his subject in an openly popular spirit. His *Life* is an exercise in British hagiography, an effort to apotheosize Nelson as "the darling hero of England!"[25] A short prefatory note describes the biography as a sort of heroic conduct book—"a manual for the young sailor, which he may carry about with him, until he has treasured up the example in his memory and in his heart."[26] The most conspicuous incident in this exemplary saint's legend is Trafalgar, in which Southey gives the *Téméraire* a leading role. It destroyed the *Redoubtable,* from which snipers, stationed in the riggings, had shot and killed Nelson. And if Nelson's captains could have had their way before the battle, the *Téméraire* might have saved him from death. Everyone knew that he made an easy target, especially since he refused to cover his uniform with a cloak, stay under cover, or allow his flagship, the *Victory,* to sail into battle behind others. In view of Nelson's bravery, and the French practice of placing sharpshooters aloft to aim for such targets, his officers begged him to allow the *Téméraire* and the *Leviathan* to sail in front of the *Victory* at the head of the van attacking the French fleet. Only at the last minute did he refuse to give (or to endorse; accounts differ) the order for the *Victory* to shorten sail and allow the other ships to pass ahead of it.

These tactical matters are important to the painter as well as the naval historian because they define a scenic structure, what we might term a topography of heroism. Southey identifies a particular landscape (or, more properly, seascape) with Trafalgar's naval valor, and that of Nelson. We encounter it immediately after Nelson's refusal to yield the first position in the attacking fleet. The act is notable, to be sure, yet still not so different from the bravery of his sailors preparing to face death. Southey's narrative suggests that this stoicism is bolstered by the stirring imagery of nature, and he represents the collective emotions by depicting the scene:

> A long swell was setting into the bay of Cadiz: our ships, crowding all sail, moved majestically before it, with light winds from the south-west. The sun shone on the sails of the enemy; and their well formed line, with their numerous three-deckers, made an appearance which any other assailant would have thought formidable;—but the British sailors only admired the beauty and splendour of the spectacle; and, in full confidence of winning what they saw, remarked to each other, what a fine sight yonder ships would make at Spithead![27]

This is writing, like Turner's painting, growing out of the most fundamental assumptions of Romantic aesthetics, and out of the earlier traditions of the picturesque and sublime. But it is less important to specify the precise source of such a description than to recognize its implications: sights are food for thought, in life as well as in art. Even a situation as fraught with peril as this—perhaps, especially such a situation—can, or must be transformed into a "spectacle," an instructive moral tableau. This is a kind of naval graveyard poetry, a self-conscious contemplation of death transfigured into the grandeur of a "view." It is an elevated version of the responses attributed to the visitors at Mr. Beatson's demolition-wharves; only here (if for the moment we regard Southey's embroidered version as accurate) the edifying sight has not been sought. That is what makes it heroic.

At this point, of course, Southey's *Life* is more concerned with effect than accuracy. It is difficult to believe that these sailors at the edge of battle really became aesthetic tourists, that while passing into the valley of the shadow of death they stopped to admire the view. Nevertheless, such rhetoric can be moving, and that is its point. Southey is creating a patriotic legend. The biography appeals for imitation of the example of Nelson and his men, an appeal all the more understandable when we recall that it was written while the Napoleonic Wars were still being fought, before Waterloo. This passage is a typical example of the way Southey uses aesthetics in the service of propaganda, and of the complex relation between the two. Aesthetic distance nurtures bravery. To face death courageously, Southey seems to say, we must conceive ourselves as figures in a heroic painting. It is not just that the sailors regard this instant in their own lives as a "spectacle," but that they can look forward and imagine a similar spectacle being used to invoke, and memorialize, a heroic past—a past that turns out to be the still-future battle they are about to enter. Perhaps a similar capacity for aesthetic detachment can help explain Nelson's simultaneous agreement to and violation of the order that might have saved his life, for it was an order that would have shifted him out of a heroic, figurative position at the head of his attacking ships. The self-conscious hero becomes a kind of spectator too, surveying his own place in a scene that stretches into both space and time. As the landscape of Southey's passage suggests, the "prospect" at Trafalgar was also prospective, a landscape of futurity; the sailors contemplating it also achieved an anticipatory glimpse of what was going to be the past. Perhaps Nelson had the same vision of his own heroic legend. This aesthetic hero transcends the limits of time, beginning in the present the process of memorializing himself.

III

By 1839, as the activities of the Nelson Memorial Committee grew increasingly controversial, the possibility of creating genuinely public memorials seemed dubious. Pugin, in "A Letter on the Proposed Protestant Memorial to Cranmer, Ridley, and Latymer ..." (1839), denounced all efforts to honor the past that were not Catholic. "Never has a nation been so deluded and hoodwinked as the English for the last two centuries; every source of historical information has been poisoned and perverted."[28] Turner's equally bitter view appears in the poetic tag he included in the Academy catalogue entry for the *Temeraire:*

> The flag which braved the battle and the breeze,
> No longer owns her.[29]

The allusion, which almost anyone at the exhibit would have recognized, is to Thomas Campbell's popular song "Ye Mariners of England," itself an appeal for a revival of Britain's naval might. Only Turner invokes it ironically: the flag has abandoned its own; the nation has forgotten, and perhaps forgotten how to remember.

The problem of memory (and patriotic memorializing) runs throughout the early responses to Turner's painting as well. Thackeray, writing in *Fraser's* as Michelangelo Titmarsh, takes some trouble to explain to a supposed correspondent why his own excitement over the picture becomes so bound up in patriotic emotion: "It is absurd, you will say (and with a great deal of reason), for Titmarsh, or any other Briton, to grow so politically enthusiastic about a four-foot canvas, representing a ship, a steamer, a river, and a sunset. But herein surely lies the power of the great artist." To illustrate his own response, Thackeray-Titmarsh recalls what he says is an anecdote from his travels. It took place, he tells us, at Weimar, with the orchestra playing Beethoven's "Battle of Vittoria." When the music of "God Save the King" entered the piece, "every Englishman in the house was bolt upright, and stood reverently until the air was played out. Why so? From some such thrill of excitement as makes us glow and rejoice over Mr. Turner and his 'Fighting Temeraire'; which I am sure, when the art of translating colours into music or poetry shall be discovered, will be found to be a magnificent national ode or piece of music." Apparently it also will be seen as a kind of pictorial mausoleum:

> I think, my dear Bricabrac (although, to be sure, your nation would be somewhat offended by such a collection of trophies), that we ought not, in common gratitude, to sacrifice entirely these noble old champions of ours, but that we should have somewhere a museum of their skeletons, which our children might visit, and think of the brave deeds which were done in them. The bones of the Agamemnon and the Captain, the Vanguard, the Culloden, and the Victory, ought to be sacred relics, for Englishmen to worship almost. Think of them when alive, and braving the battle and the breeze, they carried [*sic*] Nelson, and his heroes victorious. . . . All these things, my dear Bricabrac, are, you will say, absurd, and not to the purpose. Be it so: but Bowbellies as we are, we Cockneys feel our hearts leap up when we recall them to memory; and every clerk in Threadneedle Street feels the strength of a Nelson, when he thinks of the mighty actions performed by him.[30]

For Thackeray, then, this is memorial art, as he suggests in even his most apparently gratuitous imagery: that odd reference to naval relics as "bones" alludes to what many observers at the time saw as the peculiarly skeletal appearance of Turner's ship. And there is a need for such relics, Thackeray insists, because memory itself is at risk. The very extravagance of his style offers a proof of his own capacity to remember. Yet he worries about the future, when such reminders may be lost.

This concern becomes even more central in Ruskin's accounts of the painting. The final volume of *Modern Painters* (1860) speaks of Turner's boyhood "vow that Trafalgar shall have its tribute of memory some day." Several years earlier the *Notes on the Turner Bequest* (1856) referred to the picture as "the best memorial that Turner could give." Yet now, seventeen years after Thackeray's exuberant remarks and five years after the painter's death, the tone of criticism has shifted. For Ruskin must add the tragic corollary that such exercises in recollection may prove to have been in vain, for the significance of these noble fighting ships already has been forgotten. Like Thackeray, he makes his point by reference to a scene outside the picture.

> Perhaps, where the low gate opens to some cottage-garden, the tired traveller may ask, idly, why the moss grows so green on its rugged wood; and even the sailor's child may not answer, nor know, that the night-dew lies deep in the war-rents of the wood of the old *Téméraire*.[31]

Ruskin and Thackeray share a concern for what Paul Fussell calls, in a twentieth-century context, "modern memory," the living presence of recent history informing a sense of contemporary experience. Both agree on the need for new symbols to animate such a conception, the need to stimulate memory through the arts, through new memorials.

But what was meant by the term "memorial" in 1839? What sorts of people, or virtues, deserved such formal tribute? This is not easy to answer, particularly because the nature of heroism itself was being revaluated. In the spring of 1840, less than a year after the *Temeraire* was exhibited, Thomas Carlyle expounded the diverse modes in which that virtue could manifest itself in his lectures *On Heroes and Hero-Worship*. Perhaps the presence of a new, young queen on the throne raised such issues. Had the definitions of heroism changed? Must every age formulate new ones? The designs for the Nelson Memorial contain numerous signs of uncertainty about the proper conception of heroism generally, and about precisely what form a monument to any particular hero ought to take. They are no more unanimous about how to memorialize Nelson himself, which of his attributes (as iconographers would say) ought to receive emphasis, or how. John Goldicutt's design shows the admiral at the top of a huge globe; that of "M.M." places him at the foot of a tremendous column; R. G. Wetton introduces a pedestal without a pillar, and Nelson standing in front of it, his head bent thoughtfully; John Britton's entry is a large Gothic chapel, with no figure visible from the outside at all—perhaps suggesting that genuine heroism is inward, hidden from sight, or perhaps because Britton happened to have a Gothic chapel design on hand. Is a hero to be represented in thought, in victory, in death, in command, or inside? Almost all of the designs introduce an intricate apparatus of symbolic imagery. But all are uneasy about the use of such symbolism—its proper form as well as content. To some extent, then, their differences are disagreements over the appropriate form for any modern memorial. The problem in Trafalgar Square, in the words of one of the entrants, Thomas Bellamy, is to create "a monument worthy alike of Nelson and of the arts."[32]

This is the only issue of importance on which most of the competitors agree: a modern memorial involves special artistic problems. Most of their designs are broadly allegorical, yet they repeatedly emphasize that this does not mean allegory in the traditional sense. The challenge of memorializing Nelson is to create new symbols. "In this design, it has been as much as possible my wish to avoid remote allegorical allusion, by adhering to an alphabet of symbols, so familiar as to be legible to the plainest understanding, and to impart to the whole a naval and British character."[33] So explains T. Butler, and his views are echoed over and over by other entrants. "Allegory, and particularly the old allegory of Neptune, Tritons, nymphs and sea-horses, can only be used in commemorating a man, whose virtues are unknown, or problematical. In a monument to a man like Nelson," Patric Park insists, "such cannot be tolerated." J. G. Lough puts it more directly: his memorial will be "perfectly simple, and at the same time purely Nelsonic. . . . My idea of a monument being to make it national and intelligible to all classes. I have studiously avoided allegory."[34] What he really means is that he has avoided traditional imagery. Most of the explanations themselves are, in fact, allegorical in form, but based on the familiar "British" symbolism of ships and naval warfare, and the associations of certain fundamental architectural forms. As George Foggo notes, in connection with his own design,

> The ornaments consist entirely of objects obtainable at sea, and characteristic of our navy and illustrious leader, who dared beyond the rules of art. Objects that savour of preparation, and partake not of enthusiastic impulse, and likewise the mystic visions of antiquity, have been discarded for the more terrible features of modern warfare.[35]

John Hakewell, like many of the other entrants, recommends using a column, perhaps because, as "M. M." suggests in his published *Description of a Drawn Model . . . proposed for the Monument intended to be erected in Trafalgar Square to the Memory of Lord Nelson . . .* (1839), a column reminds us of that familiar nautical form, the mast.[36] The competition is an early example of the Victorian turn towards a more familiar, domesticated, artistic vocabulary, to bring all the arts into closer touch with the realities of ordinary life.

The problem, then, is not simply to design an impressive memorial but to design an appropriate one, a monument suited to its setting and legible to its audience. The *Penny Magazine* pointed this out in an article on the Nelson monument in Yarmouth (June 1838), clearly alluding to the competition for a London memorial.

> It is so rarely that these compositions are calculated to touch the heart and imagination, that their absence is scarcely to be regretted.... Unless ... there exist popular sentiments shared by all ranks, from the palace to the fisherman's cabin, it is in vain that even monuments are raised, for they can excite no adequate and appropriate interest.

The essay concludes recommending easy access to public buildings, as a way of bringing people back in touch with their heroes and their history.[37] But even such a measure would not close this question for a massive public monument in London. After all, it could not be placed in the contemplative atmosphere of a gallery, where it would be possible to read the most subtle imagery with deliberate, intimate attention. "That design will be best adapted to the circumstances," J. Harrison of Chester writes, "which is most calculated, to excite, at a glance, in the thoughtless idler, or hurrying man of business, the desire, by a life like Nelson's, active and honourable, to win honours like his."[38] The monument, then, must be "calculated" (and the word will turn up again) not only to pay proper tribute to Nelson, and to do justice to the modern arts, but to appeal to the actual urban audience that is likely to view it. As John Britton sums this up, the monument must be capable of making "an instant impression on the passenger," one "which will irresistibly excite inquiry, awaken curiosity, and keep up a continued stimulus of gratification,—which is calculated to arouse at once an intense reverence for, and admiration of, the dauntless British Admiral."[39]

If there was no agreement on the precise contents, or shape, of the memorial, there was a general unanimity on its proper mood. Most of the artists tried to be solemn and subdued, rather than grandiosely celebratory. James Thrupp hoped "to avoid any expression of ostentation; for Nelson's illustrious deeds were ever accompanied by a simple dignity of character."[40] G. B. Moore points out that after a space of "twenty-four years of peace," it was not appropriate—or indeed, in keeping with classical precedent—"to revive the exultation of triumph.... The present memorial should be rather a testimonial of gratitude, to one who died to obtain an honourable peace, than a record of national glory." J. Taylor, junior, makes a related observation on the inevitable differences between monuments to "heroes who have survived the conflicts in which they were engaged," like Wellington, and the ones to "those who fell in action, which event it is considered should stand recorded as well as their bravery and prowess."[41] Thus "An Architect of Middlesex," characterizing the monument that must be built as an "epico-technico poem," argues that it should refer above all to "the victory of Trafalgar, sanctified by the hero's own blood."[42]

The best way back to the painting from the perspective of these very different kinds of modern imagery is through Ruskin, who often proves remarkably sensitive to the contemporary currents in Turner's work. His remarks on the *Temeraire* explore at some length the sort of problem that is raised by the designs for the Nelson memorial and the commentaries on them: precisely what is it that makes this imagery moving—so "pathetic" or "pensive"; what is it about this particular ship that makes it worthy of "honour or affection"?[43] He attempts to explain our feelings, and the character of Turner's imagery, by comparing a ship to a special form of architecture. For we respond to this picture much as we respond to ruins, although no ruin could be as "affecting as this gliding of the vessel to her grave." A ruin can be associated with the gallant deeds of men, but "it never seems to have offered itself to their danger, and associated itself with their acts, as a ship of battle can." A ship can move and hence remind us of "a living creature, that may indeed be maimed in limb, or decrepit in frame, but must either live or die, and cannot be added to nor diminished from—heaped up and dragged down—as a building can." But it is also that this particular ship is associated with the Trafalgar victory, and with its human costs: "those sides that were wet with the long runlets of English life-blood . . . those pale masts that stayed themselves up against the war-ruin, shaking out their ensigns through the thunder, till sail and ensign drooped." A footnote retells the story of the attempt to use the *Téméraire* to shield Nelson from French sniper fire, although Ruskin embellishes it a bit: "Nelson himself hailed her to keep astern. The *Téméraire* cut away her studding-sails, and held back, receiving the enemy's fire into her bows without returning a shot. Two hours later, she lay with a French seventy-four gun ship on each side of her."[44] Ruskin's *Téméraire*, then, represents both victory and the suffering that accompanies it. He stresses the ship's vulnerability, and the assaults against it that came before that final triumph. It is as if he imagines the *Téméraire* at Trafalgar in much the form Turner presents it in on that last, powerless voyage up the Thames.

In effect, he views the Battle of Trafalgar through the medium of Turner's art after it has been adjusted to meet the demands of James' *Naval History,* which ridiculed the representation of the *Victory* in Turner's earlier Trafalgar painting: "shattered in her hull, and stripped of the best part of her sails . . . without a grazed plank or a torn piece of canvas." The "nobility" of the *Téméraire* in Ruskin's eyes is a function of its damaged but still dignified appearance. Its heroic stature, in his highly allegorized reading, is established by suffering and injury. The *Téméraire* represents triumph through self-sacrifice.

These are hardly the terms of modern art criticism. In the current standard catalogue of Turner's work, the editors, Martin Butlin and Evelyn Joll, complain that one contemporary response "personalizes the *Temeraire* shamelessly."[45] Yet the fact remains that such interpretations are widespread, not simply because of the character of nineteenth-century art criticism, or, for that matter, because of Ruskin's own influence, but because of something perceived in Turner's painting, something it was seen as. Ruskin's stress on the heroism of sacrifice appears frequently in other writers, who often personify the ship as a victim. Thus, the *Athenaeum:*

> A sort of sacrificial solemnity is given to the scene, by the blood-red light cast upon the waters by the round descending sun, and by the paler gleam from the faint rising crescent moon, which silvers the majestic hull, and the towering masts, and the taper spars of the doomed vessel, gliding in the wake of the steam-boat—which latter (still following this fanciful mode of interpretation) almost gives to the picture an expression of such malignant alacrity as might befit an executioner.[46]

The *Art Union,* making no such apologies for its comparisions, also contrasts the "venerable" warship and the "paltry steam-boat, upon whom he looks down with powerless contempt:—the old bulwark of a nation governed and guided by the mean thing that is to take his place!" As in the metaphor of execution from the *Athenaeum,* the word "governed" hints that this "little demon of a steamer" (now I am quoting Thackeray again) in some sense represents constituted authority, the necessities of order and progress. The *Téméraire* is a victim of modernization. This is in part an image of official replacement, continuity achieved through change. The *Spectator* thus compares the two vessels to "a superannuated veteran led by a sprightly boy." Such language does not make the action of the picture any less disturbing, but it does suggest that it may be inevitable, part of a larger process. Some sacrifices are necessary; some falls, including tragic falls, are fortunate. Those early critics "read" the *Temeraire* much as they read Southey's *Life of Nelson,* and in terms of the language of the contemporary debate on memorials. As we will see, that perspective makes them aware of some of the painting's most subtle and most modern elements.

IV

Turner's *Temeraire* is a study in contrasts. Steam power beside an ancient and legendary three-decker, itself nearly dismantled to contrast further with the elaborate rigging it would have carried into battle. Black superimposed on white, which is set off additionally by the brilliant flashes of fire from the steamer's chimney and deck. A slender and almost skeletal form (the *Spectator* calls it a "a ghost of her former self," and Thackeray claims to be able to see "death, as it were, written on her")[47] moves behind the lower, squatter, darker, and more visibly functional structure of the tug. The stripping of the *Téméraire* that had already taken place made it ride unusually high in the water, so that alongside it every other ship "appeared like a pigmy," as the *Times* observed.[48] Beyond all this, the picture is a contrast of peace and war, although this opposition does not fully accord with the ones already mentioned. For the *Téméraire* itself looks the more peaceful of the two , pale and powerless behind the explosive energy of the tug. This is a paradox Turner would explore further in paired paintings exhibited at the Royal Academy in 1842: *War. The exile and the rock limpet* (Figure 6.3), and *Peace—burial at sea* (Figure 6.4)—pictures referring, respectively, to Napoleon and David Wilkie, the painter (and Turner's friend) who had died recently. *War* is a contemplative seaside scene, with Napoleon at the center studying the marine animal named in the title; *Peace,* continuing this practice of opposition, not only represents a death (actually, it depicts the moment of burial), but includes the darkness, smoke and fire of a steamboat to heighten the dramatic immediacy of the event (when a steamboat actually was present). Turner's reversal of the conventional associations of the two main terms in the titles implies that each can be understood only in terms of the other. In a sense, this is true for those two central figures as well. The painter and the soldier, apparaently dissimilar beings, share an uneasy position at the margins of life and power, confronted with reminders of human weakness. Napoleon meditates stoically on this subject, as we learn from Turner's verse in the academy catalogue, supposedly taken from his literary *magnum opus, The Fallacies of Hope:*

Ah! thy tent-formed shell is like
A solder's nightly bivouac, alone
Amidst a sea of blood———
—but you can join your comrades.[49]

Wilkie achieves a similar nobility, though only in death. He becomes, as
Jack Lindsay observes, something like the limpet in *War,* "a living part of
. . . nature in the consecrated moment of death."[50] Peace and war, then, are
only temporary conditions within the ongoing rhythm of existence. An
apparent opposition reveals the embracing unity of nature. The real subject of both pictures individually and of the paired set together is the continuity between extreme conditions of life, the reciprocity of life and death.

In one respect, the *Temeraire* depicts an interruption of this continuum,
something being taken out of nature (out of circulation, we might say), for
the ship is about to be destroyed. Its rigging has been removed; it moves
now only with the aid of steam power, no longer driven by the wind. Yet
in another sense this powerlessness brings the ship closer to nature by ini-
tiating a transformation back towards the elements from which it was originally constructed. It is a transformation almost visible in the colors with
which Turner has rendered its hull: bleached by the weather, it is not
merely without paint but in a literal sense un-painted, looking as if all pig-
ment has been removed, down to the very grain. Art historians often speak
of Turner's gift for calling our attention to his materials, and preserving
on canvas the feeling of paint as paint. Here he is exploring an equivalent
in the form of the ship, and makes us aware of its frame, its timbers, as
wood. In this way, a moment of impending destruction looks forward and
backward at once—to the demolition that is about to take place and to the
time of first construction, or to the first transformation of natural materials
into the materials of shipbuilding. This simultaneity is hinted at in Turner's title (and he often uses titles to express the embedded complexities of
his paintings): the ship is being "tugged to her last Berth." Is there an allusion to midwifery here? A berth is a place of rest, but the word (whose
orgins are uncertain, according to the *Oxford English Dictionary*) also contains a punning suggestion of birth spelled with an "i"—the act of bringing
a new being into the world is remembered at the moment it is ushered out.
Construction is echoed by destruction, or should it be called
deconstruction?

This continuity and simultaneity of life processes is expressed in still
another way. The most vivid image of the linkage of life and death in this
painting is the interconnected representation of the sun and moon, occupying the sky together, framing the picture as a whole and bracketing the

two ships, its main figures, between them. In fact, it is tempting to equate those two heavenly bodies with the two ships, respectively. The *Literary Gazette* did this in speaking of the "sun of the glorious vessel setting in a flood of light." The *Art Union,* which also treated the sun as the "emblem of the aged ship," referred to the "young moon" as the "type of the petty steamer." Such typological interpretations would be even more appealing if the structure of the painting did not complicate or even reverse them. Perhaps the sun and the battleship should be linked to one another; yet the colors of the former are mirrored also in the fire bursting from the steamer, and the "ghostly" pallor of the *Téméraire* seems to associate it with the moon. It is not a question that should be settled; indeed, the painting dramatizes the artist's refusal to settle it. We will not understand its complex interdependencies unless we recognize the cross-references of these two sets of paired images, one dimension of an emphasis on pairing throughout the structure of the picture. The sun and moon define another continuity linking those two apparently opposed ships at the center of the action. It is an image of circularity, and unbroken process.

Traditionally the *Temeraire* has been viewed as depicting an ending, a destruction, or even a death. But all these signs of interconnectedness subsume destruction wtihin an unending natural cycle. The new moon, an ancient image of metamorphic change, is close enough to the *Téméraire* to be associated with it, yet the tug too is moving in the direction marked by the line of reflected moonlight, from left to right, towards the sun. Still, moonlight itself is only reflected from the sun. The two ships, then, as they glide along the path of the sunset, sailing from one source of light to another, move in two directions at once, forward and back, into a future associated with the past. Demolition docks are also construction docks; the *Témérarie* is sailing towards a "last b[i]rth." In this sense the motion backward is also forward, in time as well as space, because the work that is about to be performed ultimately will metamorphose the *Téméraire* into another ship, possibly into something like the steamer that seems to be its antagonist here. It is important to recall that the three-decker is about to be disassembled rather than simply destroyed—"broken up" so that its parts can be reused in future ship construction. Her new owner, Mr. Beatson, a "ship-broker and timber merchant,"[51] is dismantling the *Téméraire* for profit; his business depends on the possibility of reselling usable pieces and parts. Lindsay takes this as one of the dark aspects of the history of the ship as Turner understands it: British heroism victimized by capitalist greed.[52] Yet Turner would have known that some of those profits finally would accrue to the nation. The *Times* of 13 September marvels that "considering her age and the service she has seen, her timbers are in a very sound state," adding that the ship's "copper sheathing and bolts will be returned to Government [*sic*]." Even the story about that old tar's removal of a piece of oak for his new leg, like Ruskin's more obviously fictionalized fable of the garden gate, makes this point. Such recycling was not uncommon: the capital of the Nelson monument column was cast from old guns in the Woolwich Arsenal, and the bronze bas-reliefs at the base from guns captured at the battles they depict.[53] If we wish to lament this moment in the "life" of the warship as we would the last moments of a noble human being (to invoke metaphors from the contemporary interpretations of the painting), we must recognize also that it (like those moments) is part of a larger sequence of events, one phase in an ecological process of renewal.

It should be clear that I am departing from the customary readings of this painting—even departing from some of the contemporary explanations of it, although not, I think, from Thackeray's or Ruskin's. But in another way I am stressing an aspect of the responses of almost all the picture's interpreters, one to which most of them pay little attention as a clue to its significance. Almost all of them find the mood of the painting stirring (once again, we should recall Thackeray's burst of patriotic fervor), its brilliant colors impressive. Even the most hostile critics are enthusiastic, and yet that mood is never ascribed to the painting itself, or to Turner, in spite of the legend that he referred to it lovingly as his "darling." The powerful colors are noted, but the sun is usually taken as one of Turner's blood-red suns of wrath, casting, like that of *The Slave Ship* (in the words of Ruskin's famous description) "an awful but glorious light, the intense and lurid splendour which burns like gold, and bathes like blood."[54] But I believe these two paintings, and these suns, are fundamentally different, although the picture of 1839 contains suggestions of the dark possibilities that would preoccupy Turner increasingly through the 1840s. Perhaps a phrase like "dark possibilities" is out of place: although Turner's sense of alienation and gloom increased, he often would express this in images of blinding and consuming light, as in *The Angel Standing in the Sun,* with its almost Einsteinian representation of light as an explosive energy. Some of this destructive potential is present in the sun of the *Temeraire,* yet it is usually felt to be—seen as—a positive, creative element.

That sun—an almost palpable presence, for Turner's thick paint has given it substance—lies at the right of the main action of the scene. If we read visual imagery the way we read print, it is the last of the picture's central images, the one towards which the left-right motion of our eyes has advanced. It is also the direction in which the two ships are moving, although their path will bring them in front of the sun itself, to a point that touches the lower edge of the picture just where the reflection of the sun touches it. In this sense (there are others) the sun is linked to futurity and change. I am not certain that this is a setting rather than a rising sun, as every other observer has assumed; but even the conventional explanation (sunset) does not preclude that elusive Turnerian moral of hope. Consider the traditional British weather adage: Red sky at night, sailor's delight; red sky in the morning, sailor take warning. Even if we are not prepared to "delight" in the brilliant colors of this sun and sky, they cannot be explained away as merely suggesting decline. For the presence of the sun gives the rest of the painting light, and life. It is an almost painterly presence, coloring everything else, even producing (partly by the reflection of its light from the moon) the eerie pallor on the *Téméraire*. If it is in part an allegorical sun of decline, we still are forced to recognize that it can produce beauty—or, more accurately, a sublime grandeur. From such an ending, then, at least one new beginning can be traced: the creation of a magnificent visual spectacle, much like the creation of a work of art. In this way the sun alludes to the presence of Turner himself at the event, transforming it into a pictorial image. As in much of his late work the sun seems to represent both humanity and nature, the artist as well as the world he tries to capture on canvas; it contains a creative and destructive potential at once, the powers of both life and death.

The most complex locus of such interdependencies in the *Temeraire* is the dark, compact form of the steam tug that draws the battleship to the demolition dock. This is a multivalent image too, no less than the machines represented in Turner's other treatments of steam power: *Staffa; Rain, Steam and Speed;* the *Snowstorm;* and *Peace* (to name the most important). Some of its complexity emerges from the historical record I have been citing—as (to cite one example) in the name of the steamer playing such an apparently villainous role in this patriotic drama: the *Monarch.*[55] It is equally relevant to recall the story that Turner, sketching on those cards, was on board another steamship as he watched the *Téméraire* being towed. The painting could not exist without steam power; the great fighting ship is memorialized, quite literally, from the perspective of a new generation of steam vessels. Steam, then, is not so much an opposing force as a condition of perception, a technology that motivates recollection and makes it possible.[56] In a sense, we can say that steam power creates the scene, a notion Turner illustrates in the resemblance between the fires bursting from the tug and the colors of the setting sun. It is not simply that a steam vessel is one of the subjects of the picture. This new technology is part of Turner's conception of reality.

I think this accounts for his decision to represent only one steam tug, rather than the two that actually were there. It is easy enough to explain this alteration in dramatic terms: three central figures would have confused the scene, blurred the contrast at the heart of it. Of course, a contrast of two to one might have been effective in other ways, if only to emphasize the immensity of the *Téméraire* itself, a size and power incommensurate with the modern replacements that outnumber it and hem it in. But perhaps that is precisely the disparity Turner did not wish to show—wished to not show, in fact. For the contrast of two opposed images in his picture suggests an equivalence as well as difference: one tug and one three-decker, a new mythos (Carlyle's term) and the old one it will replace, future and past inseparably linked. Nor is this equivalency static: the ships are in motion, and their relationship is defined in terms of a temporal continuum. An old era is drawn towards a new one. After all, the *Téméraire* was once part of a new technology itself, a frightening or even hostile power put to the service of the nation; Turner would have known that the ship was named for another *Téméraire* captured by the British from the French and reequipped. Even such "foreign powers," then, eventually can find a place in our affections, or in popular legend; novelties finally become part of the past, and the venerable past, for that matter. This insight suggests a parallel one about the future. As the three-decker is now, so will the steamer someday be. Innovation and obsolescence are part of an endless continuum in technological history; we are viewing two items excerpted from an infinite series, extending in both directions through time. The juxtaposition of these ships, like the reciprocities in nature, represents history as an endless succession of achievements and replacements, deaths and births.

Most commentators on the *Temeraire* observe only half of this process: Turner's prophecy of decline, his grim eulogy to departing glory. There are good reasons for this. The painting was executed at a time when he was preoccupied with death. His great patron, Lord Egremont, had died in November 1837, almost a year to the day after his old friend, W. F. Wells. He had been deeply affected by the death of his father in 1829 and that of Sir Thomas Lawrence in 1830, as he would be by the deaths of Wilkie and Sir Frances Chantrey in 1841. This mood may help explain his apparently increasing attachment to the *Téméraire*. Jack Lindsay argues that it came to stand for this entire series of losses, as well as the passing of a noble phase of British tradition; and as a representation of a vanished epoch, it is also "an expression of Turner's own life."[57] Yet as Lindsay himself also observes, the painting "is permeated with a sense of historical change, of remorseless destruction and renewal."[58] It does concern decline and destruction, then, but only in part. The painting is organized around cyclic patterns that are larger than the warship itself or the tug that tows her, or even the sum of those two ships together. Turner has created an image of process and succession, of an endless evolutionary chain that links individual acts of destruction—and the destruction of individuals—to a perpetual movement of renewal. We can speak of this as a tragic painting but only if in doing so we refer to its overwhelming cathartic power, its final expression of consolation and even triumph. For Turner to have achieved less, to have attempted less, would have been to fail in providing an adequate memorial.

V

Artists have grappled with the problem of death for as long as there has been art; the use of representations in primitive ritual suggests that the problem of death is one of the origins of art, perhaps the most important. But as the intensified interest in a Nelson monument suggests, there was something unusually pressing about this problem in 1838: death, and memorializing, was in the air. The death of William IV the year before may have had something to do with it: a royal death provides a public reminder of mortality, with the accession that immediately follows politically reenacting the continuities of nature. Victoria's coronation, which took place in the summer of 1838, might be seen as a ritualization of the need to end mourning, a ceremony "calculated" to shift our vision from past to future. Of course, for many it was not calculated well enough; the Penny Coronation lacked some of the pomp it should have had, and this was seen as an offense to both queen and nation, a degradation of present festivities and a failure to venerate the past. All the more reason that memorializing Nelson would have become a matter of urgency. Without suitable ceremonies and artifacts to reassure us, we might be confronted with an unrelieved spectacle of death and decline. As John Britton, one of the entrants in the Nelson memorial competition, remarked, "the slight and quickly mouldering monuments hitherto placed over the graves of eminent men have been too trivial and insubstantial." He proposed a building "combining the elements of *Architecture, Sculpture, Painting, and Literature.* These, judiciously collected and united, will administer to each other's preservation,—to each other's influence,—to each other's attractions and beauties."[59] Britton's language indicates that all of the early Victorian arts experienced something of this sense of threat. The most notable examples in contemporary writing, as we have seen, are Carlyle's *French Revolution,* Tennyson's *In Memoriam,* and Darwin's *Journal of Researches,* books preoccupied with change and death. All are searching for an intellectual perspective that makes it possible to face the grimmest inevitabilities of nature and history. Turner is confronting the same sort of threat and searching for the same sort of consoling perspective.

Perspective in painting has a more specific technical reference than point of view; but it is useful to explore that more general question of "authorial" position, and in a form almost never introduced in discussions of the *Temeraire*. To what extent are we meant to be aware of a spectator in this painting? The best analogue elsewhere in Turner's art can be found in the *Snow Storm* of 1842, a painting of natural violence—and a steamship—that Turner invites us to view in relation to his own role as observer. There is an apocryphal story that before painting it he had himself lashed to a ship's mast (perhaps enacting the role of Ulysses, one of his favorite heroic figures) to observe and experience the power of the elements at sea.[60] It is precisely the sort of legend Turner encouraged, and perhaps helped circulate—another way to confirm the unique role of the painter suggested by so many of his pictures: the artist as hero. This role is expressed most directly in the painting's full title: *Snow Storm—Steam Boat off a Harbour's Mouth making Signals in Shallow Water, and going by the Lead. The Author was in this Storm on the Night the Ariel left Harwich.* I am not sure that Andrew Wilton is right in reading this title as a declaration that "the sublime is accessible to us all," for few would be willing, or able, to undergo such an ordeal. But the title does require us to view the painting, in Wilton's words again, in terms of "that sublime realism which accurately records a natural event as perceived by a profoundly receptive mind"[61]—as, in other words, an expression of a way of seeing as well as of something seen. The destructiveness of the storm is transformed into a representation of a kind of heroic vision. And so, I believe, is the impending destruction of the *Téméraire,* especially if we think of it as a public event that anyone at that Royal Academy exhibition of 1839 might have witnessed the year before. It is not simply that the picture would have evoked strong recollections; it is a pictorial demonstration of how to remember—how to remember both the events of 1838 and those of 1805 (when the Battle of Trafalgar took place), how to remember a venerable ship and, through it, a venerable hero. It becomes a memorial, then, and a meditation upon memorializing as well. The painting is not just about a heroic ship and a heroic admiral; it is also about a heroic vision, and the heroic potential of art.

To understand what this means, we need only turn to the classic nineteenth-century discourse on memorializing, one that Turner would have been likely to have had in mind: Wordsworth's *Essay upon Epitaphs,* a standard point of reference for decades of artists and mourners. Wordsworth recommends a lofty imagery of consolation, centered around a conception of the cyclic unity of life. The bereaved are to be reminded of "the subtle progress by which, both in the natural and moral world, qualities pass insensibly into their contraries, and things revolve upon each other." To illustrate this abstraction, Wordsworth describes a scene:

> As, in sailing upon the orb of this planet, a voyage towards the regions where the sun sets, conducts gradually to the quarter where we have been accustomed to behold it come forth at its rising; and, in like manner, a voyage towards the east, the birthplace in our imagination of the morning, leads finally to the quarter where the sun is last seen when he departs from our eyes; so the contemplative Soul, travelling in the direction of mortality, advances to the country of everlasting life; and, in like manner, may she continue to explore those cheerful tracts, till she is brought back, for her advantage and benefit, to the land of transitory things—of sorrow and of tears.[62]

There is nothing new in taking a sea voyage as an emblem of the journey of life. The same comparison was implied in Southey's picturesque description of Trafalgar before the battle (it is worth noting that Southey's biography was based on an essay of 1810, the same year Wordsworth's *Essay* appeared). But Wordsworth goes beyond Southey (and the traditional metaphor) to make the voyage an image of the mind contemplating death: it travels to the ends of the earth, surveys the beyond, and then returns to the "provisional" world of "transitory things." The voyage represents a resignation to the inevitability of death as part of the oceanic rhythm of life.

Even the landscape of Turner's painting, then, alludes to a vision of the universality of this final voyage. We are to be reminded of a real ship, its most famous battle, the admiral for whom it would have been sacrificed long before, the whole history of violence and change through which it has moved, and the pervasiveness of death in the world. The picture expresses passion, to be sure, but that passion is (in Wordsworth's words) "subdued, the emotions, controlled; strong, indeed, but nothing ungovernable or wholly involuntary."[63] For the painting is the product of a composed artistry that can recognize such a loss for what it is, and define its place in an ongoing process of renewal. It is partly a lament, but not wholly that. The days of the great three-deckers are over, and the ships themselves are nearly all gone; the task remaining is to learn to live with those facts, to incorporate them into the service of a "modern memory" that manages to return us to an acceptance of the world as it is. The very form of the painting is tragic, in a high, affirmative, realistic sense—a sense we find in Wordsworth, or in Yeats. Thus it is necessarily informed by Turner's implied presence at the scene, regarding and "transfiguring" it as do the carved figures in Yeats' "Lapis Lazuli," staring on tragedy with "ancient, glittering eyes." The same sort of clear-eyed philosophic calm is represented in the statue of Nelson in Railton's winning design. Its gaze is abstracted and meditative. It does not look down on the square below, and even though the head is turned towards Westminister its attention seems to be more general, perhaps even more distant. It seems engrossed in a contemplation of mortality, seen in nothing more particular than the curve of the Thames, the distant horizon, or even the point where the sun will set.[64] The focus of the eyes is permanent—and on permanence; that, too, is part of what heroism means.

Turner found such lifeless memorials inadequate, especially compared to the vitality of his own art. The rivalry of paint and marble is (as Professor John McCoubrey has reminded me) an old theme in the history of art, and it informs Turner's earlier pictorial treatments of Nelson. The "Great Yarmouth" watercolor for the *Picturesque Views in England and Wales* (which Eric Shanes dates 1825–1828), shows another Nelson column (erected in 1817) surrounded by various animated signs (ships, cats, human figures, a violent seascape) of Britain's need for a strong naval defense. A companion piece, "Yarmouth Sands" (1830) (Figure 6.5), represents (in the words of Ruskin, who once owned it) "Sailors explaining the position of the *Victory* and *Redoubtable* at Trafalgar by the help of models," with the same column in the background.[65] It is a picture about different ways of remembering, again dramatizing the conviction that the only valid memorial is achieved in an art that can capture images of permanence and the mood of a fleeting moment, an art that can, in effect, represent the act of recollection itself. The same note is sounded in Turner's tributes to Nelson from as early as 1805, when he sketched the Victory as it sailed up the Thames to the Medway, bearing the admiral's body. In the next year "he showed an unfinished version of *The Battle of Trafalgar* in his own gallery."[66] It is not surprising that he would have been sensitive to criticism of the version of that painting finally commissioned by the Crown in 1823—when he had been memorializing Nelson for eighteen years—or that he might have been deeply wounded when in 1829, George IV had the painting removed from St. James' Palace, where originally it was intended to be hung, to the naval hospital at Greenwich. Perhaps the *Temeraire* even alludes to that incident: a national treasure is being retired—and Rotherhithe (where Beatson had his dock) is not too distant from Greenwich; the crown is abandoning its ownership of something it ought to prize. This may be part of the significance of the poetry adapted from Campbell:

The flag which braved the battle and the breeze,
No longer owns her.

Clearly, the task of remembering cannot be left to the nation.

It is possible to read that poetic tag in still another way, one that also illuminates Turner's continuing project to memorialize Nelson and his ships. The *Temeraire* demonstrates that the ship has achieved a higher status than that of mere property, that it has passed to a higher form of ownership. "The flag . . . no longer owns her." The artistic imagination, Turner's own special form of modern memory, does. The ship has been transfigured, given inner and personal significance. In 1845, when resubmitting the poetic lines to accompany the engraving of his painting, he wrote the penultimate word as "own's."[67] Although we should hesitate to place too much weight on the frail structure of Turner's orthography, this punctuation may suggest a return to the metaphoric roots of the word ownership, a reference to the connection between objects and our own identity. We are what we have, what we can keep, even if that possession is only in memory. In one sense this ship is a piece of property that can be bought and sold; in another it embodies an idea, a set of principles, to which we may or may not admit (may or may not own up to) but through which we can express or even create our own sense of self. After the physical ship has been dismantled, it will be possible to recall and recreate its significance imaginatively, through memory. With the help of Turner's painting, we too can make it our own. And by so doing, we can begin to own up to death.

For this is the quality the painting memorializes above all, the artist's ability to see and to endure. That is the only way I can account for his otherwise inexplicable attachment to this particular masterpiece, refusing to part from his "darling" for "any consideration of money." It becomes an image of his own perseverance, hence as dear as life itself. Lawrence Gowing has remarked in connection with the event recorded, or supposedly recorded, in the *Snow Storm* that Turner "treasured the experience like a private possession."[68] The observation fits the *Temeraire* equally well, perhaps even better, since there is no doubt that the event referred to in that picture is real. It records two events, in fact: the last voyage of a particular ship, and the activity of an artist who apparently happened to observe it. And even assuming that Turner did not actually see the *Téméraire* on its final voyage, his painting defines a way of responding to such events in art. If the painting depicts the "break-up" of one visible embodiment of heroic tradition, and if it is drenched in private associations with the deaths of Turner's closest friends, it also records a refusal to be paralyzed by those facts, a refusal to bury the life of the imagination. A way of seeing comes to stand for a way of life, at once aesthetic and heroic. Turner has created a complexly symbolic memorial, not merely as a fitting public testimony to Nelson but also, equally important, as a monument to the power of the artistic imagination. As a private image, it is Turner's pictorial memorandum to himself about the necessity of continuing in the shadow of age and death. And the fervor of some of those early responses suggests that the private message also became public. Turner might have said with Tennyson, "It is rather the cry of the whole human race than mine."[69] The *Temeraire* is Turner's *In Memoriam*. The unanimity of the picture's first critics demonstrates how well, even before publication of Tennyson's poem, contemporaries were able to recognize this, to recognize, that is, the themes of memory, mourning, and consolation. That general acclaim, like Turner's own growing attachment to the painting, also suggests that it became for the public—if not for the artist himself—an expression of a stirring heroic myth: about art and the human condition, and about the potential of the age. Here, for once at least, in the last period of his career, Turner's art speaks a language accessible to all: "real nature," the *Spectator* announced, "and its poetry is intelligible."[70]

Intelligibility of this sort, for an audience of this kind, would become increasingly rare in the last decade of Turner's life. That period was marked by some of his greatest and most obscure paintings, bursts of expressionistic energy (like the *Snow Storm*) that anticipate French painting later in the century and much of twentieth-century painting as well. Ruskin would refer back to the *Temeraire* in 1856, five years after Turner's death, as the division between the last two phases of the artist's career, between a period of absolute mastery and something far less accomplished: "the last picture he ever executed with his *perfect* power . . . the last picture in which Turner's execution is as firm and faultless as in middle life."[71] Of course, what Ruskin regards as "some failure in distinctness of sight and firmness of hand" is seen a century later as the product of a deeply personal vision, without regard for any other more public standards of legibility. Now Turner's myth-making has become radically private. No wonder Ruskin's description at first sounds extreme. But Turner's contemporaries expressed Ruskin's reservations even more intensely; at times they felt the artist was not only out of control but out to play a deliberate hoax. And at least one of the paintings exhibited in that last period seems to justify their uneasiness. The title seems to mock its audience and the sorts of expectations that had been fulfilled in the "distinctness" of pictures like the *Temeraire: The New Moon; or, "I've lost My Boat, You shan't have Your Hoop"* (Figure 6.6). It is one of Turner's most elusive late works, representing in a childish incident the great theme of changeability (in people and the natural world) that was the subject of the *Temeraire*. The *Times* of May 6 1840 dismissed the subtitle as "unintelligible periphrasis."[72] But it is easy to detect one possible meaning—an ironic reference to the painting of the year before, and to the fickle enthusiasm of a briefly adulatory public. Nelson's *Téméraire,* after all, had been destroyed with little objection; when the Nelson memorial came to be built it was many decades overdue. Perhaps an appropriate monument is not appropriate for this public; perhaps some memorials can become too accessible, some imagery too distinct. A childish public "shan't have" its "Hoop." Turner well could have come to feel that memorializing too often is only toyed with, trivializing the subject and the task. I am not suggesting that he came to regard the *Temeraire* this way; but he may have become uneasy over the enthusiasm that accompanied its first public exhibition. Thereafter it was to become more exclusively, even defiantly, the "darling" picture from which he would not be parted for any price, a private image of his own. The Nelson memorial would be completed; a new memorial industry might surface in its wake. The Victorian arts generally might move towards an increasingly stable, increasingly public, mythology. Turner at least could insist that this personal image would not return to the public domain, that for the remainder of his life "The flag that braved the battle and the breeze / No longer owns her."

Conclusion
Sun Pictures

We remember, we remember,
  But we heard it on the sly,
'Twon't be finish'd next November,
  Nor the following July.

Punch (1843)

From today, painting is dead.

Paul Delaroche (1839)

It was during these thoughts that the idea occurred to me . . . how charming
it would be if it were possible to cause these natural images to imprint themselves durably, and remain fixed upon the paper!

W. H. Fox Talbot, *The Pencil of Nature* (1844)

. . . we must be on our guard against judging from what we see in the world
at a particular era.

Robert Chambers, *Vestiges of the Natural History of Creation* (1844)

A Life of Antique devoutness, Antique veracity and heroism, has again
become possible. . . .

Thomas Carlyle, *Past and Present* (1843)

In a palace in a garden—not in a haughty keep, proud with the flame, but
dark with the violence of ages; not in a regal pile, bright with the splendour,
but soiled with the intrigues, of courts and factions,—in a palace in a garden,
meet scene for youth, and innocence, and beauty—came the voice that told
the maiden she must ascend her throne!

Benjamin Disraeli, *Sybil* (1845)[1]

At the end of October 1843 the statue of Nelson was scheduled to be put in
place in Trafalgar Square. But installation, like the creation of the
memorial, was delayed. *Punch* remarked that the large crowds that assem-
bled really were there because they expected not to see the statue put up,

"for they would have been mad if they had expected anything of the sort, but to witness the mull the authorities were certain to make of it."[2] Several weeks later, the continuing delays became the subject of a "Nelson Column Drama" (as the *Punch* article is titled), "a grand architectural and historical burletta." The play's two acts "comprise the commencement and completion, and a lapse of twenty years is supposed to take place between them, in which 'the boy,' who is the principal character, becomes a middle aged man." In both roles, they/he sing(s) a duet in the second act, ending with the stanza printed as the first epigraph to this chapter. Remembering has become the subject of jokes, as has the Nelson memorial.

The *Illustrated London News* reported the near-event with very little of *Punch's* skepticism. "While we feel a satisfaction that a public memorial to him is now completed, we cannot help regretting that more than thirty years should have elapsed before so obvious a duty to his renown . . . was accomplished." The delay "seems likely to remain a reproach to us, unless the future is an improvement on the past. We are glad to see that there are some signs of an improvement." It is, then, an occasion for self-congratulation, perhaps the first of many. Other monuments are being planned; new kinds of achievements deserve their memorials, too. "There are victories of science; there are conquests of mental enquiry; and those who achieve them add to the happiness of mankind, or accelerate the progress of society to a better state."[3] The front-page article is arranged around a picture (Figure C.1) of the huge statue in the midst of staring crowds (almost all of their heads are turned towards it, away from us); and it seems to invite us to share the excitement. One hundred thousand people visited it in two days! The statue weighs nearly eighteen tons! The *ILN* has discovered the journalistic rhetoric that would characterize its reporting of such marvels as the Great Exhibition later in the century. This is contemporary history in the making, a technological triumph. The significance of the monument as a record of the past recedes beside its importance as an engineering achievement in the present and its promise of progress in the future. That is what the illustration represents as well: a monument both to Nelson and the emerging age.

All the more reason to record its completion in words and pictures. *Punch* had been founded in 1841, the *Illustrated London News* a year later. In spite of their differing political slants, apparent in the distinct tones of their treatments of the memorial, there is a way in which they exemplify a similar outlook. From the left or the right, as critics or admirers, both approach the statue in Trafalgar Square as something to be explicated simply, something knowable, and known. The problems associated with the memorial are forgotten. Contemporary history as they represent it is less a puzzle than a spectacle. As a subject of ridicule or praise, the statue and the agencies responsible for erecting it (or not) are there to be seen and described clearly, depicted in more or less accurate, more or less serious drawings. It is the *ILN,* of course, that makes solemn claims of accuracy for its images; but it is difficult to take them as seriously as they apparently were intended, or to have much confidence in their fidelity. Standardized figures reappear in supposedly accurate representations of sharply differing events; we can observe the standardization in the treatment of the crowd around the statue of Nelson. In a sense, both journals are filled with caricatures on a series of contemporary subjects; their illustrations couldn't have been printed distinctly if they weren't simplified, and beyond that necessary clarification a stylization takes place that makes most of their pictures recognizable at once. And this is in part a stylization of contemporary life: they make the age recognizable, too. We still think of the Victorians in terms of this imagery, which remained remarkably stable over the next half-century. Perhaps it is even here that the notion of a "Victorian age," or the possibility of such a notion, begins to form. It is usually claimed that the adjective only came into use in 1851, the year of the Crystal Palace and the fouding of the Australian colony of Victoria (whose citizens thus became the first Victorians officially so named).[4] The earliest example I have come across is from the second volume of *Punch,* published in 1842, in an article on "The Victorian, in Contradistinction to the Elizabethan Style." It is a satire on contemporary drama, but once again the point is that contemporary drama is itself "stylized" enough to merit such blanket treatment. In fact, the object of the humor is the "pure" domesticity of the modern stage, which "is nightly received by astonished thousands with vehement delight, and a kind of Mount Vesuvius greeting, that cannot be expressed by the English language."[5] It cannot be expressed, that is, except by that new word.

Without being prepared to assign the new age a name, the *ILN* was convinced that its existence had something to do with its own founding, with the emergence of modern pictorial journalism. "We know that the advent of an Illustrated Newspaper in the country *must* mark an epoch."[6] It is an epoch of information. Now contemporary history will become clearer and more accessible to present and future generations. The preface to the second volume proudly confesses, "Yes, these tomes are little monuments of Art, which we are building up on the broadlands of community; and on the four tablets of which Literature, Poetry, History and the Intelligence of the social world have graven inscriptions which we hope will prove as indelible as they are distinct."[7] And beyond this distinctness, the new medium produces a new kind of historical record:

> The life of the times—the signs of its taste and intelligence—its public monuments and public men—its festivals—institutions—amusements—discoveries—the very reflection of its living manners and costumes—the variegated dresses of its mind and body—what are—what *must* be all these but treasures of truth that would have lain in Time's tomb, or perished amid the sand of his hour-glass but for the enduring and resuscitating powers of art— the eternal register of the pencil giving life and vigour and palpability to the confirming details of the pen. . . . This volume is a work that history *must* keep.[8]

But what that last remark means is that now everything is history. There is a confidence in the significance of the ordinary that exceeds anything we encounter in Dickens, and a correspondingly heightened confidence in the ability of the modern journalist to capture it. We are surrounded by the materials for our newest memorials, and a new graphic technology enables us to transform them immediately into permanent images.

The medium that made that transformation most dramatically was photography, announced to the public in January 1839, almost simultaneously by Louis Daguerre in France and William Henry Fox Talbot in England. The discovery produced widespread excitement—over the beauty of the images (Talbot had called the process "photogenic drawing" in his first account of it to the Royal Society) and their almost magical power to arrest transitory effects of light. "The most fleeting of all things—a shadow, is fixed, and made permanent," the *Athenaeum* explained in an admiring account of Talbot's first explanatory lecture.[9] Talbot illustrated the same fact in his first published collection of callotypes (as he called them), *The Pencil of Nature,* published in parts between 1844 and 1846, and explicated it in the notes to the twenty-four plates. There is a characteristic example in his remarks on a "Bust of Patroclus" that appeared in the first published part. Talbot comments on the effects of light on the statue, which will lead him to rephotograph it under other conditions for inclusion in a later part of the book:

> These delineations are susceptible of an almost unlimited variety: since in the first place, a statue may be placed in any position with regard to the sun, either directly opposite to it, or at any angle: the directness or obliquity of the illumination causing of course an immense difference in the effect. And when a choice has been made of the direction in which the sun's rays shall

fall, the statue may be then turned round on its pedestal, which produces a second set of variations no less considerable than the first.[10]

These are, in the most literal sense, sun pictures. A collection Talbot published in 1845 was titled *Sun Pictures in Scotland,* and it was a term he used generally to refer to his new process. It caught on. On the back of a callotype by two of his early followers, David Octavious Hill and Robert Adamson, an inscription notes, "Sol fecit."[11]

The proper place for such Latin tags is, of course, in the lower corners of an engraving, to identify the engraver or the original artist. The use of "fecit" on a photograph (even on the back), the very use of Latin at all, is telling. While recognizing the revolutionary nature of their new medium, the first photographers also understood their own work in relation to more traditional visual art. Hill first experimented with callotypes in 1843 to record likenesses for a large historical painting of the Disruption of the Scottish Church; the result is a huge omnibus portrait, in which dozens of figures are represented in detail. *The Pencil of Nature* repeatedly points out that photography will help painters introduce "a multitude of minute details which add to the truth and reality of the representation, but which no artist would take the trouble to copy faithfully from nature" (he "would probably deem it beneath his genius," we are told a sentence later).[12] If Talbot wished to legitimize photography as an art form in its own right, it was still a form of art according to conventional definitions; it was to be separate from but analagous to painting.

> We have sufficient authority in the Dutch school of art, for taking as subjects of representation scenes of daily and familiar occurrence. A painter's eye will often be arrested where ordinary people see nothing remarkable. A casual gleam of sunshine, or a shadow thrown across his path, a time-withered oak, or a moss-covered stone may awaken a train of thoughts and feelings, and picturesque imaginings.

Talbot here is commenting on one of the earliest of his photographs, "The Open Door" (Figure C.2). Although he calls it "one of the trifling efforts" of the art in "its infancy,"[13] in a sense he also tries to persuade us that this isn't a new art at all. But it is hard for us to be convinced. "The Open Door" falls outside most of the categories of traditional painting, even Dutch realism, if only by virtue of the teasing uncertainty of the "subject" itself, or the suggestiveness of those shadows at its center. Talbot describes it in the language of the picturesque, and that vocabulary only partly fits. These are very new kinds of scenes.

The twentieth-century view of nineteenth-century photographs is predictably different from the one found in *The Pencil of Nature*. We respond first to the tensions exhibited in these early prints: between clarity and obscurity, fixity and motion. Here, as in some of the dark, blurred portraits of Julia Margaret Cameron, suggestiveness and uncertainty have a power of their own. Talbot, even while exploiting the apparently opposing qualities of photographic images, seems to have found some of the differences disconcerting. The images and explanations of *The Pencil of Nature* attempt to establish photography as an art of representational certainty, a record of fact. "It frequently happens . . . and this is one of the charms of photography—that the operator himself discovers on examination, perhaps long afterwards, that he has depicted many things he had no notion of at the time."[14] In the notes on "The Ladder," a picture including three figures (arranged with the help of a professional painter, Henry Collen),[15] he recommends photography as an art of portraiture especially, although only under certain conditions.

> If we proceed to the City, and attempt to take a picture of the moving multitude, we fail, for in a small fraction of a second they change their positions so much, as to destroy the distinctness of the representation. But when a group of persons has been artistically arranged, and trained by a little practice to maintain an absolute immobility for a few seconds of time, very delightful pictures are easily obtained.[16]

Cities are too mobile, too active; their citizens pose problems because they will not pose. In spite of his interest in changing effects of light, Talbot also wishes to record images of permanence. One of the virtues of the new medium, then, is the capacity to "fix" certain subjects (if those subjects subject themselves to this fixity in the first place), just as the final discovery that made photography possible was how to "fix" the changes of light-sensitive chemicals so an image could be preserved. Through an extension of this analogy Talbot even comes to associate photographs with social stability: "What would not be the value to our English Nobility of such a record of their ancestors who lived a century ago? On how small a portion of their family picture galleries can they really rely with confidence?"[17] In the same spirit, he compares his photograph of "Articles of China" to a "written inventory" of the same collection. There can be no doubt which gives the more complete description, especially if the pieces shown have "strange and fantastic" forms; and Talbot speculates on the legal result if such a photograph were introduced as evidence following a theft.[18] *The Pencil of Nature* is to a great extent a record of Talbot's own home and possessions: Lacock Abbey ("the Author's country seat in Wiltshire"), with its grounds and architectural features; personal collections, as in the plates showing "Articles of China" or "Shelves of Books" (Figure C.3). Early paintings often served a similar function: to document what was owned or known, and by so doing to make that knowledge more certain. (In a similar way portraits can be said to "identify" their subjects, in the sense of both acknowledging and conferring identity, an identity that is often bound up in class.) The drive for pictorial specificity thus reflects a double impulse: to extend the boundaries of the known world and to solidify them in new ways. This paradoxical mixture of experimental and conservative motives is apparent in the earliest photography, and the explanations of it.

It would not take long for photographers, Talbot included, to become aware that the new medium possessed revolutionary possibilities for departures from the aesthetics of traditional painting and graphic art. In the early 1840s, however, experimentation coexists with an impulse to align photography with visual tradition. "Sun pictures," "The Pencil of Nature": Talbot's phrases suggest a natural or even divine authority, and thus intentionality, as well as clarity of definition. He classifies photography as "photogenic drawing," an art of line and distinct detail. To some extent we are meant to overlook its obscurities, the areas of vagueness, just as the photographer is meant to overcome them in perfecting his art. Or so we are told in Talbot's text. As a means of representation (and as a product of modern technology) the photograph is an instrument of knowledge. The photographer will make every effort to make that knowledge as precise as possible. Of course, in saying this I am stressing Talbot's commentaries on his photographs more than the photographs themselves; his words may misstate (or simply miss) the true character of those images, but that is part of what makes *The Pencil of Nature* an important text. It presents a vision and a revision, a set of representations and a new representation of them in words, images followed by a text that requires us to reimagine what we have just seen. In a sense, photography is always an art of memory,[19] and here we have a double memory at work, a process through which the world represented becomes all the more distanced, that which is seen in the present all the more firmly located in a fixed and knowable past. This is what makes these images typical of a much wider and more varied set of representations, including those commentaries from *Punch* and the *ILN:* an urge to transcend the obscurities of the real, to represent the world in a legible form, as itself legible.

The issue is familiar. *The Poetry of Architecture* explores the legible meanings of nature, *Oliver Twist* those of the city; J. O. Parry's "London Street Scene" portrays the urban world as a series of texts. But most of those earlier attempts to decipher the inscriptions of reality break down:

legibility has its limits, or did in the late 1830s; the known faces the constant danger of reabsorption into the unknown. The arts of Victoria's Year return, far more often than their creators wish, to recognitions of the inscrutability of things, the intractability of the real. Not that they never embark on ambitious explanatory ventures, but those efforts all too often are frustrated, or become tangled in contradictions. A fully knowable, explicable world remains just out of reach. A fully adequate way of knowing or representing it does too. In a sense, what is lacking is a new mythos, or the confidence that one can be found. But we can detect the emergence of that confidence in Talbot's commentary on his photographs, or those articles from *Punch* and the *ILN*. And at just about the same time there are signs that that new mythos is being shaped in the literature of the 1840s as well.

The subject of Carlyle's *Past and Present* is the absence of such a myth, or its apparent absence. Like Pugin's *Contrasts,* the book shifts our gaze from the nineteenth century (1843, to be exact) to the Middle Ages, painting a gloomy modern picture of decayed monuments and vanished heroes. Beginning from "the hard, organic, but limited Feudal Ages," we then are asked to "glance timidly into the immense Industrial Ages, as yet all inorganic, and in a quite pulpy condition, requiring desperately to harden themselves into some organism!"[20] That is the requirement Carlyle's book proposes to meet: in its accounts of a new "Working Aristocracy," the modern Captains of Industry who could lead the nation back to the future; in its announcement of a new modern epic, "Tools and the Man," which promises a heroic existence for the whole nation. Present reality is dismally different. The book opens describing the blighted contemporary countryside—rich harvests and an impoverished population, England collectively "dying of inanition." By the end, this sleeping world has awakened; a new stage of history, a new kind of history, is prepared to begin. "The Present, if it will have the future accomplish, shall itself commence."[21] *Contrasts,* as the title suggests, emphasized the differences between past and present; Pugin never fully can make Carlyle's prophetic turn towards a new world. *Past and Present* concludes with a stirring, visionary "Horoscope" that stretches from 1843 into an unlimited future. A new organic society is prepared to bloom. The imagery of this final prophecy comes directly out of the conclusion of *The French Revolution:* "The World is black ashes;—which, ah, when will they grow green?" Now the possibility is no longer expressed as a question: "Chaos is dark, deep as hell; let light be, and there is instead a green flowery World."[22] The rhetoric is emphatic, but Carlyle declares that it is even more certain than that, not rhetoric at all. "This is not a figure of speech; this is a fact. . . . This is not Theology, this is Arithmetic."[23] Our vista on the future now is limitless; the nature of the present, and its direction, is absolutely clear. History has been absorbed into myth.

Nineteenth-century mythmaking did not begin with Carlyle and would not end with him, but the tradition is not unbroken. Even writers who eventually come to embrace myths, or construct private myths of their own, sometimes only arrived at that end after a struggle. The sections of *In Memoriam* composed in the 1830s record a struggle of that kind, one all the more evident in the context of the finished poem, where the fragmentariness and gloom of those evolutionary lyrics is set off by the confident clarity of the epilogue. It is worth recalling that that conclusion depended upon the (anonymous) appearance of Chambers' *Vestiges of the Natural History of Creation* in 1844, a book that almost seems to have been created to meet the poet's needs. It is as if Tennyson had been searching for just such an all-encompassing system, a structure to contain his earlier thought. In a sense, that search is described in "The Epic," which in framing the earlier, mythic "Morte d'Arthur" self-consciously explores the problem of linking modern and mythic worlds. As we have seen, the linkage doesn't completely work; in the late 1830s Tennyson did not yet find contemporary life entirely congenial to myth. It might be argued that Ruskin encountered the same difficulty in *The Poetry of Architecture,* for he invokes a traditional pastoral myth only to become ensnared in its ironies. By 1843, with the first volume of *Modern Painters,* he began constructing myths of his own, in which Turner stood at the center of a panoramic history of Western naturalism; by the time he wrote *The Stones of Venice,* this had grown into a myth accounting for the whole of history, with significant debts to Carlyle's vision of past and present. Even Darwin fits into this pattern, although the culmination of his search for a unifying vision of things would not come until 1859. We can see the beginnings of *The Origin of Species* in the *Journal of Researches* of 1839, but we also can see a good deal more. The *Beagle* record is the product of a mind still asking fundamental questions—without being prepared to provide many answers. Questioning continues in the *Origin,* but within a totalizing vision that also deserves to be considered a species of myth, within a structure of explanations and answers.

As the nineteenth century progresses, many of the same questions remain, or are asked again by others in new forms; but new answers are available too, as is a growing sense that they are available, a sense that the present can be understood and named. Victorianism finally may constitute nothing more than a collection of contradictory attitudes and opinions, a shifting, complex "frame of mind" of the sort catalogued in Walter Houghton's magisterial survey. But even within such a fluctuating field of values, the sense that there was a field provided a kind of assurance, one that emerged only after the 1830s. If the adjective "Victorian" was not yet in use in 1837 and 1838, it may have been because a word of that sort did not yet seem possible; the present was too varied, too diverse, to be identified by any sweeping, comprehensive term. Most important, as Carlyle would observe in *Chartism,* it was too much unknown. But confidence in such generalizations would grow. However complex or elusive its character, the "Victorian period" existed for those who lived in the last half of the century. We can confirm this from many sources, including those self-satisfied remarks of Walter Besant I discussed in the introduction to this book. And I believe that the existence of this growing sense of cultural identity can be traced to one last work of the 1840s, one of the most self-conscious examples of mid-nineteenth-century mythmaking: Disraeli's *Sybil.*

Disraeli's myths are both literary and political, and *Sybil* includes among its several aims the creation of a party platform. "The Two Nations" (the novel's subtitle) can be united through the firm, benevolent guidance of an enlightened post-Carlylean aristocracy, glowing with high moral purpose and the vigor of youth. But "Young England" becomes conceivable as a movement and a phrase only after the power of youth is validated in other ways. One is the magical appearance of Sybil herself, illuminated in the roseate hues of the setting sun, singing the evening hymn to the Virgin, dressed in "the habit of a Religious," conveying to the novel's hero an impression of "almost divine majesty."

> Egremont might for a moment have been pardoned for believing her a seraph, that had lighted on this sphere, or the fair phantom of some saint haunting the sacred ruins of her desecrated fane.[24]

It is a powerful image, in a book that to a great extent concerns the power of images. Disraeli prophecies both a new order and the new symbolism required to give it force. His hero, Egremont, requires this vision of a Sybil to begin his political education with sufficient passion. And the nation must have a similar ideal if it is to follow his example. Hence the famous scene I have quoted as the last epigraph to this chapter, the announcement (it reads more like an Annunciation) to Victoria that she had become Queen. In this moment, Victoria's Year itself passes into myth.

The final chapter of *Sybil* reminds the reader of two things. The rich and poor are still divided, but it is now possible for a new relation between them to be conceived.

In an age of political infidelity, of mean passions and petty thoughts, I would have impressed upon the rising race not to despair, but to seek in a right understanding of the history of their country and in the energies of heroic youth—the elements of national welfare. . . . It is the past alone that can explain the present, and it is youth alone that can mould the future.[25]

The word "Victorian" does not appear. But Disraeli quite self-consciously is constructing a historical mythology according to which such a word, or such a concept, can have meaning. In a sense the largest problem of the novel is conceiving of this world and its problems in some totalizing way. That is why Disraeli makes such deliberate use of a few powerful images, and why he writes a modern novel about events that are (in 1845) still a few years in the past, where they can be seen clearly and safely at a distance.

I will not stretch the analogy with photography any further by claiming that Disraeli creates sun pictures of his own. But I have organized this concluding chapter around those frozen images of a living reality to emphasize what our own familiarity with this technology may allow us to forget: the power and attractiveness of a medium that almost instantaneously makes our own world appear more distinct while setting it apart from us, as another object of study. Images can achieve this, as well as ideas. We should recall how eagerly the speaker of "Locksley Hall" yearned for the clarity of his youthful view of the world through an old casement window, or how eagerly Tennyson himself responded to the ideas of natural history in *Vestiges of Creation*—or should I say to its picture of natural history? For that book also translates the world into a new kind of imagery, reconsiders the facts unveiled by science from a special perspective; it asks the reader to "fully and truly consider what a system is here laid open to view."[26] Chambers is well aware that he is constructing, or reconstructing, this view for the first time: "The book, as far as I am aware, is the first attempt to connect the natural sciences in a history of creation."[27] As he ends the last long chapter of the *Vestiges* (on the "Purpose and General Condition of the Animated Creation"), he is prepared to acknowledge the existence of facts that might disturb some of his readers, or might have disturbed a reader of Lyell in 1837. Yet he remains confident of a larger unity:

Thinking of all the contingencies of this world as to be in time melted into or lost in the greater system, to which the present is only subsidiary, let us wait the end with patience, and be of good cheer.[28]

Notes

Introduction: The New Map of London

1. Walter Besant, *Fifty Years Ago* (New York: Harper, 1888), p. 18; G. M. Young, *Victorian England: Portrait of an Age,* annotated edition, ed. George Kitson Clark (London: Oxford University Press, 1977), from the "Introduction to the Second Edition," (1953), p. 18; Richard Monckton Milnes, *Poems,* 2 volumes (London: Moxon, 1838), i, 118; *The Centenary Edition of the Works of Thomas Carlyle,* ed. H. D. Traill, 30 volumes (London: Chapman and Hall, 1896–1899), xxix, 127.

2. *Times,* June 20, 1837.

3. Ibid.

4. Ibid.

5. Lytton Strachey, *Queen Victoria* (New York: Blue Ribbon Books, 1931), p. 71.

6. King William had anticipated such confusion, predicting that sailors would tatoo her face on their arms, imagining that she was named after Nelson's flagship, the *Victory.* See Elizabeth Longford, *Queen Victoria: Born to Succeed* (New York, Harper and Row, 1964), p. 24.

7. *Times,* June 28, 1837; the story is reprinted from *The Western Luminary.*

8. Carl Dawson, *Victorian Noon: English Literature in 1850* (Baltimore and London: Johns Hopkins University Press, 1979), p. 1.

9. Young, p. 18.

10. Reprinted in *Hood's Own: Laughter from Year to Year,* Second Series (London: Moxon, 1862), p. 133.

11. *Chambers' Edinburgh Journal,* no. 281, June 17, 1837; the lead article is titled "London."

12. *Penny Magazine,* January 31, 1837, from the first article in the series entitled "The Looking-Glass of London."

13. *Penny Magazine,* December 30, 1837.

14. *Blackwood's Edinburgh Magazine,* August 1837, p. 159.

15. I am grateful to Prof. Randall McGowen for pointing this out.

16. The rest of the title reads, "A Puzzle Suggested by the Stoppages Occasioned by repairing the Streets. The object is to find a way from the Strand to St. Paul's,

without crossing any of the Bars in the Streets supposed to be under repair." The author was C. Ingrey. James Howgego, *Printed Maps of London circa 1553–1850* (Folkstone, Kent: Dawson, 1978), p. 238, entry no. 326.

17. *Tallis's London Street Views, exhibiting upwards of one hundred buildings in each number . . . the whole forming a complete Stranger's Guide through London. . . .* (London: John Tallis, n.d., but dated in the copy in the British Library Map Library as 1839).

18. See James Howgego, *Printed Maps of London circa 1553–1850,* second edition (London: Dawson, 1978), entry no. 309 (3b).

19. Philippe Glanville observes that the new maps generally ignored new conditions in London, citing *Cary's New Plan of London and its Vicinity,* which first appeared in 1790 and was still on sale in 1836 with only minimal alteration of its plates; James Wyld reissued in 1838 the plates of Faden's map of *The Country 25 Miles Round London,* first published in 1788; see Glanville, *London in Maps* (London: The Conoisseur, 1972), p. 39.

20. Besant, p. 18.

21. Besant, p. vii.

22. Besant, p. 1; he does add, however, "I, who am no longer, unhappily, quite so young as some, and whose babyhood heard the cannon of the Coronation, can partly understand this time"; Jerome Hamilton Buckley, *The Victorian Temper: A Study in Literary Culture* (New York: Vintage, 1951), p. 6.

23. Besant, p. 260.

24. Carlyle, *Works* xxix, 77.

25. Besant, p. 20.

26. The remark comes from "Civilization," in *The Collected Works of John Stuart Mill,* gen. ed. J. M. Robson (Toronto and Buffalo: University of Toronto Press, 1963–), xviii, 126.

27. Brian Friel, *Translations* (London: Faber and Faber, 1981), p. 30.

28. Carlyle, *Works,* xxix, 127.

1. Signs, Scenes, and Sketches

1. *Penny Magazine,* 11 August 1838—the essay concerns "Allegorical Painting and Sculpture"; *Quarterly Review* 66 (September 1840), on "Carlyle's Works"—the anonymous reviewer was William Sewell; *Times,* September 5, 1837.

2. Marina Warner, *Queen Victoria's Sketchbook* (New York: Crown Publishers, 1979), p. 41.

3. Warner, p. 45.

4. Queen Victoria's Journal, typescript in the Royal Archives, Windsor; the Journal is noted below as RA QVJ.

5. *The Rural Life of England* (London: Longman, Brown, Green, and Longmans, 1838), p. 165.

6. RA QVJ; *The Gipsies' Advocate: or, Observations on the Origin, Character, Manners, and Habits of the English Gipsies,* by James Crabb (Author of "The Penitent Magdalen") (London: Seeley, 1831), p. vii.

7. RA QVJ, December 22, 1836.

8. John Barrell, *The Dark Side of the Landscape: the Rural Poor in English Painting, 1730–1840* (Cambridge: Cambridge University Press, 1980).

9. On Westall, see Warner, pp. 14–19; RA QVJ, December 6, 1836.

10. Edgar Allen Poe, *Essays and Reviews* (New York: The Library of America, 1984), p. 205.

11. F. S. Schwarzbach, *Dickens and the City* (London: The Athlone Press, 1979), pp. 34–37; *Westminister Review* 27 (April 1837), 202.

12. Charles Dickens, *Sketches by Boz,* in the Oxford Illustrated Dickens (London and New York: Oxford University Press, 1973), p. 75.

13. James Grant, *The Great Metropolis,* 2 volumes (London: Saunders & Otley, 1836), i, 2.

14. *Sketches by Boz,* pp. 48–49.

15. Grant, i, 17.

16. *Sketches by Boz,* p. 81.

17. *Sketches by Boz,* p. 170.

18. *Sketches by Boz,* p. 104.

19. *Sketches by Boz,* p. 202.

20. Asa Briggs, "The Human Aggregate," in *The Victorian City: Images and Realities,* 2 volumes (London and Boston: Routledge and Kegan Paul, 1976), i, 84.

21. Philip Collins, *Dickens and Crime* (Bloomington and London: Indiana University Press, 1968), pp. 33, 36.

22. See Collins, p. 27.

23. Walter Pater, *The Renaissance: Studies in Art and Poetry* (London: Macmillan, 1920), p. 235.

24. Michael Mason, "Browning and the Dramatic Monologue," in *Writers and their Background: Robert Browning,* ed. Isobel Armstrong (Athens, Ohio: Ohio University Press, 1975), pp. 258f.

25. *Sketches by Boz,* p. 144; the passage quoted below is from p. 146.

26. *Penny Magazine,* August 9, 1836.

27. See Gareth Rees, *Early Railway Prints: British Railways from 1825 to 1850* (Ithaca, New York: Cornell University Press and Phaidon Books, 1980), pp. 52–53.

28. George L. Hersey, *High Victorian Gothic: A Study in Associationism* (Baltimore and London: Johns Hopkins University Press, 1972). Associationism "involves an attitude or description that has earlier been implanted in the observer's mind and that is automatically elicited when the object is seen. The implanted description controls, or perhaps even constitutes, his response to the work of art" [p. 7].

29. Rennie is cited in Felix Barker and Ralph Hyde, *London as It Might Have Been* (London: John Murray, 1982), p. 131.

30. John Summerson, *Victorian Architecture in England: Four Studies in Evaluation* (New York: Norton, 1970), p. 22.

31. Summerson, p. 20.

32. For an account of this church, see Basil F. L. Clarke, *Parish Churches of London* (London: Batsford, 1966), where it is termed "one of the best Grecian

churches" (p. 200).

33. Kenneth Clark, *The Gothic Revival* (New York: Harper and Row, 1974), p. 145.

34. Clark, p. 147.

35. A. W. N. Pugin, *Contrasts; or a Parallel between the Noble Edifices of the Fourteenth and Fifteenth Centuries, and Similar Buildings of the Present Day. . .* (New York: Humanities Press, 1969); reprint of the second edition (London: Charles Dolman, 1841); pp. 9–10. Later references to this edition will appear parenthetically in the text.

36. Phoebe Stanton, *Pugin* (New York: Viking, 1971), p. 40.

37. Stanton, p. 45.

38. Stanton, p. 87.

39. Stanton, p. 86.

40. Stanton, pp. 86, 92.

41. Quoted in *Thomas Carlyle: The Critical Heritage,* ed. Jules Paul Seigel (New York: Barnes & Noble, 1971), p. 144.

42. Raymond Lister, *Victorian Narrative Painting* (New York: Clarkson Potter, 1966), p. 31.

43. *Sketches by Boz,* p. 104.

44. Quoted in Donald J. Olsen, *The Growth of Victorian London* (London: Penguin, 1976), p. 58.

45. Grant, i, 17.

46. Grant, i, 10.

47. Richard D. Altick, *The Shows of London* (Cambridge, Massachusetts and London: Belknap Press, Harvard University Press, 1978), pp. 181–182, 323.

48. Thomas Babington Macaulay, "Ranke's History of the Popes," *Critical and Miscellaneous Essays* (Philadelphia: Carey and Hart, 1841), 3 volumes, iii, 320–321; Gustave Doré and Blanchard Jerrold, *London, A Pilgrimage* (New York: Dover, 1970, reprint of 1st edition, London: Grant & Co., 1872), p. 190 and illustration facing p. 188.

49. Grant, i, 19.

50. Alfred Dunhill Ltd., who gave permission for reproduction of this watercolor, have called my attention to the explication of this and other allusions in notes to the reproduction of Parry's print in *Motif* (1958), prepared by George Nash of the Victoria and Albert Museum for James Shand of the Shenval Press Ltd. This particular reference is one of the proofs that although the print is dated 1835, Parry must have continued to work on it for several years after that. The entry also points out that another of the posters refers to Parry's "success in his father's 'The Sham Prince,'" performed September 29, 1836. See the typed pages on "John Orlando Parry, 1810–1879" available from Alfred Dunhill Ltd.

51. *Narrative of the Surveying Voyages of His Majesty's Ships Adventure and Beagle, between the years 1826 and 1836, describing their examination of the Southern shores of South America, and the Beagle's Circumnavigation of the Globe,* 3 volumes (London: Colburn, 1839), volume 3, "Journal and Remarks," by Charles Darwin, p. 604.

52. See F. S. Schwarzbach, "'Terra Incognita,'—An Image of the City in English Literature, 1820–1855," *Prose Studies* 5:1 (May 1982), 61–84.

2. The Golden Year

1. *The Centenary Edition of the Works of Thomas Carlyle,* ed. H. D. Traill, 30 volumes (London: Chapman and Hall, 1896–1899), xxix, 203; *The Poetical Works of Wordsworth,* ed. Ernest de Selincourt (London, Oxford University Press, 1964), p. 404; *The Poems of Tennyson,* ed. Christopher Ricks (London and New York: Longman and Norton, 1969), p. 716; *Elizabeth Barrett to Miss Mitford,* ed. Betty Miller (London: Murray, 1954), p. 14 (Barrett mistakenly dates her letter "May 2nd 1836" for 1837; *Edinburgh Review* 47 (July 1838), 356–357.

2. *The Works of the Reverend Sydney Smith,* 3 volumes complete in one (New York: Appleton, 1881), p. 421; the sermon's publication was listed in the *Times,* July 14, 1837.

3. Smith, p. 422.

4. Smith, p. 424.

5. Smith, p. 423.

6. *Blackwood's Edinburgh Magazine* 42:262 (August 1837); the irrelevance of some of these poetic tributes becomes humorously obvious in the December issue of *Blackwood's,* where a poem on "Augusta Victrix" praises Victoria as the "Salomé of the West" (in the regular column, "The World We Live In").

7. *Times,* June 19, 1837.

8. *Quarterly Review* 59 (July 1837), 246.

9. *Westminster Review* 27 (July 1837), 245–246.

10. *The Collected Works of John Stuart Mill,* gen. ed. J. M. Robson, (Toronto and Buffalo: University of Toronto Press, 1963–   ), xii, 352; Letter 218: 28 September 1837.

11. Ibid, 352. Mill adds that it is "just the writing one would expect from Miss Mitford, or any other woman who has written tragedies, and learnt to put good woman's feelings into men's words, and to make small things look like great ones" (353).

12. John Killham, *Tennyson and the Princess: Reflections of an Age* (London: Athlone Press, 1958), p. 120; *Woman's Mission,* fifth American edition (Philadelphia: William Hazzard, 1854); the copy at the University of Virginia Library is inscribed with birth and death dates and the following motto inside the back cover:

Steel not this Book
My onist Frend
for fer the Gallus may
Bee you the End the
Gallus so high the
Rope so Strong and
Remember that you have
Got tow Die.

It is written in the hand of "Fanny Wicker the Wife of John W. Wicker," March 20, 1858; on the identity of Sarah Lewis as Aimé-Martin, see also Patricia Thomson's review of Nina Auerbach, *Woman and the Demon,* in *Victorian Studies* 27:4 (Winter 1984), 239.

13. *Edinburgh Review* 67 (July, 1838), 388; the remark comes in a review-essay titled "Waagen on English Art."

14. *The Poems of Tennyson,* ed. Christopher Ricks (London and New York: Longman and Norton, 1969), p. 666; all references to Tennyson's poetry (with line numbers given in the text) will be to this volume, cited hereafter as "Ricks."

15. The German quotation from Goethe appears as the epigraph to *Sartor Resartus* and is translated by Carlyle as follows:

> My inheritance how wide and fair!
> Time is my fair seed-field, of Time I'm heir.

See *A Carlyle Reader,* ed. G. B. Tennyson (New York: Random House, 1969), p. 124.

16. Ricks, p. 717n.

17. Ibid.

18. Cited in Charles Babbage, *The Ninth Bridgewater Treatise: A Fragment* (London: Cass, 1967; reprint of 1837 edition), preface.

19. Babbage, pp. 26–27.

20. Ricks, p. 717n.

21. Ricks, p. 716n.

22. For the best discussions of Tennyson's use of the Theocritan idyll, see A. Dwight Culler, *The Poetry of Tennyson* (New Haven and London: Yale University Press, 1977), pp. 90–92, 106–128; and particularly Robert Pattison, *Tennyson and Tradition* (Cambridge and London: Harvard Unversity Press, 1979), *passim,* esp. 15–39.

23. John Dixon Hunt, "The Poetry of Distance: Tennyson's 'Idylls of the King,'" in *Victorian Poetry,* Stratford-Upon-Avon Studies no. 15 (London: Arnold, 1972), p. 95.

24. Richard Hengist Horne, *A New Spirit of the Age,* 2 volumes (London: Smith, Elder and Co., 1844), i, 187; Horne's unacknowledged co-author was Elizabeth Barrett. Culler connects the prose pastoral with Tennyson's *English Idyls* (pp. 116 f).

25. Horne, ii, 86.

26. Roy Strong has observed that the genre of Charles I paintings was intended to remind viewers of "the middle-class domestic happiness . . . of their own Victoria and Albert." *Recreating the Past: British History and the Victorian Painter* (London and New York: Thames and Hudson, and the Pierpont Morgan Library, 1978), p. 139.

27. Benjamin Disraeli, *Henrietta Temple* (New York: Routledge, n.d.), Book II, chapter ix.

28. Cited in R. K. Webb, *Harriet Martineau: A Radical Victorian* (New York: Columbia University Press, 1960), pp. 185–186.

29. *Edinburgh Review* 47 (July 1838), 356–357.

30. *Elizabeth Barrett to Miss Mitford,* ed. Betty Miller (London: Murray, 1954), p. 14.

31. *Athenaeum,* June 1, 1837; the version reprinted in Barrett's volume of 1838 is altered:

> Perhaps our youthful Queen
> Remembers what had been—
> Her childhood's rest by loving heart, and sport on grassy sod—
> Alas! can others wear
> A mother's heart for her?
> But calm she lifts her trusting face, and calleth upon God.

The Poetical Works of Elizabeth Barrett Browning (New York: Macmillan, 1900), p. 138; all further references to Barrett will be to this volume.

32. Barrett, p. 138.

33. Barrett, p. 76.

34. Barrett, p. 77. Line numbers of this poem will appear after further quotations from it.

35. See Virginia L. Radley, *Elizabeth Barrett Browning* (New York: Twayne Publishers, 1972), p. 39.

36. Barrett, p. 184.

37. Barrett, p. xi.

38. Harriet Martineau, *Deerbrook,* 3 volumes (London: Saunders and Otley, 1837), i, 204; subsequent references to this edition will appear parenthetically in the text.

39. Robert A. Colby, *Fiction with a Purpose: Major and Minor Nineteenth-Century Novels* (Bloomington and London: Indiana University Press, 1957), p. 221.

40. George Woodbridge, *The Reform Club, 1836–1978* (New York and Toronto: Clearwater Publishing Co., 1978), p. 52; £1689 was supposed to be 5 percent of £35,000, the original estimated cost of the project.

41. *The Works of Cardinal Newman,* 40 volumes (London: Longmans, Green and Co., 1918), vi, "Lectures on the Prophetical Office of the Church," 24.

42. *The Centenary Edition of the Works of Thomas Carlyle,* ed. H. D. Traill, 30 volumes (London: Chapman and Hall, 1896–1899), xxix, 32. All subsequent references to Carlyle will be to this edition.

43. Benjamin Disraeli, *Venetia* (New York: Routledge, n.d.), Book VI, chapter iv.

44. *Athenaeum,* no. 499 (May 20, 1837), 356–357.

45. *Venetia,* IV, x.

46. *Venetia,* IV, xiv.

47. *Venetia,* IV, vi.

48. *Venetia,* V,v.

49. *Venetia,* VI, iv.

50. Donald D. Stone, *The Romantic Impulse in Victorian Fiction* (Cambridge, Massachusetts and London: Harvard University Press, 1980), pp. 87–88. Stone remarks of *Venetia* and *Henrietta Temple* that "one might almost say that under

the romantic trappings of these books a Victorian conscience is struggling to be heard" (84).

51. *Venetia,* VI, xii.

52. *Venetia,* VI, vi.

53. Mary Poovey, *The Proper Lady and the Victorian Writer: Ideology as Style in the Works of Mary Wollstonecraft, Mary Shelley, and Jane Austen* (Chicago and London: University of Chicago Press, 1984), p. 164.

54. Mary Shelley, *Falkner: A Novel, by the Author of "Frankenstein," "The Last Man," &c.* 2 volumes (New York and London: Saunders and Otley, 1837; reprint, Folcroft Press, 1975), Volume II, chapter xi.

55. *Falkner,* II, xv.

56. Poovey, p. 165.

57. *Falkner,* II, xvi.

58. *The Madwoman in the Attic: The Woman Writer and the Nineteenth-Century Literary Imagination* (New Haven and London: Yale University Press, 1979), Chapter 7, "Horror's Twin: Mary Shelley's Monstrous Eve," pp. 213–247, esp. p. 230.

59. *Falkner,* I, xvi.

60. *Falkner,* II, ii.

61. Alexander Welsh, *The City of Dickens* (Oxford: Clarendon Press, 1971), p. 219.

62. Robert Browning, *Poetical Works* (London and New York: Oxford University Press, 1967), Act V, scene ii.

63. *The Youthful Queen, A Comedy in Two Acts* by Charles Shannon (*sic:* in fact the author is Jean-François-Alfred Bayard) (New York: French, n.d.), Act II, i; the play was produced in English from as early as 1828.

64. Horne, ii, 86.

65. Thomas Noon Talfourd, *Tragedies: to which are added a few Sonnets & Verses* (Boston: Crosby and Ainsworth, 1865), Act II, ii.

66. *The Athenian Captive,* III, ii.

67. Edward Lytton Bulwer, *The Dramatic Works of Edward Bulwer Lytton,* in *The Works of Edward Bulwer Lytton,* 9 volumes (New York: Collier, n.d.), ix; all references to Bulwer's plays will be to this edition; *Money,* Act II, v.

68. *Money,* V, iii.

69. *The Lady of Lyons,* IV, i.

70. *The Lady of Lyons,* II, i.

71. *The Dramatic Works of James Sheridan Knowles,* 3 volumes (London: Moxon, 1843); all references to Knowles' works will be to this edition; *Love,* I, i.

72. *Love's Disguises,* I, i.

73. *Love's Disguises,* IV, iii.

74. *Love,* I, ii.

3. Under the Volcano

1. Charles Darwin, *The Red Notebook,* ed. Sandra Herbert (London: British Museum, 1980), p. 59 (Darwin's p. 108); *The Centenary Edition of the Works of*

Thomas Carlyle, ed. H. D. Traill, 30 vols. (London: Chapman & Hall, 1896–1899), iii, 249 (all further references to *The French Revolution* will appear parenthetically in the text); *The Poetical Works of Wordsworth,* ed. by Thomas Hutchinson & Ernest de Selincourt (London: Oxford, 1964), p. 223—"To the Planet Venus, Upon Its approximation (as an Evening Star) to the Earth, January, 1838"; *The Poems of Tennyson,* ed. Christopher Ricks (London: Longmans, 1969), p. 697.

2. At the end of its review of the novel, *The Athenaeum* of September 27, 1834 interjects a report of the disaster: "At what a moment too has the novel appeared! . . . The eruption, which had been previously expected from the drying up of the fountains, is said to surpass everything which history has transmitted to us" (p. 708).

3. See, for instance, Dennis R. Dean, "'Through Science to Despair,' Geology and the Victorians," in *Victorian Science and Victorian Values: Literary Perspectives,* ed. by James Paradis and Thomas Postlewait (New Brunswick, N.J.: Rutgers University Press, 1985), pp. 116–118.

4. *British Critic, Quarterly Theological Review, and Ecclesiastical Record* 9:17 (January 1831), 185.

5. *Quarterly Review* 43, 86 (October 1830), 143; the reviewer was the geologist George Poulett Scrope.

6. Charles Dickens, *Oliver Twist; or the Parish Boy's Progress* (London and New York: Penguin, 1966), pp. 45–46; subsequent references to page numbers of this edition will appear parenthetically in the text.

7. Steven Marcus, *Dickens from Pickwick to Dombey* (New York: Simon & Schuster, 1968), pp. 66–67.

8. *Quarterly Review* 61:122 (April 1838), 479; the article is titled "Plato, Bacon, and Bentham."

9. John Fowles, *The French Lieutenant's Woman* (New York: Signet, 1969), p. 191.

10. *The Library Edition of the Works of John Ruskin,* ed. E. T. Cook and Alexander Wedderburn, 39 volumes (London: George Allen, 1903–1912), xvii, 26.

11. Michel Foucault, *The Order of Things: An Archeology of the Human Sciences* (New York: Vintage, 1970), pp. xx–xxi.

12. See Ralph Wilson Rader, *Tennyson's Maud: The Biographical Genesis* (Berkeley and Los Angeles: University of California Press, 1963), pp. 46–47; but on Amy, also compare Robert Bernard Martin, *Tennyson: The Unquiet Heart* (Oxford: Oxford University Press, 1980), pp. 215–221.

13. See Ricks, p. 688.

14. See Martin, p. 212.

15. Christopher Ricks, *Tennyson* (New York: Collier Books, 1972), p. 49.

16. The dates are from Eleanor Bustin Mattes, *In Memoriam: The Way of A Soul* (New York: Exposition Press, 1951), pp. 111–125, but these must be supplemented by those in Ricks, or in Susan Shatto and Marion Shaw, eds., *In Memoriam* (New York: Oxford University Press, 1982).

17. Hallam Tennyson, *Alfred Lord Tennyson: A Memoir, by his Son,* 2 volumes (New York: Greenwood Press, 1969; reprint of 1897 Macmillan Edition), i, 162.

18. A. Dwight Culler, *The Poetry of Tennyson* (New Haven and London: Yale University Press, 1977), p. 177.

19. John Killham, *Tennyson and the The Princess: Reflections of An Age* (London: Athlone Press, 1958), p. 286.

20. Killham, p. 287.

21. Killham, p. 280.

22. Killham, p. 287.

23. *History of the Inductive Sciences,* 3 volumes (London: Parker, 1837), ii, 392.

24. Whewell, ii, 388.

25. See John C. Greene, "The Kuhnian Paradigm and the Darwinian Revolution in Natural History," in *Paradigms and Revolutions: Appraisals and Applications of Thomas Kuhn's Philosophy of Science,* ed. Gary Gutting (London: University of Notre Dame Press, 1980), pp. 298–321.

26. Quoted by Gertrude Himmelfarb, *Darwin and the Darwinian Revolution* (New York: Norton, 1962), p. 220.

27. Cited in Himmelfarb, p. 92.

28. "Parliamentary History of the French Revolution," *Works,* xxix, i.

29. *Narrative of the Surveying Voyages of His Majesty's Ships Adventure and Beagle, between the years 1826 and 1836, describing their examination of the Southern Shores of South Ameria, and the Beagle's circumnavigation of the Globe,* 3 volumes (London: Colburn, 1839), iii, "Journal and Remarks," by Charles Darwin, 369, 373.

30. *The Poetical Works of Wordsworth,* pp. 402, 403.

31. Carlyle, *Works,* xxviii, 168. Further references will be given parenthetically in the text.

32. "Carlyle and Goethe as Scientist," in *Carlyle and His Contemporaries: Essays in Honor of Charles Richard Sanders,* ed. John Clubbe (Durham, North Carolina: Duke University Press, 1976), p. 23; and "Carlyle: Mathematics and 'Mathesis,'" in *Carlyle Past and Present,* ed. K. J. Fielding and Roger L. Tarr (New York: Barnes and Noble, 1976), p. 86.

33. Philip Rosenberg, *The Seventh Hero: Thomas Carlyle and the Theory of Radical Activism* (Cambridge, Massachusetts: Harvard University Press, 1974), pp. 66, 67.

34. *Westminster Review* 27 (July 1837), 17; reprinted in *Carlyle: The Critical Heritage,* ed. Jules Paul Seigel (New York: Barnes & Noble, 1971), p. 52; on epic qualities in the book, see also John Clubbe, "Carlyle as Epic Historian," *Victorian Literature and Society: Essays Presented to Richard D. Altick,* ed. James R. Kincaid and Albert J. Kuhn (Columbus: Ohio State University Press, 1984), pp. 119–145.

35. Rosenberg, p. 67.

36. Albert J. LaValley, *Carlyle and the Idea of the Modern* (New Haven and London: Yale University Press, 1968).

37. Quoted in *Carlyle: The Critical Heritage,* p. 84.

38. *Edinburgh Review* 71:144 (July 1840), 414, 415, 419.

39. *Quarterly Review* 66 (September 1840), 483.

40. *Quarterly Review* 66, 492–3; this passage, like the two previous ones, is omitted from the excerpts printed in the *Critical Heritage* volume.

41. *A Tale of Two Cities* (London and New York: Penguin, 1970), p. 391 (Book III, chapter 15).

42. *Hard Times* (New York: Norton, 1966), p. 125 (Book II, chapter 6).

43. See Leonard Engel's remarks on Darwin's conclusions about the Fuegians in his edition of *The Voyage of the Beagle* (New York: Anchor, 1962), pp. 214–215n, where he cites expecially E. Lucas Bridges' book on the region, *The Uttermost Part of the Earth.*

44. Rosenberg, p. 69.

45. *Carlyle: The Critical Heritage,* p. 49.

46. Sewell, quoted in *Carlyle: The Critical Heritage,* pp. 154–155.

47. *Works,* xxvii, 81.

48. Ibid. In *The French Revolution,* a similar image comes to stand for the passivity of the king and court, and by extension all available leaders of the nation, amid the turbulent "Life-sea" of the revolutionary multitude (ii, 135):

Boundless Chaos of Insurrection presses slumbering round the Palace, like Ocean round a Diving-bell; and may penetrate at any crevice. Let but that accumulated insurrectionary mass find entrance! (ii, 277)

4. The Stolen Child

1. *Morning Chronicle,* June 2, 1838; T. N. Talfourd, *Tragedies, to which are added a few Sonnets and Verses* (Boston: Crosby and Ainsworth, 1865), Sonnet X, p. 244; Richard Monckton Milnes, *Poems,* 2 volumes (London: Moxon, 1838), i, "Poems of Many Years," 127.

2. *Graphic Works of George Cruikshank,* selected and with an introduction and notes by Richard A. Vogler (New York: Dover, 1979), p. 149.

3. *Oliver Twist; or the Parish Boy's Progress* (London and New York: Penguin, 1966), pp. 56–57; all further quotations from the novel will be from this edition and noted parenthetically in the text.

4. J. Hillis Miller, *"Sketches by Boz, Oliver Twist,* and Cruikshank's Illustrations," in J. Hillis Miller and David Borowitz, *Charles Dickens and George Cruikshank* (Los Angeles: William Andrews Clark Memorial Library, 1971), pp. 55–57.

5. Robert A. Colby comments on the "proliferation of orphan tales" in the 1830s. *Fiction with a Purpose: Major and Minor Nineteenth-Century Novels* (Bloomington and London: Indiana University Press, 1967), p. 122 and pp. 105–137, passim; see also John R. Reed, *Victorian Conventions* (Athens: Ohio University Press, 1975), pp. 250–267.

6. John Galt, *The Stolen Child,* in *The Library of Romance* (Philadelphia: Carey Lea, and Blanchard, 1833). Charlotte Adams, *The Stolen Child; or Laura's Adventures with the Travelling Showman and His Family* (London: Parker, 1838). To the British Library's characterization of Adams, it is worth adding Kathleen Tillotson's remark—"the line between tales for the young and novels is a wavering one." *Novels of the Eighteen-Forties* (London and New York: Oxford University Press, 1961), p. 5.

7. Galt, part II, chapter xiv, p. 151.

8. Adams, chapter iii, p. 32.

9. Adams, chapter iv, p. 48.

10. Adams, chapter vi, p. 75.

11. Adams, chapter vi, p. 77.

12. Adams, chapter vii, pp. 80–81.

13. Adams, chapter vii, pp. 83–84.

14. Adams, chapter vii, pp. 87–88.

15. *A Statistical Account of the British Empire: Exhibiting its Extent, Physical Capacities, Population, Industry, and Civil and Religious Institutions,* by J. R. McCulloch, Esq., 2 volumes (London: Knight, 1837), i, concluding supplement on "Crimes and Punishments."

16. *London Labour and the London Poor,* 4 volumes (London: Griffin, Bohn and Co., 1861–1862; reprinted New York: Dover, 1968), iv, 501–501, map no. 14, table no. 16.

17. Nina Auerbach, "Incarnations of the Orphan," in *Romantic Imprisonment: Women and Other Glorified Outcasts* (New York: Columbia University Press, 1985), pp. 58, 72. George P. Landow points out that the "situation" of the "waif struck men who had lost their religious beliefs as a fitting metaphor for the human condition"—*Images of Crisis: Literary Iconology, 1750 to the Present* (Boston and London: Routledge and Kegan Paul, 1982), p. 91.

18. The Countess of Blessington, *The Victims of Society,* 3 volumes (London: Saunders and Othey, 1837), iii, 121.

19. Mrs. S. C. Hall, *Uncle Horace* (London: Colburn, 1837), chapter xxiv.

20. *Uncle Horace,* chapter xiii.

21. *Uncle Horace,* chapter xiii.

22. Mrs. Trollope, *The Vicar of Wrexhill,* 3 volumes (London: Bentley, 1837), ii, 151, and iii, 342.

23. *Vicar,* ii, 162.

24. *Vicar,* iii, 106.

25. *Vicar,* ii, 104.

26. *Vicar,* iii, 111.

27. *Vicar,* i, 242.

28. *Vicar,* i, 273–274.

29. *Times,* October 24, 1837.

30. *Vicar,* i. 70.

31. *Vicar,* i. 238.

32. *Vicar,* iii, 17.

33. *Vicar,* ii, 68.

34. Steven Marcus, *Dickens: from Pickwick to Dombey* (New York: Simon & Schuster, 1968), p. 86.

35. J. Hillis Miller, *Charles Dickens: The World of His Novels* (Bloomington and London: Indiana University Press, 1973), p. 57.

36. John Hogg, *London As it is: Being a Series of Observations on the Health, Habits, and Amusements of the People* (London: John Macrone, 1837), pp. 218, 219–220.

37. John Bayley, "*Oliver Twist:* 'Things as they Really Are,'" in *Charles Dickens: A Penguin Critical Anthology,* ed. Stephen Wall (London: Penguin, 1970), p. 447.

38. *Graphic Works of Cruikshank,* p. 150. For the fullest discussion of Cruikshank's role in shaping the novel, and an exploration of his astonishing claim that it was "entirely my own idea and suggestion and all the characters are mine," see Richard A. Vogler, "Cruikshank and Dickens: A Reassessment of the Role of the Artist and the Author," in *George Cruikshank: A Revaluation,* ed. Robert L. Patten, *Princeton University Library Chronicle,* 35, 1 and 2 (Autumn, Winter, 1973–74), 61–91.

39. Guilland Sutherland, "Cruikshank and London," in *Victorian Artists and The City,* eds. I. B. Nadel and F. S. Schwarzbach (New York: Pergamon, 1980), pp. 118, 114.

40. Sutherland, p. 107.

41. Cited by Sutherland, p. 114.

42. R. H. Horne, *A New Spirit of the Age,* 2 volumes (London: Smith, Elder and Co., 1844), i, 37; Horne adds, "We are with the hunted-down human being, brought home to our sympathies by the extremity of his distress; and we are *not* with the howling mass of demons outside. The only human beings we recognize are the victim—and his dog"(39).

43. G. K. Chesterton, *Charles Dickens: The Last of the Great Men* (New York: Readers Club, 1942), p. 81.

44. See Blanchard Jerrold, *The Life of George Cruikshank, In Two Epochs,* 2 volumes (London: Chatto and Windus, 1882), i, 226f.

45. For the relation of the representation of Fagin to the Satanic figures in morality plays, see Marcus, p. 75.

46. E. P. Thompson, *The Making of the English Working Class* (New York: Vintage, 1963), p. 801.

47. *Times,* June 1, 1838.

48. *Times,* June 4, 1838.

49. J. F. C. Harrison, *The Second Coming: Popular Millenarianism, 1780–1850* (New Brunswick, New Jersey: Rutgers University Press, 1979), p. 213.

50. *Times,* June 1, 1838.

51. Harrison, p. 213.

52. *Times,* June 4, 1838.

53. Quoted in P. G. Rogers, *Battle in Bossenden Wood: The Strange Story of Sir William Courtenay* (Oxford: Clarendon Press, 1961), p. 167.

54. Quoted in Rogers, pp. 191–192.

55. *Times* and *Morning Chronicle,* June 4, 1838.

56. *Times,* June 6, 1838.

57. *Morning Chronicle,* June 6, 1838.

58. *Morning Chronicle,* June 4, 1838.

59. Harrison, p. 215.

60. *Times,* June 4, 1838.

61. *Times,* June 7, 1838.

62. Quoted in Rogers, p. 203.

63. *Morning Chronicle,* June 5, 1838.

64. Quoted in Rogers, p. 150.

65. William Harrison Ainsworth, *Rookwood* (London: Gibbings & Company, 1902), Book III, Chapter v, pp. 27–28.

66. *Rookwood,* pp. 27–28 *n.* Ainsworth cites "An Essay on His Character, and Reflections on his Trial."

5. How to Observe

1. Roland Barthes, *Camera Lucida* (New York: Hill & Wang, 1981), p. 12; Harriet Martineau, *How to Observe: Morals and Manners* (London: Charles Knight & Co., 1838, p. 1; Martin Tupper, *Complete Poetical Works* (Boston: Phillips, Sampson and Company, 1851), p. 430; *Edinburgh Review* 69:140 (July 1839), 477—the passage appears in a review of the volumes by King, Fitz Roy, and Darwin (406–466); Adam Zagajewski, "Franz Schubert: A Press Conference," translated by Renata Gorczynski, from *The Threepenny Review,* no. 22 (Summer 1985), 25; William Whewell, *The Philosophy of the Inductive Sciences,* 2 volumes (London: Parker, 1840), ii, 486.

2. *Harriet Martineau's Autobiography,* 2 volumes (London: Virago, 1983; reprint of 3rd edition, London: Smith Elder & Co., 1877), ii, 7. All subsequent references will be in the text, parenthetically, to *A.*

3. Andrew Bell ("A. Thomson"), *Men and Things in America* (London: W. Smith, 1838), pp. 20ff; Peter Conrad, *Imagining America* (New York and London: Oxford University Press, 1980).

4. Valerie Kossew Pichanick, *Harriet Martineau: The Woman and Her Work* (Ann Arbor: University of Michigan Press, 1980), p. 75.

5. *Edinburgh Review* 46, 309; quoted in *Society in America,* 3 volumes (New York: A. M. S., 1966; reprint of first edition, London: Saunders & Otley, 1837), i, v–vi. All subsequent references will be in the text, parenthetically, to *SA.*

6. *How to Observe,* p. 52. All subsequent references will be in the text, parenthetically, to *HO.*

7. *The Collected Works of John Stuart Mill,* gen. ed. J. M. Robson (Toronto and Buffalo: University of Toronto Press, 1963–), xviii, 126.

8. William Whewell, *The Philosopy of the Inductive Sciences,* 2 volumes (London: Parker, 1840), ii, 398–399.

9. Mill, *Collected Works,* x, 77.

10. Mill, *Autobiography,* in *Collected Works,* i, 219.

11. Harriet Martineau, *Retrospect of Western Travel,* 2 volumes (London: Saunders and Otley, 1838), i, 33. Subsequent references to this edition will be in the text, parenthetically, as *R.*

12. *Illustrations of Political Economy,* 9 volumes (London: Charles Fox, 1832–1834), ii, 99. Subsequent references will be to *Illustrations.*

13. Her remarks on the realism of *Deerbrook* appear in the *Autobiography,* ii, 111. *Quarterly Review* 59:97 (April 1833), 136.

14. *Illustrations,* ii, vi.

15. David J. Rothman, *The Discovery of the Asylum: Social Order and Disorder in the New Republic* (Boston: Little, Brown, 1971), p. 81.

16. Michael Foucault, *Discipline and Punish: The Birth of the Prison* (New York: Vintage, 1979); Max Byrd, *Visits to Bedlam: Madness and Literature in Eighteenth-Century England*, (Columbia: University of South Carolina Press, 1974).

17. Foucault, *Discipline and Punish*, esp. the chapter on "Complete and austere Institutions," pp. 231–256.

18. *Times,* 30 May 1837.

19. R. K. Webb, *Harriet Martineau: A Radical Victorian* (New York: Columbia University Press, 1960), pp. 161, 172.

20. *The Library Edition of the Works of John Ruskin,* ed. E. T. Cook and Alexander Wedderburn, 39 volumes (London: George Allen, 1903–12), i, 5. All subsequent references to *The Poetry of Architecture* will be given by page number only, in the text. George Hersey traces the phrase "the poetry of architecture" to Jacques-François Blondel's *Cours d'architecture* (1771–1773) [4, liv)]: *High Victorian Gothic: A Study in Associationism* (Baltimore and London: The Johns Hopkins University Press, 1972), p. 7.

21. Elizabeth K. Helsinger, *Ruskin and the Art of the Beholder* (Cambridge, Massachusetts and London: Harvard University Press, 1982), see pp. 67–110.

22. *On Photography* (New York: Dell, 1977), pp. 3–4.

23. *The Darkening Glass: A Portrait of Ruskin's Genius* (New York and London: Columbia University Press, 1961), p. 25.

24. See John Rosenberg, "Style and Sensibility in Ruskin's Prose," in *The Art of Victorian Prose,* ed. George Levine and William Madden (New York and London: Oxford University Press, 1968), p. 177.

25. I have discussed this imagery in an unpublished paper titled "The King's Buttermilk: Victorian Painting, *The Life of Sterling,* and Carlyle's Unheroic Biography." On the genre of cottage paintings, see Rosemary Trebel, "The Victorian Picture of the Country," in *The Victorian Countryside,* ed. G. E. Mingay, 2 volumes (London and Boston: Routledge and Kegan Paul, 1981), i, 169.

26. Ruskin, *Works,* xxxv, 225.

27. *The Rural Life of England* (London: Longman, Brown, Green, and Longmans, 1838), pp. 1–2, 608–609, 406–409, 410.

28. "England and Brittany," by "H. F.," in *Westminister Review* 31:2 (August 1838), 372.

29. Howitt, p. 254.

30. Charles T. Dougherty, in "A Study of *The Poetry of Architecture,*" in *Studies in Ruskin: Essays in Honor of Van Akin Burd,* ed. Robert Rhodes and Del Ivan Janik (Athens, Ohio: Ohio University Press, 1982), argues that the last parts of *The Poetry of Architecture* should be read as satire (p. 23); John Dixon Hunt suggests that Ruskin's "strict division of imaginative work into 'Rhyme' and 'plain prose'" begins to break down with *The Poetry of Architecture—The Wider Sea: A Life of John Ruskin* (New York: Viking, 1982), p. 76; Hunt's quotation is from *The Ruskin Family Letters,* ed. Van Akin Burd, 2 volumes (Ithaca and London: Cornell University Press, 1973), i, 324.

31. See Richard L. Stein, *The Ritual of Interpretation: The Fine Arts as Literature in Ruskin, Rossetti, and Pater* (Cambridge, Massachusetts, and London: Harvard University Press, 1975) p. 40.

32. *Works,* xvii, 282–283.

33. *The History of the Inductive Sciences,* 3 volumes (London: Parker; third edition, 1857), iii, 398.

34. Howitt, pp. 388, 403.

35. *The Encyclopedia Britannica, a Dictionary of Arts, Sciences, and General Literature,* seventh edition, 24 volumes (London: Black, 1842), iii, 239.

36. *Encyclopedia Britannica,* iv, 518; *Chambers' Edinburgh Magazine* describes the traps set for ants by the ant-lion as having been constructed "as methodically as the most skillful architect or engineer amongst ourselves"—"Contrivances of the Ant-Lion," no. 275 (30 July 1836), 215—the article is taken from the series title, the *Library of Entertaining Knowledge,* "Insect Architecture."

37. John Macculloch, M.D., *Proofs and Illustrations of the Attributes of God, from the Facts and Laws of the Physical Universe: Being the Foundation of Natural and Revealed Religion,* 3 volumes (London: James Duncan, 1837), i, 552.

38. Macculloch, i, 546.

39. Macculloch, i, 544, 546.

40. *Ruskin Family Letters,* i, 387.

41. *Ruskin Family Letters,* i, 417n., ii, 462–3.

42. Cited in Richard Ormond, *Sir Edwin Landseer* (London and Philadelphia: Tate Gallery and Philadelphia Museum of Art, 1981), p. 104.

43. Adrian Desmond, "Robert E. Grant: The Social Predicament of a Pre-Darwinian Evolutionist," *Journal of the History of Biology* 16: 1 (Spring 1983), 189.

44. *Works,* iii, 88–89.

45. Macculloch, i, 534.

46. *Works,,* v, 387.

47. Gillian Beer, *Darwin's Plots: Evolutionary Narrative in Darwin, George Eliot, and Nineteenth-Century Fiction* (London and Boston: Ark Paperbacks, 1985), p. 67.

48. Charles Darwin, "Journal and Remarks," volume 3 of the *Narrative of the Surveying Voyages of His Majesty's Ships Adventure and Beagle, between the years 1826 and 1836, describing their examination of the Southern Shores of South America, and the Beagle's Circumnavigation of the Globe* (London: Henry Colburn, 1839), 3 volumes; iii, 1–2. Subsequent references to this volume will appear parenthetically, in the text; subsequent references to other volumes of this edition in these notes will be to *Narrative.*

49. *Narrative,* ii, 52; this is the volume by Captain Fitz Roy.

50. Peter J. Vorzimmer, "The Darwin Reading Notebooks (1838–1860)," *Journal of the History of Biology (JHB)* 10: 1 (Spring 1977), 107–183; the citation of Reynolds appears on Darwin's p. 6, for 12 October 1838; Malthus is listed on October 3, 1838; for the date of Darwin's composition of *Journal of Researches,* see Sandra Herbert, "The Place of Man in the Development of Darwin's Theory of Transmutation: Part I, to July 1837," *JHB* 7: 2 (Fall 1974), who suggests that Darwin was trying to meet a publisher's deadline of July 1837; also see Howard E.

Gruber, *Darwin on Man: A Psychological Study of Scientific Creativity,* second edition (Chicago: University of Chicago Press, 1981), p. 261; on the importance of Darwin's thinking of 1837–1838 for the formation of his hypotheses, see also Silvan S. Schweber, "The Origin of the *Origin* Revisited," *JHB* 10: 2 (Fall 1977), 229–316, and Frank J. Sulloway, "Darwin's Conversion: The *Beagle* Voyage and Its Aftermath," *JHB* 15: 3 (Fall 1982), 325–396; on the dating of the "Malthus insight," see Gruber, 150–174.

51. Carol T. Christ, *The Finer Optic: The Aesthetic of Particularlity in Victorian Poetry* (New Haven and London: Yale University Press, 1975).

52. *The Autobiography of Charles Darwin,* ed. by Francis Darwin (New York: Dover Books, 1958), p. 54.

53. Sandra Herbert, "The Place of Man in the Development of Darwin's Theory of Transmutation," Part II, *JHB* 10: 2 (Fall 1977), 155–227; "he moved from field to field with unusual ease" (215).

54. *Narrative,* ii, 104.

55. Stephen Jay Gould, *Ever Since Darwin: Reflections in Natural History* (New York: Norton, 1977), p. 33.

56. See John C. Greene, "The Kuhnian and the Darwinian Revolution in Natural History," in *Paradigms and Revolutions: Appraisals and Applications of Thomas Kuhn's Philosophy of Science,* ed. Gary Gutting (London: University of Notre Dame Press, 1980), p. 314.

57. *Journal of Researches into the Natural History and Geology of the Countries Visited during the Voyage of H.M.S. Beagle round the World, under the Command of Capt. Fitz Roy, R.N.* (London: Murray, 1845), p. 375; cited in Gruber, pp. 287–288.

58. *Narrative,* ii, 494.

59. *Narrative,* ii, 466; ii, 486, 487.

60. Gruber, p. 289.

61. *Narrative,* ii, 503.

62. *Narrative,* ii, 252.

63. *Narrative,* ii, 106–107

64. Gertrude Himmelfarb, *Darwin and the Darwinian Revolution* (New York: Norton, 1962), p. 70.

65. Himmelfarb, p. 374.

66. See the Anchor edition (in "The Natural History Library") of *The Voyage of the Beagle,* ed. Leonard Engel (New York: Doubleday, 1962), pp. 207–208.

67. John Stuart Mill, "Civilization: Signs of the Times," in *The Collected Works of John Stuart Mill,* ed. J. M. Robson (Toronto and Buffalo, 1963–), xviii, 120.

68. *The Voyage of the Beagle* (Anchor edition), p. 213.

69. Herbert, Part II, 194.

70. *Narrative,* ii, 650.

71. Beer, pp. 60–61.

72. A. Dwight Culler, "The Darwinian Revolution and Literary Form," in *The Art of Victorian Prose,* pp. 224–246. Edward Manier comes to similar conclusions in emphasizing Darwin's debts to Wordsworth for an ethic based on self-sacrifice,

benevolence, and love: "The young Darwin's positive theological views were similar to the central theses of the natural religion expressed by Wordsworth's character the Wanderer." *The Young Darwin and his Cultural Circle* (D. Reidel Publishing Company: Dordrecht, Holland, and Boston, 1978), pp. 196, 171, passim.

73. Francis Darwin, ed., *The Foundations of the Origin of Species* (Cambridge: Cambridge University Press, 1909); see also Peter J. Vorzimmer, "An Early Darwin Manuscript: The 'Outline and Draft of 1839,'" *JHB* 8: 2 (Fall 1975), pp. 191–217, which dates this as early as 1839; but for a rejoinder, see also David Kohn, Sydney Smith, and Robert C. Stauffer, "New Light on the Foundations of the Origin of Species: A Reconstruction of the Archival Record," *JHB* 15: 3 (Fall 1982), 419–442.

74. *Foundations,* p. 52.

75. Quoted in Leonard G. Wilson, *Charles Lyell: The Years to 1841, The Revolution in Geology* (New Haven and London: Yale University Press, 1972), p 439; the letter is dated June 1, 1836.

76. *Edinburgh Review* 62: 86, 301: the author of the anonymous essay was David Brewster; it is listed in Darwin's reading notes.

77. *On the Origin of Species,* (A. L. Burt Publishing Co., n.d.), p. 502; a facsimile of the version of this passage from 1842 is printed opposite p. 50 in the *Foundations.*

78. *Narrative,* i, xvii; this is King's volume.

79. *Origin,* p. 1; the phrase "mystery of mysteries" was also "in the air" (as Darwin indicates in citing it); for its use by Herschel and Lyell, see Wilson, *Charles Lyell,* pp. 438–441.

80. *Metaphysics, Materialism, and the Evolution of Mind: Early Writings of Charles Darwin,* transcribed and annotated by Paul H. Barnett, with a commentary by Howard E. Gruber (Chicago: University of Chicago Press, 1974), p. 196; Darwin, *Autobiography,* p. 43.

81. Himmelfarb, p. 160.

82. Stephen J. Gould, "Darwin's Middle Period," in *The Panda's Thumb: More Reflections on Natural History* (New York: Norton, 1980), p. 66.

83. Robert M. Young, "Darwinism *is* Social," in *The Darwinian Heritage,* ed. by David Kohn (Princeton, N.J.: Princeton University Press, 1985), pp. 609–638.

84. John Cornell, "Analogy and Technology in Darwin's Vision of Nature: An Essay on Some Foundations of Modern Biological Thought," *JHB* 17: 3 (Fall 1984), 303–344. Stanley Edgar Hyman has remarked that "Darwin's viewpoint is that of an English squire, a sporting breeder writing for other breeders." *The Tangled Bank: Darwin, Marx, Frazer and Freud as Imaginative Writers* (New York: Atheneum, 1962), p. 69. On breeding, see also Robert M. Young, *Darwin's Metaphor: Nature's Place in Victorian Culture* (Cambridge and London: Cambridge University Press, 1985), pp. 79–88; Young's remarkable book, which I encountered only just before this volume went to press, is a rich source of insights into the cultural situation of Darwin's thought.

85. *Edinburgh Review* 69: 140 (July 1839), 467–468.

86. "The Darwin Reading Notebooks (1838–1860)," 107–183; the reference to

Macaulay's essay appears on Darwin's p. 19, probably from 1840; cf. *The Life and Letters of Charles Darwin,* ed. Francis Darwin, 2 volumes (New York: Appleton, 1899), i, 266; Silvan S. Schweber, who cites this letter, notes that Lyell thought of using Macaulay's remark on the "law" of science as progress as the motto for his *Elements of Geology* (see Lyell's *Life and Letters,* p. 37)—"The Origin of the Origin Revisited," p. 241.

87. Darwin, *Autobiography,* pp. 42–43.

88. Vorzimmer: "The Darwin Reading Notebooks . . ."; the reference to Martineau appears on Darwin's p. 4, probably from late 1838.

89. *How to Observe,* pp. 66–67; One more curious parallel is worth adding, although I think it unlikely that Darwin would have run across it. *The English Annual* for 1837 includes a story by H. W. Woolrych, Esq., called "The Dark Water King—A story of the Niger," which includes the rescue of a native queen from a sultan who is torturing her to test her loyalty. The rescuers, a party of Englishmen, subdue the sultan by the power embodied in a steamboat:

> the Niger had never borne so grand a pageant as that which now moved majestically upon its blue stream. Again the cannon roared, and the monarch of the Dark Water beheld a vessel with its colours flying in sight, and scudding along the great river with a speed which the African had never yet conceived. It was a mighty steam-ship, baffling in triumph both wind and stream, with guns which could sweep a thousand sun-burst savages from their lair, and a crew whom neither sickness nor strangers could subdue. The Sultan beheld with awe the hastening mast; his rich turban studded with gems shook wildly as he bowed his head in homage to his fearful guest, and his warriors, with equal wonder, made obeisance after the manner of their chief.

The English Annual for 1837 (London: Edward Churton, 1837), pp. 339–340.

90. *Narrative,* ii, Appendix, 199.

91. Michel Foucault, *Power/Knowledge* (New York: Pantheon, 1980), p. 129.

92. George Levine, "Darwin and the Problem of Authority," *Raritan* 3: 3 (Winter 1984), 59.

6. *Remember the Téméraire!*

1. John Macculloch, M.D., *Proofs and Illustrations of the Attributes of God, from the Facts and Laws of the Physical Universe: Being the Foundation of Natural and Revealed Religion,* 3 volumes (London: James Duncan, 1837), i, 422; *Penny Magazine,* 21 May 1836, 200; *The Poems of Richard Monckton Milnes,* 2 volumes (London: Moxon, 1838), i, *Poems of Many Years,* 94; *The Poetical Works of William Wordsworth,* ed. Ernest de Selincourt (London: Oxford University Press, 1964), p. 290; Edward Lytton Bulwer, "The Death of Nelson," in *Richelieu; or, The Conspiracy* (New York: Harper & Brothers, 1839), p. 148.

2. Charles Dickens, *The Life and Adventures of Nicholas Nickleby, Containing*

a Faithful Account of the Fortunes, Misfortunes, Uprisings, Downfallings, and Complete Career of the Nickleby Family. Edited by "Boz." Facsimile edition, ed. Michael Slater, 2 volumes (Philadelphia: University of Pennsylvania Press, 1982), ii, 623.

3. Donald J. Olsen, *The Growth of Victorian London* (London: Penguin, 1979), pp. 57–58.

4. *Flora Tristan's London Journal, 1840* (Charlestown, Massachusetts: Charles River Books, 1980), p. 251.

5. Tristan, pp. 1–5.

6. Mark Girouard, *The Return to Camelot: Chivalry and the English Gentleman* (New Haven and London: Yale University Press, 1981), p. 93.

7. Girouard, p. 90.

8. Girouard, pp. 90–91.

9. *The Collected Correspondence of J. M. W. Turner,* ed. John Gage (Oxford: Clarendon, 1980) includes a letter probably written in 1845 to J. Hogarth, who had exhibited the *Temeraire,* in which Turner declares that "no consideration of money or favour can induce me to lend my Darling again" (p. 211). Finberg links this to the *Temeraire,* although the reference is not certain. A. J. Finberg, *The Life of J. M. W. Turner, R. A.* (Oxford: Clarendon, 1961), p. 417.

10. This selection from contemporary reviews, and many of the others I will cite, can be found in Martin Butlin and Evelyn Joll, *The Paintings of J. M. W. Turner,* 2 volumes (New Haven and London: Yale University Press, published for the Paul Mellon Center's Studies in British Art and for the Tate Gallery; 1977), i, 208ff. The quotation from the *Athenaeum* appears on i, 209.

11. Louis Hawes, "Turner's *Fighting Temeraire,*" *Art Quarterly* 35: 1 (1972), 23–48; Jack Lindsay, *J. M. W. Turner: His Life and Work* (Greenwich, Connecticut: New York Graphic Society, 1966), p. 188.

12. To avoid confusion between Turner's painting and the name of the actual ship in it, by which it is often identified, I will use the accented form of the ship's name only when referring to the actual ship (and Turner did not use accents in his title): thus, Nelson's *Téméraire,* Turner's *Temeraire.*

13. Woolner is quoted in Butlin and Joll, i, 208. Ruskin offers a slightly different account, according to which Turner was going downriver to dine at Greenwich; Clarkson Stanfield, with him on the journey, called his attention to the "fine subject" (*The Library Edition of the Works of John Ruskin,* ed. E. T. Cook and Alexander Wedderburn, 39 volumes (London: George Allen, 1903–1912), xiii, 167n–168n. Prof. John McCoubrey (in a letter to me, commenting on the present chapter) takes a more sceptical view of such accounts. "Turner could have painted the picture from newspaper accounts, and, though he may have seen it pass, he could have been sailing or on the shore. He did take the steamer to Margate often because that was the best way to go. The public love stories of how the scene was taken; it feeds the positivistic attitude toward art." Ruskin's claim was denied by Stanfield; see Butlin and Joll, i, 208.

14. *Times,* 13 September 1838.

15. The 1845 title is quoted in Butlin and Joll, i, 208.

16. Hawes, pp. 25ff.

17. Sir John Barrow, *The Life of George Lord Anson* (London: John Murray, 1839), p. 421; italics in original.

18. Rodney Mace, *Trafalgar Square* (London: Lawrence and Wishart, 1976), p. 56.

19. *Times,* August 2, 1838.

20. *Correspondence,* pp. 69–70; the remark comes in a letter of 1816.

21. *Times,* 4 March 1839.

22. William James, *The Naval History of Great Britain,* 6 volumes (London: Macmillan, 1902), iii, 473; Oliver Warner remarks that the *Battle of Trafalgar* is "an interesting pointer in the direction of thought whose most popular expression was undoubtedly "The Fighting Temeraire,'" "Turner and Trafalgar," *Apollo* 62 (Ocober 1955), 104.

23. James, iii, 474. Butlin and Joll (i, 140) cite a review of James' *Naval History* in the *Literary Gazette* for 1826 (pp. 389–90), which complains that *The Battle of Trafalgar* is "full of glaring falsehoods and palpable inconsistencies"; in fact, these remarks are also quoted from James, iii, 474.

24. *The Life of Nelson, with Original Anecdotes, Notes, &c.* by the Old Sailor [Matthew Henry Barker] (London: Tegg, 1867), p. 6.

25. Robert Southey, *The Life of Nelson* (London: J. Murray, 1830), p. 327.

26. Southey, prefatory note.

27. Southey, p. 334.

28. A. Welby Pugin, "A Letter on the Proposed Protestant Memorial to Crammer, Ridley, and Latymer, Addressed to the Subscribers to and Promoters of that Undertaking" (London: Booker and Dolman, 1839), p. 22.

29. Butlin and Joll cite the poetry, and its variations, i, 208.

30. W. M. Thackeray, "A Second Lecture on the Fine Arts," *Fraser's Magazine* 19:114 (June 1839), 744; compare a letter to the *Times* on April 19, 1838 from a correspondent called "Roger Oldstyle"—one of a series he submitted objecting to the parsimony of the Penny Coronation: "there is still a thrilling force in our 'God Save the Queen.' Here is still deep reverence paid to the crown. We are not yet (howl, ye fiends!) on the brink of a republic."

31. Ruskin, *Works,* xiii, 171–172. The quotation from *Modern Painters* is from the famous chapter on "The Two Boyhoods": *Works,* vii, 379.

32. Mace, p. 256. Some even wondered if any appropriate modern solution could be found. Before the competition closed, the *Times* printed a letter (April 13, 1838) from a relative of Sir Edward Berry, Nelson's captain at the Battle of the Nile, proposing that Cleopatra's Needle be moved into Trafalgar Square to form the center of the memorial.

33. Mace, p. 241.

34. Mace, pp. 246–247.

35. Mace, p. 257.

36. Mace, pp. 273–274.

37. *Penny Magazine,* June 23, 1838.

38. Mace, p. 249.

39. Mace, p. 277.

40. Mace, p. 262.

41. Mace, p. 265.

42. Mace, p. 263.

43. Ruskin, *Works,* xiii, 171.

44. Ruskin, *Works,* xiii, 170n.

45. Butlin and Joll, i, 209. The closest approximation to such personification among recent critics can be found in Andrew Wilton: "The old ship . . . provides a substitue for the human protagonist whom Turner so often makes the focus of his idea, if not of his composition." *J. M. W. Turner: His Art and Life* (New York: Rizzoli, 1979), p. 212.

46. Butlin and Joll, i, 209.

47. *Spectator,* quoted in Butlin and Joll, i, 209; Thackeray, 744. Prof. McCoubrey has suggested that "skeletal" is a less apt term for the appearance of the ship than "ghostly," a quality he explains in terms of the Téméraire's pallor: "its ghostliness stems from its having been taken over by the advance of the color of night" (he is paraphrasing Ruskin). I suspect that Victorian audiences would have accepted such an argument but still might have advanced others for the appropriateness of the first term. In *The Harbours of England* Ruskin speculates that Turner must have seen a violent shipwreck in 1818, adding his conviction that thereafter the painter never saw a ship at sea "without, in his mind's eye, at the same instant, seeing her skeleton" (*Works,* xiii, 43).

48. Hawes points out that the ship rode higher without its guns, stores, crew, etc. (pp. 24–25); the remark in *Times* comes from 13 September 1838; Finberg quotes Benjamin Haydon on the representation of the *Victory* in *The Battle of Trafalgar*—"The principal ship stands high and bravely in her element, as if proud of Nelson's flag"; Finberg, *J. M. W. Turner,* p. 284.

49. Butlin and Joll, i, 226.

50. Lindsay, 203.

51. *Times,* October 12, 1838.

52. Lindsay, 187.

53. Sir George Gates, *Trafalgar Square and Neighbourhood (The Parish of St. Martin-in-the-Fields, Pt. III), Being the 20th Volume of the Survey of London* (London: London County Council, 1940; reprinted A. M. S. Publishers, 1979), p. 18.

54. Ruskin, *Works,* iii, 572. Cf, vii, 437n.: "And remember also, that the very sign in heaven itself which, truly understood, is the type of love, was to Turner the type of death. The scarlet of the clouds was his symbol of destruction."

55. Alex L. Parks, *Law of Tug, Tow, and Pilotage* (Cambridge, Maryland: Cornell Maritime Press, 1971), p. 1; I am indebted to the students in Prof. Kathleen Nicholson's University of Oregon art history seminar on Turner for calling my attention to this reference.

56. Lancelot Hogben makes a similar observation about Darwin and the *Beagle* voyage: surveying journeys of that sort were made possible by improvements in oceanic navigation under steam power. "Darwinism and Human Society in Retrospect," in *Darwin and the Study of Society,* ed. Michael Benton (London: Tavistock, 1961), p. 37.

57. Lindsay, pp. 187, 188.

58. Lindsay, p. 187.

59. Mace, p. 278.

60. Prof. McCoubrey remarks: "At least two marine painters, Backhuysen and Vernet, supposedly had themselves tied to masts. To match their reputations someone was bound to think of it for Turner."

61. Andrew Wilton, *Turner and the Sublime* (Chicago: University of Chicago Press, 1981), p. 99.

62. Wordsworth, *The Poetical Works,* ed. Ernest de Selincourt (London: Oxford University Press, 1964) 729–730.

63. Wordsworth, p. 732.

64. James Hakewill, one of the entrants in the design competition, raised the question of the direction of Nelson's gaze: "Is it correct in principle or feeling that the statue of a subject be placed looking down upon royalty, as the statue of Nelson would be, if placed on the summit of the column immediately over that of Charles the First?—Certainly not." Mace, 255.

65. See Eric Shanes, *Turner's Picturesque Views in England and Wales, 1825–1838* (New York: Harper & Row, 1979), p. 30, and Ruskin, *Works,* xiii, 558.

66. Lindsay, 92.

67. Butlin and Joll, i, 208.

68. Lawrence Gowing, *Turner: Imagination and Reality* (New York: Museum of Modern Art, 1966), p. 45; John Gage observes that many of Turner's "pictures of travel" tell "a story of the painter's journey . . . and in each case he underlined his personal involvement in a vivid verbal record."—*Turner: Rain, Steam and Speed* (New York: Viking, 1972), pp. 42–43.

69. Tennyson's remark to John Knowles about *In Memoriam* is quoted from Christopher Ricks' edition of his *Poems* (London and New York: Longman and Norton, 1969), p. 859.

70. Butlin and Joll, i, 209.

71. Ruskin, *Works,* xiii, 168.

72. Butlin and Joll, i, 216.

Conclusion: Sun Pictures

1. *Punch or the London Charivari* 5: 124 (25 November 1843), 236; Paul Delaroche, quoted in Gisele Freund, *Photography and Society* (Boston: Godine, 1980), p. 84; William Henry Fox Talbot, *The Pencil of Nature* (New York: Da Capo, 1968), "Brief Historical Sketch of the Invention of the Art"; Robert Chambers, *Vestiges of the Natural History of Creation* (New York: Humanities Press, 1967), p. 368; *The Centenary Edition of the Works of Thomas Carlyle,* ed. H. D. Traill, 30 volumes (London: Chapman and Hall, 1896–1899), x, 236; Benjamin Disraeli, *Sybil* (New York: Penguin, 1980), Book I, chapter vi, p. 66.

2. *Punch* 5: 122 (4 November 1843), 236.

3. *Illustrated London News* 3: 79 (November 4, 1843); hereafter abbreviated *ILN.*

4. See, for instance, Richard D. Altick, *Victorian People and Ideas* (New York: Norton, 1973), p. 73.

5. *Punch 2:* 49, 249.

6. *ILN* 1 (January 7, 1843), preface.

7. *ILN* 2 (July 8, 1843), preface.

8. *ILN* 1 (January 7, 1843), preface.

9. Quoted in Gail Buckland, *Fox Talbot and the Invention of Photography* (Boston: Godine, 1980), p. 44; the article is dated Febrary 2, 1839.

10. Talbot, plate V.

11. Quoted in David Bruce, *Sun Pictures: the Hill-Adamson Callotypes* (Greenwich, Connecticut: New York Graphic Society, 1973), p. 13.

12. Talbot, plate X.

13. Talbot, plate VI.

14. Talbot, plate XIII.

15. Buckland, p. 87.

16. Talbot, plate XIV.

17. Ibid.

18. Talbot, plate III.

19. Professor Stanley Tick, in a paper delivered at the 1984 annual meeting of the Philological Association of the Pacific Coast, discussed this issue in a fascinating survey of the beginnings of photography; in the photographic image, he pointed out, the subject "is already memory."

20. Carlyle, *Works,* x, 249.

21. Carlyle, *Works,* x, 296.

22. Carlyle, *Works,* iv, 323; x, 298.

23. Carlyle, *Works,* x, 229, 231.

24. *Sybil,* II, v, p. 97.

25. *Sybil,* VI, xiii, p. 496.

26. Chambers, p. 386.

27. Chambers, p. 388; as Robert M. Young comments, "Chambers leaped over the inhibitions and reservations of his scientific contemporaries and conveyed the whole sweep of naturalism, embracing man, his mind, and society." *Darwin's Metaphor: Nature's Place in Victorian Culture* (Cambridge and New York: Cambridge University Press, 1985), p. 183.

28. Chambers, p. 386.

Index